Regions and Regionalism in History

12

NORTHERN LANDSCAPES

REPRESENTATIONS AND REALITIES OF NORTH-EAST ENGLAND

Regions and Regionalism in History

ISSN 1742–8254

This series, published in association with the AHRB Centre for North-East England History (NEEHI), aims to reflect and encourage the increasing academic and popular interest in regions and regionalism in historical perspective. It also seeks to explore the complex historical antecedents of regionalism as it appears in a wide range of international contexts.

Series Editor
Prof. Peter Rushton, University of Sunderland

Editorial Board
Dr Joan Allen, University of Newcastle
Prof. Don MacRaild, University of Northumbria
Dr Christian Liddy, University of Durham
Dr Diana Newton, University of Teesside

Proposals for future volumes may be sent to the following address:

N E England History Institute,
School of Arts and Media,
University of Teesside,
Middlesbrough,
TS1 3BA.

NORTHERN LANDSCAPES

REPRESENTATIONS AND REALITIES
OF NORTH-EAST ENGLAND

Edited by

THOMAS FAULKNER, HELEN BERRY and JEREMY GREGORY

THE BOYDELL PRESS

First published 2010
The Boydell Press, Woodbridge

ISBN 978–1–84383–541–7

The Boydell Press is an imprint of Boydell & Brewer Ltd
PO Box 9, Woodbridge, Suffolk IP12 3DF, UK
and of Boydell & Brewer Inc.
668 Mt Hope Avenue, Rochester, NY 14620, USA
website: www.boydellandbrewer.com

The publisher has no responsibility for the continued existence or accuracy of
URLs for external or third-party internet websites referred to in this book,
and does not guarantee that any content on such websites is,
or will remain, accurate or appropriate.

A catalogue record for this book is available
from the British Library

This publication is printed on acid-free paper

Printed in Great Britain by
CPI Antony Rowe, Chippenham and Eastbourne

Contents

Illustrations

Foreword

Northern Landscapes:
Representations and Realities of North-East England

MARGARET DRABBLE, DBE

The essays in this volume illustrate the interest in landscape that has been growing and changing so remarkably in recent decades. Together, they present a portrait of the North East seen from complementary perspectives, which includes much pioneering research. The popular histories of and attitudes towards land and architecture exemplified in the works of well-known writers such as W.G. Hoskins and Nikolaus Pevsner are examined and updated here in scholarly and scrupulous detail, yet with a commitment of energy and enthusiasm that makes the armchair traveller in London long to take the first train north, or to head off up the Great North Road. The spirit of place is alive and particular, and the landscapes of the North East are vividly evoked.

We travel through time, from prehistoric and medieval Prudhoe to the unfinished stories of Darlington and Middlesbrough, and through a wide social spectrum, from the ill-recorded turf-covered and mud-floored hovels of labourers and the stone cottages and colliery rows of miners to the grander terrain of Northumbria's great houses and the public parks of the nineteenth and twentieth centuries. We travel through geographical regions, through the agricultural, the industrial, and the maritime: the humble hay bogie, the growth of the railways, and the aesthetic priorities in landscaping of a land of coal and slag are all discussed in a close sociological detail that often questions received opinion. This is a broad panorama, enlivened by some striking personal histories: the tale of the Victorian development of Gibside is full of bizarre and extraordinary human drama as well as interesting new information about the 'gardenesque' vogue, and the story of the rise and fall and possible restoration of Hardwick is poetic and no less dramatic. The influence of Northumbrian-born 'Capability' Brown and Newcastle architect John Dobson threads through the composite narrative and is charted here in many a reference and record, some rescued from unpublished sources. Thomas Bewick has his own chapter, but we also hear the voices of topographers, town planners, developers, civic dignitaries, gardening experts and enthusiasts, painters and novelists.

One of the events that prompted this collection was a conference at the University of Northumbria in September 2000, which I had the good fortune to attend. It surveyed many of the topics discussed here, and introduced me to the writing of Mary Linskill and to the distinctive social and artistic legends inspired by Cullercoats, a place which I had visited with my parents in the late 1950s when my father was county court judge of Northumberland. The 'place-myths' of Cullercoats and Whitby are tellingly explored here, and add to what I learned then: the North-East coast inspires strong loyalties. The distinctive qualities of Northumbria had impressed me deeply, although I lived there only briefly, and the conference reminded me of much that I had seen, with pleasure but without much understanding, in my youth. These essays cover far more ground than a conference can, and increase one's appreciation of the history of a whole region. My parents lived for some years in Wylam-on-Tyne, and my youngest son was born in Jesmond, Newcastle, which gives me a lasting sense of connection to the area, but many (perhaps most?) of the contributors to this volume have a long association with Northumbria, and strong local roots.

The industrial sublime is well covered, and so is the way in which travel writers and residents alike have accommodated themselves to (or distanced themselves from) the dirt and ravages of coal and iron workings. The relationship between traditional landowners, nouveau-riche industrial magnates, the workforce and the land itself is observed over time and from many angles – those of the sportsman, the aesthete, the tenant, the Quaker manufacturer and philanthropist, the passionate gardener, the hired labourer, the migrant worker. The conflict between the desire to create a pleasing rural idyll and the demands of industry and productivity is a perennially fascinating topic, with many new illustrations provided here which will be grist to the mills of those who labour in this field. Splendid quotations illustrating a fastidious recoil from industry and labour pepper the text, exemplified by Elizabeth Montagu's description in 1758 of the mining communities of Tyneside as 'an anthill swarming with black creatures no better than savages', but just as marked is the impulse in some quarters to include, to embrace, to dignify and exalt the labourer.

We find the landscapes and the texts we need, and we re-interpret vanished or vanishing landscapes in accordance with our own changing desires and perceptions. The transition of our concept of 'barren and inhospitable' to 'wild and romantic' has by now been well documented: less well covered has been the shift from the romantic to the civic, from the civic to the public. Those interested in these shifts, and the way they have evolved naturally and been manipulated by individual writers and by interest groups, will find much to challenge and interest them here.

A concept of 'Northern-ness' or 'North-Eastern-ness' also lies behind this collection. In their Introduction Thomas Faulkner and Jeremy Gregory discuss the geography of their project and the boundaries they have drawn for themselves and their contributors, but all who have lived in or visited the North East (and some who have not) will have their own view, their own notion of the region. For some, the coastline of Cullercoats and Whitby and Lindisfarne (with its walled garden designed by Gertrude Jekyll) is quintessential Northumbria. Others will think first of Durham's cathedral and its ancient city walks, or of

Newcastle with its steep streets and alleys, its quays, its magnificent bridges, its long and active history, its public parks. Some will see those long moorland uplands, or the wooded river valleys, or the market town of Hexham, or the brave optimism of MIMA, the Middlesbrough Institute of Modern Art. All these are part of the larger portrait. Some of what we remember, as one or two of these essayists remind us, is already vanishing, and we do well to record it while we can. Northumbria is full of antique ruins, sham ruins, lost ruins and dynamic new projects. This book expands our vision of North-Eastern-ness, and adds shade and colour and historical perspective to the places we already know.

Preface

This book is about the landscape of North-East England, a region with a distinct identity yet one which from the point of view of landscape has been curiously under-researched. It consists of a substantial Introduction and a series of essays which, while making no claim to comprehensiveness, explore the subject from a wide variety of perspectives. These range from the historical and the literary to the archaeological, art-historical and geographical. Many examine hitherto under-explored topics, including country-house landscapes, village landscapes and the 'townscapes' of some of the region's major cities and towns, and reflect some of the differing approaches to and ways of understanding the subject. They also serve to illustrate the ever more diverse uses of the concept of landscape in contemporary thinking.

Our subtitle may need some explanation, as although the binary polarity of 'representations' and 'realities' is a useful way of describing some of the overall themes of the volume, the essays themselves suggest that there is often no hard and fast distinction between the two: our images of the landscape can shape our reality, and vice-versa.

The book had its first origins in the rather similarly titled conference 'Northern Landscapes: Representations and Realities' that was held as long ago as September 2000 at the University of Northumbria, Newcastle upon Tyne, under the auspices of the North East of England History Institute (NEEHI). It was organised by the present editors. Since then they and other contributors have continued to work in the general field that formed the subject matter of this conference. They have also dealt especially with North-East England, which accounts for the more precise geographical focus of this book than was the case with the original conference; this is something which is doubly appropriate in view of what can be perceived as a burgeoning interest in regionality in general, and the location of the conference in Newcastle.

Many of the chapters presented here are based on papers originally given at this conference, but a significant number of additional contributions by other scholars not in attendance or not having given papers at the conference have also been solicited in order to provide a fuller perspective. *Northern Landscapes: Representations and Realities of North-East England* is organised thematically into five sections: (1) The Lie of the Land, (2) Parks and Gardens, (3) Living in the Landscape, (4) Urban Landscapes, and (5) Perceptions and Representations; the chapters within these sections are arranged in chronological order of subject matter. The book is illustrated with a wide selection of photographs, historic engravings and maps. Also, as readers will already have seen, it benefits from a foreword by the distinguished novelist and critic Dame Margaret Drabble, who kindly contributed to and supported the original conference and whose *A Writer's Britain: Landscapes in Literature* (London, 1979, currently under revision) was a pioneering study of the genre.

Contributors

THOMAS FAULKNER was Senior Lecturer in the History of Architecture and Design at the University of Northumbria (1974–2004) and is now a Visiting Fellow in the School of Historical Studies at Newcastle University, where he also teaches in the School of Architecture, Planning and Landscape. He is a member of the Society of Architectural Historians of Great Britain, the Georgian Group and the Victorian Society, and is a Fellow of the Society of Antiquaries of London. He has written and lectured extensively on many aspects of the history and architecture of North-East England.

HELEN BERRY is Reader in Early Modern History at Newcastle University. Educated at Durham and Cambridge Universities, and a winner of the Royal Historical Society's Alexander Prize (2000), she is the author of *Gender, Society and Print Culture in Late-Stuart England* (2003), and of numerous articles on early modern English history. She is co-editor with Jeremy Gregory of *Creating and Consuming Culture in North-East England, 1660–1830* (2004) and with Elizabeth Foyster of *The Family in Early Modern England* (2007).

JEREMY GREGORY was Principal Lecturer and Head of History at the University of Northumbria and is now Senior Lecturer in the Department of Religions and Theology at the University of Manchester. Both his first degree and doctorate are from the University of Oxford. He has published widely on eighteenth-century history, including *The Speculum of Archbishop Thomas Secker* (1995) and *Restoration, Reformation and Reform, 1660–1820: Archbishops of Canterbury and their Diocese* (2000). He edited *John Wesley: Tercentenary Essays* for *The Bulletin of the John Rylands University Library of Manchester* (2005), and was co-editor of *Culture, Politics and Society in Britain, 1660–1800* (1991), *The National Church in Local Perspective: the Church of England and the Regions, 1660–1800* (2003) and *Creating and Consuming Culture in North-East England, 1660–1830* (2004). He was co-author with John Stevenson of *The Longman Companion to Eighteenth Century Britain, 1688–1820* (1999, new edition 2007). He has been a co-editor of *Studies in Church History*, and is currently working on a monograph on the Church of England in Colonial British North America, c.1680–1780.

JUDITH BETNEY completed her MA in the History of Ideas at the University of Northumbria in 2000. She is currently living and working in Devon.

STEPHEN CAUNCE is Senior Lecturer in History at the University of Central Lancashire, having previously worked at Leeds University and in various museums in northern England, including the Beamish Museum, County Durham. His research interests centre around a long view of northern history since 1550, attempting to synthesise aspects normally studied in isolation. The rural north has been a particular interest throughout.

GILLIAN COOKSON was county editor of the *Victoria County History of Durham* for ten years to 2009, writing and overseeing the publication of books on Darlington and Sunderland. She is now a freelance historical consultant working on community projects and films in Yorkshire and the North East. Her academic interests lie in industrial and landscape history, particularly in the eighteenth and nineteenth centuries.

STEVE COUSINS (also known as 'The Green Man Potter') is an independent land-scape designer, landscape archaeologist and ceramic artist based in Durham. His work is heavily influenced by his love of history, ethnology and the natural environment.

STEVEN DESMOND is an independent landscape consultant specialising in the conservation and management of historic gardens in Britain and Europe.

HUGH DIXON is from a Northumbrian family of shopkeepers, soldiers and engineers, and has been National Trust Curator for the North-East Region (now including Yorkshire) since 1986. After studying fine art at Edinburgh he became the first researcher for the Penguin Books series *The Buildings of Ireland*. He is a former Fellow of the Institute of Irish Studies and Lecturer at the Queen's University of Belfast, and, before his return to Northumberland, was also Senior Inspector of Historic Buildings for Northern Ireland for twelve years. He is Chairman of the Bewick Society and is active in heritage and conservation matters both regionally and nationally.

VERONICA GOULTY has been much involved in plant conservation, after an earlier botanical education at Cambridge University. The history of plants, and of the gardens they are grown in, became subjects of great interest to her, leading also to her current passion for walled gardens.

HILARY J. GRAINGER is a Professor and Dean at the London College of Fashion, University of the Arts, London, having taught previously at the Universities of Leeds, Staffordshire, Keele and Wolverhampton. She is the leading authority on both the late Victorian domestic architect Sir Ernest George (the subject of her doctorate from the University of Leeds) and the architecture of British crematoria. Her book *Death Redesigned: British Crematoria, History, Architecture and Landscape* was published in 2006.

ADRIAN GREEN is Lecturer in History at Durham University. His publications include 'County Durham at the Restoration: A Social and Economic Case Study', in *County Durham Hearth Tax Assessment Lady Day 1666* (British Record Society, 2006) and 'Heartless and Unhomely? Dwellings of the Poor in East Anglia and North-East England', in *Accommodating Poverty: Households of the Poor in England, 1650–1850* (eds P. Sharpe and J. McEwan, forthcoming).

FIONA GREEN is a garden historian who provides specialist advice to a wide variety of clients. Her work involves researching, analysing and defining the historic significance of designed landscapes and advising on the restoration and conservation of historic parks and gardens.

JAN HEWITT is Senior Lecturer in English Studies at the University of Teesside. She works on regional writing and colonial literature in the nineteenth and early twentieth centuries.

LAURA NEWTON specialises in art and design history of the late nineteenth and early twentieth centuries and was for some years a Research Associate at the University of Northumbria. Her publications include works on the Cullercoats Artists' Colony (2003), British art colonies (2005) and the 'Glasgow Boys' (2005). She also curated the exhibition 'Cullercoats: a North-East Colony of Artists' at the Laing Art Gallery, Newcastle upon Tyne (2003).

LINDA POLLEY is Senior Lecturer in History at the University of Teesside, where she is Programme Leader of the History MA courses. Her teaching and research interests include eighteenth- and nineteenth-century urbanisation, the local and regional urban and suburban experience, and professional architectural practice in Victorian North-East England.

A.W. (Bill) PURDUE was, until his recent retirement from the post, Reader in British History at the Open University. His books include: *Merchants and Gentry in North-East England 1650–1830: the Carrs and the Ellisons* (1999) and *The Ship That Came Home: the Story of a Northern Dynasty* (2004).

MARTIN ROBERTS came to the North East as a student, qualified as an architect and settled in the region. A long-standing fascination with historic buildings and landscapes led to a career in conservation first as Durham City Conservation Officer, then later as Historic Buildings Inspector for English Heritage. A Fellow of the Society of Antiquaries of London, he has written and lectured widely on historical subjects, particularly those relating to the North East. His publications include the book *Durham: A Thousand Years of History* (2003).

WINIFRED STOKES is a retired university lecturer and currently Chair of the Durham County Local History Society. She is a contributor to various local history journals and has interests in business history, particularly with regard to mining and railways.

Acknowledgements

We would like to record our gratitude to the University of Northumbria for financial support in the production of this book. We would also like to thank Peter Sowden, of Boydell & Brewer, for his enthusiasm, encouragement and many helpful suggestions, while the highly constructive comments of the publisher's anonymous adviser were similarly invaluable. Thanks are also owed to the Universities of Durham (Department of History) and Newcastle (School of Historical Studies and School of Architecture, Planning and Landscape) and to the following individuals: Professor Dana Arnold, Hilary Arnold (for information about the Hardwick estate), Russell Baston (for photographic work), Dr Helen Berry (for editorial assistance to her co-editors in the writing of the Introduction), Ian Chilvers, Dame Margaret Drabble, Janet Dunn-Muse, Dr Martin Harrop, Michael Johnson, Paul Jones, Alex Kidd, Rachel Nesbitt, Colm O'Brien, Richard Pears, Robin Whalley and Dr Tom Yellowley (for much useful advice as well as for the generous supply of original photographs).

Introduction: Landscape and 'North-Eastern-ness'

THOMAS FAULKNER AND JEREMY GREGORY

With the current increased interest in regional matters, there have now been several recent accounts of northern-ness or 'North-Eastern-ness' which can claim to have something approaching as wide a chronological range as the present book. These include H. Jewell, *The North/South Divide: the Origins of Northern Consciousness in England* (Manchester, 1994), T.E. Faulkner (ed.), *Northumbrian Panorama: Studies in the History and Culture of North East England* (London, 1996), N. Kirk (ed.), *Northern Identities: Historical Interpretations of 'The North' and 'Northerness'* (Aldershot, 2000), D. Russell, *Looking North: the North in the National Imagination* (Manchester, 2004), R. Colls (ed.), *Northumbria: History and Identity 547–2000* (Chichester, 2007) and A. Green and A.J. Pollard (eds), *Regional Identities in North-East England, 1300–2000* (Woodbridge, 2007). Of these texts, however, only three – namely *Northumbrian Panorama*, *Northumbria*, and *Regional Identities* – focus on the North East itself, rather than on the north as a whole.[1]

Furthermore, none of the works listed above deals with landscape *per se*, and specialist publications on North-Eastern landscape are similarly sparse. In this context there is, of course, Peter Willis's pioneering study of Lancelot 'Capability' Brown in Northumberland (1983),[2] to say nothing of Robert Newton's even earlier *The Northumberland Landscape* (London, 1972), in *The Making of the English Landscape* series edited by W.G. Hoskins. This latter text adopts an essentially topographical approach. So too do Geoffrey N. Wright's popular but by no means negligible North-Eastern studies *View of Northumbria* (London,

---

1   For more on the North East, see N.J. Higham, *The Kingdom of Northumbria AD 350–1100* (Stroud, 1993), D. Rollason, *Northumbria, 500–1100: Creation and Destruction of a Kingdom* (Cambridge, 2003), R.A. Lomas, *North-East England in the Middle Ages* (Edinburgh, 1992), C.D. Liddy and R.H. Britnell (eds), *North-East England in the Later Middle Ages: Regions and Regionalism in History*, 3 (Woodbridge, 2005), D. Newton (ed.), *North-East England, 1569–1625* (Woodbridge, 2006), H. Berry and J. Gregory (eds), *Creating and Consuming Culture in North-East England, 1660–1830* (Aldershot, 2004) and G. Milne, *North-East England, 1850–1914* (Woodbridge, 2006). Recent studies of major aspects of North-Eastern architecture include T.E. Faulkner, 'Architecture in Newcastle', in W. Lancaster and R. Colls (eds), *Newcastle upon Tyne: A Modern History* (Chichester, 2001) and T.E. Faulkner, P. Beacock and P. Jones, *Newcastle and Gateshead: Architecture and Heritage* (Liverpool, 2006).

2   P. Willis, *Capability Brown in Northumberland* (Newcastle upon Tyne, 1983, reprinted from *Garden History*). Mention should also be made of an innovative conference on 'The Pre-Industrial Landscape of North-East England', held at Durham in October 1997 and organised by the North East of England History Institute (NEEHI).

1981) and *The Northumbrian Uplands* (Newton Abbot, 1989). Another valuable survey, more historical in nature, is *Northumbria* by Constance Fraser and Kenneth Emsley (London, 1978), although this work is almost as much about architecture as landscape. Meanwhile, aimed at least in part at a more academic readership, and more informed by modern archaeological, historical and geographical methodologies, is *England's Landscape: the North East*, edited by Fred Aalen with Colm O'Brien (London, 2006). This impressive book is part of an ambitious and lavishly illustrated new series of landscape studies produced by English Heritage. However, like many of its companion volumes, it adopts an unconventional definition of its particular region, based more on geology than on possible cultural and historical identity. Thus *England's Landscape: the North East* includes, in addition to the historic counties of Durham and Northumberland, all of North and East Yorkshire as well as much of the former West Riding of Yorkshire, as far as Sheffield in the south and Halifax in the west.

Developing the theme of landscape, the detailed essays within *Northern Landscapes: Representations and Realities of North-East England*, many examining historically neglected topics, reflect some of the differing approaches to and ways of understanding this subject. They also serve to illustrate the ever more diverse uses of the concept of landscape in contemporary thinking. Thus, for example, a recent semi-official definition of the term suggests that 'landscape is about the relationship between people and place ... it is the setting for our lives ... it can mean a suburban area as much as a mountain range.'[3] Similarly, more specific notions such as 'urban landscape'[4] and even 'cultural landscape' – however difficult the latter, especially, may be to define precisely – have become common intellectual currency.[5]

In addition, as these varied definitions illustrate, landscape is an interdisciplinary and multidisciplinary subject *par excellence*. It has attracted the attention of archaeologists, geologists, geographers and environmentalists, while, over the past twenty years or so, further specialists, in literature, history and art history,

---

[3]   Definition published by the Countryside Character Network (see website: www.ccnetwork.org.uk), an organisation funded by the Countryside Agency and co-ordinated by Countryscape, which promotes 'Landscape Character Assessment', a tool that helps to identify features that give a locality its 'sense of place'. Meanwhile, at the time of writing there is now even a UK Minister for Landscape, Barry Gardiner. His portfolio also includes Biodiversity and Rural Affairs. Appropriately for the purposes of this volume, Mr Gardiner recently visited the Northumberland National Park to mark its 50th anniversary and went on a guided walk to Winshields, the highest point on Hadrian's Wall, commenting that 'These living landscapes are a source of our most precious resources. People think of them as timeless but they are actually living and dynamic.'

[4]   An early study in this field was G. Eckbo, *Urban Landscape Design* (New York, 1964).

[5]   Cultural landscapes may be defined as geographic areas that include cultural and natural resources associated with historic events, activities, persons or groups. They will be human-made or modified. Such landscapes can include, for example, landed estates, farmland, public parks, historic sites, gardens, scenic highways, college and university campuses, cemeteries and industrial sites. The concept of 'cultural landscape' is now recognised by the United Nations via the themes of Museums and Heritage, Visual Culture, Identities and Communities, Tourism and Economics, Architecture, Education, and Management and Protection; see website: www.ncl.ac.uk/unescolandscapes. See also K. Anderson and F. Gale (eds), *Inventing Places: Studies in Cultural Geography* (Melbourne and New York, 1992), B.J. Graham, G.J. Ashworth and J.E. Tonbridge (eds), *A Geography of Heritage: Power, Culture and Economy* (London, 2000) and J.H. Jameson jr (ed.), *The Reconstructed Past: Reconstructions in the Public Interpretation of Archaeology and History* (Walnut Creek, CA, 2004).

as well as heritage and arts managers and other professionals, have increasingly turned their attention to exploring the ways in which landscapes have been used, shaped and represented.[6]

The definition of North-East England adopted by such a major recent publication as *England's Landscape: the North East* (see above) contrasts with our own view of the North East as a more circumscribed region, admittedly with highly permeable borders that are open to debate, but centring on the historic counties of Durham and Northumberland (see Figs 0.1 and 0.2). This more restricted definition, one to which the name 'Northumbria' is also often applied,[7] is surely substantiated by both geography and history. The region as now proposed is demarcated by the North Sea to the east, the Cheviots and the Tweed to the north, the Pennines to the west and the area of the Tees valley or perhaps the North Yorkshire Moors to the south (here the regional 'boundary' is less definite, with similarities on either side of administrative divisions). For Charles Phythian Adams, the North East qualified as one of his English 'cultural provinces' by virtue not only of these physical demarcations but also of its clear cultural division from other peripheral regions.[8] Moreover, it has also been argued that 'Northumbria', as defined above, is one of only two regions (the other being Yorkshire) which have constituted distinct entities throughout the course of English history.[9]

Historically, the Anglo-Saxon kingdom of Northumbria had at its core the area later occupied by the two counties (even if extending from the Humber to the Forth at the height of its power in the seventh and eighth centuries AD). By the late tenth century the kingdom had become reduced to little more than this area because of the appropriation of all lands north of the Tweed by the Scots and of substantial territory north of the Humber by the Danes. Similarly, of the two previously independent kingdoms from which Anglo-Saxon Northumbria was created, Bernicia and Deira, the former also approximated to the core, if not the totality, of the area we have defined as the modern North East, the boundary between them almost certainly being the Tees.[10] So too did the later earldom of

---

6   Thus the present editors calculate that there are over 25 journals devoted to the study of 'landscape', including, for example: *Landscape History: Journal for the Society of Landscape Studies; Landscape Journal; Landscape Management; Landscape and Urban Planning; Landscape Planning; Landscape Research;* and *Studies in the History of Gardens and Designed Landscapes.* For examples of texts illustrating different approaches to landscape, see M. Andrews, *Landscape and Western Art* (Oxford, 1999), J. Barrell, *The Idea of Landscape and the Sense of Place, 1730–1840: An Approach to the Poetry of John Clare* (Cambridge, 1972), M. Dorrian and G. Rose (eds), *Revisioning Landscapes and Politics* (London, 2003), D. Matless, *Landscape and Englishness* (London, 1998), and S. Schama, *Landscape and Memory* (London, 1996).

7   This usage is followed in the works *Northumbrian Panorama: Studies in the History and Culture of North East England* (ed. T.E. Faulkner) and *View of Northumbria* (by Geoffrey N. Wright), referred to above. Confusingly, however, in Wright's other work *The Northumbrian Uplands* (1989), he uses the term 'Northumbrian' in its other sense of appertaining to the county of Northumberland.

8   See C. Phythian Adams, *Societies, Cultures and Kinship, 1580–1850: Cultural Provinces in English Local History* (Leicester, 1993). For more see the same author's 'The Northumbrian Island', in R. Colls (ed.), *Northumbria: History and Identity 547–2000* (Chichester, 2007), pp.334–59.

9   P. Wormald, 'The Making of England', *History Today* (February 1995), pp.26–32; he further developed his ideas during an appearance on *Start the Week* (BBC Radio Four, 6 February 1995).

10 See P. Hunter Blair, 'The Boundary between Bernicia and Deira', *Archaeologia Aeliana*, 4th ser., 27 (1949), pp.46–59.

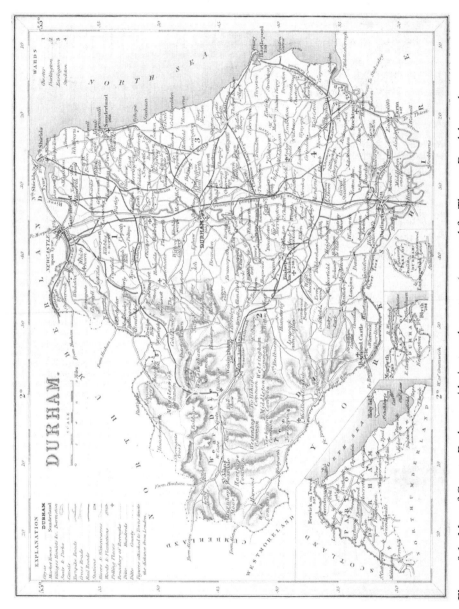

Figure 0.1. Map of County Durham, mid-nineteenth-century (engraved for Thomas Dugdale et al., *England and Wales Delineated*, c.1850).

Northumberland, ratified by the Anglo-Scottish Treaty of York in 1237, under which the Scottish king also forfeited any remaining claim to the northern counties in exchange for lands within them, held subject to the English king.[11]

It was probably a perceived sense of surviving independence that led to the need for savage repression after the Norman Conquest. Yet, in spite of this repression, it has been suggested that 'the ancient kingdom of Northumbria retained its identity as a single administrative area throughout the Middle Ages',[12] with William the Conqueror turning the situation to his advantage by creating the so-called 'Prince-Bishops' of Durham. These prelates ruled over what was in effect a buffer state against the Scots. The consolidation by 1189 of the 'palatinate' (i.e., a border area with a ruler having special powers) gave the Prince-Bishops jurisdiction over eastern England between the Tees and the Tweed. This, incidentally, helped to hold the region together for many centuries, despite the competing power of local magnates.

Furthermore, historians such as Keith Wrightson have argued that this sense of regional identity for 'Northumbria' became stronger still following the Union of the Crowns in 1603 (and even more after the Act of Union of 1707), after which Northumberland and County Durham could to a greater extent look inwards, rather than constantly north towards the threat from the Scots.[13] Later, industrialisation, particularly the coal industry – coal mining was a major activity in much of the North East from medieval times – as well as the enclosure movement in agriculture, seem to have accelerated this process. A strong pattern of what Professor Wrightson calls 'commercial connectedness' was thereby created, being further underpinned by the presence of an unusually large and well-integrated elite (centring mainly on Newcastle: see also Chapter 13) that was balanced in turn by a very substantial industrial workforce. Both groups shared economic, cultural and linguistic points of reference and by 1800 there existed a definite sense of a 'shared, if not quite common' regional identity.[14]

Significantly, too, the North East's elite was highly literate and members of Northumberland and County Durham's polite society, many becoming genteel through success in commerce, industry or agriculture, seem also to have had a deep sense of a regional past. This awareness was manifested in their enthusiastic subscription to the new county and topographical histories that resulted from the upsurge of antiquarian and historical endeavour in the eighteenth and early nineteenth centuries, and which themselves further reinforced feelings of local and regional identity. Important in this context were, among others, the writings of Henry Bourne, John Brand and Eneas Mackenzie on Newcastle, Robert Surtees and William Fordyce on County Durham, and James Raine,

---

11 J. Cannon (ed.), *The Oxford Companion to British History* (Oxford, 1997), pp.1011–12.

12 R.R. Reid, *The King's Council in the North* (London, 1921), p.1.

13 Although there was for many years a certain amount of anxiety on the part of the Church of England regarding the possible threat posed by Scottish Presbyterianism. See F. Deconnick-Brossard, '"We live so far north": the Church in the North-East of England', in J. Gregory and J.S. Chamberlain (eds), *The Church of England and the Regions, 1600–1800* (Woodbridge, 2003), pp.223–42.

14 These ideas, and some of those in the subsequent paragraph, were developed by Prof. Wrightson in his paper 'The Re-making of the North East, 1500–1760', given before the School of Humanities at the University of Northumbria, 12 May 2004, and further developed in his 'Elements of Identity: The Re-making of the North East, 1500–1760', in Colls, *Northumbria*, pp.126–50.

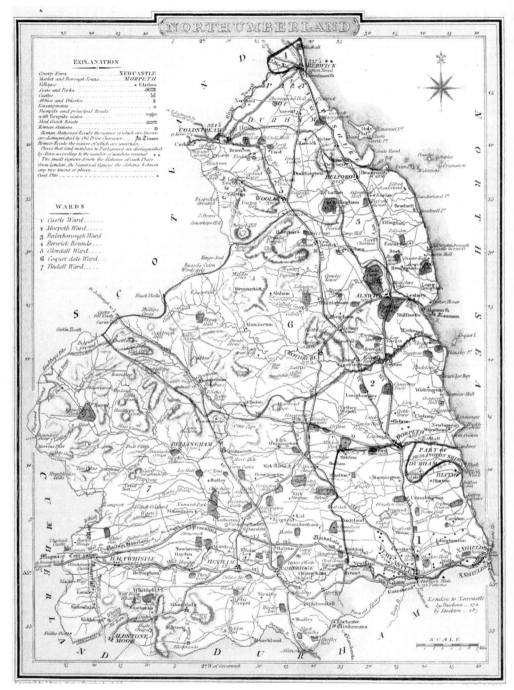

Figure 0.2. Map of Northumberland, early-nineteenth-century (engraved for *The Beauties of England and Wales*, 1808).

John Wallis and John Hodgson on Northumberland. Mackenzie also produced histories of both County Durham and Northumberland, as did an earlier historian, William Hutchinson.[15] Hutchinson's *View of Northumberland* (1778) is discussed in detail by Helen Berry in the last part of this book. His work is doubly interesting in that it explores the received notion of 'Britishness' that was being continually promoted throughout much of the eighteenth century. As Dr Berry explains in her essay 'Landscape, Taste and National Identity: William Hutchinson's *View of Northumberland* (1776–8)', this latter work brings into especial focus the point of contact between English and Scottish cultures in this North-Eastern border county and, like Hutchinson's other county histories, 'both reflected and informed opinion on the meaning of local identity within the context of British national culture' (see Chapter 15). Dr Berry further argues that Hutchinson's contribution to the genre of county history writing was to marry an earlier antiquarian tradition with his own blend of digression, philosophical reflection and empirical observation, based on the idea of the 'man of taste' as the standard-bearer for the good British subject.

Notwithstanding the powerful historic resonances of the traditional counties of Durham and Northumberland, for the purposes of the present volume we have found it useful, as intimated earlier, to include within our definition of the North East an additional area formerly constituting the far north-eastern part of North Yorkshire. This is denoted by the modern, albeit now abolished, county of Cleveland. Here we follow the demarcation adopted by Fraser and Emsley, as shared by numerous government economic surveys and other official and semi-official publications.[16] There is further precedent for this extension. According to the geographer A.E. Smailes, in his classic study *North England*, 'the northernmost parts of Yorkshire, in Cleveland and Teesdale' are essentially part of North-East England.[17] His colleague G.H.J. Daysh agreed: 'the words North-Eastern England are well known and understood in their applicability to the counties of Northumberland and Durham and the northern portion of the

---

[15] See, for example: H. Bourne, *The History of Newcastle upon Tyne, or, the Ancient and Present State of that Town* (Newcastle upon Tyne, 1736); J. Brand, *The History and Antiquities of Newcastle upon Tyne*, 2 vols (London, 1789); W. Fordyce, *The History and Antiquities of the County Palatine of Durham*, 2 vols (Newcastle upon Tyne, London and Edinburgh, 1855–7); J. Hodgson, *A History of Northumberland*, 7 vols (Newcastle upon Tyne, 1820–58); W. Hutchinson, *A View of Northumberland, with an Excursion to the Abbey of Mailross in Scotland*, 2 vols (Newcastle upon Tyne, 1776–8) and *The History and Antiquities of the County Palatine of Durham*, 3 vols (Newcastle upon Tyne and London, 1785–94); E. Mackenzie, *A Descriptive and Historical View of Northumberland,, Newcastle, Berwick, etc.*, 2 vols (Newcastle upon Tyne, 1825) and *A Descriptive and Historical Account of the Town and County of Newcastle upon Tyne*, 2 vols (Newcastle upon Tyne, 1827); E. Mackenzie and M. Ross, *An Historical, Topographical and Descriptive View of the County Palatine of Durham*, 2 vols (Newcastle upon Tyne, 1834); J. Raine, *The History and Antiquities of North Durham ... now united in the County of Northumberland* (London, 1852); R. Surtees, *The History and Antiquities of the County Palatine of Durham*, 4 vols (London, 1816–40); J. Wallis, *The Natural History and Antiquities of Northumberland, etc.*, 2 vols (London, 1769).

[16] See, for example: The British Association, *Scientific Survey of North-Eastern England* (Newcastle upon Tyne, 1949); J.W. House, *Recent Economic Growth in North-East England* (Newcastle upon Tyne: University of Newcastle upon Tyne, Department of Geography Research Series No.4, 1964); and *The North East: A Programme for Development and Growth* (London, 1963).

[17] A.E. Smailes, *North England* (London, 1960, revised edition 1968), p.1

Figure 0.3. The beach at Seaham, Co. Durham (photograph: Tom Yellowley).

North Riding of Yorkshire'.[18] Indeed, for Professor Daysh this unit, which, interestingly, corresponds roughly with the domain of Viking Age Northumbria, had
an emphatic natural cohesion, forming 'one of the most clearly defined regions
of these islands'.[19] The historian A.J. Pollard also includes parts of Yorkshire
in his definition of the North East, contending that the Tees was not such a
clear-cut regional boundary as is usually supposed. Certainly the bishopric of
Durham once included land south of the Tees and in Professor Pollard's view
the river actually brought people from its north and south sides closer together,
many individuals owning property on both banks, for instance.[20] Moreover,
as M.R.G. Conzen argued, the position of the river Tees 'is marginal between
North-Eastern England and Yorkshire, and the routeway from Scotland and the
North-East crosses the Tees at a considerable distance from the coast ... and
offers no point of special distinction'.[21]

This body of opinion justifies us in including within the scope of this volume
the major conurbation of Middlesbrough (see Chapter 14), founded and developed by more northerly entrepreneurs from Newcastle and Darlington; and, in
order to explore similarities in the area immediately to the south, we may even
be permitted to take the short step along the coast to Whitby (see Chapter 17).

[18]   The British Association, *Scientific Survey*, p.xi.
[19]   Ibid.
[20]   See A.J. Pollard, *North Eastern England during the Wars of the Roses* (Oxford, 1990), esp.
       chapter 1.
[21]   M.R.G. Conzen, 'Geographical Setting of Newcastle', in The British Association, *Scientific Survey*,
       p.192.

Figure 0.4. The Alcan Aluminium Smelter, Lynemouth, Northumberland; designed by architects Yorke, Rosenberg & Mardall and opened in 1972, this is directly served by a nearby coal-fired power station of c.1970 (photograph: Tom Yellowley).

This town is technically just outside our region but has many links northwards. For example, it was a designated member of the port of Newcastle until as late as the second quarter of the eighteenth century and for generations had close links to the Newcastle coal trade.

As we have seen, the North East, notwithstanding problems of precise definition, has strong claims to a distinct general identity, something greatly reinforced through a sense of isolation created by the lengthy stretches of open country around its borders. To the south these extend down to York and Leeds and, to the north, as far as Edinburgh. In the west lies the immense and largely rural county of Cumbria. Yet the region could hardly be less physically homogeneous. Its landscapes differ widely, perhaps more so than in any other region of the United Kingdom. This diversity applies not least within the core historic counties of Durham and Northumberland themselves (see below). Indeed, the landscape of the North East has a history of stark contrasts: man's limited planting essays set against the vast backdrop of the upland wastes of the Cheviots and the Pennines; coastal settlements bracing themselves against the unforgiving examination of the sea (see Fig. 0.3); and the ever-increasing drift of mineral exploitation, industry and commercialisation into rural areas (see Fig. 0.4 and cover photograph). The North East is what Gordon Cherry called 'a region of extremes', with the natural beauty of its hills, rivers and expansive beaches contrasting with 'its spoil heaps, quarries and industrial waste ... its landscape witness to an industrial structure of coal, steel, ships and chemicals'.[22] These factors, especially the carving of the landscape due to its heritage of coal (and lead) mining and, more recently, its subsequent greening, make the region truly distinctive. Industrial and rural areas merge and the North East's landscapes also have a multi-layered character, revealing plentiful evidence of prehistoric, Roman, Anglo-Saxon, medieval and later settlement patterns, as cogently demonstrated in the first part of this book in S.M. Cousins's case study of the area around Prudhoe, south Northumberland (see Chapter 1). Dr Cousins adopts a multidisciplinary, 'retrogressive' approach, concentrating on land-use history, which allows, via the use of estate plans, tithe maps and other archival data, the restoration of the area's historical topography.

Notwithstanding its outstanding industrial heritage, the North East remains extensively agrarian. In the eighteenth century the region was noted for its agricultural improvements (although no less an authority than Arthur Young found in the third quarter of that century large areas of fertile land still wastefully unenclosed, particularly in the more remote, northern parts).[23] There is arable farming, especially in Northumberland, along the coastal plain, accompanied by large areas of pasturage on the higher ground to the west. This agriculture was fostered by the watering of the region by a number of important rivers. These are, principally, from north to south: the Aln, the Coquet, the Wansbeck, the Blyth, the Tyne (the region's largest river; at Warden, near Hexham, it divides into the North and South Tyne), the Wear and the Tees. Yet only small sections of these rivers are navigable and, compared to much of Yorkshire, for example, inland waterborne transport in the region was fairly insignificant. For a time this handicap actually impeded the development of agriculture (see Chapter 3).

Roads and, later, railways have proved to be much more crucial. Prehistoric routeways definitely existed and may be the basis of many later roads, lanes and footpaths, but most of the main alignments for land routes in the region were established in Roman times. For example, the northern branch of the Roman Dere Street (forerunner of the modern B6275 and A68), linking near Catterick with a road from York, led up to Corbridge via what is now Bishop Auckland and thence to Hadrian's Wall and beyond. It became the main link between the Anglo-Saxon kingdoms of Bernicia and Deira and remained a major north–south route until the turnpike era and the redevelopment of the Great North Road (A1), itself partly of Roman origin.[24]

It is also worth noting that the North East has comparatively few inland towns. Of these, the most important, apart from Durham itself (see Chapter 11), are

[22] G.E. Cherry, 'The Ambience of the North: The Image of an Unfavoured Region', *Northern Architect* (July 1967), pp.834–5.

[23] See A. Young, *Six Months Tour Through the North of England, etc.*, 3 vols (Dublin, 1770), ii, pp.146–200, esp. pp.199–200. Similarly, at about the same time the topographer P. Russell noted that 'Between Wooler and Rothbury, and also between Alnwick and Rothbury, are vast tracts of mountainous moors; indeed all the latter fifteen miles are absolutely uncultivated' (P. Russell et al., *England Displayed, being a New, Complete, and Accurate Survey of the Kingdom of England, etc.*, 2 vols (London, 1769), ii, p.178.)

[24] For more on routes and transport within the North East see R. Muir, 'Communications and Routeways', in F. Aalen with C. O'Brien (eds), *England's Landscape: The North East* (London, 2006), pp.183–200.

Alnwick and Morpeth (both lying on the main north–south overland route) and Chester-le-Street and Darlington (again strategically placed on the Great North Road and on the main north–south railway line: see Chapter 12). Hexham, Rothbury and Bishop Auckland are of similar status. Current or historic ports, all significant at one time or another for the export of coal, include Blyth, Newcastle (see Chapter 13), North Shields, South Shields, Sunderland and Hartlepool, while Yarm and Stockton, both on the Tees, are examples of small inland ports originating in medieval times, which were at their most prosperous during the eighteenth century. Middlesbrough (see Chapter 14) was founded as coal port but soon became much more important for the production of iron and steel.

Of the two historic counties, central, if not exclusively so, to our concept of the North East, Northumberland is far less industrial. Coal mining and other industrial development was largely restricted to a substantial segment occupying the south east of the county, where two-thirds of its population still live. At the height of mining activity at the turn of the twentieth century it was said of this area that 'industrial activity has deprived the district of any natural beauty which it may have once possessed. Its monotonous level stretches are for the most part only varied by pit heaps and wagonways, and by colliery villages of one prevailing type.'[25] As late as the 1950s, when this coalfield was still supplying at least a sixth of the nation's output, a topographer noted 'the great slag heaps that raise their pyramidal shapes above the blackened cottages'.[26] Yet even here agriculture did and does exist and this section of the county, now environmentally much improved following the demise of the coal industry,[27] has a distinctive quality of its own that is characteristically North-Eastern, being neither rural nor urban but somehow a mixture of the two. Industrial and agricultural elements are often strikingly juxtaposed (see again, Fig. 0.4). Overall, however, Northumberland does remain essentially rural. It still contains much undeveloped moorland and approximately a quarter of its area is designated as the Northumberland National Park, established in 1956, where one can find some of England's most remote and tranquil countryside. This lies westwards, extending north of Hadrian's Wall.

The Tyne valley constitutes one of Northumberland's most fertile and densely wooded sections. The Tyne divides 'Hexhamshire' into two parts, with the northern part rising steeply up towards Hadrian's Wall and the southern – a magnificent blend of woods and moors, penetrated by deep valleys – extending right down to the County Durham border. Here lead was mined for centuries. Further north, another extremely attractive river is the Coquet, with much appeal for naturalists, anglers and historians. Rising in the Cheviots, it traverses the entire width of the county, passing by Harbottle, through country rich in prehistoric earthworks, to Rothbury, Brinkburn (with its twelfth-century priory)

---

25 E. Bateman et al. (eds), *A History of Northumberland*, 15 vols (Newcastle upon Tyne, 1893–1940), ix, p.1.

26 S. Moorhouse, *Companion Into Northumberland* (London, 1953), p.174.

27 This is perhaps more the case than with the equivalent parts of County Durham, where many of the former mining villages seem more evidently disused and dilapidated.

and Felton. Now 'a deep and purposeful river',[28] the Coquet then flows into Warkworth, with its hermitage and castle, before reaching the sea at Amble.

The predominantly flat landscape on Northumberland's eastern side, bordering its nearly eighty miles of North Sea coast, becomes more undulating as one moves westwards, culminating in the county's most mountainous portion (including the Cheviots) to the north west. This latter area, with its wide moors, green hills and fast-flowing streams, contrasts with much of the rest of the county, where 'the countryside is ... orderly with a neatness that stems from the fact that for so many centuries Northumberland belonged to great landowners who cared for their estates and even built whole villages for their employees.'[29] One such village is Cambo, near Wallington Hall, where one of Northumberland's favourite sons, the landscape gardener 'Capability' Brown, went to school.[30]

Northumberland, discussed in more detail by A.W. Purdue in Chapter 2, has never been populous and still remains the most sparsely populated county in England. In the sixteenth century it possessed only eight market towns, compared to, for example, forty-five in Devon at this time,[31] and as late as 1832 William Cobbett was surprised to find that it had a mere 88 parishes compared to the 510 of Suffolk, a county a quarter less in size.[32] Northumberland is also England's most northerly county, and probably one of its least-known.[33] For centuries it was very much a frontier zone, vulnerable to incessant conflict with the Scots. Consequently it remained backward in terms of agriculture and architecture – except for fortified structures such as castles, towers and bastle-houses – until at least the early eighteenth century.

After this, country-house architecture and other 'polite' forms developed apace. Nationally known architects such as Sir John Vanbrugh, James Paine and Robert Adam and, later, the North East's own pre-eminent practitioner, John Dobson (1787–1865), played their part.[34] Major improvements to the landscape were now also being made, notwithstanding the strictures of Arthur Young and others regarding areas of unimproved land (see above). Thus, as Mr Purdue points out, William Hutchinson in particular emphasised the 'happy reverse' of the 'opulent and beautiful', Northumberland of the third quarter of the eighteenth century when compared to its situation 150 years earlier. In Hutchinson's words:

[28] C. Fraser and K. Emsley, *Northumbria* (London, 1978), p.53.
[29] *Northumberland: the County Handbook*, 5th edition (Cheltenham and London, for the Northumberland County Council, n.d. but c.1969), p.25.
[30] For a modern account of Brown and his followers, see T. Williamson, *Polite Landscapes: Gardens and Society in Eighteenth-Century England* (Stroud, 1998), pp.77–99.
[31] R. Newton, *The Northumberland Landscape* (London, 1972), p.146. Northumberland's market towns were Alnwick, Bellingham, Berwick-upon-Tweed, Haltwhistle, Hexham, Morpeth, Newcastle and Wooler.
[32] W. Cobbett, *Rural Rides, etc.* (first published 1832, ed. G.D.H. Cole and M. Cole, 3 vols, London, 1930), iii, p.740.
[33] See, for example, Moorhouse, *Companion*, p.vii.
[34] For more on the country house in Northumberland, see P. Lowery, 'Patronage and the Country House in Northumberland', in T.E. Faulkner (ed.), *Northumbrian Panorama: Studies in the History and Culture of North East England* (London, 1996), pp.49–73, T.E. Faulkner and P. Lowery, *Lost Houses of Newcastle and Northumberland* (York, 1996) and T.E. Faulkner and A. Greg, *John Dobson: Architect of the North East* (Newcastle upon Tyne, 2001).

Figure 0.5. Bothal Castle, Northumberland (an engraving of 1774).

'What blessings have flowed in upon this land, from the union of the kingdoms and the excellent police of the age ... cultivation, with all the comeliness of plenty, laughs in the valleys', while scenes of desolation are now replaced by 'rising woods, inclosed [*sic*] farms, villages and hamlets ... disposed under the smiles of prosperity.'[35]

Hutchinson's assessment, despite his perhaps exaggerated enthusiasm, would appear to have been substantially correct, to judge from numerous topographical engravings of the period and earlier. These show the county's antiquities, country seats and other objects of picturesque interest usually set, when not within impressive landscape parks, then amid well-cultivated landscapes with enclosed fields and well-ordered hedges and trees (see Fig. 0.5). Indeed, it is even tempting to speculate that the origin of many features of the much-imitated 'Capability' Brown style of landscape gardening may lie in what the youthful Brown saw in much of the landscape of his native Northumberland during the 1730s. A study of contemporary topographical prints does seem to suggest that the county possessed, even then, in its less wild parts, substantial areas with proto-Brownian pastures and fields characterised by a gentle rise and fall to the ground and clumps of trees.

Compared to Northumberland, County Durham possesses a much more consistently 'up hill and down dale' character. Deeply incised by rivers and streams, its scenery is marked by numerous steep valleys or 'denes', quite small in scale, which gradually give way to the more open yet remote dales and moors

---

[35] Hutchinson, *View of Northumberland*, i, p.133.

Figure 0.6. Gibside, Co. Durham (engraving by T.A. Prior from a design by T. Allom, 1835).

that lie towards the county's western boundary high in the Pennines (see cover photograph). The county, bounded by the river Tees to the south and by the rivers Tyne and Derwent to the north, can be visualised as a triangle lying on its side, with its base formed by the coastline between the Tyne and the Tees and its apex by a narrow tongue of land bordering the Cumbrian hills towards Cross Fell, the source of the Tees. It is generally less wooded than Northumberland – although eighteenth- and nineteenth-century topographers did admire such exceptions to the rule as the verdant, picturesque scenery of the Wear valley near Chester-le-Street ('wild, romantic, and sublime'[36]), the magnificent gardens at Gibside, at Rowlands Gill, near Gateshead[37] (see Chapters 5, 7 and 8 and Fig. 0.6), and the well-planted landscape parks at Raby and Ravensworth Castles[38] (see Figs 0.7 and 0.8). In addition, it was much more dominated by coal mining (see especially Chapter 9), consistently employing twice as many men in this trade than was the case in Northumberland. Thus, with further heavy industry developing not only in such towns as Consett but also on the strip of flatter land towards the coast, the county had gained by the late nineteenth century a population almost

---

[36] See, for example, Russell et al., *England Displayed*, ii, p.169.

[37] Fordyce, *County Palatine of Durham*, ii, p.342, Surtees, *History*, ii, p.254.

[38] The park at Raby Castle greatly impressed Arthur Young: 'Upon the whole, I have no where seen plantations disposed with more taste – sketched with more judgment for setting off the natural inequalities of the ground' (Young, *Six Months Tour*, ii, p.119). For Ravensworth Castle see Fordyce, *County Palatine of Durham*, ii, pp.641–2 and Surtees, *History*, ii, p.208, while for a later historian Ravensworth was 'the most picturesque monument of the romantic medieval revival in the county' (N. Pevsner, *The Buildings of England: County Durham* (Harmondsworth, 1953), p.195).

Figure 0.7. Raby Castle, Co. Durham (an engraving of 1775).

exactly twice that of its northern neighbour, compared to a position of equality just fifty years before.[39]

Politically, thanks to its position further south – and closer to the source of power represented by the Prince-Bishops – County Durham always remained slightly more secure than Northumberland. From the Middle Ages onwards this allowed the development of reasonably prosperous, (mainly) small-scale agriculture, despite the setbacks of the Black Death, and, later, a certain amount of depopulation in the sixteenth century. And, despite the acknowledged importance of coal mining, it was probably only from the late eighteenth and nineteenth centuries that this and other heavy industrial development radically transformed the county's landscape.[40] However, in Part 3 of this book Adrian Green argues that, in the northern part of the county at least, its modern landscape of (former) mining villages actually originated as far back as the seventeenth century (see Chapter 8).

Turning now to a more detailed account of the contents of this volume not already alluded to above, it is important to note that, despite differences of approach and subject matter, all the individual contributions are informed by reference to at least one of the following major themes: the relationship of build-

---

[39] By the 1880s the Durham coalfield employed over 130,000 men, reaching a peak of 170,000 shortly after the First World War. Even in the mid-1950s there were still over 100,000 miners in the county, not least because here, curiously, the industry was slower to adopt mechanisation than in Northumberland. For more on the region's coal (and other) mining see A. Wedgwood, 'History of Coal Mining', in Sir C. Headlam (ed.), *The Three Northern Counties of England* (Gateshead, 1939), pp.140–58.

[40] For a good summary of County Durham's history see K. Emsley, 'An Historical Introduction', in J. Dewdney (ed.), *Durham County and City with Teesside* (London, 1970), pp.181–90.

Figure 0.8. Ravensworth Castle, near Gateshead, Co. Durham, by John Nash, c.1808–22, enlarged 1840s, now demolished (engraving by W. Le Petit from a design by T. Allom, 1832).

ings to landscape; the response to landscape of artists, writers and topographers; and, above all, the impact of the crucial period c.1750–1914, when agricultural improvements, industrialisation and urbanisation combined to fashion so much of the character of the region's landscape that we know today.

For example, as we have seen, agriculture is and has been a very significant element in the economy of the North East, and in the first part of this book S.A. Caunce examines agrarian development during the key period indicated above (see Chapter 3). His research reveals an unexpected pattern of mechanisation that indicates that this region was more advanced and specialised than previously thought, thus overturning the accepted notion of North-Eastern rural districts as followers of an advanced and specialised agricultural south, and suggesting that urbanisation in the North East actually promoted agricultural prosperity and productivity. Also crucial to agricultural change within the region, especially in Northumberland, was the rapid progress of the enclosure movement from the eighteenth century onwards, even if much of this was of common pasture and waste. This, together with the concomitant growth in the landowning class, led to the development of major new landed estates as well as the enlargement of existing ones. Many of these estates included substantial landscape parks. However, it should be noted that Northumberland was always much more a county of such estates than its southern neighbour (see again, Chapter 2).

Even so, in the next part of the book, on 'Parks and Gardens', we do examine two of the most interesting of County Durham's comparatively limited number of eighteenth-century landscape parks. These, at Hardwick, near Sedgefield (a hitherto rather obscure example), and the much more celebrated Gibside, are discussed in essays by Steven Desmond and Judith Betney respectively (Chapters 4 and 5), the latter from the novel point of view of the attention the estate received during the nineteenth century. Very little has hitherto been known about Gibside as a Victorian pleasure garden, even though large sums of money were spent on it at this time by owner John Bowes and his tenant and step-father William Hutt. However, Ms Betney argues, the estate still became increasingly vulnerable in a rapidly changing society.

Like the famous example of Stourhead in Wiltshire,[41] both Hardwick and Gibside comprise layouts that are virtually independent of the houses to which they belonged. These contain numerous architectural features that create, especially in the case of Hardwick, the sense of a predetermined circuit, rich in aesthetic and symbolic meaning and involving a remarkable sequence of visual and atmospheric experiences. The Hardwick estate, which is now being restored after decades of neglect, was acquired by the immensely wealthy John Burdon in 1748 and transformed into an elaborate landscape garden with extensive water features and ornamental buildings of exceptional quality.

Interestingly, we find that elsewhere in the county at almost the same time the very extensive landscape park at Raby Castle, mentioned above, was being laid out by Thomas White, with garden buildings by Daniel Garrett. It was commissioned by the second Lord Barnard. Yet the fact that, by contrast, the proprietor of Hardwick was not an aristocrat, or even initially a landed gentleman, but a South Shields lawyer and industrialist, is perhaps more typical of general social and economic conditions in the North East. George Bowes, the original creator of Gibside, was also not titled (although he was the son of a knight) and again had substantial mining and other industrial interests.[42] Indeed, it is interesting to note – especially in view of some of the themes explored in Part 3 of this book ('Living in the Landscape') – that Bowes ensured that views outwards from his park were designed to take in the nearby industrial landscape, most of which he owned and in which he took considerable pride (see Chapter 8, by Adrian Green). Even so, as Ms Betney points out, his nineteenth-century successor John Bowes was reluctant to build a large number of miners' dwellings, despite a great shortage, in case they would be visible or a 'nuisance' in some way.

Another significant, if comparatively unpublicised, component invariably found within the eighteenth- and nineteenth-century landed estate was the walled garden. In Chapter 6, Veronica Goulty catalogues the evolution of this type of garden in Northumberland, where the building of such gardens by the gentry began only in the seventeenth century, when country houses no longer needed to be fortified. In particular, she highlights the fact that in these parts many earlier walled gardens were completely redesigned during the nineteenth century, so that the imprint of the Victorian era is very evident in most of those examples that survive today. Fiona Green then concludes this part of the book by demonstrating how, from the later nineteenth century, changed social and

---

41 See K. Woodbridge, *Landscape and Antiquity: Aspects of English Culture at Stourhead 1718 to 1838* (Oxford, 1970).

42 For more on George Bowes and on Gibside generally, see M. Wills, *Gibside and the Bowes Family* (Chichester, 1995).

economic conditions caused many of the parks and gardens of the gentry and aristocracy to become redundant and ultimately appropriated for public use (see Chapter 7).[43] This topic also relates to Thomas Faulkner's discussion of public open spaces in Newcastle, again mainly during the Georgian and Victorian periods (Chapter 13, in Part 4, Urban Landscapes), which also illustrates the city's propensity for radical reinvention and regeneration.

Further developing the theme of the relationship between buildings and landscape, in Part 3, 'Living in the Landscape', Hilary Grainger looks at ways in which a direct response to the austerity of the North-Eastern landscape seems to have conditioned the fashionable Edwardian architect Sir Ernest George's choice of a late classical style in his design for a major regional country house, Crathorne Hall, near Yarm (Chapter 10). Professor Grainger also demonstrates how Crathorne, one of the largest houses built in Britain during the Edwardian period, clearly reflects contemporary attitudes towards architecture, patronage and landscape, while also exemplifying the changing relationship between the wealthy middle classes and the countryside.

Earlier in this part of the book, in Chapters 8 and 9 respectively, Adrian Green and Winifred Stokes examine housing at the other end of the social scale: namely, the terraced cottages of the County Durham mining villages. These cottages were as much a part of the landscape as the collieries themselves and in many places have outlasted them. In Dr Stokes's words, they 'constituted the archetypal vernacular architecture of the North East', as well as being important centres of a community spirit since lost. Adrian Green explores how houses in the landscape manifested in built form the social relations underpinning economic and landscape change; indeed, they were integral to this change. He also emphasises the curious mixture of the industrial and the agricultural that once again characterises the landscape of so much of the county, a dichotomy continuing to this day as the mining villages' rigid rows of urban-style terraced housing, sometimes single-storey, proceed relentlessly across this landscape, seemingly without reference to the contours of the (often quite hilly) moorland terrain. Both grid-pattern and ribbon-development layouts can be found. Appositely, Dr Green quotes the early-nineteenth-century local historian Robert Surtees, who describes how these mining settlements formed 'at every point the strongest contrast to the varied and picturesque appearance of the genuine village – consisting, in general, of long uniform lines of low brick buildings, running along each side of a public road, black with coal dust.' Even today, this still creates a strange though distinctive effect.

Yet, while some County Durham villages were entirely the creation of mining colonisation, some older ones successfully absorbed industrial workers and terraced dwellings without forsaking their agricultural roots,[44] and in both

43 As Ms Green also points out, many estates and mansions had been accessible even when privately owned, at least to the 'polite' visitor. A good example of this practice was at Hardwick, Co. Durham (discussed in detail in Chapter 4), where there was 'liberal permission afforded to strangers to examine and admire the grounds' (Mackenzie and Ross, *Historical, Topographical and Descriptive View*, i, p.440).

44 See R.I. Hodgson, 'First Threat to the Environment', *Northern Architect*, 54 (January 1971), pp.288–93.

core North-Eastern counties housing for farm labourers was also an important feature of the landscape. As Adrian Green again explains, houses in good repair enabled farmers to attract better-quality workers; such houses were both a perquisite and a prerequisite of respectability in the community. Yet the standard was often deplorable. For example, a typical land agent's report on two cottages in north Northumberland in 1850 describes one as containing just one mud-floored living-room, and the other as decayed beyond repair.[45] S.A. Caunce also emphasises the importance of farm-workers' housing.

Moving from the rural or semi-rural to the urban, the next part of the book, 'Urban Landscapes', examines the concept of urban landscape in the senses both of landscapes within an urban situation, and of what Thomas Faulkner calls 'the totality of a town or city's appearance and topography ... involving its layout, buildings, public spaces, and streets' (see Chapter 13). Detailed reference is made to four of the region's most important towns and cities, Durham, Darlington, Newcastle and Middlesbrough, in essays by Martin Roberts, Gillian Cookson, Thomas Faulkner and Linda Polley respectively (Chapters 11 to 14). These multiple case studies combine to offer an interesting contrast, highly characteristic of the North East, between unique historic city, regional capital, major market town and archetypal nineteenth-century industrial settlement.

Newcastle was always the undisputed, if unofficial, capital of the North East (there was no comparable rival), developing thanks to its position as the most eastward convenient crossing point of the Tyne. This point was 'the natural focus of North-Eastern England, not only gathering the radial routes of the region but also forming the junction between the main route from Scotland to the South and the shortest route from the east to the west coast of northern England'.[46] By the fourteenth century Newcastle had become extremely wealthy, mainly through the coal trade. It was walled, and its centre of commercial activity was the waterfront. The antiquary William Camden, writing in 1586, found it 'the glory of all the towns in this country'.[47] During the eighteenth century Newcastle possessed a remarkable number of gardens and public open spaces (see Chapter 13) and this period also saw the construction of many elegant new buildings. In the early nineteenth century the city was further redeveloped, again along classical lines.

Durham was a much smaller settlement, but one of great political and religious significance. During the Middle Ages it developed around the fortified enclave of castle and cathedral, sited on a dramatic promontory formed by a loop of the river Wear, and, with road links north, south, east and west, became established as the crossroads of the county. By the end of the thirteenth century a street layout had been established that remained largely unchanged until about the last hundred years. Durham was famously described by Nikolaus Pevsner as comparable architecturally only to Avignon and Prague.[48] Its topography is

45 Northumberland County Record Office, Society of Antiquaries MSS, ZAN Bell 61/10.
46 Conzen, 'Geographical Setting', p.191.
47 W. Camden, *Britannia, or, a Chorographical Description of England, Scotland and Ireland* (1586, first English edition 1610, revised and republished by E. Gibson, 1695; facsimile edition, Newton Abbot, 1971), p.855.
48 Pevsner, *County Durham*, p.77.

explored by Martin Roberts in Chapter 11, with particular reference to the spectacular river banks that contribute so much to the unique visual character of the city. Here redundant fortifications were transformed into objects of interest for the landscape movement of the eighteenth and nineteenth centuries.

Further south, the sizeable market town of Darlington is also of medieval origin. In the nineteenth century it became more industrial, thanks to major activity in coal, leather, iron and textiles, and, although not the equivalent of a Crewe or a Swindon, it was an important railway town. However, as Gillian Cookson explains in Chapter 12, Darlington retained a broad-based economy and thus, somewhat untypically for the North East, emerged relatively unscathed even from the serious depression of the 1920s and 30s. Dr Cookson's chapter also considers the role of the town's main landowners in developing housing after 1860 and examines the extent to which such schemes were prompted by the growth of railway-related industry. By contrast, Middlesbrough, with its grid-pattern of terraced streets, originated (in 1830) as an unequivocally industrial settlement and has always proved much more vulnerable to economic fluctuations. Its early years, though, were prosperous. Astonishingly, by 1871 its population had grown to nearly 40,000 and with this expansion came prestigious public buildings and even a number of substantial middle-class suburbs, the development of which is a major focus of Linda Polley's essay (see Chapter 14).

In the final part of the book, 'Perceptions and Representations', we examine ways in which, particularly during the last two centuries, many creative artists have found inspiration in the landscape of the North East. These include, most famously, the painters Thomas Girtin and J.M.W. Turner, working in the early nineteenth century. At this time, too, the region became the location for an increasingly well-established 'Picturesque Tour';[49] indeed, no one responded more eloquently to the picturesqueness of the Northumberland landscape, especially that around the Tyne valley, than William Hutchinson, discussed by Helen Berry in Chapter 15. Also active during this period was the North East's own Thomas Bewick (1753–1828), the Newcastle trade engraver whose refined wood-engraving transformed the standard of late Georgian book illustration. He is the subject of an essay by Hugh Dixon, who examines the settings, both architectural and landscape, for Bewick's graphic representations of figures, animals and birds (see Chapter 16). These settings provide a hitherto untapped source for linking representations with the realities of the time, such as the impact of industrialisation upon the hitherto comparatively unspoilt North East. Although Bewick himself bemoaned this process, for others the region's new industrial landscapes had a beauty, or at least a fascination, of their own. Thus during the mid nineteenth century these landscapes were depicted by such outstanding local artists as J.W. Carmichael, T.H. Hair, H.P. Parker and H.B. Richardson. Their approach was taken up a century later by the Ashington Group of pitmen

---

[49] For more on this see *The Picturesque Tour in Northumberland and Durham, c.1720–1830* (exh. cat., the Laing Art Gallery, Newcastle upon Tyne, 1982). See also M. Andrews, *The Search for the Picturesque: Landscape, Aesthetics and Tourism in Britain, 1760–1800* (Aldershot, 1989).

artists (which included Harry Wilson) and also Norman Cornish of Spennymoor, with their uncompromising mining scenes.[50]

During the intervening period the North-East coast began to be particularly attractive to painters searching not only for undiscovered scenery but also for what they saw as unspoilt, quasi-primitive social types, arguably offering a reflection upon the impact of landscape upon moral character that was represented especially by local communities of fisherfolk. The fishing villages of Staithes, in North Yorkshire, and Cullercoats, in Northumberland, became so popular that around the turn of the twentieth century they were able to support substantial artists' colonies during the summer months. Laura Newton provides an appraisal of artistic activity in Cullercoats in Chapter 18. With nationally known artists coming to the village and mingling with local practitioners, a tension seems to have been created which, Dr Newton argues, contributed substantially to 'the local construction of an alternative regional identity'. This in turn circumvented the unacceptability of urban or industrial imagery, replacing it with an imagery which combined a pre-modern subject with a modern aesthetic.[51]

Curiously, comparatively few writers have responded significantly to the North East's landscape, but in this context the once-popular Victorian poet Algernon Swinburne should not be forgotten. Although born in London, he spent much time in his family's ancestral home, Capheaton Hall in Northumberland; he regarded the county, with highly romanticised ardour, as the finest in England. Its scenery provided inspiration for many of his poems, especially *Tristram of Lyonesse* (1882), and is also depicted in his novel *Lesbia Brandon* (published posthumously, in 1952). Another celebrated Northumbrian was the historian G.M. Trevelyan (1876–1962). His family home was Wallington Hall (where, earlier, Swinburne had been a frequent visitor); his own residence was nearby Hallington Hall. Over the years Trevelyan walked nearly every mile of his native county:

> In Northumberland alone both heaven and earth are seen: we walk all day on long ridges, high enough to give far views of moor and valley, and the sense of solitude above the world below … It is the land of far horizons, where the piled or drifted shapes of gathered vapour are for ever moving along the farthest ridge of hills like the procession of long primaeval ages that is written in tribal mounds and Roman camps and Border towers …[52]

In the twentieth century, other literary figures whose work reflected a strong involvement with the North East included the poets W.H. Auden and Newcastle-born Basil Bunting. The latter's semi-autobiographical *Briggflatts* (1966) effectively mingles themes of Northumbrian history, language and landscape. Auden

---

50 See W. Feaver, *Pitmen Painters: The Ashington Group* (London, 1988), and M.-H. Wood and W. Varley (eds), *Norman Cornish: Paintings, Drawings, Sketches* (exh. cat., University Gallery, Northumbria University, Newcastle upon Tyne, 2005).

51 For more on art in and of North-East England generally, especially Northumberland, see P. Usherwood, 'Myths of Northumberland: Art, Identity and Tourism', in Colls, *Northumbria*, pp.239–55.

52 Quoted in A. Myers, *Myers' Literary Guide: The North East* (Ashington and Manchester, 1995), p.86; much of the general literary information in this Introduction is derived from this publication. See also the same author's 'Swords at Sunset: The Northumbrian Literary Legacy', and N. Everett, 'Basil Bunting's *Briggflatts*', both in Colls, *Northumbria*, pp.293–313 and 314–33 respectively.

became fascinated with the rugged landscape of the North Pennines, in both Northumberland and County Durham, and some of his early poems describe the desolate landscape of Weardale, for example at Rookhope (see cover photograph), and the work of the lead-miners around Alston. He also successfully collaborated with the composer Benjamin Britten on their radio documentary *Hadrian's Wall* (1937).

For the now rather neglected late Victorian novelist Mary Linskill it was the rugged beauty of the region's coast that was the inspiration. Following the earlier example of Elizabeth Gaskell in *Sylvia's Lovers* (1863), Linskill set most of her novels and stories in a fictionalised version of Whitby. She uses this location to powerful effect, arguably contributing towards the construction of identity at both an individual and a communal level. Her *The Haven under the Hill* (1886) is analysed in Chapter 17 by Jan Hewitt, who argues that we have become used to present-day heritage designations such as 'Brontë' or 'Thomas Hardy Country' aligning predominant meanings of 'region' with the 'classic' texts of English literature to reinvent our ideas of both, and that in this context Linskill went far beyond mere local description: 'if visiting artists and writers had discovered a "new" romantic landscape, full of rugged beauty and spiritual power, Linskill was encouraged by their visions to create her own – part real, part imagined – with a distinctive moral and spiritual transformative power.'

In conclusion, it can be argued that in linking the topics of 'North-Easternness' and 'landscape', the essays in the present book address two subjects which have attracted significant scholarly attention during the last decade or so: regionality, and landscape itself. Thus their emphasis on landscape is self-evidently timely, as is their concentration on the North East, an area that can too easily be forgotten or misunderstood in a country in which power and population have for so long been radically skewed towards London and the South East. The focus of these essays can also be seen as part of the wider interest in regionality, both at home and abroad, which has made such an impact on contemporary academic and political debate in recent years. In addition, by attempting to explore the distinctiveness of the North-Eastern landscape, wild yet 'civilised', as well as a number of significant responses to it, this text attempts to demonstrate that this landscape is more subtle, layered and varied than is often supposed. It may therefore have the overall effect of helping to revise and even discard some long-standing but enduring stereotypes about the region, such as that based on the notion that it is or was grimly and overwhelmingly industrial. In so doing, it seeks to make a useful contribution to our understanding of North-East England as a whole, and therefore of more general issues concerning regional identity.

PART ONE

THE LIE OF THE LAND

1

The Prudhoe Landscape History Project:
A Retrogressive Study of the Landscape History of
Part of Southern Northumberland

S.M. COUSINS

The main value of applying a 'retrogressive' approach to landscape analysis is that it recovers evidence of human activity from periods that might otherwise be missed or wrongly assigned if one started one's analysis forward from some fixed point. Therefore, the retrogressive approach does not start with a fixed agenda, and it is not known how far back one will be able to go. Additionally, as demonstrated in the present chapter, when looking backwards at individual layers of activity within the time-continuum of change to the landscape, it is possible to view that landscape as the occupants of that time saw it, with all the richness of development that occurred before that period. Arguably this approach, which utilises as wide a range of historical data as possible, is the best way to view past landscapes, as we, after all, are only living in the past landscape of tomorrow.

Accordingly, this chapter is based on a project which aimed to recover the landscape history of the Prudhoe area since the end of the last Ice Age.[1] However, the chapter's necessarily limited scope means that it covers only the last 3,000 years; nor can a full explanation of every term used be given here. The area studied was located in the very south of Northumberland and covered the two high east–west ridges lying between the rivers Tyne and Derwent (Map 1, see Fig. 1.1). This area also consisted of the southern half of the old parish of Ovingham, and contains the townships of Prudhoe, Prudhoe Castle, Dukeshagg, Hedley-on-the-Hill and Hedley-Woodside, in the former medieval barony of Prudhoe or Umfraville, and the townships of Mickley-on-the-Hill and Eltringham, which were once parts of the barony of Bywell or Balliol.

---

[1] See S.M. Cousins, *A Retrogressive Study of the Landscape History of Part of Southern Northumber-land (The Townships of Prudhoe, Prudhoe Castle, Hedley, Hedley-Woodside, Dukeshagg, Mickley and Eltringham, in the former Parish of Ovingham)* (unpublished PhD thesis, University of Newcastle upon Tyne, 2000).

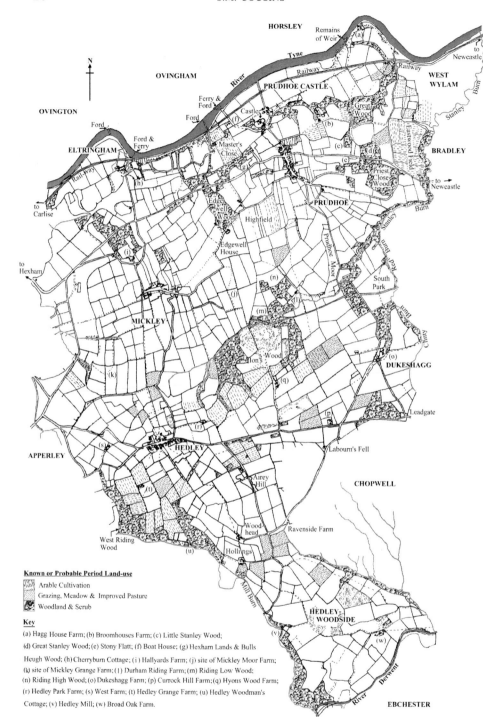

Figure 1.1.   Map 1: Prudhoe and part of southern Northumberland: the landscape at the time of the tithe maps.

Retrogressive analysis and total archaeology

Retrogressive analysis is not a new technique of historical analysis and was used by Bloch[2] and others for their historical studies, but despite its early use by archaeologists such as Petrie,[3] it has rarely used by landscape archaeologists. The main exceptions are those influenced by the work of Christopher Tolan-Smith at the University of Newcastle upon Tyne,[4] such as Gladys Bettess,[5] Myra Tolan-Smith[6] and the present writer.[7] Retrogressive analysis of the landscape involves the removal of known dated features backwards in time to reveal all the features of the landscape that existed at certain layers within its development history. So, for example, to recover the landscape of the nineteenth century, one would remove all features from the modern landscape that dated from after that period, and to recover the landscape of the eighteenth century, one would remove the nineteenth-century features. In effect, the landscape archaeologist excavates the whole landscape, layer by historical layer, recovering successively earlier periods of landscape development. Each resulting map, from the first showing the current landscape, to the last depicting all those features underlying the earliest dateable landscape, are retrospective maps of the landscape at that particular time: that is, they show their own contemporary landscape and include all the developments in the landscape up to that point in time.

Typically, the analysis described here is based on an examination of all the available historical documents, maps and aerial photographs that could be found in a variety of different archives, libraries and museums. Additionally, field studies of the landscape were made, via the examination of hundreds of field boundaries, the exploration of several local woods and the viewing of any earthwork features that survived.

The mid-nineteenth-century landscape

Map 1 depicts the study area in the mid nineteenth century at the time of the tithe assessments of the 1830s and 40s. The main changes that occurred to the landscape after this date were major urban developments around Prudhoe, Mickley Square and Painshawfield, along with various industrial developments such as coal mining and gravel extraction. Otherwise the field system shown on this map is more or less the same today because, except for the amalgamation of many small farms into larger units, the agricultural landscape has seen little other development. Although the two main existing villages of Mickley and

---

2   M. Bloch, *The Historian's Craft* (London, 1954).
3   W.M. Flinders Petrie, *Proceedings at meetings of the Royal Archaeological Institute* (1878), pp.169–75.
4   C. Tolan-Smith, *Landscape Archaeology in Tynedale*, with contributions by M. Macklin, D. Passmore, J.E. Smith and M. Tolan-Smith (*Tyne-Solway Ancient and Historic Landscape Research Programme, Monograph 1*, Dept. Archaeology, University of Newcastle upon Tyne, 1997).
5   G. Bettess, 'Alnmouth, a Retrogressive Archaeological Study of its Landscape, Economy and Social History' (unpublished MA dissertation, University of Newcastle upon Tyne, 1994).
6   M. Tolan-Smith, 'Landscape Archaeology and the Reconstruction of Ancient Landscapes: a Retrogressive Analysis of Two Tynedale Townships' (unpublished PhD thesis, University of Newcastle upon Tyne, 1995).
7   See Note 1.

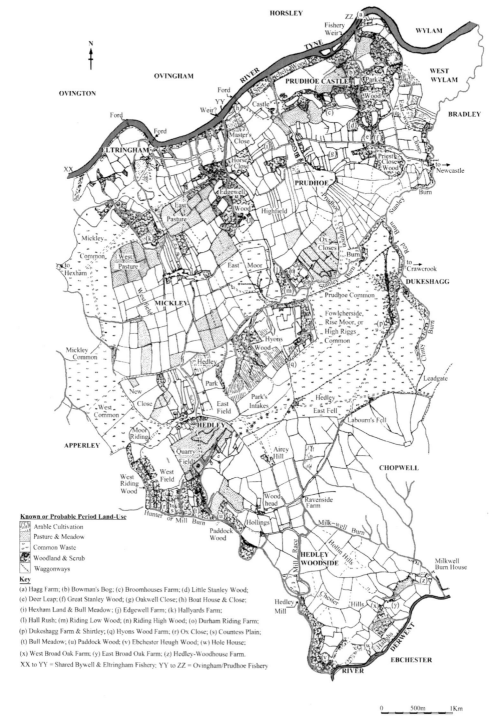

Figure 1.2. Map 2: Prudhoe and part of southern Northumberland: the landscape in the mid eighteenth century.

Hedley are essentially similar to their modern layout, anyone familiar with the Prudhoe area will be surprised to see how small the town was and that, rather than sprawling along the main Newcastle to Hexham road, it was still in its original north–south orientation along what is now a minor route.

The eighteenth-century landscape

Map 2 (Fig. 1.2) displays the landscape of the study area in the mid–late eighteenth century, and catches the countryside in the process of change from the much more open medieval landscape to the fully enclosed landscape seen in Map 1. What draws the eye most of all are the two large unenclosed areas, Mickley Common and Rise Moor or High Riggs Common; the latter was enclosed in 1778–80, but the former not until 1812–15. Another large common had existed up until about 1767 in Hedley-Woodside and the map displays this area immediately after enclosure. The field pattern of the village of Mickley is very similar to that of today; any open arable fields in this area were enclosed in the 1760s. This map also shows that one area of former open common was still not fully enclosed at this time: that is, the area labelled East Moor. Features on both East Moor and Hedley East Fell are the series of bell-pits and small galleried coal-mines, which had wagon-ways leading away from them towards the Newcastle area. Another small colliery, Bewick's Pit, also existed at this time on an extension of Mickley Common, which was leased to the father of Thomas Bewick, the engraver, who was born at nearby Cherryburn Cottage (in 1753).

Except for the urban development that has covered large parts of Prudhoe, the field system there was much as it is today. The main exception is that many of the minor boundaries have since been removed to create larger fields and a golf course now occupies the area labelled Eastwood Closes. This latter area was formerly the medieval open field for the township and was enclosed sometime between the 1650s and 1730s. Additionally, most of the large area of wood and scrub shown to the east of Prudhoe Castle has also disappeared. This map also depicts the townfields of Hedley before their enclosure in around 1770, and shows that much of the area was very open, although it is uncertain whether these were large pasture or arable fields at this date. In the medieval period most of this area had been arable, but eighteenth-century maps suggests that by this period the area was under pasture.

The landscape of the later Middle Ages

The next stage backwards is shown on Map 3 (Fig. 1.3), and it is considerably different from the landscape seen today, although many of the features shown on this map still exist. This map was arrived at only after the removal of many features that proved to date from after about 1550, and involved a careful study of both contemporary documents and post-medieval sources. Among the most important of these was a detailed early-seventeenth-century survey of the townships in the barony of Prudhoe carried out by William Mason,[8] which contains

---

8   Alnwick Mss. A ii.

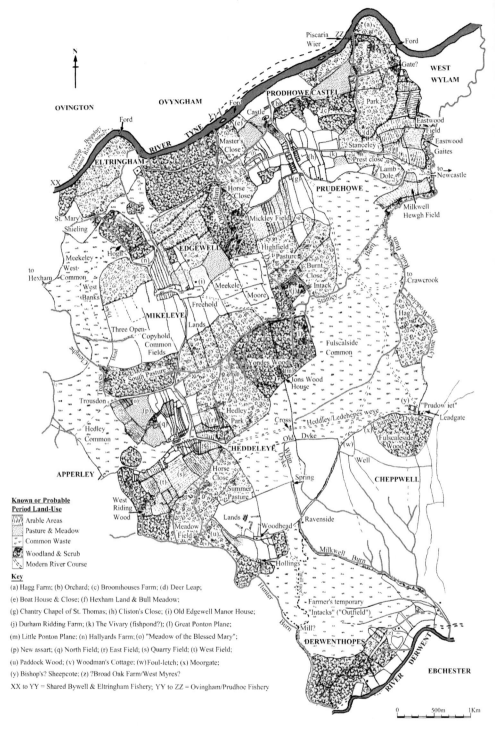

Figure 1.3. Map 3: Prudhoe and part of southern Northumberland: the landscape of the later Middle Ages.

a series of maps drawn by Robert Norton depicting the survey information and shows us the appearance of much of the early post-medieval landscape. Unfortunately, the survey did not cover the townships of Mickley or Eltringham. Very little is known about Eltringham prior to the late eighteenth century and much of the landscape here has been assumed. However, much of the topography of Mickley was recreated through the meticulous study of sixteenth- and seventeenth-century estate surveys and the retrogressive analysis of field boundaries and from the pattern of land ownership recorded in the eighteenth century, revealing the main underlying features of this area.

Of all the villages in this area, Hedley appears to have the only field system approximating to the stereotypical view of medieval agricultural techniques: that is, a series of three open arable fields that are divided into furlongs and further subdivided into a series of long thin strips, resulting in the classic ridge-and-furrow earthworks of much of the English landscape. However, even this village is not as conventional as it seems, as it appears that an attempt was made to force the normal three-field stereotype on to an earlier system in the late fourteenth century. The three-field system appears to have based upon the North Field, the East Field, the Quarry Field and the West Field, with the North Field and the East Field being combined together to create one of three similarly sized open fields. The village was composed of two rows of farmsteads with a series of long, thin closes, known as 'long tofts' or 'long crofts', running north and south from them. A similar arrangement can be seen in Mickley, and this is a pattern common to many other villages in North-East England, with Cockfield in County Durham being the most famous example.[9] This type of arrangement is known to result from village planning and colonisation in the early medieval period (see below).

The field system of Prudhoe departs even further from the stereotypical model. The area is in fact made up of two townships, Prudhoe and Prudhoe Castle, the whole of the latter of which was a demesne estate farmed separately along with an area called Edgewell that had been part of Mickley prior to the early thirteenth century. This demesne estate mainly consisted of a number of fairly large arable and pasture fields, as well as several wooded and semi-wooded areas, along with Prudhoe Park, a hunting reserve dating from before 1245. The field system of Prudhoe village, therefore, consisted of many small enclosures around a central large square arable area called Mickley Field (later called High Field), and the main common open arable field some distance away from farmsteads in the Eastwood area. Mickley Field seems rather unusual, as it probably consisted of a series of long narrow enclosed arable strips (certainly by the early seventeenth century), and probably had early origins. The main Eastwood arable fields are quite extraordinary, partly because of their distance from the village centre, but also because of the arrangement of the arable strips here. More will be said of the earlier origins of this field system in the next section, but here we will examine the field arrangements of the later Middle Ages.

9   B.K. Roberts, 'Village Plans in County Durham', *Medieval Archaeology*, 16 (1972), pp.33–56 and 'The Northern Village: An Archaeological Perspective', in P.A.G. Clack and P.F. Gosling, *Archaeology in the North* (ed. D. Harding) (Durham, 1976), pp.255–64.

As with Hedley, it appears that in Prudhoe there was also an attempt to create three open arable fields of similar size to allow crop rotation. These three areas were made up of the north end of the Eastwood Field, its south end, and the area known as Milkwell Heugh. When the early-seventeenth-century strip distribution of the individual farmers is studied, a very strict pattern is repeated again and again in each furlong, and where there are not enough strips for everyone to get an equal number within an individual furlong, the pattern continues directly into the next furlong, therefore ignoring the furlongs as individual units. However, the pattern does respect the two major north–south divisions of Eastwood Field and the confines of Milkwell Heugh. This pattern of strip distribution also reflects, almost exactly, the pattern of tenancy within the village centre, following the four rows of farmsteads and cottages in a clockwise direction. This sort of distribution has the appearance of being an adapted form of the Scandinavian *solskifte* or 'sun division' system,[10] and shows the possibility of 'new' ideas being introduced into the area sometime before the early seventeenth century.

Some clues as to when these new ideas were introduced can be derived from looking at the strips listed in the Mason Survey as being 'Late Chantry'. There were several large blocks of these strips and many other individual strips that sometimes could be related to individual farmsteads in the village centre. Most of this land had been given by the Umfravilles, lords of Prudhoe, to various chantry chapels during the thirteenth and fourteenth centuries and the existence of large blocks suggests that these strips were grouped together at the reorganisation and that additional strips were granted after this. As the village was emptied of all its occupants by Scottish devastation in the early and middle part of the fourteenth century, it is probable that the townfields were rearranged after the village was repopulated in the later part of that century. At this time, new populations were brought into many northern townships from the Midlands and south of England, and these people, while taking over the remains of the earlier agricultural arrangements, are likely to have brought their own ideas of how field systems should be organised.

The reconstruction of the field system of Mickley, as shown on the map, is very patchy because of a lack of information and depends upon the careful interpretation of post-medieval information. For example, late-sixteenth- and early-seventeenth-century surveys indicate that there were three common open fields in the village, but these were apparently used only by the leaseholders ('copyholders') of the village. In the eighteenth century the freeholders held their land separately in a series of long enclosures and the leaseholders mostly had their land in an area to the west and south west of the village. As the total sizes of the three common fields in the early surveys and the land held by the eighteenth-century leaseholders are comparable, and they are apparently in similar locations, then there is a strong possibility that a comparable pattern existed in the medieval period. This pattern of separate freehold/leasehold occupation is also reflected in the village street plan, as the two rows of farmsteads and cottages

---

[10] B.K. Roberts, *The Making of the English Village* (London, 1987), p.46.

were occupied only by leaseholders (except for one freehold occupying an area at the western end of both rows); the freeholders were all based together at the eastern end of the village and were not part of the planned two-row system.

Sizeable amounts of woodland are another striking aspect of this landscape. The large wood-pasture areas have been mentioned above, but it can be assumed that a coppicing system was employed in much of the formal woodland, as evidenced by such field names as 'Spring' and 'Spring Bank' and the mention of underwood in contemporary documents. However, because of the quantity of woodland it seems not to have been as highly valued as in other parts of England, where woodbanks were normally erected to deter theft and grazing by cattle and deer. At least in this part of the Tyne valley, there appears to have been little need or desire to erect these classic woodland archaeology features to defend this resource. Map 3 also shows several large open commons, often referred to in contemporary documents as the 'waste'. They should not be considered of little value, however, as these extensive areas of unenclosed land were important for the grazing of sheep and cattle as well as the provision of some woodland products from scrub areas, bracken for bedding and heather for thatching.

Finally, in this section, some mention should be made about the area labelled Derwenthopes, which later became known as Hedley-Woodside. In this area, at least in the sixteenth and seventeenth centuries, there existed a field system based upon small enclosures around a loose scatter of farmsteads, which were mostly occupied by closely related family groups. There was also a series of temporary arable fields ('Intacks/Intakes') on the common waste, which were left to recover as unenclosed grazing after a couple of crops had been removed. This sort of arable system is known elsewhere, in other parts of Northumberland and in Scotland, as an 'infield-outfield' system, but does not seem to have been used in other parts of the study area at the time. So this may reflect either the activities of a small group of farmers from outside the immediate area, or the survival of earlier agricultural practices.

The Anglo-Saxon/Anglo-Norman landscape

To discover the origins of the field systems and village plans we need to deconstruct the previous landscape back to the late Anglo-Saxon and Anglo-Norman periods. Map 4 (Fig. 1.4) shows the results of this deconstruction, and these are deliberately vague because many aspects of the origins of the medieval townships are far from clear. What is fairly certain is that the manorial system shown in the previous section was established in about 1100, and that all the main villages existed by then (except Prudhoe), although they are not definitely recorded until the early thirteenth century.

As can be seen, much of the landscape consisted of areas of woodland with uncertain boundaries, although one may assume that they were similar to those shown on later sources. Additionally, woodland is likely to have covered a much larger area in this period, so those areas that are thought likely from botanic and field-name evidence to have had woodland on them at the time have been added. The large open commons discussed above were also probably in existence by this stage, but, again, their exact shape is unknown.

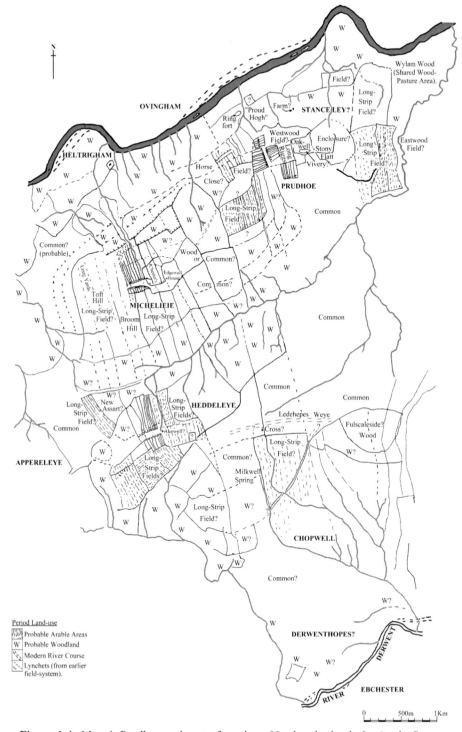

Figure 1.4. Map 4: Prudhoe and part of southern Northumberland: the Anglo-Saxon and Anglo-Norman landscape.

Despite later being in two separate baronies, the villages of Hedley and Mickley appear to have had similar origins, as both have similar layouts. For example, they both have two rows of farmsteads on an east–west alignment, with a rectangular village green between, and these features are typical of many villages throughout northern England, resulting from the insertion of planned settlements or from landscape reorganisation in the Anglo-Norman period. The place-name element 'ley' was also often applied to many villages founded at this time, but was frequently used to name settlements from the mid Saxon period through to the mid thirteenth century.[11] However, although Prudhoe village has a similar planned layout, it is orientated north–south on the route between the castle and the large common wastes. This, along with some other evidence, suggests that Prudhoe may have been laid out at a different date, or took a form more suitable for its topographical situation.

A common feature of all the arable fields shown on Map 4 are the long thin co-axial arrangements known as 'long strip fields', a pattern far from the stereotypical patchwork of strips in the classic 'Midland' open-field system. Whereas in the latter the strips are normally around a furlong in length (c.200m), the strips in a long-strip system can be 300–500m long, or even more than 1,000m in length, and can stretch from one side of the settlement to the other, ignoring local drainage and soil conditions. Where research has been carried out, this type of plan has been recovered in Cumbria[12] and from areas of North Yorkshire,[13] and it is becoming increasingly likely that they underlie many of the Midland field systems further south[14] and in other parts of Western Europe.[15] Therefore, it is not too surprising to find them here, but little research has so far been carried out to show the extent of their use in other parts of the North East. It is probable that this is actually the normal form of field system for large parts of the country throughout the Saxon and early medieval period, but it is uncertain as to why this style was used. However, there are plausible reasons for the change to shorter arable strips: when climatic conditions worsened, with the onset of the 'Little Ice Age' from the middle of the fourteenth century,[16] field systems apparently had to be rearranged to allow for local drainage conditions, but during warmer and drier conditions in the tenth to early fourteenth centuries field drainage had not been such a problem.

It is also apparent that the previously mentioned 'long toft' compartments of both Mickley and Hedley have a very close relationship with the long-strip fields, and Roberts has shown that these toft compartments and the double farmstead rows are often laid out over pre-existing long-strip fields.[17] And this seems to be the case here, as in Hedley arable strips in the Eastfield and individual toft

[11] M. Gelling, *Place Names in the Landscape* (London, 1993), p.206.
[12] B.K. Roberts, 'Norman Village Plantations and Long Strip Fields in Northern England', *Geografiska Annaler*, 70B (1988) and 'The Great Plough: a Hypothesis Concerning Village Genesis and Land Reclamation in Cumberland and Westmorland', *Landscape History*, 18 (1996), pp.17–30.
[13] W. Matzat, 'Long Strip Field Layouts and Their Later Subdivisions', *Geografiska Annaler*, 70B (1988), pp.133–47.
[14] D. Hall, *Medieval Fields* (Aylesbury, 1987, first pub. 1982), pp.43–55.
[15] Matzat, 'Long Strip Field Layouts', pp.136–44.
[16] M. Bell and M.J.C. Walker (eds), *Late Quaternary Environmental Change* (London, 1992), p.73.
[17] Roberts, 'Norman Village Plantations', pp.169–70.

compartments were found to run across the village green and the Lead Road. Therefore, the presumably twelfth-century planned villages with long tofts and double farmstead rows replaced or augmented existing long-strip arrangements.

There are some other hints as to the nature of the landscape immediately prior to the establishment of the long-toft development phase. For example, we have seen that in Mickley the freeholders occupied one distinct part of the village, and it seems that the leaseholders were deliberately moved into the double farmstead rows from an earlier settlement. In parts of North Yorkshire Matzat points to an association of the field name Toft Hill with earlier settlement foci in some long-strip villages, especially where the names Long Tofts and Long Lands also occur,[18] and in Mickley there is an area called Toft Hill that associated with two fields called Long Yards. This is basically within the area of the later leasehold open field, and it is probable that this is where the unfree tenants of Mickley lived before the settlement was amalgamated together into one nucleation. It also seems that the freehold farmsteads were based within a roughly circular enclosure that also included the ancient manor house belonging to the Edgewell demesne estate. Additionally, it is possible that another similar enclosure existed to the east of Prudhoe between the village and its own long-strip field system. It is probable that an early settlement focus existed within this enclosure, and I suggest that this village was called Stanceley (Stanley), as this was the name of the area in later sources. In fact, the existence of an earlier settlement here would explain why Prudhoe's common arable fields were so far from the village centre, and the name of the Stanley Burn. It seems likely that Stanceley was founded at the same time as Mickley and Hedley, and that the Scottish army destroyed this settlement when they devastated the area in 1173–4. Then Prudhoe village was founded soon afterwards, closer to the protection of the castle, with the villagers continuing to use the Stanceley field system even though the settlement was abandoned.

Eltringham also probable existed during this period and its name, supposedly meaning the 'hamlet' or 'homestead' of 'Aelfhere's people' might represent a combination of a Scandinavian personal name with an Anglian settlement name. It used to be thought that these names belonged to a period of Anglo-Scandinavian settlement in the eighth to ninth centuries,[19] but work by Roberts in Cumbria points to the Anglo-Norman period. He suggests that the men who organised and laid out the planned villages, called 'locators',[20] were often granted a freehold within or near the villages they created. In this case, if the man who set out Mickley and some of the other villages in the area was of Scandinavian descent, he may have been given Eltringham, and this could explain its name.

[18] Matzat, 'Long Strip Field Layouts', pp.138–9.
[19] C.D. Morris, 'Northumbria and the Viking Settlement. the Evidence for Land-holding', *Archaeologia Aeliana*, 5:5 (1977), pp.81–103, and V.E. Watts, 'Scandinavian Settlement-Names in County Durham', *Nomina*, XII (1988–9), pp.17–63.
[20] Roberts, 'Norman Village Plantations', p.179.

The late prehistoric/Romano-British landscape

The reconstruction of the late prehistoric/Romano-British landscape is in some ways very speculative (Map 5, see Fig. 1.5), but is also more certain than the depiction shown in Map 4, as many pre-existing boundaries were reused during the Anglo-Saxon/Anglo-Norman periods. Actually, several of the boundaries depicted on Map 5 proved to underlie many later features, as well as areas of woodland, which regrew over much of the landscape in the cold and damp climatic conditions that coincided with a period of low population after the Roman occupation and before the late Saxon period. The best evidence for this comes from a series of east–west lynchets to the north of Mickley, with hedges that frequently contain woodland species and often have drystone revetments that are in places 2m high. Some of these boundaries can be traced into areas of modern woodland, proving that this field system must be older than these woods. Also, in recent centuries, this area has mostly been used for pasture or woodland, so the existence of such large lynchets demonstrates that there was a long period of ploughing before the woodland regrowth. Additionally, there is a small round cropmark feature in the area, which may indicate the site of an Iron Age/Romano-British roundhouse. It is likely that this lynchet system extended further west to include the western end of the Mickley ridge and eastwards into parts of Prudhoe, where further lynchets exist to the south of the High Field.

Running at right angles to the Mickley lynchet system is another system of co-axial boundaries aligned north–south, which may be of an earlier or later date. Owing to later developments it is difficult to tell whether these north–south boundaries overlie or underlie the east–west system or the roughly circular enclosure that later contained the freeholders of Mickley. However, the enclosure does have a shape similar to some Iron Age enclosures and a field name within it, 'The Chesters', is normally associated in North-East England with Iron Age or Romano-British occupation. Both this enclosure and the one in the Stanceley area may have had boundaries ('antennae') running out from them which could have been used to guide cattle into them. This suggests that they were not in use at the same time as the long lineal arable fields of the north–south system. It is also possible that a small square Iron Age farmstead existed near what would later be Hedley village.

Finally, much of this landscape is dominated by long linear features, which are less regular than those in the Mickley area and in some places form parts of the Northumberland–Durham county boundary. Although the name 'Ravenside Dyke' dates from before the twelfth century and that of 'Horse Close Dyke' from before the sixteenth, most of the other dyke systems shown on Map 5 have been named by myself. An interesting common feature of these named dykes is that they were often used later as townships boundaries, which implies that they were considered to be well-established features of the landscape and symbols of permanence. In addition, despite appearing to be continuous and splitting the landscape into two halves, when they are examined closely it can be seen that the situation is more complicated: they appear to relate to the Stanley Burn and two other east–west boundaries that probably ran close to the crests of the two main ridges. It is hard to prove these boundaries, as they are now mostly

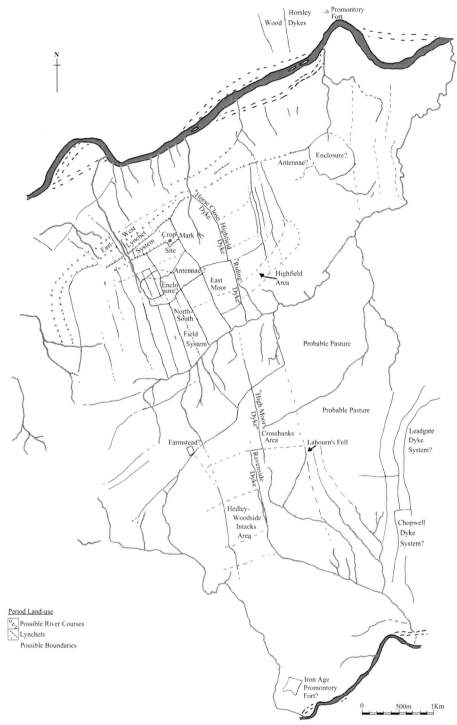

Figure 1.5. Map 5: Prudhoe and part of southern Northumberland: the late prehistoric/Romano-British landscape.

removed, but they were probably laid out before the north–south dykes, and the whole system divides the landscape up into eight roughly equal sections. Exactly when this occurred is difficult to establish but their character does point to a late Bronze Age or early Iron Age date, when they may have been used as part of a cattle ranching system. These boundaries and the many other smaller north–south features that seem to underlie later developments in the area also have similarities to other Bronze Age systems found on Dartmoor and in other highland areas of Britain, but such systems have been difficult to locate at lower altitudes owing to continuous changes to the landscape.

In addition, a programme of fieldwalking was carried out within this area in order to recover details of the earlier prehistoric landscape via the distribution of flint tools. This data has not yet been fully analysed so it is difficult to take this landscape back any further. However, needless to say, although the analysis presented here ends at around 1000 BC, the fieldwalking programme has revealed human activity in this landscape since at least 8,000 BC.

Conclusion

It can be seen from my results that by applying a 'retrogressive' approach to the analysis of so many different data types, that I was able to recover far more evidence of past human activity from periods that I may otherwise not have been able to access with so much confidence. This also reveals that decisions made by Mesolithic hunter-gatherers or Neolithic or Bronze Age farmers may have led to the creation of some of the boundaries still in use today. Certainly, the activities of later prehistoric people affected the use and layout of this landscape and all those who have occupied it since and will continue to do so for many years to come. It is now possible to view these changes to the landscape chronologically, if necessary, viewing the topography, land-use patterns and socio-economic developments of this area of landscape as the people who used it knew it, within their own rich cultural heritage. As stated at the beginning of this chapter, we are only living in the past landscape of tomorrow.

2

The Landed Estate and the Making of
the Northumberland Landscape, 1700–1914

A.W. PURDUE

When Macaulay reached for an example of a wild and desolate area of late-seventeenth-century England in order to illustrate his argument as to the great progress that England had made between the Glorious Revolution and the early years of Queen Victoria's reign, he chose Northumberland:

> Many thousands of square miles which are now rich corn land and meadow, intersected by green hedge-rows, and dotted with villages and pleasant country seats, would appear as moors overgrown with furze, or fens abandoned to wild ducks. Within memory of some whom this generation has seen, the sportsman who wandered in pursuit of game to the sources of the Tyne found the heaths round Keeldar [sic] Castle peopled by a race scarcely less savage than the Indians of California, and heard with surprise the half-naked women chanting a wild measure, while the men with brandished dirks danced a war dance.[1]

William Hutchinson, writing a century before Macaulay, also emphasised the 'happy reverse' of the prosperous and refined Northumberland of his day, which had emerged from its recent brutal and desolate past.[2] Both may have exaggerated the contrast but, if we go back to the early seventeenth century, much of rural Northumberland was, indeed, bleak and barren, though there were many in Macaulay's generation who might have chosen words like 'sublime' and 'romantic'.

By the late seventeenth century greater changes to the landscape and society of the county had taken place than Macaulay recognised. The Union of the Crowns had greatly reduced endemic lawless and cross-border raiding and enabled retainers to become tenants, while enclosures by agreement transformed the pattern of landholding in much of the coastal plain. Nevertheless, defence in seventeenth-century Northumberland only gradually ceased to be a primary consideration in domestic architecture and towers and bastles still dotted the landscape. There was a great difference between the area around Newcastle and

---

[1] T. B. Macaulay, *The History of England from the Accession of James I* (London, 1906 edition), p.222.
[2] W. Hutchinson, *A View of Northumberland, with an Excursion to the Abbey of Mailross in Scotland*, 2 vols (Newcastle upon Tyne, 1776–8), i, pp.133–4.

lower Tyneside together with the coastal plain, and the Cheviot foothills, the north and south Tyne and the debateable lands to the west.

While in nearly all of England comfort, elegance and display had long been the aims of the aristocracy and gentry when they built their country houses, only a few such houses were built without thought of defence in Northumberland until late in the century. Denton Hall (1622) is an early example but then it was only a couple of miles away from Newcastle, and it is from the 1660s that we find a number of houses being built by or attributed to Robert Trollope, the first architect of country houses in Northumberland that we know of: Eshott Hall (c.1660), Netherwitton Hall (c.1685) and Capheaton Hall (1668). A parallel development was the alteration of existing houses, of which the most interesting examples were the replacement of the buildings which had adjoined towers by much grander and more comfortable wings, as at Belsay (1614) and Chipchase (1621), where Jacobean mansions were built on to the towers (see Chapter 6, Figs 6.2 and 6.3, p.98 and p.99).

Such houses were harbingers of the rapid social and economic changes which transformed the landscape of Northumberland in the eighteenth century. After the Act of Union, even north and west Northumberland were relatively safe, stable and increasingly prosperous societies. 'What we have in the north at this time', wrote Edward Hughes, 'is rather like a Caucasian spring, a sudden blossoming of civilisation with the sudden melting away of political and social disorder under the warming influence of economic prosperity.'[3]

We can discern a number of factors in the making of the modern rural landscape of Northumberland. Perhaps the most important is the pattern of land ownership. Northumberland is *par excellence* a county of great estates. Bateman's survey of 1873 showed that it was the second county in terms of the proportion of the total area occupied by estates of over 10,000 acres, with 50 per cent of the total covered by such estates, and eighth in terms of the proportion covered by substantial gentry estates of 1,000 to 10,000 acres, which occupied 35 per cent of the total area. Thus 85 per cent of Northumberland consisted of estates of over 1,000 acres.[4] Intimately connected with this profusion of large estates were changes in farming practice that occurred as a body of largely tenant farmers, working on the consolidated farms facilitated by enclosures, perceived in the emergent peaceful environment new market opportunities and availed themselves of up-to-date farming techniques.

In much of Northumberland changes in agricultural practice and land tenure, which took place gradually in other counties, were concentrated into a shorter period. By the early seventeenth century enclosures by what was, at least ostensibly, private agreement had, as part of a general rationalisation by lords and tenants, already resulted in changes to the landscape in areas close to Newcastle and in parts of the fertile coastal plain, areas which were well placed to take

[3] E. Hughes, *North Country Life in the Eighteenth Century: The North-East 1700–1750* (Oxford, 1952), p.30.
[4] J. Bateman, *The Great Landowners of Great Britain and Ireland* (London, 1883). See F.M.L. Thompson, *English Landed Society in the Nineteenth Century* (London, 1963), pp.32–5 and 109–19, for an analysis of Bateman's figures.

advantage of expanding markets for agricultural produce. The picture was very different elsewhere. In the uplands and the Middle and Western Marches open fields had never existed but farming practices were very backward; in upper Tynedale such an ancient practice as transhumance still existed, while, in many parts of the county, defensive considerations remained important in the lord and tenant relationship until the Union of the Crowns provided a fillip for enclosures and old patterns of tenure based on military needs gave way to commercial pressures. We can trace the effects of this in the demise of fortified farmhouses and bastles and the appearance from the late seventeenth century of farmhouses designed for modest comfort.

Nevertheless, much of the Northumberland landscape remained bleak and the villages have been described as unkempt and often mere 'clusters of turf-covered huts, surrounded by open fields – oases in a wilderness of whim, broom and heather'.[5] Much of the county had meagre amounts of trees and hedges, heath and moorland remained unenclosed and the drystone walls we think so typical of the uplands had yet to be erected.

It was in the eighteenth century that the real transformation of the landscape took place. Agricultural development was based upon burgeoning markets, the more effective division of holdings due to enclosures, the more intensive cultivation of land and major progress in the breeding of cattle and sheep. By the mid-century the enclosure of moorland, mainly effected by private acts of parliament, was well under way, with the east and west commons of Hexham (about 4,000 acres) enclosed in 1753, though this was a long-drawn-out process, with the 42,000 acres of the Hexham and Allendale commons to the south not enclosed until 1800, while enclosures continued in the county until the mid nineteenth century. Northumberland, rather than a byword for agricultural backwardness, was seen by the end of the eighteenth century as a centre of advanced farming practices. The Culley brothers, who began by renting a farm at Fenton, ended up among the major landowners of north Northumberland and were famous for their new techniques of crop cultivation and for the breeding of cattle.[6] The high prices for agricultural produce, and especially corn, in the last half of the century made many fortunes. The landscape revealed the impact of such development, with its substantial farmhouses surrounded by their own fields demarcated by hedges and walls and dotted with lime kilns, barns, byres, stables and the roundhouses for horse-propelled threshing machines.

The emergent pattern of the countryside was largely the result of the mutual interests of farmers and landlords, though such interests were not always in harmony. Landowners were just as concerned to extract the maximum economic gain from their estates as were tenants from their farms, but the country house and estate were more than just a business. The landed estates' other dimensions, the taste, the prestige, the way of life they represented, did almost as much to shape the county's landscape as agriculture. The approaches to the big houses were 'allées d'honneur', concerned to impress and excite visitors, as were the

5   C. Bosanquet, 'John Horsley and his times', *Archaeologia Aeliana*, 4th series, 10 (1933), p.59.
6   See D.J. Rowe, 'The Culleys, Northumberland Farmers 1767–1813', *Agricultural History Review*, 19 (1971), pp.156–74.

Figure 2.1. Rothley Lake, near Wallington Hall, Northumberland. Some four miles from the mansion itself, Rothley Lake was created as part of a picturesque pleasure ground enhancing the far northern end of Sir Walter Blackett's estate. Laid out by 'Capability' Brown around 1765, it comprises two sheets of water, lying either side of the Cambo to Rothbury road, and is overlooked by a mock fortification called Codger Fort (by Thomas Wright of Durham, 1769). Nearby lies the castellated Gothick folly of Rothley Castle (an earlier design, by Daniel Garrett, c.1745) (photograph: Tom Yellowley).

views of the houses from the surrounding parkland and of the parkland from the houses. The lakes, follies and eye-catchers were all part of the culture of the big house (see Fig. 2.1). Sir Walter Blackett's sham ruin, Rothley Castle, on his Wallington estate, Lancelot Allgood's Gothick dog kennels at Nunwick Hall (Fig. 2.2) and the Duke of Northumberland's Brizlee Tower near Alnwick were all designed to enhance the view from mansion or castle or to entrance a guest as he or she walked in the park.

The whole of the surrounding countryside was treated as a landscape to be sculpted and moulded as part of a great scheme, at the centre of which was the house itself (see Fig. 2.3). The building of a new church might be a pious act but it could also improve the view. Old villages might be considered an eyesore or too close to the house; they could be removed and rebuilt on more appropriate sites, as at Capheaton, Netherwitton, Shawdon, Wallington and Haughton. Partly owing to philanthropy and partly for aesthetic reasons, the results were usually more pleasing and had better housing than their predecessors.

Planned villages, of which Northumberland has many, tended to be extensions of the aesthetic and social vision of the estate and big house. All over

Figure 2.2. Dog kennels at Nunwick Hall, Northumberland. These unusual structures, part folly, part functional, are an early example of the Gothic Revival in Northumberland. Looking like a ruined monastery, they were in fact converted from an old watermill in 1768. Nunwick Hall itself is a classical design of 1748–52, almost certainly by Daniel Garrett (see also Fig. 6.6, p.103) (photograph: Tom Yellowley).

Figure 2.3. Hesleyside Hall, Northumberland. A good example of a Georgian country house, set within what was once one of the wildest parts of Northumberland. The facade seen in this view dates from c.1796, and the surrounding park, traditionally ascribed to 'Capability' Brown but without firm evidence, probably from about twenty years earlier. The mansion seems both to dominate, and harmonise with, the landscape (photograph: Tom Yellowley).

Figure 2.4. Blanchland village, Northumberland. A quasi-medieval village, based on an amalgam of genuine and eighteenth-century Gothic architecture and very much reflecting the antiquarian spirit of its period. The village square incorporates part of the original abbey buildings, while the embattled gatehouse seen in this view is largely fifteenth-century (photograph: Tom Yellowley).

the county villages were built or rebuilt during the eighteenth and nineteenth centuries, often reflecting the aesthetic and historicist fancies of landowners. Blanchland was built by the Lord Crewe Trustees for the lead miners of Blanchland and Shildon in the mid eighteenth century and is an exercise in ecclesiastical medievalism based on the existing monastic buildings (see Fig. 2.4). Stamfordham was built after the common lands were divided largely between Sir John Swinburne and Balliol College, Oxford, and has been described as 'one of Northumberland's finest examples of harmonious architecture in brick and stone'.[7] At Ford, the Marchioness of Waterford, having turned the castle into a dream of Camelot, built a village which was an exercise in cosy Victorian paternalism. Cambo, where Sir Walter Blackett rehoused the villagers of Wallington, has cottages sympathetic in design to its refurbished bastle house. Etal was built in the late eighteenth century but is in fact one of the most recent of the new but historicised villages of Northumberland, having been rebuilt by the 'coal baron', Lord Joicey, in the early twentieth century; it is unusual in its whitewashed houses (see Fig. 2.5), many of which retain the thatch once so common in Northumberland. Rock, basically a row of Tudor-style cottages, was built with wealth garnered in more distant lands, namely the West Indies.

Such closed villages were undoubtedly a valuable aesthetic addition to the Northumberland countryside and also provided greatly improved living condi-

---

[7] R. Newton, *The Northumberland Landscape* (London, 1972), p.133.

Figure 2.5. Cottages at Etal village, Northumberland. The 'model' village of Etal, with its neo-vernacular cottages, is dominated by its medieval castle, and Etal Manor, a modestly proportioned Georgian mansion; the main street runs between the two. The cottages shown in this view are roofed with large stone slabs (photograph: Tom Yellowley).

tions for their inhabitants. Those built or remodelled in the nineteenth century often, however, imposed a moral as well as an aesthetic vision of improved rural life, as was demonstrated by the absence of public houses from villages such as Ford and Simonburn and, indeed, by their paucity in many stretches of the county. Outside such villages housing in Northumberland could be pretty dismal. James Caird thought labourers' housing worse than in Ireland.[8] Upright timbers forming the frame with wattle and mud-plaster between, and turf or thatched roofs, as at mid-eighteenth-century Rothbury, were common characteristics. Gradually more comfortable houses, roofed with red pantiles in the north, stone slates in the south west and blue slates elsewhere, became general throughout the county. Charitable landowners formed the Cottage Improvement Society in the early nineteenth century, which resulted in more commodious and healthier living conditions, though the results had rarely the aesthetic merits of the planned villages. A contribution by both farmers and landowners was the revival of an older idea, the self-contained hamlet based on one large farm. Examples of this abound in north Northumberland, as at Elford near Bamburgh and at Ilderton in the foothills of the Cheviots. There are, however, many instances elsewhere, as at Chollerton in the North Tyne valley.[9]

8   J. Caird, *English Agriculture in 1850–51* (2nd edition, London, 1852), p.390.
9   Newton, *Northumberland*, pp.138–9.

Roads, too, could be incorporated visually into the estate plan and, as with Matfen and Wallington, it is often difficult to see where the public road ends and the private drive begins. At Wallington the road was moved from the west to the east side of the Hall and was given a grand entrance in the shape of a Palladian bridge across the Wansbeck, but it was cleverly lowered between the bridge and the house so that passers-by would not intrude into the view or be able to peer at the house from close quarters.

Road development generally owed much to landowners. The development of turnpikes improved communications throughout the county and modified the landscape; the aristocracy and gentry were invariably the motive force. Turnpikes proffered generous returns on the investment of shareholders but often the aim was to increase the value of estates via easing the transport to markets or ports of the produce of farms, quarries or rural industries. The so-called Military Road between Newcastle and Carlisle (now the B6318), constructed approximately parallel to Hadrian's Wall, was only partly encouraged by perceived military needs in the light of the Jacobite Rebellion of 1745 – partly, as well, it was impelled by the desire of local landowners in west Northumberland for better east–west communications. Similarly, the term 'Corn Road' for the Hexham to Alnmouth road is a partial misnomer, for corn was only one of the many goods the transport of which this road facilitated across a great stretch of the county, and few goods of any kind were transported along the whole route.[10] Again, its construction was due to landowners and principally to Lancelot Allgood of Nunwick.

Several railways, destined never to show a profit, were constructed in the late nineteenth century, largely as the result of the ambitions of groups of landowners concerned for better access to markets for the agricultural produce of their tenants or the materials from the quarries, coal mines and lead mines on their estates: the Beaumonts encouraged the Hexham to Allendale railway in the hope of cutting the cost of the transport of lead from the declining lead mines and smelting mills of the Allen Valley; the plans for a Northumberland Central Railway, of which only thirteen miles of track was eventually built, were drawn up by landowners in the mid nineteenth century to link their estates to Newcastle and the Scottish borders;[11] and the North Tyne Railway was an example of aristocratic entrepreneurship on the part of the Duke of Northumberland intended to further the interests of his north Tyne estates.

All over England landowners were remodelling the countryside around their houses, but the effect in Northumberland was particularly marked because of the great number of estates in the county, because the contemporary prestige, status and power of landowners was reinforced by tradition in a county where the feudal past was close, and because wealth made in Newcastle and on Tyneside reinforced rental incomes.

A further impact of the aristocracy and gentry on the landscape was the effect of their love of sport. As the deer parks and 'forests' of the medieval period demonstrate, sport had long been an aristocratic obsession, but from the

---

[10]   S. Linsley, *Ports and harbours of Northumberland* (Stroud, 2005), pp.114–15.
[11]   See N.D. Mackichan, *The Northumberland Central Railway* (Whittingham, 1997).

late eighteenth century the tendency to alter the landscape to facilitate hunting and shooting became marked. Whereas previous generations had been content with hunting as a privately and loosely organised activity and with shooting as largely a matter of going out with friends and a dog in order to shoot what game the environment provided, in the early nineteenth century both sports became organised activities. The coming of the subscription fox hunt and of rivalry between hunts resulted in a new hunting ethos with its codes, rules and discipline, testified to by the great hunting journalist 'Nimrod' and lovingly satirised by R.S. Surtees. One result was landscaping to suit the fox and his hunter. At the same time, the desire for great numbers of game grew, as landed society began to adopt the practice of the shooting party provided with driven game; such *battues* had previously been regarded as un-English. Whereas the eighteenth-century sportsman made use of the land and the fauna he found, the nineteenth century saw the land specially shaped and nurtured for quarry and game.

It is naïve to think that copses, coverts and hedgerows are there just for agricultural purposes. The woodland edge is of prime importance for game, providing refuges and nesting sites close to open feeding areas. The estate designed for shooting tends to have shelter belts and small copses, which bring variety to otherwise monotonous landscapes and encourage a variety of wildlife. Great estates usually have a big home covert, a base not only for pheasants but also for other birds and animals. For the convenience of the fox, land had to be set aside for coverts, while gorse patches were often specially laid out to provide suitable habitations for the quarry. Fences, hedges and walls had to be high enough to be a challenge to the hunter but not so high as to totally impede the progress of a good rider, while hunting gates and bridges had to be maintained. As F.M.L. Thompson wrote:

> Strict preservation of game, begun in the eighteenth century on some estates, became very much more widespread and highly organised in the early nineteenth century, forming one of the more noticeable effects on the living standards of the landed interest produced by agricultural progress and increased incomes. Technically the spread of root crop husbandry and the cultivation of grain crops two years in four instead of one year in three provided a farming environment palatable to the pheasant and partridge. Financially the elaboration of permanent gamekeeping staffs, the running of hatcheries, and the provision of winter feed for game birds, were products of buoyant landed incomes. Preservation itself was made feasible and enforceable by the compactness of estates in ring fences, and to perfect its arrangements was a common motive for buying out small intermingling properties; enclosure therefore made a great contribution to the practicality of strict preservation where it sorted out open-field country into the manageable pattern of fields and compact farms.[12]

An important result of the combination of the economic self-interest of landlords and tenants and Northumberland's landowners' aesthetic vision and love of sport was a new greening of the county. If enclosures led to a great increase in the number of hedgerows, landscaping by landowners led to a similar increase

---

12 Thompson, *English Landed Society*, p.137.

in trees and woodland. Pressure upon woodland in the late Middle Ages had resulted in a landscape denuded of tree cover in many areas. From the mid eighteenth century this process was reversed. Sir William Loraine of Kirkharle planted 24,000 forest trees, 488,000 quicks and 580 fruit trees. The first Duke of Northumberland was said to have planted some 2 million trees. Trees were at once a crop, an adornment and an aid to country sports. If Admiral Lord Collingwood is supposed to have planted acorns on his walks in order to provide for future ships of the line, Mr Davison of Swarland Park, somewhat whimsically, planted trees to delineate the positions of the fleets at the Battle of the Nile.[13]

Behind these developments lay the relative openness of the Northumberland elite and the erosion of distance that resulted from improved communications. New families which had made their way in the merchant houses of Newcastle, in the coal and lead trades or in the legal profession moved cautiously from the late seventeenth century towards the status of landowners, often, like the Blacketts and the Ridleys, maintaining a half-merchant, half-gentry status for several generations. When Sir William Blackett purchased Wallington in 1688 he probably conceived of it as a hunting lodge rather than a main residence but, even by the mid eighteenth century, better roads had brought it closer to Newcastle, and for the nineteenth-century Trevelyans it was a seat within easy distance of the town; similarly, for a twentieth-century Minister of Education[14] it was somewhere to which he could return after a week at Westminster. The highly successful Newcastle merchant Ralph Carr considered Hedgeley Hall a rural retreat when he bought it in the late eighteenth century (for north Northumberland was not easily accessible then), but by the 1820s one could catch the mail coach at Alnwick in the late afternoon and be in Newcastle in time for dinner, and by the end of the nineteenth century Hedgeley Hall had become the main residence of the Carr-Ellisons.[15]

During the nineteenth century the speed of transition quickened as the Claytons, Strakers and many others invested wealth made in Newcastle or on Tyneside in land and country houses. The career of James Joicey demonstrates an exceptional and rapid rise in wealth and status in less than half a century and his houses mark the stages of his elevation: the Orchard House in Gateshead, Dissington Hall, Longhirst Hall, Ford and Etal. In the same period established families found their mansions on industrialising Tyneside and the outskirts of Newcastle unfitting and moved further up the Tyne valley. The Newcastle–Carlisle Railway enabled such families to combine ownership of country estates with frequent contact with their urban and industrial interests.

The Northumberland gentry experienced something of an Indian summer in the late nineteenth and early twentieth centuries. Whereas over much of England

---

[13] Davison, a friend of Nelson, acquired the estate in 1793. The Battle of the Nile took place in 1798 (eds).

[14] Sir Charles Philips Trevelyan, 3rd Baronet, of Wallington Hall (1870–1958), was President of the Board of Education in 1924 and 1929–31 (eds).

[15] For more, see A.W. Purdue, *Merchants and Gentry in North-East England, 1650–1830: The Carrs and the Ellisons* (Sunderland, 1999), and *Squires, Scholars and Soldiers: The Carr-Ellisons, 1830–2000* (2003).

agricultural depression cast a shadow over country estates, in Northumberland agriculture was not so badly affected as its main strengths were in stock rearing rather than in grain. Many landowners could call upon incomes from industrial Tyneside and from coal mines to supplement any decline in incomes from farms. Country houses were enlarged and ballrooms became *de rigueur*. The parklands surrounding estates were walled, while imposing and often castellated lodges guarded the access to sweeping drives. A way of life, with the big house at the centre of a small empire, with substantial farmhouses and farm-workers' cottages surrounding it, continued until 1914 and beyond.

In much of rural Northumberland the countryside became more purely agricultural in the course of the nineteenth century. The small ironworks of the north Tyne and upper Wansbeck were wound up, the tanning and glove-making manufactures of Hexham declined and by the end of the century even the agriculture-related mills and local breweries were closing down. Coal mines became the ubiquitous feature of south-east Northumberland, with even more northern and western areas having scattered mines, while quarrying expanded, but the greater part of the county remained overwhelmingly agricultural. However, until late in the century the Allen valleys were different. The Beaumont family, long the 'richest commoners' in England, ran their lead mines with the aid of their capable manager Thomas Sopwith, and the landscape and social organisation, with miners' smallholdings, mines, smelting works and Methodist chapels, were distinct from those of most of rural Northumberland. The Blacketts and the Beaumonts left their marks in schools, chapels, churches and almshouses but, until one dropped down to Whitfield, this was not an area dominated by country houses. From the 1870s, however, lead mining was in decline.

Along with improved roads and railways, it was the need of Newcastle and Tyneside for water that now drew new patterns on the countryside, but here, too, the influence of the estates and the gentry was felt. Not only were the gentry major investors in water companies, but it took a country gentleman to negotiate with his fellow landowners as to on whose lands the water network would be established. Reservoirs, pumping stations and the housing for water-company staff bear witness to a careful accommodation of the interests of the view from the big house and the desire to maintain a rural and historicist ethos for a utilitarian activity[16] (see Fig. 2.6).

By 1914, the Northumberland landscape as designed by aristocracy and gentry was largely complete. Whether the transformation that landowners did so much to bring about retained or diminished an intrinsic 'northern-ness' can be debated. Certainly the impact of much eighteenth-century landscaping of estates and the building and rebuilding of the great houses at their centre can be seen as reflecting an aesthetic spreading from the south of England and even as the imposition of an image of Italian landscapes seen via the paintings of Claude Lorraine. Yet, even by the end of the eighteenth century, romanticism and antiquarianism introduced an alternative aesthetic which valued the county's border history, its castles and tower houses, a taste reflected in the architecture of

---

[16] See R.W. Rennison, *Water to Tyneside: A History of the Newcastle and Gateshead Water Company* (Newcastle upon Tyne, 1979).

Figure 2.6. Whittle Dene Reservoir, near Welton, Northumberland: Keeper's Cottage and Directors' Rooms, 1848. This design by the Newcastle architect John Dobson, in his favoured 'Tudor-Gothic' style, conveys an air of antiquity. It reflects the revivalist tradition in Northumberland and above all ensures that this essentially functional building blends harmoniously into the landscape (photograph: Thomas Faulkner).

country houses, castellated lodge houses and even mock-medieval farm buildings. Constants, however, were the influence of the landed estate and the relationship of the big house to its grounds and the farmland beyond.

Changes were to come – primarily the forests of conifers on the uplands and the pylons for electricity which march across the countryside, while the rising demands of industry and towns were to see the building of the biggest reservoir of all at Kielder. But much of the view from and of the big houses remains, together with a carefully planned landscape which served agricultural, aesthetic and sporting purposes. Probably more great houses in Northumberland remain inhabited by families than in other parts of England and, where the family residences have gone, country parks, conference hotels and golf courses utilise the aesthetics of the gentry and a vision of gracious living. The landscape that the Northumberland gentry did so much to create is still with us, magnificent but fragile.

3

Agriculture in North-Eastern England, 1750–1914: Relic, Parasite or a Key Part of Development?

S. A. CAUNCE

All modern landscapes are the product of many interacting factors, some fixed, but many contingent. Recognising this is particularly important for the region made up of Northumberland, Durham and Yorkshire north of the North York Moors, which displays highly differentiated human and economic geographies superimposed upon a jumble of widely varying geological and climatic zones.[1] Since 1750, some of England's most industrialised districts have been found here, but also some of its most rural. Large areas are located at high altitudes by English standards, with the Cheviot reaching 2,681 feet, but substantial tracts also lie virtually at sea level. Some pockets of land are as good as any in the country for growing wheat, close by some of its most difficult hillscapes. In 1843 Sir F.H. Doyle reported to the Poor Law Commissioners that generalising about work available for women in Yorkshire rural districts was very difficult because it depended 'mainly upon the nature of the soil, and the nature of the crops [which] fluctuates by the mile', a remark that applies throughout the North East.[2]

Human activity was heavily conditioned, until recently, by this varied natural endowment, and the extraction and processing of minerals have obviously had a tremendous impact on the regional landscape. However, though coal and heavy engineering were certainly the most distinctive and productive sectors of the regional economy before the 1960s, their location and growth patterns are more complex than many realise. The existence of coal did not lead automatically to mining, for instance, since local demand was low before 1850, and proximity to navigable water, or the possibility of creating waggonways to convey coal to staithes, was therefore essential. In addition, while mining led to urbanisation in Northumberland, in Durham an extensive network of self-contained, specialised pit villages developed instead.[3]

---

[1] Boundaries of traditional counties are used throughout, since they are the basis on which statistics were collected and analyses of all types conducted before 1974. Above this level, as with all English regions, boundaries can never be precise.

[2] Sir F.H. Doyle, *Report on the Employment of Children and Women in Agriculture, Reports of Special Assistant Poor Law Commissioners*, PP. LXII, 1843, *Yorkshire and Northumberland*, p.282.

[3] D. Levine and K. Wrightson, *The Making of an Industrial Society, Whickham 1560–1765* (Oxford, 1991) is the classic study of the origins of North-Eastern industrialisation.

Agriculture is generally assumed to have become distinctly secondary, with labour and capital priced out of reach by the more 'modern' sectors, though the general thesis on which such assumptions rest has rarely been subjected to critical examination. It interlocks with an equally unproven belief that eighteenth- and nineteenth-century England saw a progressive specialisation of its regions, with the south (outside London) improving its agriculture while the north concentrated on mining and manufacturing.[4] However, in settings like the North East the evidence indicates that agriculture could increase both production and profitability even while forming a steadily shrinking percentage share of the regional economy, declining relatively but not absolutely, and finding a new role for itself.[5] F.M.L. Thompson has confirmed the excellent performance of agriculture in the north and throughout much of Scotland, even when southern English counties were gripped by depression after 1870.[6]

Operating in and around an industrial zone obviously affected styles of farming intensely, both by altering the profitability of differing crop and livestock combinations and by modifying attitudes towards the use of labour. However, much of the landscape remained outside the direct influence of the new industries, and, in addition, a true global market in foodstuffs and agricultural raw materials developed only a little more than a century ago, and until it functioned reliably industrial development provided more opportunities for northern farmers than competition. Recent rhetoric of an inevitable and irretrievable divide between town and country rests on an emotional rather than a rational, evidential basis, and it should not determine our view of the past. If it applies anywhere it is in the southern half of England, with its very distinctive pattern of urbanisation, but even here East Anglia's early modern agricultural pre-eminence developed under the stimulus of London as a massive centre of consumption, and also during its own earlier phase as a dynamic and successful textile manufacturing area. It is often forgotten that London always had first claim (as a highly accessible, well-organised and rich market) on the food production of the south, and its demand expanded on a massive scale after 1750.

We can thus acknowledge the primacy of the newer industries of the North East and unequivocally accord them the role of triggers of economic development while still having things to say about regional agricultural history which are important. The question considered here, then, is whether the rural North East in the nineteenth century was simply a poorly utilised residual area surrounding the vibrant new sectors, and essentially making do with whatever resources they did not need, or whether it was actually a vital part of the general growth. This is not about showing deviation from an accepted norm established by the existing research into southern English patterns, but asking whether this region estab-

---

[4]   C.H. Lee, 'Regional Growth and Structural Change in Victorian Britain', *Economic History Review*, 33 (1981), pp.438–52, is an attempt to establish regional economic types, but the methodology plays down diversity in order to bring clarity, and agriculture simply disappears in any industrial region.

[5]   See S. Caunce, 'A Golden Age of Agriculture?', in I. Inkster and S. Rowbotham (eds), *The Golden Age: Essays on Industrial England, 1851–1870* (Aldershot, 2001), pp.46–60.

[6]   F.M.L. Thompson, 'An Anatomy of English Agriculture 1870–1914', in B.A. Holderness and M.E. Turner (eds), *Land, Labour and Agriculture 1800–1929, Essays for Gordon Mingay* (London, 1991), pp.223–40.

lished its own successful path within a multi-stranded British agriculture that performed so well precisely because it was so different from region to region, and even from area to area within each region. Such a study will contribute to building a much more rounded picture of the reality of rural Britain than has been achieved in the past.

Certainly, the apocalyptic images conveyed by visitors to coalfields, iron-works and engineering plants did not reflect reality in the majority of the land area of the northern counties. C.W. Percy could still write in 1970 that 'in spite of the dominance of industry in the local economy, the general appearance of Durham County is to a large extent agricultural'.[7] Large parts of Northumber-land have always been among the most lightly populated and least involved in non-agricultural pursuits of any in England. A.W. Fox noted that in 1892 Glendale in the far north was still 'entirely agricultural', with its population of 10,156 people in an area of 147,000 acres so thinly scattered that he noted a 'scarcity of villages' which remains striking today.[8] This in turn had stunted the market towns: most never developed urban institutions, nor were regarded as urban by the census, nor functioned as local government urban districts. They had populations numbered in hundreds rather than thousands.[9] In fact, in this region Fox's enquiries for the Royal Commission on Labour took much longer than anywhere else because of the scattered nature of the population, while the public meetings routinely held elsewhere to get labourers' views were regarded as impracticable here.[10] South Northumberland was relatively densely populated, of course, for this coal-mining district was compact, but that also limited its environmental reach. Moreover, the Newcastle/Gateshead/Tyneside conurbation is the smallest in England, and though it has always formed the region's main centre of population, administration and commerce, as a port and shipbuilding complex it had a natural tendency to focus on the river, and to spawn rivals along its banks rather than to expand over its hinterland, so its physical impact has always been very limited.

The chronology of regional agricultural growth is also distinctive. The disturbed conditions created by the border and the lack of local commercial demand for produce together hindered both peasant cultivation and commercial-isation for centuries. Brassley has shown that far from the spread of coal mining changing this, it actively stunted agriculture in the North East since the coastal coal trade encouraged the importation of grain as a return cargo into the heart of the densely populated area. It was carried very cheaply since no other cargo was available, and it could be picked up at many places along the return journey up the east coast.[11] Internal communications, by contrast, were dreadful. The lack

7   J. Dewdney (ed.), *Durham County and City with Teesside* (London, 1970), p.284.
8   *The Royal Commission on Labour*, PP 1893–4, XXXV, B-III, Poor Law Union of Glendale, pp.101–2. The census shows that Coquetdale Ward (the equivalent of a southern hundred) had only 6.79 residents per hundred acres in 1871, *Northumberland*, vol. I, table 4.
9   Even in 1971 Alnwick, for instance, was only an urban district with a population of 7,489. Most market towns were then civil parishes: Wooler had a population of 1,976, Rothbury 1,784, and Belford, 1,070.
10 *Commission on Labour*, p.101, paras 2 and 3.
11 P. Brassley, *The Agricultural Economy of Northumberland and Durham in the Period 1640–1750* (London, 1985), pp.47–8.

of navigable rivers north of the Tyne left farmers unable to supply towns even a few miles away economically, and north Northumberland was in a hopelessly uncompetitive position. However, by the mid nineteenth century a threshold had been crossed as internal transportation systems were first improved and then transformed, largely to assist industry. Local demand soared, and southern England had less food to spare, not more. Northumberland, with crop yields as good as any in the country, was suddenly seen by informed contemporaries as the epitome of effective arable farming, alongside lowland Scotland. Durham and north Yorkshire had achieved similar status for their cattle-breeding, and Northumbrian sheep had a good reputation.[12]

Farmers thus changed their methods of food production, and thereby changed the landscape, not as some abstract, intellectual game, but because there was money to be made as there had not been before. That, allied to the respect and status derived from running a thriving estate, encouraged landlords to invest a good share of their plentiful mineral royalties and profits, and to play an active role in shaping the new working methods in all types of setting.[13] The result was not one uniform agricultural system or even several, but a widely differentiated response to the limits and opportunities of their situation. This was achieved initially by copying the best practices of other regions, but it was never slavish imitation. The variety of local conditions meant that several external models had to be adapted, and all very quickly became distinctively localised. The lack of a long tradition and the observation of so many different ways to farm success-fully seem to have made and kept minds flexible.[14] Farmers would plant or rear whatever made money for them, and if the mix that succeeded in one decade worked less well in another, adaptation occurred with no sense of betraying a sacred tradition. Landlords would spend, sometimes heavily, to provide farm-steads suited to high intensity, cost-effective operations.[15]

Agriculture and the landscape were therefore transformed not according to a master plan, but through an evolutionary process where radical change combined with the preservation of aspects of the traditional North-Eastern system which still met farmers' needs. Thus, a combination of the very small initial rural population, competition from industries able to absorb large numbers of generi-cally skilled manual labourers and immigration that focused on industrial jobs, not farms, drove rural wages to great heights in the early nineteenth century

---

[12] D.J. Rowe, 'The Culleys, Northumberland Farmers, 1767–1813', *Agricultural History Review*, 19 (1971), pp.156–74; G.E. Mingay (ed.), *The Agrarian History of England and Wales, Vol. VI, 1750–1850* (Cambridge, 1989), pp.320 and 338–89.

[13] P.S. Barnwell, 'Farm Buildings and the Industrial Age', *Industrial Archaeology Review*, XXVII (2005), pp.113–20, also P.S. Barnwell and C. Giles, *English Farmsteads 1750–1914* (Swindon, 1997), esp. chapter 7.

[14] On modern North-Eastern agriculture, J.A. Hanley, A.L. Boyd and W. Williamson, *An Agricultural Survey of the Northern Province* (Newcastle upon Tyne, 1936) and H. Pawson, 'Agriculture', in The British Association, *The Scientific Survey of North Eastern England* (Newcastle upon Tyne, 1949), are accessible and well-informed studies of Northumberland and Durham (most comments can be extended down into North Yorkshire). For the nineteenth century, see J. Caird, *English Agriculture in 1850–51* (London, 1852), pp.346–7. On northern North Yorkshire, see C. Hallas, *Rural Responses to Industrialization: The North Yorkshire Pennines 1790–1914* (Bern, Switzerland, 1999).

[15] P.S. Barnwell, 'Rural Industrial Revolutions: The Evidence of Agricultural Buildings in Northumber-land and Cheshire', *Northern History*, 37 (2000), pp.160–67.

compared to most other regions. Far from needing to encourage a bloated rural sector to 'release' labour to the factories and mines, the issue that has driven so much debate in studies of true peasant economies, the question here was of just maintaining levels which were already far below those perceived as essential to intensive cultivation elsewhere. Hence Northumbrian farming sometimes most resembled that in Scotland, since the extent of the lack of local labour and of settlements resembled the situation across the border more than that prevailing even in other northern counties.

All North-Eastern farmers learned to use available labour with great care, whether their own or that of hired workers. Relying on family members was one solution, since the family that took pride in its independence might be the only operational unit capable of delivering labour near to the better-paid opportunities of industry. Public attention has always focused on farmers with large arable acreages, but many North-Eastern landscape types suited family operations, and northern experience generally showed that shaping farms of all types to family operations could be highly successful.[16] This was never more than part of the solution, however, and yet far from moving towards casualisation, which Marxists and disciples of classical economists alike have seen as the future for the early-nineteenth-century farm labour force, the reverse happened.

Farm service became the basis of a large proportion of paid farm work. With its six-monthly and yearly hires, which were legally binding on both sides, and with wages that were agreed in advance and paid regardless of performance, service has generally been associated with pre-capitalist farming, but here we see it steadily adapting to modern needs.[17] This was clearest north of the Tyne, where it became nearly universal and where married men enthusiastically hired out their entire families. As Doyle remarked in 1843, 'the Northumberland system ... is peculiar to itself and the south of Scotland; it has at any rate nothing in common with Yorkshire.'[18] Thus, south of the Tyne, the picture of classic early modern English service, mostly involving single lads and young men, continued to flourish long after it was felt to have died, and with no hint of ossification. The North-Eastern region as a whole was, in fact, part of the majority of Britain where this method of employing labour continued, not an odd, peripheral region of England, as generally portrayed by English historians. Given recent Scottish willingness to investigate farm service without preconditions, there is much to be gained in the North East by investigating the system and by engaging with the rural literature from north of the border in preference to that from southern England.[19]

---

[16] See, for instance, M. Winstanley, 'Industrialization and the Small Farm: Family and Household Economy in Nineteenth-century Lancashire', *Past and Present*, 152 (1996), pp.157–95, and A. Mutch, *Rural Life in South-West Lancashire, 1840–1914* (Lancaster, 1988).

[17] S. Caunce, *Amongst Farm Horses: The Horselads of East Yorkshire* (Stroud, 1991). Summarised in 'Twentieth-Century Farm Servants: the Horselads of the East Riding of Yorkshire', *Agricultural History Review*, 39 (1991), pp.143–66, and the links to capitalism are further explored in 'Farm Servants and the Development of English Capitalism', *Agricultural History Review*, 45 (1997), pp.49–60.

[18] Doyle, *Children and Women in Agriculture*, p.281.

[19] See, for instance, T.M. Devine, *Farm Servants and Labour in Lowland Scotland 1770–1914* (Edinburgh, 1984); I. Carter, *Farm Life in Northeast Scotland 1840–1914*, (Edinburgh, 1979); and R. Anthony, *Herds and Hinds: Farm Labour in Lowland Scotland 1900–1939* (East Linton, 1997).

The distinctive nature of the Northumbrian system was most visible at the end of a hiring term, when roads were full of families flitting from farm to farm. Elaborate codes regulated the handing over of gardens so that people could harvest what they had planted, thus ensuring that cultivation remained worthwhile even when a house was occupied only for one year at a time. Single servants moved with less fuss, but there was a regular, massive movement of both sexes at every term end throughout the whole region.[20] Farmers could thus shape their workforce to their needs despite the apparent rigidity of long contracts. They also economised greatly on the need for cash to pay wages whether they hired single or married servants, since board and lodging made up at least half a single servant's wage, and a substantial part even of the married men's wages was paid in kind throughout the nineteenth century. Oatmeal remained the basis of the rural diet, so farmers and workers agreed that cutting out the wholesaler and retailer in the supply of this necessity made sense. There was also no need to create new villages for those employed on the expanding cultivated area; farmsteads capable of housing, in a utilitarian fashion, those workers seen as essential were all that was required. If conditions changed, then employment could be reduced without any great loss in terms of wasted investment in redundant infrastructure.

The traditional hiring fairs of the market centres therefore boomed to facilitate the operation of this system. At Hexham on 14 May 1892, for instance, it was reported in the local press that:

> the May hirings for single men and women were held on Monday. The weather throughout the day was cold, but notwithstanding there was a large influx of visitors. Though masters and servants were strongly represented, engagements were only slowly made, servants holding out for higher wages. Men received from £13 to £16 for the half-year, strong lads from £5 to £12, women from £6 to £8.10s, and girls £3 to £5.[21]

All these payments were over and above board and lodging. Durham hirings were busy in 1900, as were those at Newcastle a year later, where women field workers were hired alongside the lads and men for £14 for the half-year.[22] In 1910, Stockton, Darlington, Bishop Auckland and Bedale all reported such large attendances of servants at the Martinmas hirings in November that wages fell, while Guisborough reported the reverse.[23] Newcastle and Stockton were still busy in 1922, and innumerable further illustrations could be added for later dates, as well as for the region's other fairs, held at Cornhill, Berwick, Lowick, Belford, Alnwick, Rothbury, Morpeth, Barnard Castle, Richmond and Northallerton.[24] Dunbabin has showed how some workers used fairs both to increase

---

[20] H.M. Neville, *A Corner in the North: Yesterday and Today with Border Folk* (Newcastle upon Tyne, 1909; new edn, Newcastle upon Tyne, 1980).

[21] *Hexham Courant*, 14 May 1892, reprinted on 19 May 1917.

[22] *Yorkshire Post*, 12 November 1900, and 5 November 1901.

[23] *Yorkshire Herald*, 12 November (supplement), 16 November, 17 November, 18 November and 22 November 1910.

[24] *Yorkshire Post*, 29 November 1922, for Newcastle and Stockton. Note that Cornhill and Lowick had 1971 populations of 401 and 666 respectively. Berwick held separate hirings for men seeking work on either side of the border: *Hexham Courant*, 13 March 1915.

wages and to press for changes to terms of employment.[25] A trade union movement therefore briefly flourished around the Northumberland fairs, which did
not resemble and had little connection with the mainstream that dominates the
historical literature.[26]

Women remained an essential part of the labour force. Some were hired as
part of a hiring package, notably the controversial 'bondagers', the terms of
whose inclusion caused much negotiation at fairs, some of it bitter, while others
used fairs in their own right, as shown above. Migrant workers, mostly Irish,
helped manage the harvest peaks in the North East long after the south ceased
to make much use of them.[27] This allowed a core labour force hired as servants
to be employed fully outside peak periods like harvest, and that in turn helped
farmers to pay higher wages, to pay all year round, and still to make good
returns on their capital. The newspapers also show that wages at the hiring fairs
altered year by year according to demand and supply. The system preserved the
self-respect of workers and avoided much of the social tension that soured class
relations in the areas upon which historians have mostly concentrated. To some
scholars a lack of conflict was in itself a hindrance to a move to a fully capitalistic mode of production, but for those not constrained by a pre-existing vision
of how development 'ought' to proceed, it is a fascinating alternative outcome
which enables us to gain comparative perspectives from within English agriculture.[28] However, its very success has rendered it virtually invisible to historians,
and that obscures how contingent and how localised patterns of labour management really were on British farms.

The social system that resulted both reflected and helped to maintain a distinctive landscape that at the extreme almost managed without either villages or
scattered small farms. High cash wages might have encouraged inward migration, but they were combined with a continued acceptance of a traditional diet
and single-storey housing of very modest dimensions which, alongside obvious
cultural and linguistic barriers, largely ruled out such movement despite the
desperate conditions southern English agricultural labourers frequently endured.
The difficulties were reinforced by the much higher expectations of all northern
employers in terms of effort by labourers.[29] Neo-classical economics has no
explanation for the lack of significant northward migration, and it is baffling
why economic historians have given so little thought to explaining how wages
that were sometimes double those paid in East Anglia could persist for most of

[25] J.P. Dunbabin, 'The Revolt of the Field: The Agricultural Labourers' Movement', *Past and Present*,
      26 (1963), pp.68–97; *Rural Discontent in Nineteenth-Century England* (New York, 1974), Chapter 7.
[26] J. Arch, *The Story of his Life, Told by Himself* (London, 1898), p.221.
[27] *Second Report on the Wages, Earnings and Conditions of Employment of Agricultural Labourers in
      the United Kingdom*, PP. 1905, XCVII, pp.138–9 and *Report on the Wages and Conditions of Employ-
      ment in Agriculture*, I, *General Report*. PP. 1919, IX, p.382.x.
[28] T.M. Devine, 'Social Stability and Agrarian Change in the Eastern Lowlands of Scotland, 1810–40',
      Social History, 3 (1978), pp.331–46, is a rare attempt to investigate this contrast within a hiring
      system like that of North-Eastern England, and shows the sense that serious social conflict had
      somehow been avoided rather than accepting that it did not arise.
[29] See E.H. Hunt, *Regional Wage Variations in England* (Oxford, 1974).

Figure 3.1. A farmstead at Chollerton, Northumberland. Within the complex of buildings, the farm's steam engine chimney is clearly visible (photograph: Tom Yellowley).

the century before the First World War in an industry characterised at a national level by its huge surplus of workers.[30]

Given this picture, the general belief that it was a southern shortage of labour developing in the second half of the nineteenth century that provoked the main surge of mechanisation in Britain seems a particularly odd aspect of the accepted narrative of agricultural history.[31] The overwhelming availability of labour seen there in the middle decades of the nineteenth century at all seasons, except at the very peak of intensity of work, may have diminished, but numbers of workers per acre and wage levels in the south still did not then compare with those experienced in the North East decades before, and as the southern workforce declined, moreover, so did that of the North East.[32] The southern case seems to rest entirely on expectations of a desire for excellence for its own sake despite a social imperative to use more labour than necessary, coupled to an

---

[30] R.E. Prothero (Lord Ernle), *English Farming Past and Present* (London, 1912; 6th edn, 1961), Appendix ix is the best summary of wage levels. A. Redford, *Labour Migration in England 1800–1850* (Manchester, 1926, 3rd edn, 1968) shows clearly the lack of movement to the north.

[31] D. Grace, 'The Agricultural Engineering Industry', in Mingay (ed.), *The Agrarian History*, pp.538–9, makes an explicit statement that East Anglia was the cradle of most significant developments. E.J.T. Collins, 'The Age of Machinery', in G.E. Mingay (ed.), *The Victorian Countryside*, 2 vols (London, 1981), ii, talks of the 'labour problem' after 1835, pp.200–201 and 210–11.

[32] Caunce, 'Golden Age', table 4.2, p.51; Prothero, *English Farming*, appendix IX. The census shows that North-Eastern counties all saw a reduction of around a third in numbers of male farm-workers, 1861–91.

implicit thesis that in industrial areas all available engineering capacity would be absorbed by industrial demand.[33] Neither seems convincing.

During the pioneering era of agricultural mechanisation, in fact, the lack of extra labour whatever the wage and the manifestly superior availability of coal, iron, engineering expertise and manufacturing facilities in the north made it a more likely leader. Tradition clearly did not block general innovation there and the rapid increase in the general intensity of operations was an ideal inducement to such innovation. Thus, threshing machines developed north of the border and were welcomed, rather than wrecked and burned, in the early nineteenth century in the North East.[34] Especially for very large farms whose farmsteads were provided by large estates, the power to drive them might be provided by waterwheels, while some on the coalfields acquired steam engines. A cheaper alternative was simply to add extensions behind the farmstead to house a horse wheel. Though they often pre-date more elaborate installations, they were not primitive devices but a cost-effective way of using a labour-saving power source already available to the farmer, and which did not need either coal or a suitable stream. Horses were already paid for, whereas a waterwheel required heavy initial investment and a steam engine was all expense. The wheelhouses and the steam engine chimneys (see Fig. 3.1) remain distinctive features of the region today.[35] A survey of nineteenth-century farm sales conducted for the Beamish Museum, County Durham, offers a unique opportunity to observe a real mechanisation process in operation. It showed that we must be careful of assuming either that the traditional equipment of farms before 1850 was seriously deficient, or that the logic of machinery, especially steam-powered machinery, as a solution to labour shortages or other production problems applied throughout the economy.[36] Farm machinery is used for such short periods during the year that only massive real savings can justify its own cost, and few machines actually did jobs significantly better than people. Thus, though the processing of crops and animal feed at the farmstead provided an opportunity to develop simple stationary machinery which could operate under cover, starting an engine up simply to break some cattle cake, say, was unlikely to make operational sense, whereas a simple hand-powered device could provide work for a man temporarily at a loose end no matter how short a time was involved. Therefore, while estate farmsteads did become carefully planned and had extensive ranges of specialised buildings, no tendency to create steam-powered food processing

[33] See A. Charlesworth, *An Atlas of Rural Protest in Britain 1548–1900* (London, 1983) and E J. Hobsbawm and G. Rude, *Captain Swing* (London, 1969).

[34] S. Macdonald, 'The Progress of the Early Threshing Machine', *Agricultural History Review*, 23 (1975), pp.63–77.

[35] Hanley et al., *Agricultural Survey*, p.41; A. and J.K. Harrison, 'The Horse Wheel in North Yorkshire', *Industrial Archaeology*, 10 (1973), pp.247–65; J. Hellen, 'Agricultural Innovation and Detectable Landscape Margins: the Case of Wheelhouses in Northumberland', *Agricultural History Review*, 20 (1972), pp.140–54; Barnwell, 'Rural Industrial Revolutions', pp.160–62.

[36] *Farm Equipment Database, 1850–1914*, compiled by S. Caunce for the Beamish Museum, Co. Durham, in 1999. Roughly a thousand sales advertised in newspapers were analysed by type of implement and by decade. A much more detailed summary and analysis of the results can be found in S. Caunce, 'Mechanisation in English Agriculture: the Experience of the North-East, 1850–1914', *Rural History*, 17 (2006), pp.23–45. The full database can be consulted at the Beamish Museum.

factories along the lines suggested by propagandists or the literature issued by machinery manufacturers actually emerged.[37]

The general adoption pattern revealed for all machinery, in fact, was that the region's farmers started and finished with a remarkably similar and extremely heavy dependence on ploughs, harrows and carts.[38] There were some changes to the design of these implements, and new, specialised types were introduced, but nothing transformed them and the basic designs always predominated. Even the automatic assumptions of the superiority of iron over wood as a construction material only prevailed clearly in cultivation implements for light soils. Elsewhere, local conditions might leave a more traditional design superior in performance, and wood was always seen as the best material for vehicles. Even apparently archaic devices like field rollers made of stone could remain common because they worked well and did not wear out. In this context, the late-nineteenth-century adoption of grass- and grain-harvesting machinery stands out as driven by its own narrow logic, like the mechanisation of threshing decades earlier, rather than by a general urge to use machines for all operations. Other devices which have received much attention because of favourable reviews by contemporaries, notably Crosskill's clod crusher, had a limited success, but it was transitory.[39] Perhaps the most surprising local failure was of corn drills, often cited as the epitome of improved grain farming and as one of the few cases where hand operations were seen as inferior. North-Eastern farmers took to drilling turnips very early, but they preferred to broadcast grain over a field carefully ploughed into narrow ridges, which produced the same effect but apparently was more economical.[40]

Particularly significant was the regional success of two-wheeled carts, which replaced the four-wheeled waggon on all types of North-Eastern farms despite being smaller and apparently less sophisticated. The light construction of carts and the fact that loads balanced over the single axle meant that fewer horses were needed for any given load, and a farm with only carts could more readily meet the needs of several jobs.[41] Carts were especially suited to moving small loads more economically, but extending the sides with light frames allowed surprisingly large quantities to be carried at harvest. When heavy loads had to be moved, the use of waggons might seem more appropriate, but the carts that all farms possessed would then stand idle, no small matter since vehicles were probably the most expensive items on most farms. That carts were not so

---

37 See, for instance, J. Brown, *Farm Machinery 1750–1945* (London, 1989), where an imaginative illustration of an outhouse converted to a veritable factory is reproduced on p.44 from S. Copland, *Agriculture Ancient and Modern* (London, 1866). More generally, N. Goddard, *Harvests of Change: The Royal Agricultural Society of England, 1838–1988* (London, 1988), part II, is an authoritative view of top-down pressures for mechanisation more or less for its own sake, and with a strong emphasis on steam for all purposes.

38 Brassley, *Agricultural Economy*, and S. Macdonald, 'The Development of Agriculture and the Diffusion of Agricultural Innovation in Northumberland, 1750–1850' (unpublished PhD thesis, University of Newcastle upon Tyne, 1974) together suggest that this pattern was of long standing.

39 See Goddard, *Harvests*, pp.51 and 54.

40 Caird, *English Agriculture*, p.337, describes the North-Eastern system. For the conventional view see Brown, *Farm Machinery*, p.18; see also Rowe, 'Culleys'.

41 This is analogous to the leverage built into wheelbarrow design, though less pronounced, and it is striking today that farm vehicles are almost all two-wheeled.

Figure 3.2. A hay or pike bogie in use in 1914 at St John's Chapel, Weardale, Co. Durham. This is on the farm of the Rev. James Pattison, hence the smart dress of some participants. An entire pike or cock of cured hay has just been winched up on to the platform ready to be taken away. The winch itself is visible on the near edge of the bogie; note how low-slung the vehicle is to facilitate operations in the field (photograph © Beamish: The North of England Open Air Museum, Co. Durham).

impressive evidently cut no ice, and if they wore out more quickly, that could be an advantage as long as the price was right.[42] Even more clearly, a significant innovation which was not seen elsewhere in England, the hay bogie, was adopted widely though it was a pragmatic, fairly crude device (see Fig. 3.2). A flat bed was mounted on very small wheels, making it very low-slung, and a simple winch mounted behind the shafts meant that a haycock could be winched directly onto the bogie in its entirety.[43] For small farmers the need for extra labour to load harvested crops, which was actually made worse once cutting was mechanised, was thus addressed economically.

As late as 1914 really new implements found on North-Eastern farms, other than those associated with harvesting and feed processing, were counted in their tens and very occasionally in their hundreds, whereas the traditional types were present in thousands. Even successful new types did not rival the old ones numerically, though sufficient threshers, mowers and reapers were bought for all the appropriate work. Reaper-binders apart, agricultural machinery remained simple: it had few moving parts and little need for extreme precision, and the hostile conditions in which it was used militated against sophistication (see Fig. 3.3). Names that historians have made famous over the last century, notably

---

[42] See G. Sturt, *The Wheelwright's Shop* (Cambridge, 1923).

[43] J.R. Bond, *Farm Implements and Machinery* (London, 1923), chapter 11. See also W. Page (ed.), *The Victoria History of the County of Durham*, 3 vols (London, 1905–28), ii, p.368.

Figure 3.3. Alwyn Charlton ploughing, with an implement made of iron, in the 1950s. The exact location is unknown but the high peaks on the collars would confirm that it is on a North-Eastern farm. The operation of the implement, and its various components, can be clearly discerned here. A slice of the stubble is turned under after the coulter and share separate it off, ready for the mouldboard to lift and rotate it before dropping it back into place, but upside down and tilted against the previous furrow slices. The large wheel helps to keep it straight, but primarily determines the depth of the furrow being ploughed (photograph © Beamish: The North of England Open Air Museum, Co. Durham).

Ransome's of Ipswich as plough manufacturers, are rarely to be met in these farm sale lists, whereas local ones recur.[44] Grass-cutting machinery became a northern speciality, understandably. Most corn-harvesting machinery was of American design, and dealing in such implements supplemented the income from the traditional implements that small northern firms carried on making. Thus, far from dwindling away in the face of competition from specialist agricultural engineers further south, many small and medium-sized firms flourished through meeting the region's needs. However, they did not stand out within the regional economy as their southern counterparts did owing to operating in industrial deserts.

The avoidance of dependence on specialised, expensive machinery and the extensive trading of older machinery at relatively low prices were both a consequence and a reinforcement of the mixed farming characteristic of Britain in general, since this mix of equipment placed no barriers in the way of regular

[44] Grace, 'Agricultural Engineering Industry', uses evidence entirely drawn from the south, for instance. Collins, 'Age of Machinery', pp.203–4, lists many firms which were also general and railway engineers, which has inflated their importance.

changes of cropping. That such a pattern was observed in this high-wage manufacturing area helps to explain why Britain did not develop machinery in as dynamic a fashion as the USA and colonial countries, where extensive monocropping for long-distance sales produced very different attitudes, which Bogue has described as 'a whirl of technological change' starting after 1840 but beginning from the same sort of implement mix in the 1830s.[45] Even so, the farmers of North-East England generally emerge as very pragmatic and aware. Very small or extensive farms, a distinctive type found on the barren hill pastures, both married a general avoidance of expenditure on equipment of even basic types to a willingness to invest in the hay harvest and the dairy, because there the monetary gains were clear and significant for the enterprise as a whole. All this suggests that our present understanding of the mechanisation process is deeply flawed.

Overall, the geologist's cliché that Britain is a very varied and variable place is fully borne out when North-Eastern agriculture is examined in detail. The North-Eastern landscape must, therefore, be studied in several dimensions, not just as a natural or modified environment. It had a human dimension and an economic dimension that spilled over both into the hiring of labour and agricultural mechanisation, which then influenced types of farming and the fields, farmsteads and labourers' accommodation created by the landlords and farmers. It is often rural in a way that nowhere in southern England was, and yet it was located in a region generally classed as dominated by heavy, polluting industry. Only when we look at all these dimensions together do we understand what we see.

The patterns that emerge challenge the accepted national picture of agriculture and its contribution to economic development, suggesting that in the north it formed a vital and effective partnership with the industrial towns. It was not a residual sector, and it had ready access to appropriate, affordable technology that suited its operations. In the North East farming had been backward and limited in the early modern period, yet by 1850 crops were being grown wherever they could be, poor grazing was fully utilised and remote moors could be exploited for shooting. Agricultural technology was developed and tweaked, and if it was only transformed for a few operations it was because the apparent advantages of aping manufacturing industry could not yet be realised economically. National and international factors increasingly set the parameters within which the North-Eastern agricultural system operated, but the response was regional and local, and was all the more effective for that. Thus, the Great Depression could not be ignored, but it led to no substantial retreat. This may be at variance with conventional economic modernisation theory, but it reflects northern English reality, which was where so much of the industrialised economic patterns first emerged. Appreciating what Britain is today means examining and understanding all its parts, and the legacy of many aspects is still all around us in the shape of the landscape.

---

[45] A.G. Bogue, *From Prairie to Corn Belt: Farming on the Illinois and Iowa Prairies in the Nineteenth Century* (Chicago, 1963), p.148 and see pp.148–67 generally.

PART TWO

PARKS AND GARDENS

4

A Walk Through Hardwick Gardens

STEVEN DESMOND

The Hardwick estate, to the west of Sedgefield in County Durham, was purchased by John Burdon from the Lambton family in 1748. Over the next ten years Burdon oversaw the laying-out of one of the most extensive and important, though neglected and comparatively little-known, landscape gardens in the North East. It was based on a circuit walk around water features, punctuated at intervals by ornamental buildings designed by no less an architect than James Paine and decorated by a series of the leading artists and craftsmen of the day. A second campaign of improvement, to include a new house as well as further garden buildings, got no further than the drawing board, and Burdon continued to occupy the old house until his death in 1792. The estate was purchased by the Russell family, who carried out further improvements.

Hardwick was tenanted from the mid nineteenth century, and a gradual decline began. By 1945 the garden was in poor condition, with the buildings largely derelict, and the estate became fragmented and overgrown. Despite periodic expressions of concern and tentative schemes of repair, the coherence of the design and much of its detail was all but lost by 1998. Since then a programme of research has led to a better understanding of the design intentions and the prospects for revival, and the first steps to restoration have now been taken.

John Burdon is a curiously obscure character, only now gradually emerging, like his garden, from the shadows. He was born at South Shields, at the mouth of the river Tyne in County Durham, in 1711. The Burdon family were established merchants in the town, having interests in the salt and shipping industries. John appears to have been the last-born of eighteen children, which might not have predestined him for much of an inheritance, but his elder brothers died young, so that on his father's death in 1747[1] he inherited the enormous sum of £140,000. Understandably abandoning his intended career as a lawyer, he embarked on a much grander scheme. During his busy life he controlled a business empire including collieries, limeworks and other mineral interests as well

---

[1] *The Newcastle Courant* recorded on 10 January 1747 the recent death of 'Nicholas Burdon Esq. late an eminent sea captain & salt owner, and Three Times Master of Trinity House, immensely rich'.

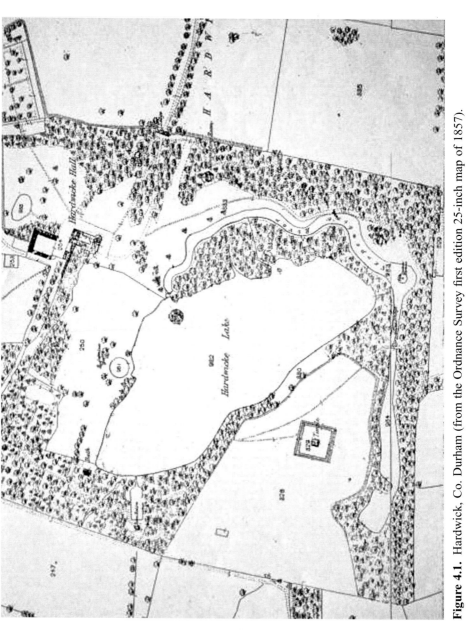

Figure 4.1. Hardwick, Co. Durham (from the Ordnance Survey first edition 25-inch map of 1857).

as banking and the existing family concerns, and took his place as 'an active magistrate and public man'[2] in South Shields.

With these considerable resources at his disposal, Burdon sought to establish himself as a county gentleman with rural property. Various possibilities offered themselves in connection with his extensive landholdings across the county, but he is most closely associated with two estates to the south east of Durham. The first of these was at Coxhoe, where he had important coal, lime and clay workings. Armstrong's map of County Durham,[3] published in 1768, attaches the name of 'Jno Burdon Esq' to Coxhoe Hall, a box of a villa on a south-facing slope. The house, bought by Burdon in 1749, was demolished in the 1950s, but surviving photographs reveal a perfunctory Gothick dress on the entrance facade and tantalising glimpses of extravagant Rococo decoration within, suggesting a date of around 1750 for the new or remodelled house, later the birthplace of Elizabeth Barrett Browning.[4]

At the same time as Burdon was investing at Coxhoe, he was making a more significant acquisition at Sedgefield, a few miles south along the road towards Stockton-on-Tees. The Lambton family had owned the Hardwick estate here since the seventeenth century, but Thomas Lambton's death in 1746 left no male heir. Lambton's six surviving daughters put the Hardwick estate up for sale in 1747. The sale advertisement in *The Newcastle Courant* described

850 acres ... of Meadow, Arable and Pasture Ground, with a good Mansion-House and Gardens well planted with the best kinds of Fruit-trees, and convenient Barns, Stables, Coach-house, Granaries and Dove-coat, all in good Repair, and the Trees growing upon the Premises are very valuable ... the situation is pleasant and healthful ....[5]

The estate lay immediately to the west of the market town of Sedgefield and occupied a low-lying area of gently undulating sand and gravel farmland with numerous springs. The house stood on a slight rise to the north of an area including a meandering stream and a pond, both fed by the springs. The pond was used for fowling; the sale particulars speak of a boat, decoy ducks, nets and dogs. The core estate was surrounded by a ring of tenanted estate farms (see Fig. 4.1).

The order of events which led to the development of the new garden is unclear owing to the loss of John Burdon's papers, but a combination of site evidence and contemporary descriptions, together with comparative research at related sites, has enabled a reasonably clear picture to be assembled. Burdon's priority appears always to have been the garden. The house remained outwardly unimproved, to the extent that the historian William Hutchinson remarked in

2   G.B. Hodgson, *The Borough of South Shields, from the Earliest Period to the Close of the Nineteenth Century* (Newcastle upon Tyne, 1903), p.470, n.3.
3   Captain Armstrong (surveyor) and T. Jefferys (engraver), *The County Palatine of Durham*, 1768.
4   For more on Coxhoe Hall see P. Meadows and E. Waterson, *Lost Houses of County Durham* (York, 1993), pp.54–5.
5   Advertisement, *Newcastle Courant*, 30 May 1747.

1787 that 'Mr Burdon has not yet thought proper to build a mansion-house'.[6] In this preference for spending his money on the garden rather than the house, Burdon was in tune with other enthusiasts for the new taste, including Charles Hamilton at Painshill in Surrey, Henry Hoare at Stourhead in Wiltshire and his own illustrious relation by marriage, George Bowes at Gibside.

Burdon's new layout included a Serpentine River running along the southern and eastern sides of the garden, which discharged into a lake via a cascade. The lake, screened by plantations from the River, was secured by a substantial earth dam built along its western margin. In the middle of the dam was the outflow, in the form of another cascade, whence the water was led away westwards out of sight to join a natural watercourse. In constructing the Serpentine River, lake and cascades, Burdon had the satisfaction of providing proper drainage for his marshy grounds and making splendid ornamental water features as a consequence. The source for his waterworks is as much a mystery today as it must have been in 1748, there being no stream flowing into the Serpentine River. Levels appear to have been maintained, then as now, by the constant flow of springs percolating down through the surrounding sands and gravels. Thus Burdon was able to present himself as practical man as well as beautifier, in tune with the prevailing philosophy commending the seamless blending of beauty with utility.

The loss of Burdon's papers means that evidence for designers at Hardwick is hard to come by, but James Paine's involvement as architect is not in doubt.[7] It is possible that Daniel Garrett may also have been involved at an early stage.[8] There is good evidence regarding the identities of the various artists and craftsmen involved in the construction and decoration of the garden buildings, however; they included the Durham architect John Bell, who carried the buildings into execution,[9] the stuccoist Giuseppe Cortese and the painters Francis Hayman, Samuel Wale, Giuseppe Mattia Borgnis and Martin Ferdinand Quadal. The fact that several of these workers had been associated with the work of James Paine at other sites emphasises the latter's central role in the developments at Hardwick.

The designer of the garden is not known. It is tempting to ascribe the layout to Burdon himself, working, like his contemporaries Henry Hoare at Stourhead and Charles Hamilton at Painshill, to develop a circuit walk of alternating atmosphere and scenery, with Paine acting the part played by Henry Flitcroft at Stourhead of architect of the various focal points. Frustratingly, none of the

[6]   W. Hutchinson, *The History and Antiquities of the County Palatine of Durham*, 3 vols (Newcastle upon Tyne and London, 1785–94), ii, p.66.

[7]   Finished drawings by Paine for features built and proposed at Hardwick survive in the Durham County Record Office, ref. D/Br/P 209–13 (shown are the east and west front of a proposed house, an elevation, ground plan and section of a proposed temple and an elevation and ground plan of a proposed banqueting house).

[8]   Paine succeeded to Garrett's contracts in the north in 1753, five years after Burdon's purchase of Hardwick. Stylistic elements in the design of the Gothick Seat at Hardwick suggest the hand of Garrett rather than Paine.

[9]   P. Leach, *James Paine* (London, 1988), pp.25, 188. Note that Bell was a subscriber to Paine's own *Plans, Elevations and Sections of Noblemen and Gentlemen's Houses, etc.*, 2 vols (London, 1767–83), as was John Burdon himself (eds).

descriptive writers, the first of whom, William Hutchinson, had visited Hardwick during Burdon's tenure, suggest an author for the overall layout. An interesting comparison exists in the grounds of Belford Hall, Northumberland, where a number of features, including a Gothick tower, a ha-ha and (formerly) a building in the Chinese taste, are grouped around a serpentine lake, all within a carefully planted woodland setting. Belford Hall was built by Paine for Abraham Dixon, a man of similar background to John Burdon, in 1754, when the developments at Hardwick were in full flow. It is possible that the same hand designed both layouts.

Burdon showed 'a distinguished liberality to the public by the free admission of all visitors'.[10] The tourist was enjoined to leave his horse (and dog) at the village inn and walk the short distance across the fields to the lodge, where the gardener would meet him and conduct him along the circuit walk, pointing out the various felicities of the scene as they unfolded. The lodge itself was the first indication of ornamental grounds. It was essentially a double pediment decorated with battlements, with a Gothick arch in the centre section forming the entrance to the garden. It was strikingly similar to the surviving gardener's cottage in the kitchen garden at Raby Castle in the same county, where James Paine was at work in the 1750s.

From this point we have a good knowledge of the visitor experience at Hardwick. Apart from a series of revealing descriptions published between 1787 and 1857,[11] an anonymous guidebook to the garden entitled *A Walk through Hardwicke Gardens* was published in 1800.[12] This, the earliest known guidebook to any garden in County Durham, follows the circuit walk and comments in some detail on the buildings and scenery. It clearly sets out the sequence of visual and atmospheric experiences which unfolded as the tour progressed – a series of vignettes and surprises of a theatrical or operatic character building inexorably from a mysterious beginning to a splendid conclusion. The 1811 edition of the guidebook includes an appended poem, 'Hardwicke Plantation', which further elaborates on the nature of the visitor experience and gives some important insights into the appearance and operation of some now-lost features along the route. The collective evidence of the site and its documentation demonstrates that Hardwick was no superficial 'Cit's Country Box', a pale imitation of its social betters, but a comprehensive and original work which stands comparison with any of its contemporaries and deserves attention as a prime example of early landscape garden design.

With the gardener as his guide, the visitor was led through a grove of trees underplanted with ornamental shrubs. This contrasted with the agricultural

---

10 Hutchinson, *History and Antiquities*, ii, p.65.
11 See Hutchinson, *History and Antiquities*; J. Britton and E.W. Brayley et al, *The Beauties of England and Wales, etc.*, 18 vols (London, 1801–15), v (1803), part 1; R. Surtees, *The History and Antiquities of the County Palatine of Durham*, 4 vols (London, 1816–40); E. Mackenzie and M. Ross, *An Historical, Topographical and Descriptive View of the County Palatine of Durham*, 2 vols (Newcastle upon Tyne, 1834); W. Fordyce, *The History and Antiquities of the County Palatine of Durham*, 2 vols (Newcastle upon Tyne, London and Edinburgh, 1855–7). A further useful contemporary description occurs in the travel journals of J.M. Fisher, 1775–9; see K. Morgan (ed.), *An American Quaker in the British Isles: the Travel Journals of Jabez Maud Fisher 1775–1779* (Oxford, 1992) (eds).
12 Anon., *A Walk through Hardwicke Gardens* (Stockton on Tees, 1800).

Figure 4.2. The view from the Grand Terrace at Hardwick, Co. Durham (engraving by John Bailey from William Hutchinson, *The History and Antiquities of the County Palatine of Durham*, 1787).

scenery he had just left behind and served as a kind of overture. Its covert purpose was to control the sequence of visual events so that each scene could be presented and felt with the maximum force and surprise. Emerging from the grove, therefore, the visitor suddenly found himself on the Grand Terrace, a straight gravel walk 'upwards of 560 paces in length'[13] on the northern shore of the lake. Looking along the terrace, the classical facade of the Bath House faced him. In the opposite direction the tower of Sedgefield church could be seen across the fields, revealed by an opening in the plantations and a ha-ha. The view across the lake revealed, near at hand, a gushing cascade flowing into it under a rock-faced bridge. On the far side of the lake a half-ruined Gothick structure with several towers, some shattered and one intact, loomed above the trees on the left, while in contrast a smooth lawn opened on the right to lead the eye up to a colonnaded classical building on a hill. This initial view is represented in an engraving by John Bailey accompanying Hutchinson's description of 1787 (Fig. 4.2).

From this point the visitor was led along the Grand Terrace to its nominal halfway point. Here was a circular pond, overlooked from the north by the Gothick Seat, an open stone structure backed by a semicircle of ornamental trees. The Gothick Seat gave its occupant a controlled view out across the lake, undesirable objects (such as the dam) or those items reserved for a later stage of the tour (such as the Serpentine River) being screened out by carefully sited groups of trees and shrubs. Continuing to the western end of the Grand Terrace, the visitor soon came to the Bath House. This was a conventional temple-

13 Hutchinson, *History and Antiquities*, ii, p.65.

fronted building of the Doric order, containing a bedroom, a breakfast room and the bath itself, fed from the lake. The path then led round the back of the Bath House and entered the woods behind the dam, changing from a straight walk in open surroundings to a meandering path through disorientatingly dark woodland, densely planted to make the most of the relatively small area of the design. Curious pieces of old buildings, described by Hutchinson as 'works, in the stile of the last age'[14] were scattered here and there, emphasising the unreal quality of the new experience. Soon the visitor arrived at the next scene, centred on the Bono Retiro. Coming upon this feature from behind in order to heighten the surprise, the visitor found a two-storey building with a rendered Gothick facade with flanking towers, liberally decorated with large quatrefoils. The building looked straight along a short canal to a trickling cascade, in fact built into the outflow of the dam. At this point the gardener disappeared: 'The guide is vanish'd when you look behind;/To heighten the surprise a cascade roars,/As when huge billows break upon the shores.'[15]

The gardener had lowered the sluice to allow a greater weight of water to foam down the cascade. Not content with this theatrical gesture, the gardener would then lead the visitor into the Bono Retiro, in the porch of which was a mirror reflecting the cascade. Thus the visitor's sense of departing from reality was confirmed by appearing to walk into the building through a waterfall. Once inside, the mystery continued. The visitor would climb the stairs, lined with busts of worthies in niches, to the upper chamber. This was bathed in ethereal light, achieved by a combination of close tree-planting and the use of stained glass windows. The subjects depicted in these windows are skated over by most writers, though Britton and Brayley in 1804 referred to 'The likeness of things so foul to behold/That what they are is not fit to be told.'[16] Perhaps only particular visitors got into this inner sanctum. Looking around, the visitor would see a domed, painted ceiling and walls lined with a 'library' composed of carved panels of 'books' painted in the minutest detail.

Moving on from the Bono Retiro, the route continued through the wood along 'confined and winding walks'[17] until it emerged across a ha-ha into an open meadow. From here the path led up to the classical building which had first been seen on its height across the lake. This was the Temple of Minerva, designed by Paine: a domed octagonal building on a square base surrounded by an Ionic colonnade (see Fig. 4.3). Stylistically, it is related to Paine's Temple of Diana at Weston Park, Shropshire. From its colonnade a series of dramatic views opened up. Looking north, the visitor saw the reverse view across the lake to the Grand Terrace, with the house and the adjacent Tuscan Alcove, a temple-fronted garden seat, beyond. Looking west, the view led out into the open countryside. To the east, parts of the next stage of the walk were revealed, rising above groves of wood: a second view of the Gothick Ruin, and for the first time, the facade of

---

[14] Ibid.

[15] Anonymous poem, *Hardwicke Plantation*, appended to the 1811 edition of *A Walk through Hardwicke Gardens*.

[16] Britton and Brayley, *The Beauties*, v, part 1, p.99.

[17] Hutchinson, *History and Antiquities*, ii, p.65.

Figure 4.3. Hardwick, Co. Durham: the Temple of Minerva (recently restored) (photograph: Tom Yellowley).

the Banqueting House, 'on rising ground, having a spacious lawn in front, and surrounded by an amphitheatre of wood'.[18]

Entering the Temple, the visitor found a single large cubic room. The domed ceiling was decorated with a central painting by Borgnis and his son of Minerva with the Gorgon Shield, and Apollo offering her the laurel wreath, with the Arts and Sciences at her feet. Below, the eight compartments contained paintings depicting Music, Painting, Sculpture, Architecture and the four cardinal virtues of Justice, Prudence, Fortitude and Temperance set in writhing Rococo stucco frames by Cortese. Busts of classical heroes on brackets lined the walls, along with the inscription 'This Temple begun by John Burdon, Esq., in the year 1754, and finished in 1757'.

From the Temple the visitor continued down through the meadow, grazed by sheep in due season, and once more entered dense groves of woodland. Passing the Rustic Seat, he turned right onto the Gothick Bridge, a single-span structure with its parapet pierced with quatrefoils. Under the bridge flowed the Serpentine River, encountered here by the visitor for the first time. Looking east from the bridge, the visitor would see the River stretching ahead to a small circular island carrying a statue of Neptune on a plinth, a copy in lead of the original made by

18 Anon., *A Walk through Hardwicke*, p.9.

Figure 4.4. Hardwick, Co. Durham: the Gothick Ruin (recently restored) (photograph: Tom Yellowley).

Andries Carpentière for George Bowes in 1729 and still standing in the Market Place in Durham. Behind the island a turf bank rose up to reveal the Gothick Ruin with its tall slender turret flanked and backed by plantations (see Fig. 4.4).

Crossing the bridge and proceeding along the southern bank of the River, the visitor soon approached the Ruin, now seen in its fourth manifestation. It was a sandstone building in the form of a gatehouse with a central vaulted arch, with three carefully 'ruinated' square towers and a fourth tower that was intact, tall, slender and circular. Above the vault was a single room with a short external walkway leading to the circular turret. A newel stair led to the top of this turret, from which an extensive view of the country to the east and south, as well as a return view to the Temple and over part of the lake, was gained. When first built the ruin had a number of fragments of medieval stonework incorporated into its fabric. These included part of the celebrated Brus Cenotaph and other items from the ruins of Gisborough Priory in Yorkshire. One of Burdon's nieces had married a Chaloner of Guisborough, on whose land the abbey ruins stood. Hutchinson found himself gazing at these relics with mixed feelings, noting that the fragments included 'a delicate piece [which] … it is to be lamented, is exposed to the weather'.[19]

---

[19] Hutchinson, *History and Antiquities*, ii, p.66.

Resuming the path, the visitor walked through the arch and once again into a grove of wood. After a short interlude a large, plain building (the Banqueting House) presented itself. Ushered in, the visitor found himself in a small green baize room of no obvious significance. Another door was then opened, and the visitor entered the finest room of all, to be 'struck with the magnificence and splendour which everywhere prevail in this noble apartment'.[20] The principal room was to some extent a reworking by Paine of some of his rejected interior designs for the Mansion House in Doncaster, and formed the culmination of the visitor's tour. The room, a double cube, was elaborately decorated in stucco and gilding by Cortese. A chimneypiece of coloured marbles occupied the centre of the back wall, with a full-length portrait by Martin Ferdinand Quadal over it of John Burdon standing with his spaniel on the Grand Terrace. Busts on brackets represented suitable artistic patrons of this enterprise, including Vitruvius, Palladio and Inigo Jones. The ceiling was divided into bold geometric compartments featuring painted panels of mythological scenes by Francis Hayman and Samuel Wale, whose work also decorated the overdoors. A separate 'neat retiring apartment'[21] at the rear provided a couch and a suggestive painting of Diana admiring the sleeping Endymion.

Stepping out on to the lawn, the visitor could now see the Banqueting House facade at close hand for the first time. An ashlar sandstone front of three bays of blind arches surrounding windows, it was based on of one of Inigo Jones's proposals for Whitehall Palace. Corinthian pilasters, coupled at either end, supported an entablature with a parapet above. Canted bays projected from the north and south fronts, housing column screens inside. Turning to look outwards, the visitor would see that the lawn fell away to a view of the Serpentine River below. Above the trees, the Temple of Minerva could be seen in its meadow. At this point the visitor's tour would end; presumably only the owner's private guests would visit the narrow peninsula between the lake and the Serpentine River. This was densely planted, partly in order to achieve the necessary visual screen between the two water bodies. Access was gained via the little footbridge over the first cascade. A few feet beyond this was the Boathouse, where Burdon kept his 'painted barge'[22] for excursions on the lake. Further along the peninsula stood the Grotto, an isolated dome of rubble limestone with its back turned to the circuit walk, gazing silently westward across the lake.

A number of developing themes became apparent if the garden tour was followed by the prescribed route. Burdon appears to have been keen to establish himself as the leading resident in Sedgefield, and had a gallery pew, approached from a private external staircase, built in the church. On the front of the pew was his coat of arms. When the visitor first arrived on the Grand Terrace and saw the initial *coup d'oeil*, he would see the framed view back to the church tower, establishing a (spurious) chain of suggestion that Burdon's family was anciently associated with the town. This notion would be reinforced on approaching the

---

[20] Anon., *A Walk through Hardwicke*, p.9.
[21] Mackenzie and Ross, *Historical, Topographical and Descriptive View*, i, p.440.
[22] Ibid.

Bath House, where Burdon's arms appeared in a Rococo cartouche in the pediment facing along the terrace directly towards the church.

The initial panorama from the terrace introduced further artistic associations. Looking south across the lake, the engraving shows the classical Temple at the top of a smooth lawn carefully framed in uniform plantations. For comparison, the visitor also sees the dramatic outline of the Gothick Ruin rising above wilder and more mixed vegetation. Correspondingly, the vista at one end of the Grand Terrace is closed by a Gothic building (Sedgefield Church) and at the other by a classical building (the Bath House). This alternation of classical and Gothic features continues throughout the circuit, and the association of Gothic buildings with dramatic scenery recurs at the Bono Retiro. The Gothic settings can thus be seen as both 'Picturesque' and 'Romantic', contrasting with the 'Beautiful' settings of, for example, the Temple and the Banqueting House, where smoothness and intellectual order are the predominant characteristics.[23]

Burdon's rigorous command of iconography continues in his placement of the classical buildings along the route, which advance through the Orders with the visitor's steps. First we come to the Doric Bath House, a building of manly straightforwardness of design and function; then to the Ionic Temple of Minerva, a place of feminine dedication and intellectual engagement; and finally to the Corinthian Banqueting House, a place filled with 'gorgeous classical and mythological display'.[24] Burdon may also have had Masonic themes in mind for his knowledgeable gentlemen visitors. Perhaps these were touched upon in the black and white marble floor of the Gothick Seat, but were surely developed in the alternation of darkness and light along the route, unexpected effects and intellectual challenges all bound together into a journey of expectation and enlightenment. Certainly the Hardwick layout exemplified William Shenstone's ideal that 'When a building, or other object has been once viewed from its proper point, the foot should never travel to it by the same path, which the eye has travelled over before. Lose the object, and draw nigh, obliquely.'[25]

In its combination of formal and informal components, its relative crowding of buildings and visual incidents and its small scale, the design looked back to the Kentian layouts of earlier years (Stowe, Rousham) rather than to the more expansive contemporary work of Lancelot 'Capability' Brown, as at Croome Court. Hutchinson, indeed, was struck by the extent to which Burdon's garden seemed to be a working model from the pages of Horace Walpole's *History of the Modern Taste in Gardening*:[26] 'We cannot quit these delightful scenes without referring the reader to what Mr Walpole says in his fourth volume of 'Anecdotes'; the works here bearing every expression of that taste and art, which he speaks of with so much spirit and delight.'[27]

---

[23] The 'Beautiful' in the sense given above had earlier been defined by Edmund Burke in his *Philosophical Enquiry into the Origin of our Ideas of the Sublime and the Beautiful* (London, 1757) (eds).
[24] Fordyce, *County Palatine of Durham*, ii, p.342.
[25] W. Shenstone, 'Unconnected Thoughts on Gardening', in *The Works in Verse and Prose, of William Shenstone, Esq.*, 2 vols (Dublin, 1764), ii, p.81.
[26] H. Walpole, *The History of the Modern Taste in Gardening* (1780; modern edition, New York, 1995).
[27] Hutchinson, *History and Antiquities*, ii, p.66.

Following completion of the garden layout, Burdon seems to have envisaged a further phase of development, including a house of exceptional grandeur, a lodge intended for Burdon's occupation 'at the time he is building his mansion house'[28] and presumably a triumphal arch also shown in Burdon's portrait. Paine was sufficiently confident of the commission to exhibit three illustrations of the proposed lodge at the Society of Artists in 1764, but in fact nothing came of these projects. This has led some commentators to suggest that Burdon had bankrupted himself through his overspending at Hardwick, but there is no evidence for this. At the time of his death in 1792 John Burdon was comfortably in funds, having sold the estate to William Russell two years previously, and held a number of responsible positions which do not suggest financial embarrassment.[29] It seems more likely that Burdon was unable to generate the capital for a second campaign of improvement, or quite possibly saw the futility of building a grand residence for a bachelor.

The new owner, William Russell, was the richest commoner in England through shrewd financial intervention in the coal industry. It was, however, his son, Matthew Russell, who instituted a new scheme of improvement at Hardwick in the years either side of 1800. Britton and Brayley, writing in *The Beauties of England and Wales* in 1804, described how the fields between the garden and the town of Sedgefield had recently been turned into parkland with clumps. Russell had also made a new drive through his park, and apparently built a new south front onto the house to resolve its hitherto unsatisfactory appearance.

The garden layout at Hardwick was by now looking antiquated, and Matthew Russell's enthusiasm for all things medieval meant that his attention would be bound to wander. In 1817 he began spending huge sums on the conversion of Brancepeth Castle, west of Durham, to become the family seat. From this point on Hardwick was a secondary estate, and herein lay the seeds of its long and gradual decline. From as early as 1834 the Hardwick estate was tenanted to a succession of minor aristocrats, merchants and military men. This had the effect of preventing significant development within the grounds, which were maintained to a high standard, but the lack of personal involvement inevitably led to a fossilisation of the layout and a disinclination to carry out expensive repairs. The Ordnance Survey map of 1857 shows Burdon's layout just as he had known it, together with Matthew Russell's eastern park, but within a few years, and certainly before 1873, the lake was drained. This disastrous event, robbing the whole design of its unifying centrepiece, has yet to be explained. The most probable scenario involves unacceptable silting and perhaps leakage at the cascade outflow. In any event this proved the beginning of the end, and a local trade directory lamented in 1894 that:

---

[28] Note on section drawing of proposed lodge at Hardwick, office of James Paine 1764. One of three 'geometrical plans' exhibited at the Society of Artists of Great Britain. See A. Graves, *The Society of Artists of Great Britain, 1760–1791, etc.* (facsimile reprint, Bath, 1969), p.186.

[29] A codicil to Burdon's will commended his fellow partners at the Commercial Bank of Newcastle upon Tyne to continue to invoke his name in their affairs after his death as long as it continued to generate the usual confidence.

These beautiful grounds have lost much of their attractiveness owing to the disappearance of the lake ... All the busts, with the exception of one, which are mentioned as adorning the exterior of the Temple, were stolen one winter's night about thirty years ago. The splendid mantelpiece, as well as the paintings in the ceiling of the Banqueting Hall, have been removed, the latter to Brancepeth Castle.[30]

The pattern of a lack of proper repair, along with theft and asset-stripping, continued after this date, by which time the Bath House was already described as a ruin. The family, by now Hamilton-Russell, Viscounts Boyne, withdrew to their Shropshire estate in the 1920s and more or less left Hardwick to its fate. Although the Temple, for example, was still in good order when its ceiling paintings were photographed in 1938, the whole garden was pillaged for scrap in the late 1940s. By the end of the 1950s, Hardwick was a wreck. The house was in use as a maternity hospital, but the grounds were virtually beyond recognition. The lake bed was half under the plough and half abandoned to self-set fen–carr woodland. The buildings were in various states of collapse or demolition, the Banqueting House suffering the indignity of having some of its fabric reused in the new cinema at nearby Trimdon. John Burdon's portrait was sold at Sotheby's in 1956 for the miserable sum of £12. There appeared to be no way back.

Better times seemed in prospect when Durham County Council bought part of the site in 1972 for use as a country park. The urgent need for the repair of the garden buildings was recognised, but the political will was lacking to begin such an expensive project; reports were written and shelved, and the situation continued to deteriorate. The Serpentine River was dredged, but the Grotto was demolished, the Temple dismantled and the Ruin partially rebuilt following almost complete destruction by vandals. In 1995 the Gothick Bridge became dangerous and a programme of repair was announced. A press conference was held to witness the start of the project, during which to general horror the bridge collapsed, much to the excitement of the assembled press photographers. A decision was immediately taken that it would be rebuilt, but the facing stone was found to be in such poor condition that a replica was built on the same site. This is hardly the ideal solution, but this traumatic event and its resolution marked a turning point in Hardwick's modern history.

The fate of Hardwick remained a pressing concern among many residents of Sedgefield, leading to the formation of the Friends of Hardwick in 1998. In the same year the Northumbria Gardens Trust held a conservation workshop at Hardwick. In 1999 Durham County Council, aided by a grant from the Heritage Lottery Fund, commissioned a Historic Landscape Survey and Restoration Management Plan[31] which drew together the historical development and significance of the site and made proposals for its conservation. During its preparation one of the major private landowners at Hardwick announced their intention to sell, and the County Council was able, with assistance from,

---

[30] F. Whellan & Co., *The History, Topography and Directory of the County Palatine of Durham ...* (Newcastle upon Tyne, 1894), p.686.

[31] S.C. Desmond, *Historic Landscape Survey and Restoration Management Plan for Hardwick Park, Sedgefield, County Durham* (unpublished report for Durham County Council, 1999).

among other parties, the Heritage Lottery Fund, to secure the single ownership of the entire former ornamental layout at Hardwick except for the house and its immediate grounds.

Since then immense progress has been made at Hardwick. Following detailed campaigns of site survey and archaeology, the dam has been reconstructed and the famous lake successfully refilled. The Gothick Seat and the Temple of Minerva (see Fig. 4.3) have risen from rubble to regain much of their former glory. Once again the visitor can look across the lake from the Grand Terrace to the slender tower of the Ruin, now rising once again to its original height (see Fig. 4.4). Even Neptune, newly refashioned, has returned to his plinth in the Serpentine River. Great schemes of tree and shrub planting look set to reinstate the noble backdrop to these Arcadian scenes.

Hardwick can never be what it was, but it has been brought back from the brink of extinction. There is good reason to believe that the facades of the Bath House and the Bono Retiro may be reassembled from the mass of surviving masonry. A site which in 2000 seemed an awful warning, a Stourhead in ruins, perhaps a monument to the uselessness of good intentions without action, has gained new life and vigour. It has been rescued from oblivion because local people cared, and because garden conservationists have been able to demonstrate that this lately isolated, unfashionable, overgrown place is, despite its difficult history, a unique and endlessly fascinating survival of the Kentian landscape garden in the North East.

5

The Shadow in the Garden:
Pleasure, Profit and Protection at Gibside, 1840–1860

JUDITH BETNEY

The pleasure gardens of Gibside, County Durham, are acknowledged to be one of the North East's most outstanding examples of an eighteenth-century land-scape garden (see Fig. 0.6, p.14). Very little is known, however, about Gibside as a Victorian garden, which is the subject of this chapter. Gardens are like a palimpsest, with one 'text' overlaying another as tastes, fashions and fortunes change, and often it is only on the remaining structures and trees that we can base ideas about how a garden looked or was used. These tend, however, to fix a garden into a particular period, leaving out other eras of its evolution which may be just as interesting to garden historians. With this in mind, the aim here has been to find out as far as possible what was done to create a Victorian garden out of Gibside's eighteenth-century structure and interpret what this tells us about nineteenth-century culture.

The main sources for the present research have been the correspondence in the Bowes papers held by the Durham County Record Office and by the Bowes Museum at Barnard Castle. John Bowes (1811–85), who inherited Gibside in 1820, was a diligent letter-writer who was almost obsessive in his need to be involved in every aspect of his estates. There are consequently thousands of letters within the Bowes papers which give a vast wealth of detail about the management of Bowes's inheritance, including the gardens.

In addition, these letters specifically reveal the dynamics of the relationship between Bowes and his friend and stepfather William Hutt. Bowes (see Fig. 5.1) leased Gibside, rent-free, to his mother and Hutt in 1831. So Hutt was a grace-and-favour tenant, but he was careful never to be seen to take advantage of his position and consulted Bowes on all his plans for Gibside. In addition, Hutt struck up a friendship with the land agent Ralph Dent, since they were both overseeing the estate whilst Bowes lived mainly in Paris.[1] The three men shared a keen interest in gardening, exchanging plants, seeds and information.

[1]   Here Bowes and his wife Josephine amassed most of the large art collection which they later housed in the Bowes Museum, founded in 1869. For more, see S. Kane, 'When Paris meets Teesdale: the Bowes Museum, Barnard Castle', in T.E. Faulkner (ed.), *Northumbrian Panorama: Studies in the History and Culture of North East England* (London, 1996), pp.163–94.

Figure 5.1. Portrait of John Bowes, by Eugène Feyen (1815–1908), oil on canvas, 181 × 119 cm (The Bowes Museum, Barnard Castle, Co. Durham).

The letters in the Bowes papers prove beyond doubt that Hutt, Bowes and Dent were all highly enthusiastic gardeners. They regularly visited local and national horticultural exhibitions, belonged to horticultural societies and subscribed to gardening magazines. All three were also hard-nosed businessmen for whom the land was a source of profit. Bowes owned vast estates but their upkeep was equally vast and he was almost always short of money. Dent's fortunes were dependent on his success in managing the estates and Hutt was a career politician – Gibside was a showcase for his growing political and economic influence, an arena for entertaining and networking. Use co-existed with beauty: hunting, shooting, forestry and farming interests were all incorporated. Other profits could be reaped from the land – in particular, mineral rights for coal and iron and way-leaves from the expanding railway network. All these brought useful income but had negative impacts on the pleasure garden. The letters show a constant anxiety to protect the garden from the railway, the pits and their smoke, urban sprawl, trespass, poaching and vandalism. Drunkenness and indiscriminate violence were feared. The high wages to be earned in the mines made it increasingly hard to get and keep efficient, reliable and above all honest servants. Gardeners in particular proved problematic.

Bowes, Hutt and Dent were protecting the estate from despoliation and intrusion but they were also protecting their exclusive rights to a refined and polite society away from the squalor and barbarism of the industry that was funding the garden. Part of the pleasure to be had from the garden was its perceived ability to refine and civilise, a common theme in the garden literature of the time. Cultivation of the garden and cultivation of the mind were inextricably linked. The outer belts of trees and dense shrubberies of the Victorian garden shielded it from unpleasant facts of life as well as protecting it from intrusion; within the garden was an unsullied paradise, nurturing the soul.

Hutt began his improvements to Gibside by increasing the range of hothouses – being able to serve a wide range of exotic fruit for much of the year was an essential indicator of the wealth and taste of the landowner. In 1834 *The Gardener's Magazine* reported that at Gibside 'A Range of dilapidated hothouses … are giving place … to a range of metallic houses on the curvilinear plan, to be heated by hot water.'[2] The cost of this heating, to produce strawberries in March, for example, or orchids, which required constant temperatures of 80–90 °F, was ruinous. The fact that such expense could only be afforded by the very wealthy was an important part of the appeal. Hutt was at an advantage here – his wife's coal-mining interests provided cheap fuel – and he made other improvements to suit Victorian tastes for convenience and show. In 1843 he built a new coach road which would enhance the drive into the estate, giving views of all its splendours. Part of the drive was made into an avenue using trees, underplanted with evergreens, chosen by Hutt from local nurseries.[3]

2   S.C. Desmond, 'The Landscape of Gibside' (unpublished MA Dissertation, University of York, 1994).
3   See Durham County Record Office (hereafter DCRO), Strathmore Archives. A vast collection of letters, bills, maps, etc., including private correspondence to John Bowes from his employees, friends and family. Also ditto, the Bowes Museum Archives, including the private correspondence of John Bowes, his employees, friends and family, all undergoing preliminary cataloguing at the time of writing this chapter.

In 1842 Hutt contemplated altering the Greenhouse into a conservatory by replacing the roof with curvilinear glass. Local architects John and his son Benjamin Green (John had designed the first Scotswood Bridge) were consulted and produced a plan showing typical features of early glasshouse construction. The price was to be £1,060, however, and it seems Bowes would not countenance the expense.[4] In 1844 Hutt began the major innovation of planting up the Long Walk, the raised terrace of Switzer's eighteenth-century plan for Gibside, with Norfolk Oaks, 'Quercus Ferris', to form a grand boulevard. Later he introduced James Duke swans and a canoe to the Octagon Pond.[5]

Hutt was particularly interested in new plant introductions from abroad: Dent gave him Cedar Deodara seed, and he planted three monkey puzzles beside the Greenhouse. He consulted the local glass manufacturer, Swinburn, regarded as a 'great florist', on the choice of rose and carnation seeds from Paris, which were destined for the walled garden. His relation-by-marriage Susan Davidson, of Ridley Hall, sent him some Himalayan seeds (possibly rhododendrons). Bowes sent him anything he thought interesting from France. Hutt also visited the gardens of the Horticultural Society to see all the new exhibits and in 1845 began growing orchids, which became an absorbing and expensive hobby. Probably spurred on by his visit to the Great Exhibition at the Crystal Palace in 1851, Hutt revived his plans to alter the Greenhouse into a conservatory. This time Hutt brought in the acclaimed Newcastle architect John Dobson to draw up a new plan. No copy of this has come to light so far, but archaeological investigations and clues from the letters show Dobson's proposed alterations to have been very similar to those of the Greens ten years earlier, except that the roof was to be crossed in a single span and there was to be a central shelved stone structure to display plants. By the time the Crystal Palace was built there was greater confidence in applying iron and glass to buildings and this was reflected in their prices. Dobson's plan was eventually completed in 1854 at a cost of £756, considerably cheaper than the earlier design.[6]

Hutt next planned to build an orchidaceous house to provide plants for display in the new conservatory. He also bought plants through the *Horticultural Society Journal* and Dent became a 'magnificent benefactor', as did Bowes. Hutt bought four orange trees to stand outside the conservatory in summer.[7] Meanwhile, the walled garden continued to be developed as a flower garden, in particular for the latest fashionable roses from Paris, which were planted in large numbers beside the hothouses.[8] In 1856 Hutt again consulted Dobson over the Bath House, already a ruin. Dobson's suggestion was an ornamental seat which would preserve the columns and adapt the sides. This plan has not survived and was never executed.[9]

In 1860, Hutt's wife, Lady Strathmore, died but Hutt stayed on at Gibside as he was still a local MP, though he leased only part of the estate. In 1862 he

4   DCRO: D/St/C5/38/72/a.
5   DCRO: Strathmore Archives (uncatalogued at time of writing).
6   Ibid.
7   DCRO: Strathmore Archives, Bowes Museum Archives (uncatalogued at time of writing).
8   DCRO: Strathmore Archives (uncatalogued at time of writing).
9   DCRO: Strathmore Archives, Bowes Museum Archives (uncatalogued at time of writing).

called in Dobson to design an ornamental stone screen to the west of the house. A faded, unsigned and undated design for just such a screen, which could be an early working drawing, survives in the Bowes papers. However, the plan was never carried out, although Hutt was still keen on the idea in 1865.[10] Instead, he built a grand new lodge entrance to the estate on the Whickham Road, the principal carriage entrance from Gateshead and Newcastle. The lodge replicated the 'Strawberry Hill' garden building erected by George Bowes in 1748 in the woods near the house. Dobson submitted a plan for the lodges but Hutt and Bowes thought his estimate was 'no joke' and instead got a local builder to do the job for £160.[11] In 1865 Hutt provided the Octagon Pond with a piped water supply and began stocking it with an exotic bird collection, protected by railings. By 1871, however, he confessed that he had not visited Gibside for two years, pleading pressure of parliamentary work in London. In 1874 he came into his own family's property on the Isle of Wight and gave up Gibside, which was never lived in by a Bowes again.[12]

It is intriguing that so much money was spent on Gibside in the mid-Victorian period, despite the fact that Bowes chose not to live there himself and had no children to inherit. Hutt was similarly childless and in any case was only a tenant. One reason for their extravagance must have been their love of gardening, as the letters show. Another was that Bowes undoubtedly wanted to please his mother. She had been a housemaid and then his father's mistress for many years until he had married her on his deathbed in an effort to legitimise their son. Her position was anomalous and Bowes seems to have felt this deeply. Lady Strathmore loved gardening, especially flower-gardening, which was considered an especially refining and 'ladylike' pastime, reflecting woman's primarily acquiescent, ornamental position in this Victorian society. As mistress of the flower garden, Lady Strathmore was demonstrating appropriate cultural behaviour for a woman of high social status, presumably an important point to prove for someone with her dubious past.

Then again, for Hutt the garden increasingly became a refuge from the stresses of a parliamentary career and from the squalor of the growing industry of the North East. For both him and his wife the garden acted as a recovered Paradise: a perfected and protected world recreated for their personal use. This, of course, has always been a familiar role for the garden – the gardener's own view of what 'Paradise' is, providing a key to interpretation throughout the history of landscape.

Yet the nature of Bowes's and the Hutts' interest in the garden was typical of their culture and status. The dominant aesthetic influence in this mid-Victorian period was John Claudius Loudon's 'gardenesque', which he described as 'the imitation of nature, subjected to a certain degree of cultivation or improvement, suitable to the wants and wishes of man.'[13] Total environmental control

---

10 DCRO: D/St/P6/2/8.
11 DCRO: Strathmore Archives (uncatalogued at time of writing).
12 Bowes Museum Archives (uncatalogued at time of writing).
13 J.C. Loudon, *The Suburban Gardener*, 1838, quoted in B. Elliott, *Victorian Gardens* (London, 1986), p.34.

was attempted – the perfect plant in the perfect place, as exuberant as a William Morris wallpaper but controlled and contained in ordered patterns. The plants became like exhibits in a display case and the garden a kind of gallery or museum, a collection of specimens artistically arranged to best effect and scientifically managed. The more complete and perfect the collection, the more status accrued to the 'exhibitor'. This accounts for the competitiveness with which these busy, wealthy men sought out new additions to their gardens. Hutt collected orchids, roses, fuschia, ornamental trees and exotic birds. Bowes collected roses, rhododendrons and, of course, went on to build his own grand museum at Barnard Castle. Dent, with his collection of pansies and holly-hocks, was imitating their behaviour and thus signalling his own upward social mobility. As Shirley Hibberd, the prolific garden writer of the 1860s, described it: 'An eminent author called this the Age of Veneer, and another dignifies it with the title of the Age of Fustian. I shall call it the Age of Toys. Our rooms sparkle with the products of art, and our gardens with the curiosities of nature.'[14]

Historians have linked this urge to collect natural phenomena with the distancing of human experience from nature that began with the enclosure movement. The enclosed landscape became increasingly alien in its appearance and at the same time there was a rapid industrialisation which resulted, in the nineteenth century, in far more people living in an urban environment than in a rural one. The effect was that nature itself became a foreign experience, to be visited rather than lived in. A garden, with its perfect 'specimens' of nature, then became a nostalgic reference point as well as a protected natural paradise.[15] This united the garden as refuge with the garden as exhibit in Victorian culture, linking the garden's private and public functions.

Another reason for the substantial horticultural expenditure of these men was that Hutt, Bowes and Dent used their interest in gardening and collecting to build up a strong, equalising friendship. They had to deal with an enormous quantity of business matters, but their mutual interest in the garden brought relaxation and engendered mutual respect and gratitude as they exchanged advice, plants and seeds. All three were in invidious positions to each other – Dent the employee, Hutt the grace-and-favour tenant and Bowes the benefactor, but also the stepson and the absentee landlord relying on the others to secure his best interests. The garden was a mechanism by which they could, usually successfully, negotiate these sensitivities.

Finally, it is significant that these men, like many landed Victorians, were encumbered with an eighteenth-century landscape park which would have been ruinously expensive to alter significantly. Their pragmatic approach was to enhance what was there, mainly with new plant introductions, rather than attempt any sweeping changes. The earlier, 'incorrect' aesthetic could be disguised by switching the focus from buildings to plants and it is interesting to note how rarely, apart from the conservatory, Gibside's garden buildings are

---

[14] S. Hibberd, *Rustic Adornments for Homes of Taste* (first published 1856, this edn., London, 1987), Preface.

[15] A. Bermingham, *Landscape and Ideology: the English Rustic Tradition 1740–1860* (London, 1986), p.160.

mentioned in the letters – and then only once in a pleasurable context. Hutt and Lady Strathmore usually ran round the dining room table when one of Bowes's horses won a race; when the Column Stakes was won in 1843, they ran around the Column to British Liberty.[16]

However, the Victorian landed estate had to be economically viable. The improvement of family fortunes, the wealth of the nation and human progress were as important to the Victorians as they were to previous generations. Man could and should strive for perfection and in the nineteenth century the rapid pace of scientific and technical progress made all things seem possible, especially in the garden. As Loudon wrote, 'The grand drawback to every kind of improvement is the vulgar and degrading idea that certain things are beyond our reach.'[17] The 'gardenesque' style aimed at achieving perfection. In the wider context this was also the era of Samuel Smiles's hugely popular book *Self Help*, which urged that with application, perseverance and good will anyone could improve prospects for himself and his progeny; indeed, it was his moral obligation to do so.[18] Idleness and profligacy were heinous sins, a moral that was not lost on the Bowes family, since the estate had been brought to virtual penury in the previous century.

Therefore the Gibside estate had to pay its way as much as possible. Far and away above the farming income, coal mining was the main breadwinner; Lady Strathmore's coal-mining interests brought Hutt £18,000 a year on average. Other industrial ventures were iron smelting, brick kilns, quarrying and paper mills. The woodlands were managed for profit. The new American conifers turned a quick profit for pit props, paper and bark for the tanning industry. The English hardwoods were slower-growing, but reaped larger sums of money. In 1857 the sale of wood fetched £1,400. In 1859 a much greater cull in the wake of huge financial pressures fetched over £5,000. Income could also be generated from way-leaves as the railway companies paid for the right to cross private land, and this was doubly advantageous since the railway enabled quicker and easier, and therefore cheaper, transport of coal from the mines to the ports.[19] Gibside was surrounded by and invaded by the industrial processes which paid for its upkeep.

A more nebulous but perhaps even more important source of profit to be gained from the landed estate was the opportunity it gave to wield power and influence locally. Political clout had financial effects; the landowner could influence the routes of railways and turnpike roads, and could expect co-operation in matters of enclosure and policing. The landed estate helped generate this power but it was also an expression of it. In building the castellated entrance lodge and the grand carriage drive to the house Hutt was declaring his wealth and influence as a man with the power to exclude or include people. It is unlikely to be a coincidence that this work coincided with Hutt's promotion to Vice-President

---

16 DCRO: D/St/C5/32/40.
17 J.C. Loudon, *The Encyclopaedia of Gardening*, 1830, quoted in M.L. Simo, *Loudon and the Landscape: From Country Seat to the Metropolis 1783–1843* (New Haven, 1988), p.157.
18 S. Smiles, *Self Help* (London, 1859), pp.8, 128.
19 DCRO: Strathmore Archives, Bowes Museum Archives (uncatalogued at time of writing).

of the Board of Trade and Privy Councillor, and Gladstone's visit in 1864.[20] The estate was as much an arena for impressing acceptable visitors as it was a private paradise providing escape from the financial and occupational pressures which paid for it.

So Bowes and Hutt combined a strong interest in gardening and a love of nature with a keen eye for profit and advantage. These were not always easy bedfellows, however. Whilst the landed estate was perceived as an essential item for anyone with pretensions to power and wealth, maintaining it as a protected, private paradise was another matter. Balanced with Hutt's and Bowes's time, effort and expense in developing Gibside as a beautiful Victorian pleasure garden were the anxiety, disappointments and misery that they frequently endured from the intrusions and depredations upon it. These took a variety of forms, not least those arising from the weather. Hutt was grief-stricken when a run of severe winters killed his monkey puzzle trees, despite his careful nurturing. When the cold destroyed his orchids, he was even more disappointed. Total environmental control was not possible, however much expense and care was lavished on the plants.[21] It is ironic to note, of course, how much this care contrasted with the lack of consideration given to their native habitats. The Victorian garden historian Alicia Amherst commented that:

> the orchid-growing portions of the globe have been ransacked ... leaving in some cases their native habitats bare ... The sight of this glorious wealth of flowers will be denied to future generations, if the searchers are not more moderate in their demands on the virgin forests of the Old and New World.[22]

But damage and despoliation was a feature of the Victorian English garden also. In 1859 the great cull of the trees of Gibside to offset financial catastrophe created enormous anxieties for Hutt and for Bowes. The encroachment of their own industries required strategies for protection. Bowes got into the iron trade locally in order to prevent anyone else doing so and the works being seen as an unpleasant 'ornament' from his grounds. Despite the great shortage of pithouses for the coal mines, Bowes was reluctant to build at Tanfield Moor in case they would be visible or a 'nuisance' in some other way. In addition, smoke caused both visual and environmental damage.[23]

The routes of the railways brought repeated anxieties. Would the railway be used as a public road by all and sundry? Would it be disagreeably visible from the house? Political clout counted here and Bowes, with Hutt's advice and help in parliament, successfully managed in 1860 to have the Derwent Line moved out of sight 'several chains to the north', incurring for the railway company the vast expense of crossing the river twice and burying the line in a deep cutting. This process was taken to an extreme: the railway company had to build wooden frames across the ravines as a model to see if they could be seen from the house.[24] Gibside was not the only local estate to be developing its industries,

---

[20] C. Hardy, *John Bowes and the Bowes Museum* (Newcastle upon Tyne, 1970), p.31.
[21] DCRO: Strathmore Archives (uncatalogued at time of writing).
[22] A. Amherst, *A History of Gardening in England* (London, 1896), p.296.
[23] DCRO: Strathmore Archives, Bowes Museum Archives (uncatalogued at time of writing).
[24] DCRO: D/St/C5/137/104.

and a creeping urbanisation was the result. Bowes spent twenty years trying to buy the Townley land opposite Gibside to prevent its being developed, but was never successful.[25] (Significantly, twentieth-century developments on the Townley land completely ruin the prospect from the house across the Derwent today.)

The railway brought other social problems in the form of the 'navvy' builders, who had a reputation for drunkenness and crime. In their letters Hutt, Bowes and Dent frequently discuss their fear of these rough strangers roaming around the neighbourhood armed with dogs and guns. Trespass and poaching were rife. There was a thriving black market for game and organised gangs of poachers took full advantage of Gibside's secluded buildings and woodlands. In 1856 an estate worker on rent-collection was brutally murdered at Gibside. Vandalism was a common problem, particularly at the Banqueting House, which seems to have been used as a venue for drunken binges. Sundays were the commonest day for trespass and Hutt employed watchers then, and on holidays.[26] The Public Parks Movement was a national response to the problems caused by the leisure demands of the masses, and one in which Hutt became closely involved in the 1870s.

These constant incursions intruded upon the essentially private world of the landowner. The appeal of the landed estate was largely in its 'polite exclusion', as Humphry Repton said: 'the exclusive right of enjoyment, with the power of refusing that others should share our pleasure'.[27] The privacy of hearth and home was an increasingly powerful myth in Victorian England. The entertainment of the wealthy became more and more concentrated in a round of country-house visits rather than the eighteenth-century public balls and assemblies. When Hutt built his fortress-like lodges he gave 'strict orders about the gates', asserting his power to exclude and include, and he wielded this power carefully. The Gateshead Mechanics' Institute, requesting permission to hold a picnic at Gibside, was only permitted if this was restricted to known members. The Tyneside Naturalists' Club was permitted to visit because its members were 'respectful like-minded' people.[28] The Victorian garden, with its screening woodlands and evergreen shrubberies, locked gates, wandering watchmen and inner sanctum of the enclosed flower garden adjacent to the house and available only to family and friends, was a direct expression of the divisions and inequalities of the society that made it. It cohered the ruling, wealthy elite, excluding all others except by strict invitation; it was an unpolluted vast space when clean air and green areas were at a premium; and it was under constant threat from the mob.

But the letters show that there were greater threats within these protected boundaries. Firstly there was the servant problem. Hutt's first gardener, Layton, was dismissed for misconduct; his woodman, MacQueen, was found drunk at the Banqueting House; his second gardener Barclay is described as 'unscrupu-

25 DCRO: D/St/C5/19/2.
26 DCRO: Strathmore Archives (uncatalogued at time of writing).
27 Quoted in J.C. Loudon, *The Landscape Gardening and Landscape Architecture of the late H. Repton* (London, 1840), p.113.
28 Bowes Museum Archives (uncatalogued at time of writing).

lous'; and Dent's brother John, his deputy at Gibside, was an habitual drunk who absconded to Australia without notice. Dent was himself a servant and despite their friendship he was reprimanded if he strayed over the boundary of familiarity.[29]

Hutt, Bowes and Dent used the garden to negotiate and strengthen their mutual relationships. For thirty years they amicably exchanged plants, information and ideas with a profound respect and warmth, but this was all to change in 1861 when Hutt married Fanny Hughes following the death of Lady Strathmore. Hutt became caught in an increasingly bitter battle between Dent, used to coming and going as he pleased at Gibside, and Fanny, who refused to accommodate him. Dent expected Hutt to stick by their long friendship but Hutt took his wife's side and denied Dent access to the house.[30] This was a calculated insult as it put Dent lower down the social scale, unacceptable within the inner sanctum reserved for intimates, and Dent never forgave Hutt the slight.

Gibside, already constantly threatened from outside its protected boundaries by pollution, vandalism and trespass, was now undermined by strife and divisions from within. The garden became a medium for tormenting Hutt in his carefully protected private world. The servants at Gibside lined up behind Dent or Hutt and fought among themselves, and Hutt had constant problems retaining and managing staff. The servants spread mischief and rumour and Hutt and Dent carried their versions of events to Bowes to arbitrate. Hutt wrote to Bowes in 1864: 'I have some reason to fear that there is a disposition to misrepresent to you systematically all that passes at Gibside in connection with me.'[31] Bowes was caught in the middle, between being a close personal friend of Hutt and the absolute necessity of appeasing Dent, who knew so much about the workings of his many interests that he simply could not manage without him.

There are too many disputes to describe in detail but a typical example is the argument over the Long Walk, which Hutt had always used but had not formally leased. Dent accused Hutt of damaging the trees by keeping stock on it, so in 1864 Hutt asked to rent it. Dent infomed Bowes that he heard that Hutt wanted the Walk to grow turnips on. Hutt replied that he 'should as soon have hatched chickens in the dining-room'.[32] Hutt complained to Bowes that Dent had ordered potatoes to be grown in view of the drawing room windows and for linen to be dried outside the chapel. He wrote that he dared not pick so much as a wild-flower for fear of being snubbed by Dent's men. This is probably the reason for the plan to build a stone screen to the west of the house, as it would give Hutt greater privacy and make his every action less open to scrutiny. In the event, the Hutts retreated more and more to London. Gibside was no longer their refuge and recreated paradise.

The Victorian garden at Gibside provides a complex and ambiguous 'text' encompassing both the public persona and the private personality of its creators, as well as their aspirations, achievements, feelings, fears, concerns and

29   DCRO: Strathmore Archives (uncatalogued at time of writing).
30   Ibid.
31   DCRO: D/St/C5/155/Part 4 161/164 File J 13/1/1864.
32   Bowes Museum Archives, unindexed 27/3/1863.

failures. It reveals a complicated hierarchical society in which upward mobility was possible among those with shared elite values; but its efforts to exclude others demonstrate its sense of vulnerability. The ownership of land conferred higher social status than commercial wealth, in terms of a 'stake' in the nation, yet disguised its dependence on the supposed self-seeking industrial wealth which was paying for it. In the letters that Hutt, Bowes and Dent exchanged, the gardens are a direct expression of these paradoxes, divisions and inequalities within society, as well as being a medium for their personal feelings and relationships.

Hutt tried to recreate a private paradise at Gibside but the shadow of insecurity, rooted in his lack of ownership, was always lurking to spoil and corrupt the view. His protective measures were in place to assure his status as a landed gentleman, with aristocratic, inherited allegiances, as much as to protect his personal domain from intrusion and despoliation. But Hutt did not own Gibside and his connections to inheritance and aristocracy through it were tenuous at best. He was always conscious of his difficult position and his lack of real power to do as he liked. This chink in his armour was fully exploited by his enemies in his last years, when the garden at Gibside became the weapon in the power struggle between Dent's real inequality of social status and Hutt's inequality of real property ownership. The cost of upward social mobility was high.

Acknowledgements

With thanks to Harry Beamish and Hugh Dixon from the National Trust, Howard Coutts from the Bowes Museum and to members of the Northumbria Gardens Trust for their encouragement and assistance with this project.

6

The Walled Garden: A Northumberland Perspective

VERONICA M.J. GOULTY

The enclosed world of the walled garden in Northumberland can best be seen against the background of the way in which North-East England developed historically, and especially alongside the evolution of the country house. The development of the Northumbrian walled garden also ran parallel to that of the larger garden landscape, as well as responding to the unique historical circumstances of the region, where centuries of border unrest inevitably affected the general development of gardens.[1] Whether made for pleasure or produce, a garden needs the hand of a secure creator – secure in place, time and finance. During the sixteenth century in particular, when many private gardens were being laid out in other parts of England, very few were being created in Northumberland. However, the number of walled gardens proliferated in the county between the mid seventeenth century and the mid nineteenth century in response to more stable political conditions and the wealth created by a burgeoning industrial and agricultural economy. The inventiveness associated with the Industrial Revolution is also evident in the elaboration of the types of growing systems used and the variety of plants that were successfully cultivated. There was a continuous interest in growing the many new types of plants available, and, perhaps surprisingly in the light of popular misconceptions about the perceived backwardness of the North East, it seems that as many fashionable plants were grown in Northumberland as in the south of England.

Within the Northumbrian context (and elsewhere), the walled garden can be defined by three main developmental stages. The earliest gardens belonged to monasteries. Later, gardens were directly attached to the dwelling houses of noblemen and of the gentry, where the integral proximity of the garden was a direct response to the need for defence and protection from external attack, both imagined and real. Throughout this stage of development there was an increasing desire for the garden to become more decorative and to serve a more social function. Finally, the walled garden became a distinct and independent

---

[1] For more about conflict in Northumberland see R. Lomas, *County of Conflict* (East Linton, 1996); for more about the country house see P. Lowery, 'Patronage and the Country House in Northumberland', in T.E. Faulkner (ed.), *Northumbrian Panorama: Studies in the History and Culture of North East England* (London, 1996), pp.49–73.

Figure 6.1. The walled garden at Lilburn Tower, Northumberland. Lilburn Tower, near Wooler, is a 'Tudor-Gothic' house designed by John Dobson of Newcastle for H.J. Collingwood in 1828–9; it was modified by Dobson c.1843–4 (photograph: Tom Yellowley).

feature of the garden landscape, commonly positioned at a distance from the dwelling house. It now became a specific area for the intensive production of a wide range of produce for the house, with its walls utilised to optimise the conditions for plant growth (see, for example, Fig. 6.1).

The present author is attempting to record as many surviving walled gardens in Northumberland as possible, in order to document them, in some cases, before they are destroyed. In so doing she also hopes to be able to understand and appreciate them better and to find any unique factors in their development. Sites are identified by the study of Ordnance Survey maps (first edition, where possible, although later editions are also useful to show developments within the garden and surrounding landscape), estate maps and other relevant archival material, as well as by word of mouth. To help in the collation and classification of the gardens an inventory recording basic details and any important features of the gardens is being assembled on a computer database. A photographic record is also being kept. The part of the county currently under investigation divides itself geographically into three main areas radiating out from Newcastle upon Tyne: the north–south corridor, adjacent to the coast; the east–west corridor, following, principally, the course of the rivers Tyne and North Tyne; and an intermediate sector between the other two areas that straddles the A696 road to Otterburn. The condition of the more than 130 walled gardens so far identified in this programme of research (within a county covering a total area of just under 2000 square miles) varies widely, ranging from a state of complete dereliction in some cases to that of full working cultivation in others. From the recording point of view, a blessing is that neglect has left many Northumbrian gardens as 'sleeping beauties'. Unfortunately, however, this is a situation that is changing fast as it becomes a more lucrative proposition to develop the sites, while written records and plans of individual sites are not easy to find, if indeed they ever existed.

As already mentioned, early walled gardens were predominantly those attached to monastic or other ecclesiastical buildings. Their primary purpose was the growing of medicinal and culinary herbs, although they may also have provided a peaceful environment for thought and contemplation. The early ecclesiastical enclosed garden at Blanchland Abbey was in existence by the twelfth century, while at Black Friars in Newcastle, a Dominican friary begun in 1239, it is still possible to see some of the original walls and appreciate the thirteenth-century garden layout (see Fig. 13.5, p.216). However, after the Union of the Crowns in 1603, there was an upswing in the development of houses and estates (even though border incursions continued for most of the next fifty years) which accelerated with the further easing of tensions during the latter half of the seventeenth century. Houses that had been built for defensive purposes were extended and rearranged to provide more pleasing accommodation, with surroundings that reflected the greater security of the time. Chipchase Castle, in the North Tyne valley, originally a defensive tower, was transformed into a Jacobean house – 'easily the best example of its time in the county'[2] – by Cuthbert Heron in 1621 (see Fig. 6.2). Rock Hall, four miles north east of Alnwick and constructed in 1670 by the Salkeld family, was another manor house that was built upon existing defensive towers, and here there is evidence of an early and very successful walled garden. In 1695 Samuel Salkeld (d. 1699) wrote *A New Book of Geography*, in which he describes this garden. It was considered to contain some of the best-grown fruit, of the widest selection, in the north of England. Some of the original walls still exist, incorporating castle-like projections that housed the heating boilers. Enclosed walled gardens attaching directly to the house, as with the earlier monastery gardens, are also known to have existed at Capheaton Hall and at Belsay Castle, both in the A696 corridor. This style is clearly shown at Capheaton, in a painting of the house and garden as they were before major alterations of the mid and later eighteenth century,[3] and at Belsay in the engraving by the brothers Buck of 1728 (Fig. 6.3).

The greatest period of garden development in Northumberland was during the eighteenth century, reflecting new wealth from the industrial revolution, especially from coal mining and glass manufacture, as well as from agrarian improvement. The walled gardens of Wallington Hall and Seaton Delaval Hall (Sir John Vanbrugh's magnificent creation close to the Northumberland coast and to Newcastle), both of the 1720s and 1730s, are notable examples. A contemporary description of the latter estate is instructive in giving some idea of the relative positions of house, landscape and garden:

2   N. Pevsner et al., *The Buildings of England: Northumberland* (London, 1992), p.231.
3   This painting is in a private collection.

Figure 6.2. Chipchase Castle, Northumberland (engraving by John Stewart for
The Beauties of England and Wales, xii, 1813). A Jacobean mansion was added to
a medieval castle (retained for defence) in 1621. The walled garden lies behind the
elevations shown in this illustration. William Hutchinson wrote of Chipchase: 'Its
situation is beautiful, on a declivity, on the eastern banks of North Tyne, commanding
an elegant prospect. The river forms a fine canal in front, washing a woody steep
projecting cliff ... whilst woods [and] rocks ... mingle their various beauties with the
cultivated lands upon the landskip' (*View of Northumberland, etc.*, i, pp.178–9).

> Before the fourth front is a grass-lawn, edged with plantations; and beyond
> it, a spacious avenue, with shady walks on each side ... to the east, through
> several openings in little groves, are seen pieces of statuary; also a large and
> spacious riding-house; and a beautiful garden, with a conservatory or green
> house; and a delightful view of the sea, which gives Seaton Delaval, in this
> particular, infinitely the advantage over Blenheim.[4]

From the beginning of the century there was a change of emphasis in the ways
in which both natural and man-made landscapes were perceived and understood.
For those with the means and desire to follow the prevailing intellectual fashion,
an aesthetic view of the landscape as a whole became more important than a
highly formal arrangement or the mere creation of an environment in which to
grow plants. The traditional pattern of garden design that had for so long meant
enclosure by walls, providing a sheltered environment for plants, now became a
hindrance in people's desire for vistas of the wider garden and parkland, prefer-
ably in the style of Lancelot 'Capability' Brown.

---

[4] P. Russell et al., *England Displayed, being a New, Complete, and Accurate Survey of the Kingdom of
England, etc.*, 2 vols (London, 1769), ii, p.189.

Figure 6.3. Belsay Castle and Old Hall, Northumberland (detail of engraving by S. and N. Buck, 1728). Again a Jacobean mansion was built on to a medieval castle, on this occasion in 1614. The walled garden shown here in this early-eighteenth-century view was completely swept away later in the same century as part of a typically Georgian scheme of landscaping. Belsay Old Hall itself was then subsequently abandoned in favour of a new neo-classical villa (Belsay Hall, 1807–17), built nearby on his estate by the then owner of the estate and talented amateur architect Sir Charles Monck, to designs based on the Greek temples he had studied abroad.

This style of gardening certainly did not encourage the foreshortening of beautiful vistas by the presence of walls. The view from inside the house, and from the outside looking at the house in its wider setting, was to be an endless rolling scene of pastoral, controlled nature. As what became known as 'polite society' evolved during the eighteenth century, the use and positioning of the walled garden began to reflect this ethos within an overall garden or park. Ultimately, a combination of aesthetic and practical considerations led to the walled garden – still a highly regarded and necessary part of the estate but not one that should impinge upon visual sensibilities – being repositioned.

The size of the larger garden or landscape park was used as a means of display, reflecting the desire of many owners to enhance and show off their social status, their political horizons, the magnitude of their disposable income or their intellectual, scientific or cultural interests. This 'social' garden became an extension of the house and was used as an area for pleasurable rides or perambulations. There was generally a well-thought-out planned route for these excursions around the garden, as undertaken by the owner, friends and family. The preferred route could take in particular views that were intended to impress by extensive vistas over the coterminous estate or by their beauty. The walled garden was usually an integral part of this planned route.

By examining the layout of a garden or park, either by reference to maps or by walking the site, or both, it is often possible to appreciate the thought behind such a planned route. For example, at Fowberry Tower, east of Wooler, it is possible to identify a planned circuit route on the Ordnance Survey second edition map of 1897. This route would have started from the terrace of the house, passing through the developing plantation of American conifers (having been raised from seed imported in 1859–60[5]), where there were views over the main expanse of parkland, and continuing through more mixed shrub and conifers to the main entrance of the walled garden at its north-east corner. On entering, it would have been possible to gain an overall impression of the walled garden, including the gazebo in the north-west corner that would have been the next destination. The ornately decorated room on the first floor of the gazebo offered further views over the walled garden and the wider landscape.

By its very nature the walled garden could be a private place to escape to, which in a busy household would be a blessing. A protected space, the walled garden was also a place to walk when the weather prevented excursions further afield; this recreational use was particularly valuable for women and children. Thus the paths in a walled garden were made wide enough to allow walking side by side, and were well kept so as to provide a good surface for walking, while being sufficiently durable for the frequent passage of loaded wheelbarrows. The eminent late Georgian garden designer Humphry Repton did much to encourage and popularise the pleasure to be gained from the walled garden, believing that it could be used for the 'comfort and utility of the family all the year round'. He continued: 'the kitchen garden ... is a different climate. There are many days in winter when a warm, dry but secluded walk under the shelter of a south wall, would be preferred to the most beautiful but exposed landscape.'[6] Repton also advocated the use of evergreens to enhance the pleasure of using such a garden in winter. Within the walled garden the individual plant beds were generally slightly raised and edged with wooden boards, brick, tiles or tight clumps of low-growing plants such as various species of *saxifraga* or *sempervivum*. The designs for the walled garden at Ewart Park, north of Wooler, of 1790, show that the edges of the beds were to be formed by 'box, daisys [sic] or a green sward'.[7] Such firm, planted edges helped to keep the paths demarcated and drained.

As the development of the estate landscape responded to the changing circumstances and fashions of the wider world, the walled garden was able to expand and become a specific feature within this landscape. It became a more independent structural unit and the purposes for which it was used were taken more into consideration when its positioning was decided. The conditions that would maximise the successful cultivation of plants could now be more readily provided, and this was to become increasingly relevant as more and more new plants were introduced from overseas. Thus the walled garden was now often established in a position that would maximise growing potential, such as a south-facing, slightly sloping site. This topographic requirement could result

[5]   (Northumberland County History Committee), *A History of Northumberland*, 15 vols (Newcastle upon Tyne, 1893–1940), xiv (ed. M.H. Dodds, 1935), p.220.
[6]   Quoted in J.C. Loudon, *The Landscape Gardening and Landscape Architecture of the late H. Repton* (London, 1840), p.332.
[7]   Northumberland County Record Office (hereafter NCRO), ZBU BS/5.

Figure 6.4. 'Chesters Herb Garden', Northumberland. This garden attaches to Chesters, or 'Chesters House', a mansion designed by John Carr (of York) in c.1771 and remodelled by John Dobson in 1832 and 1837. Later, Chesters was greatly enlarged in neo-Baroque style by R. Norman Shaw, 1891–3 (photograph: Tom Yellowley).

in a walled garden being located in an isolated and in some ways inconvenient position, up to a mile away from the house, as, for example, at Hesleyside.

With many gardens, their east- and west-facing walls were built at a slight outward angle in order to embrace as much as possible of the sun's rays, and the two corner angles of the south-facing wall were sometimes smoothly rounded rather than sharp. This may have been as much to make the expanse of brick more pleasing to the eye, enabling fruit trees to be trained in an unbroken pattern, as to maximise the effect of the temperature. The north-facing wall at some sites was built low, to allow in as much sunlight as possible. This can be seen at 'Chesters Herb Garden', three-quarters of a mile west of Chollerford, formerly the kitchen garden of Chesters House and now a semi-commercial enterprise and visitor attraction (Fig. 6.4).[8] Here the north-facing wall is not only lower (less than five feet tall) but, most unusually, heated as well. It had small boilers and connecting flues built into it and would most probably have been used to keep the frost from fruit that was being grown in a very highly pruned and controlled state.

The boundary walls of walled gardens were made either of brick or of stone, or of a combination of both. At Matfen Hall, near Stamfordham, the massive

---

[8]   At the time of this book going to press, it has been announced that this garden will shortly no longer be open to the public (eds).

Figure 6.5. A heated wall at Gosforth Park (formerly House, now Brandling House), near Newcastle. This mansion, in what is now Newcastle Racecourse, was built for the coal-owner Charles Brandling between 1755 and 1764 to the designs of James Paine, who, as can be seen from numerous references in this book, worked widely in the North East. With its later appropriation mainly for a racecourse but also for two golf courses, rather than for the usual urban development, Gosforth's former estate retains more than a semblance of the effect of the original landscape park, possibly laid out by Paine himself, and the architect was probably also responsible for the two surviving walled garden layouts on the west side of the estate. One of these is now the premises of a commercial garden centre (detail illustrated here), while the other, although having a monumental arched entrance, is semi-derelict (photograph: Tom Yellowley).

Figure 6.6. The walled garden at Nunwick Hall, Northumberland. Nunwick Hall is a Palladian mansion of 1748–52, designed almost certainly by Daniel Garrett, an immediate predecessor of James Paine in the North East and elsewhere (see also Fig. 2.2, p.45) (photograph: Tom Yellowley).

south-, east- and west-facing walls are of stone on the outside and brick on the inside, with a central rubble core. Heated walls, usually the south-facing ones, were always double-layered and built either entirely of brick or of stone and brick, with flues to allow the circulation of hot air from the boilers (see Fig. 6.5). Brick is important for the cultivation of plants because of its ability to absorb and store solar heat and heat from fires, in the case of heated walls, to be given out during the night. Raising the temperature around plants planted against the walls helped to prevent damage from frost when they were in the budding stage and encouraged development. Bricks were very often made by local workmen on or near to the site of the walled garden. For instance, the bricks for the walled garden at Nunwick Hall, in the North Tyne valley (see also Chapter 2), were made nearby at Nunwick Common: here, over a period of three years in the late 1740s, 204,000 bricks, of which 170,000 were useable, were made for the walled garden at a total cost (at 4s 6d per thousand) of £38 4s[9] (see Fig. 6.6). Heated walls were an essential feature of gardens coping with the severe Northumbrian climate, and here the easy availability of coal was a major encouragement in their development and use. Another material in plentiful supply that could be used for gentle heating was horse manure; when the weather was particularly hard, horse manure would be piled up directly against the outside of a south-

---

[9] NCRO, 2AL No. 5.

facing wall to boost the temperature and act as insulation. 'Tide marks' can still be seen along some of these walls.

The many new plants introduced from warmer climes during the eighteenth and nineteenth centuries needed very specific cultivation. The great interest of owners, and their competitive attitude, especially in the growing of pineapples, meant that an extensive body of expertise was built up. Tanner's bark was a recycled commodity put to important use in the making-up of hot beds for pines. After the bark, usually oak, was used in the tanning of animal skins to make leather, it was reused to make deep beds in special structures called pine pits. Pots of young pineapple plants were plunged into the bark, where they would be encouraged by the heat produced by its fermentation to grow into mature fruit-producing plants. When managed well the bark could provide sufficient heat for between three and six months and there was much discussion about its use in publications of the day.[10] The use of bark for hot beds was widespread in many gardens in Northumberland, and, for that matter, in County Durham, where at Gibside there are several references in the surviving accounts to the purchasing of bark, as, for example, in July and November 1774.[11] Even earlier, in April 1747, there are details of 'local tanner's bark' being obtained from Newcastle for the hot bed at Fenham Hall.[12] In 1807, Sir Charles Monck at Belsay Hall created a fine heated wall independent of a walled garden. Built for the specific cultivation of exotic fruits such as guavas, citrus and bananas, it is positioned so that it could be seen and enjoyed from the house.

In walled gardens where there was no heating it was still possible to grow a wide variety of fruit using varieties that were particularly well adapted to local conditions. Apple trees grown in trained fan shapes or espaliered against the wall could be fruited to perfection. At Ewart Park, the home of Count Horace St Paul, one walled garden was devoted in 1790 to the cultivation of espaliered apples, including such old varieties as Nonesuch, Golden Renet, Yorkshire Green, Wine or Queen Apple and the Kent Codlin.[13] Similarly, the 1820 planting plans and lists for the walled garden at Fowberry Tower have survived, giving another insight into the many varieties of fruit grown, as well as their quantities and style of planting. Local interest is evident in the naming of one variety as 'Sir Walter Blackett's Favourite Apple'.[14] Buildings within the walled garden were used to enable the cultivation and display of the most varied and extravagant of delicate, non-hardy plants. A wide range of glasshouses of specific design, in which were grown the very latest plants, such as pineapples, vines, apricots and orchids, can be identified at many sites.[15] Further documentary evidence is

---

[10] For example, see J. Anderson (ed.), *The New Practical Gardener* (London, 1857), p.586.

[11] July 1774: 'for New Hott House paid John Pescod for wherryage of Bark 15/-' and November 1774: 'for Hott House paid Anthony Dodd for 14 fothers of bark @1/8d. £1.1/-' ref. Durham County Record Office DRO/ST/ES/11 (note: wherryage = transporting by wherry boat).

[12] Gateshead Library, Local History Section, E 27.

[13] NCRO, ZBU 85/8/37.

[14] NCRO, ZCU/34.

[15] For more details of glasshouses, see R. Thompson, *The Gardener's Assistant* (Glasgow, 1859, London, 1878, and subsequent editions), and also Chapter 5.

needed to discover the uses of those many glasshouses that are now reduced to an outline of brick foundations.

At Seaton Delaval Hall, the walled garden produced in 1766 enormous quantities of specialist fruit. There are records of pineapple plants being selected in London, particularly from the nursery of James Shiells of Lambeth, who sold the New Providence pine that was supposed to fruit on the king's birthday, or thereabouts. Plants and seeds were sent by sea from London, and there is much correspondence complaining of the length of time it took and the poor condition of plants on arrival, much of it because of salt damage. The pineapple fruits, in particular, were sent annually to many friends and acquaintances, including the Lord Mayor of Newcastle. Between July and December 1806, 114 separate parcels of fruit were sent out from the walled garden to a variety of destinations; on eleven different occasions grapes, peaches and nectarines were dispatched to the Officers' Mess at Tynemouth's Castle Barracks.[16]

Particularly important features of the walled garden in the early nineteenth century were glasshouses (see Fig. 6.1) housing either a general winter garden or specific plants whose season was during the winter. It became very fashionable to have winter-flowering collections; the *erica* house at Seaton Delaval Hall is a case in point. Here there was an extensive collection of heathers, as can be deduced from a plant order given to the plant nursery of William Falla, of Newcastle and Gateshead, in 1804.[17] Individual plants of such specialities as *erica vestita coccinea* were ordered at 7s 6d per plant, along with a further thirty-one different species. These were chosen from a nursery list catering for the now-popular fashion for erica houses that offered ninety-five different varieties.

Other buildings were specifically used for entertaining and were often built into the corners of the walls – a design feature with a very long pedigree. At Fowberry Tower, the Kelso architect James Nesbit, who was employed a great deal in the north of the county, enlarged the mid-seventeenth-century house in 1776, and laid out the grounds in keeping with the fashions of the day. In addition to pleasure gardens and a bowling green, he included a magnificently sited walled garden to the west of the house. In the north-west corner of this garden, built into the angle of the south- and east-facing walls, is a wonderful two-storey Gothick gazebo with an elaborate Rococo-style ceiling. It is easy to imagine this garden room being the end point of an after-dinner stroll: a very suitable location in which to enjoy dessert, tobacco and conversation.

The last decades of the nineteenth century were the heyday of the labour-intensive Victorian kitchen garden. However, the establishment of an entirely new walled garden after the 1880s was rarely attempted, at least in this area, and soon, following the First World War and its shattering loss of men, there was a need to completely readapt to a changed world order. This brought about the rapid decline of an entire way of life in the garden. Even so, interest and new developments still continued in some places. In the walled garden at Blagdon Hall a new design feature was incorporated in the late 1920s at the behest

---

16 NCRO, 2DE 33/11/25.
17 NCRO, 2DE 34/6/10.

of the famous garden designer Gertrude Jekyll. This was a pergola lining the main path with brick uprights which would, originally, have had rope or metal swags strung between them parallel to the path. On these, roses would have been trained, a favourite Jekyll device. Such an attractive visual detail, set within a walled garden in which so much crop production had taken place, indicates a continued intention to make the experience of the walled garden – an integral part of the larger garden – a pleasurable one.

An interesting note in the final evolution of the Northumbrian walled garden, again involving Miss Jekyll, is provided by the example at Lindisfarne Castle, one of the most unusual in the whole country. Now owned by the National Trust, the castle has a beautifully wild and historic location on Holy Island, a tidal island off the Northumberland coast six miles north of Bamburgh. At the beginning of the twentieth century it was purchased by Edward Hudson, owner and founder of the magazine *Country Life*, who, with his architect Edwin Lutyens, breathed new life into the site. His own vision of a garden was probably severely constrained by the exposed position, but, with the advice of his friend Miss Jekyll, a small walled garden was built. It is located over fields to the north of the castle and may be viewed directly from the windows. Set into the long stone wall of a field boundary, it seems very much part of the landscape, and yet simultaneously appears as an extraordinary intrusion in this rugged coastal setting. The enclosing walls are about six feet high, with the south wall being at shoulder height, and so it is just possible to see over the top into it while the plants are reasonably protected from the coastal wind. Miss Jekyll designed a colourful flower garden, using plants that would cope with extreme conditions and provide pleasure over the summer when the castle would be most occupied.

In conclusion, it is probably true to say that the general perception of a walled garden today is of a run-down or derelict area enclosed by a crumbling wall. And, if such a garden is visualised in a historic context, it is imagined as a bustling workplace dedicated to fruit and vegetable production. Yet these perceptions are too shallow to do justice to the long tradition and varied uses of the enclosed walled garden, a form which can be seen as a key part of a horticultural world that also reflected the social customs, habits and attitudes of the times. At different points in their development such gardens catered for spiritual considerations, as well as the political and economic states of both the individual house owner and wider society, through the choice of plants grown. The aesthetic attitudes of the eighteenth century affected the location of walled gardens within the grounds of country houses, while contemporary scientific knowledge and understanding are evident in the specific buildings for the cultivation of particular plants and in the many different ways of treating them.

So far, the gardens documented in Northumberland under the terms of the present research have followed a rather standard basic rectangular plan. Unusual forms seen in other parts of the country, such as circular or double walls, have for the most part not been found, although one exception is the pentagonal walled garden at Matfen Hall, which has a very low north-facing wall, now almost destroyed. There is still much research to be done in order to document a wider sample of Northumbrian walled gardens. As this work proceeds, it will become possible to take a broader view of their development and to put this into a more comparative context, looking northwards to Scotland, to the Borders in particular, as well as southwards. The history of the walled garden encapsulates much that was at the forefront of horticultural knowledge and endeavour. Sadly, however, too many of these gardens have been lost to modern development. Even so, those examples that survive as gardens provide sites for cultivation in optimal positions with soil enriched by years of care, while some have found a new use as commercial garden centres, as at Gosforth Park (formerly Gosforth House, now Brandling House: see Fig. 6.5) near Newcastle. The walled garden is a landscape jewel that has lost its sparkle, but with renewed awareness could once again become a worthwhile gem.

7

Impolite Landscapes: Making Private Parks Public

FIONA GREEN

This chapter examines the changing aspirations for eighteenth- and nineteenth-century landscaped gardens in the industrial areas of northern, especially North-Eastern, England. In this latter region a pragmatic approach was often taken to designing landscaped estates adjacent to industrial activity. Inevitably, industry led to increased urbanisation and frequently made for unpleasant living conditions. Then, following the later abandonment of landscaped estates, those who had toiled to fund them were allowed to use the grounds as their retreats. Recent research assessing public parks in the north of England has highlighted the fact that many have been created from modified landscaped estates.[1] These estates have followed a transition from private sanctums to parks opened up to the very people who were often excluded from them, and whose working activities (at the very least) had been screened from important landscape views.

Eighteenth-century polite society was highly commercial. Inevitably this knocked the edges off the implementation of the approach advised for landscaped gardens by authors such as Horace Walpole, who wrote in 1785: 'We have discovered the point of perfection. We have given the true model of gardening to the world; let other countries mimic or corrupt our taste; but let it reign here on its verdant throne.'[2] Thus during recent years authors such as Tom Williamson and Stephen Daniels have discussed the dichotomy between the belief that landowners were single-minded in their determination to create polite landscapes and the fact that they were also intent upon accommodating their agricultural and sporting interests.[3]

The reality of a society where commerce took precedence was described by William Hutchinson when he visited Whickham, Gateshead, in 1767: 'The adjacent country wears an unpleasant affect to the traveller, cut and harrowed up with loaded carriages, from whence swarm forth innumerable inhabitants maintained

---

1   Other examples researched by the present author include Towneley Park, Burnley, and Taylor Park, St Helens. However, this was not purely a northern phenomenon. Castle Park, Colchester, was developed in the grounds of a mansion but without the proximity of industrial interests.

2   H. Walpole, *On Modern Gardening* (London, 1785), p.81.

3   See, for example, S. Daniels, *Humphry Repton: Landscape Gardening and the Geography of Georgian England* (New Haven, 1999) and T. Williamson, *Polite Landscapes: Gardens and Society in Eighteenth Century England* (Stroud, 1998).

by working the mines; where many a sooty face is seen by every hedgeway side; the workmen earn great wages which recompense every other evil.'[4] He further described the Dunston Hill estate, also in Whickham, commenting that 'Dunston is on a pleasant situation and Mr. Carr's delightful villa commands a beautiful prospect of the town of Newcastle and adjacent country.'[5] The practical Mr Carr had planted woodland to screen evidence of the mines, an approach taken by many of his contemporaries in the region.

As landscapes on the edge of towns became despoiled by industrial activity there was a necessity for industrial profiteers to wrap themselves in a rural idyll. The 'nouveaux riches' bought up agricultural land on the outskirts of Newcastle upon Tyne, Gateshead and other northern towns such as Leeds and Sheffield,[6] building mansions and extravagant pleasure grounds. Once abandoned, the houses and gardens were often designated to the workforce for use as civic buildings and public parks.

Public access to North-Eastern landscape parks during the eighteenth century and later

As Adrian Tinniswood illustrates in his *History of Country House Visiting* (1989),[7] the contrast between the vogue for visiting country estates today and that during the eighteenth century is that we venture to discover the 'old' whilst our forbears were examining the 'new'. The 'polite' visitor was invariably allowed to enter estates and mansions to view architecture, paintings, pleasure gardens and other indices of taste. In 1756 a description of a tumultuous hurricane on Tyneside began with the words, 'Though it is the pleasure of people of taste in the North to pay an annual visit to Gibside Woods [near Gateshead], yet few of your readers can form an idea of their present desolation by the late dreadful hurricane.'[8]

There is also evidence that there were those who were *not* encouraged to visit Gibside; 'watchers' were posted in sentry boxes on the Great Walk.[9] Fears of intruders were realised when in 1768, Richard Stevenson, the agent at Gibside, put up reward money for information which might help identify the culprits who threw the statue of Venus from the Bath House into the river, quite some distance below.[10] Another popular venue in the region was Raby Castle at Staindrop (see Fig. 0.7, p.15), which was later made accessible by the spread of the railway. The closest station to Raby Castle was Cockfield, approximately two miles to the north, which was opened in 1830. Raby was a honey-pot for hoards

[4]   W. Hutchinson, *The History and Antiquities of the County Palatine of Durham*, 3 vols (Newcastle upon Tyne and London, 1785–94), ii (1825 ed.), p.568.
[5]   Ibid., p.567.
[6]   For more on the latter towns see G. Sheeran, *Landscape Gardens in West Yorkshire, 1680–1880* (Wakefield, 1990), pp.153–91.
[7]   A. Tinniswood, *A History of Country House Visiting: Five Centuries of Tourism and Taste* (Oxford, 1989), p.1.
[8]   *Monthly Chronicle of North-Country Lore and Legend* (October 1888), pp.466, 477.
[9]   Durham County Record Office, Gibside Account Books D/St/E5/4/16.
[10]   W. Bourne, *The Annals of Whickham* (Consett, c.1890), p.76 (courtesy of Harry Beamish).

of tourists, whose access was limited to periods when the Vane family was not in residence.[11]

Those who were unable to contemplate tours of private estates were sometimes invited to visit as a philanthropic gesture. Lord and Lady Armstrong opened Jesmond Dene in Newcastle and in 1873 the appreciation of local worthies was voiced as follows:

> Even his private residences are made to serve the public, as witness Jesmond, with its splendid banqueting hall, erected for public use, and its beautiful gardens and grounds, for regular admission to which only a small charge is made, while the sum realized is handed over to the funds of the Infirmary.[12]

The most ironic invitation to visit a landscaped estate was probably issued by the Durham Church Commissioners in the late nineteenth century, when Auckland Park was opened to the public. Having been confirmed as an episcopal residence when it was recorded in the Boldon Book of 1183, Auckland Park first served as a hunting park for the omnipotent Prince-Bishops, men of vast wealth whose possessions included numerous other hunting parks throughout Durham and Northumberland. However, although extremely prestigious, the park was also a working landscape. Following the Restoration wild cattle were recorded in the park and later there were mining activities on the outskirts.[13] In 1754 the renowned landscape gardener Joseph Spence was asked by Bishop Trevor to advise on improvements to the parkland.[14] Shortly afterwards a new gateway to the palace and park was built,[15] as was the majestic deer shelter.[16] The Newcastle artist J.W. Carmichael painted a flower show in Auckland Park in 1859 (Fig. 7.1). By 1890 the park was open from sunrise to sunset each day and Bishop Lightfoot had allowed local gentry, the police and doctors to drive their carriages through it.

Coal-owners' estates

During the seventeenth century North-East England was embedded in conservatism, and was relatively backward in development in comparison with the rest of the country. This backwardness was partly due to the distance from central government but also seemed to be engendered through limitations caused by border conflicts, which continued until the mid seventeenth century. As late as 1640, the Scots occupied the city of Durham. However, following the Restoration the region saw a surge of business enterprise. By the beginning of the eighteenth century those already profiting from coal, such as William Cotesworth (see below), were able to purchase forfeited estates after the Jacobite Rising of

11 P. Mandler, *The Fall and Rise of the Stately Home* (New Haven, 1997), p.79.
12 W.D. Lawson, *Tyneside Celebrities* (Newcastle upon Tyne, 1873), pp.254–62.
13 J. Raine, *Historical Account of Auckland Castle* (Durham, 1832), pp.124, 125.
14 R.W. King, 'Joseph Spence of Byfleet', *Journal of Garden History*, 8:2 (1980), p.47.
15 The gateway was designed by the amateur architect Sir Thomas Robinson (1760); see Raine, *Historical Account*, p.127.
16 Architect unknown but the building is suggested by Eileen Harris to be similar in style to the work of Thomas Wright (1711–86); see E. Harris, *Arbours and Grottos – A Facsimile of the Two Parts of Universal Architecture 1755 and 1758 by Thomas Wright* (London, 1979).

Figure 7.1. J.W. Carmichael, *Flower Show in Auckland Park*, 1859 (© Bishop Auckland Library; courtesy of Durham County Council).

1715. Similarly, although gentry such as the Liddells were resident at Ravensworth, Gateshead (see Fig. 0.8, p.16), they took the opportunity to expand their landholdings and purchased the Eslington Estate in Northumberland after it was forfeited to the crown.[17]

The North East is well known as an early field of industrial development. However, the biggest change occurred during the eighteenth century, when the organisation of the coal trade was transformed by cartels. The North-Eastern coalfield formed the mainstay of supplies to London and the south and by the 1750s the impact of the burgeoning profits was clearly evident on Tyneside. In particular, affluence was demonstrated by the opulence of coal owners' estates. Landed gentry altered their mansions and estates thanks to monies often borrowed against their profits from the 'black diamonds'. For example, having inherited Gibside, George Bowes engineered between 1721 and 1767 a monumental landscape with garden buildings (see Fig. 0.6, p.14, and also Chapters 5 and 8), culminating with his Palladian chapel and mausoleum, a masterpiece by James Paine.

Large country estates had long signified wealth and a landholding extending beyond the distant prospect was then, as now, a symbol of power. Armstrong's maps of Northumberland (1769)[18] and Durham (1768, see Fig. 7.2) show a number of estates which had been recently completed by the time the maps were

[17] N. McCord and R. Thompson, *A Regional History of England: The Northern Counties from AD 1000* (London, 1998), p.158.

[18] *A Map of the County of Northumberland with that Part of the County of Durham that is North of the River Tyne. Also the Town of Berwick and its Bounds taken from the Actual Survey and laid down from a Scale of an Inch to a Mile; By Lieu[tenan]t And[re]w Armstrong and Son* (London, 1769).

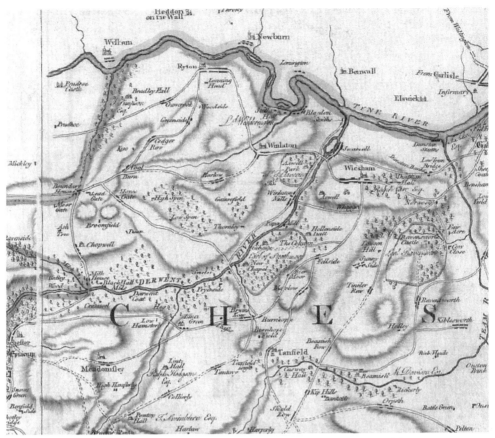

Figure 7.2. Detail of map of 'The County Palatine of Durham', surveyed by Andrew Armstrong and engraved by Thomas Jefferys, London, 1768 (reproduced by permission of Durham University Library).

published. North of the Tyne Woolsington Hall, Gosforth House (see Chapter 6), Heaton Hall, Benton Hall[19] and Fenham Hall are shown. South of the Tyne (Fig. 7.2), in what appears to be admiring proximity to Gibside and Ravensworth, Axwell Hall, Stella Hall and Dunston Hall were all built by coal owners, some of whom were 'self made'.

Gardens of North-Eastern entrepreneurs

As commerce in Newcastle escalated, the new profiteers began to build 'mini-estates' in the suburbs. Previously they might have owned winter townhouses, such as those in Charlotte Square, Newcastle (built from 1770 by the local architect William Newton), but affluent merchants found themselves in a posi-

---

19 For more on Benton Hall and Heaton Hall, both now demolished, see T.E. Faulkner and P.A.S. Lowery, *Lost Houses of Newcastle and Northumberland* (York, 1996), pp.9 and 21–2 respectively (eds).

tion to create their own large houses and landscaped estates in proximity to their
business interests.

By the eighteenth century society had diversified to such an extent that industrial entrepreneurs were also able to afford to lay out country estates, entering
a sphere of influence which had previously been exclusive to the gentry. The
changes brought about by 'new wealth', much from industry, affected responses
to the laying-out of estate landscapes. Firstly, there was the growth of large
suburban villas for industrialists who needed to live near to their businesses and,
secondly, there was the opportunity for the middle classes to develop personal
aesthetic tastes. The new 'mini-estates' were located on the outskirts of towns
and they were often close to other settlements rather than being situated in open,
rolling countryside; this influenced the dynamics of these gardens. There was
a greater requirement for privacy and the screening of unwanted views, while
within the garden the creation of an appropriate setting for the mansion was
necessary, with impressive displays of landscape gardening.

Garden design and its implementation

The flow of ideas between members of the new elite was affected by their
eagerness to illustrate discernment in taste, but at the same time they were not
unwilling to reinforce their relationship with the economy. Styford Hall, near
Bywell, was built in about 1800 for Charles Bacon, a man who, it appears, was
not averse to the 'rude hands of industry' being visible in the landscape outside
the park boundary. He may also have been keen to include the novelty of the
railway as part of the view; one of the earliest railway lines was opened here
in 1835, and the attraction is understandable. At the Ravensworth estate and at
Dunston Hill in Gateshead there were early examples of mining reclamation in
landscaped parks, where coal pits were screened by planting.[20]

Gateshead Park, another such estate, belonged to the famous entrepreneur
William Cotesworth from 1716. Although he began his career as a tallow
chandler, Cotesworth built an exceptional career as a leading figure in the
formation of a successful cartel and was High Sheriff of Northumberland by
1715.[21] The Ordnance Survey first edition map shows the estate with all the
conventional features of the period, but a colliery is also shown to the south
east of the mansion.[22] The house was approached from the north, where the
drive entered an oval-shaped turning area lined with trees and shrubs. A terrace
below the south front of the hall gave views over a parterre with small diamond-
shaped and circular beds. The house, pleasure grounds and kitchen gardens were
protected from ugly views and odours by woodland plantations (Fig. 7.3).

The letters of Henry Ellison, a later owner, reveal how in 1733 a London
nurseryman, Henry Woodman, was usurped in his role as advisor on the laying-

[20] J. Pendlebury and F. Green, *Impolite Landscapes? The Influence of Local Economic and Cultural
Factors in Garden History: A Case Study of Tyne & Wear* (Newcastle upon Tyne, 1998), p.10.
[21] A.W. Purdue, *Merchants and Gentry in North-East England, 1650–1830: The Carrs and the Ellisons*
(Sunderland, 1999), p.38.
[22] Ordnance Survey 6-inch map (1862).

Figure 7.3. Detail of Ordnance Survey first edition map showing layout of gardens at Park House, Gateshead. Note the proximity of the colliery lying south east of the mansion.

out of the grounds of Gateshead Park by the writer and landscape designer Stephen Switzer (1682–1745).[23] Switzer wrote to Ellison (who took over the estate on his marriage to Cotesworth's daughter) suggesting that Ellison's former gardener, Woolley, was a cheat working in collusion with Woodman. Such rivalry illustrates the degree of interest from London in a job located so far away that the plant stock had to be shipped. The Ellison papers also include a note from Woodman to Woolley, on 25 November 1731: 'I have at last shipp'd your trees I had indeed sent 'em almost a fortnight ago'; the order included 200 hedge Dutch Elms (6 foot high), 1500 Hornbeam, 34 Cherries, 20 apples, 31 plumbs and damsons, 17 pears, and 80 Gooseberrys and currants among others, the 'wharfedge' on the bill of £10.8.00 was £5.0.0.[24] Switzer was also commissioned to produce a plan for George Bowes in 1731, for Gibside, and was obviously aware of the potential for rich pickings in the area.[25]

23 Cited in J. Harvey, *Early Nurserymen* (Chichester, 1974), p.171.
24 Ibid., p.179.
25 Cited in M. Wills, *Gibside and the Bowes Family* (Chichester, 1995), p.15: (Durham County Record Office D/St/V985 Cash Accounts 24 June 1731).

The larger audience for landscape gardening inevitably meant a greater freedom for interpretation. Switzer's popular *Iconographia Rustica* (1718) listed subscribers in the North East such as Alexander Brown, who lived at Doxford Hall in Northumberland. The remains of modest terracing west of Doxford Hall suggest that Brown may have followed his own ideas, however. In common with much art history, studies in garden history often linger over the 'greats' such as Stowe (Buckinghamshire). Yet, as Doxford demonstrates, for all the sites by grand designers there were hundreds of local variations in all areas, the North East being no exception. Here, rising entrepreneurs developed the confidence to experiment with their own ideas rather than simply emulating the great and the good.

Pleasure grounds and coal pits in the Ouseburn valley

The main example discussed in this chapter is the Ouseburn valley and its development. Located on the eastern outskirts of Newcastle, the river Ouseburn, a tributary of the Tyne, runs from north to south through Jesmond to Heaton. Its valley, having evolved during periods of both industrial and aesthetic use to finally offer the setting for a munificent gesture at the end of the nineteenth century, provides a vivid example of changes to an urban landscape. This valley is a dene incised by the river Ouseburn, which, during the eighteenth and nineteenth centuries, was fast-flowing, sustaining water mills along its banks between South Gosforth and the Tyne.[26] There, at the mouth of the Ouseburn, was a great variety of industrial activity, including shipbuilding, with leadworks and glass making further upstream.

The aspirations for each stage of development of the Ouseburn valley were profoundly different. Initially, the vale between Gosforth and Heaton was riddled with coal mines; it then became a wealthy merchant's landscaped park. Subsequently it was divided and partly planted as a Victorian woodland garden and then, at the end of the nineteenth century, it was given to the City of Newcastle upon Tyne as a public park.

Heaton Hall, Newcastle

By the eighteenth century two powerful merchants, Matthew White and Richard Ridley, owned many collieries in Heaton. Both families were heavily involved with coal trading during a critical stage in the development of the industry's technology and marketing. The earliest available plan of the Heaton Estate, from the eighteenth century but undated, shows an extensive property divided by the river Ouseburn with Heaton Hall sited at the south end; the landscape was dotted with a total of seventeen coal pits.[27]

The original site of Heaton Hall is a matter for speculation. However, the later Hall was built in 1713 by Richard Ridley, Mayor of Newcastle.[28] Heaton

---

[26] *Busy Cottage Iron Works* (Newcastle City Council Historic Environment no. 5680).

[27] Northumberland County Record Office, *Plan of Heaton Estate with the old pits & co.* (eighteenth-century: no date): ZR1 50/9.

[28] Newcastle City Library, Local Newspaper Cuttings (10 October 1885, vol. 92, p.19).

Figure 7.4. Heaton Hall, Newcastle (now demolished): a late-eighteenth-century engraving.

Hall is shown on Armstrong's map of Northumberland 1769 as one of the principal estates in the county, although we have to wait for Greenwood's map of Northumberland (1828) to see any detail of the mature landscaped park. By this time the landscape had matured sufficiently to channel views to pleasant prospects while blocking out the industrial world of noise, unpleasant smells and pollution blown on the prevailing wind from the Tyne. The grounds of Heaton Hall are shown laid out with plantations and lawns to the west of the buildings (see Fig. 7.4). North of the Hall, hidden by a dense belt of trees, lie two abutting areas of kitchen garden. The east prospect from the Hall is screened with perimeter planting, while to the south views have been left open. Bourne described the grounds of Heaton Hall in 1736:

> Its conveniences and beauties about it, are on the west-side a fish pond, and groves. Wilderness, gardens, avenues, and numbers of plantations. On the east a very large and beauteous quadrangle, whose walls are shared with the choicest fruit-trees and whose area is adorn'd with variety of knots and flowers. In this area, at a due distance, are two images tall as life, which declare the hand of curious statuary. On the north are gardens and plantations and on the south an area adorned with images and a pleasing gravel-walk, beset with trees and bordered with flowers.[29]

Bourne provides a valuable view of a well-developed landscape divided by plantations and avenues into numerous interconnecting areas. The walled garden is noted as having fruit trees cultivated against the walls, and also being adorned with a variety of knots and flowers, all of which suggests that it was used as a

---

[29] H. Bourne, *The History of Newcastle upon Tyne, or, the Ancient and Present State of that Town* (Newcastle upon Tyne, 1736), p.114.

pleasure garden as well as a productive garden. Many walled gardens were used similarly at the time (see Chapter 6). Alnwick Castle's walled garden is a model example and was documented as having extensive ornamental gardens within the enormous expanse of terraced grounds.[30] Walls offered shelter from the trying North-Eastern climate and at Heaton they would have provided a screen from the mills and mining activity along the river Ouseburn.

Heaton Hall was altered by Sir Matthew White Ridley (1745–1813), who commissioned William Newton, from 1778 onwards, to alter the front with a facing of stone and the addition of two towers.[31] His father, Matthew Ridley, had earlier purchased land between the Hall and the 'Shields Turnpike', where he built a folly. Wallis described Heaton Hall in 1769, before Newton was commissioned to work there:

> The seat is at the south end of the village, modern and handsome. Before the south front is a park like enclosure, small clumps of young forest trees, extending to the Shields Road, which is in sight; also an artificial ruin on the hill at Biker. On the south west and west side are shrubberies, flower borders, and groves of trees with a tempiato.[32]

A 'tempiato' is a small temple or open rotunda and the fact that such a structure was juxtaposed with a landscape scarred by bell pits is an example of the pragmatic approach to landscape design taken by landowners in the region. The rotunda was located on a terrace which is still discernible at the Heaton end of the public park which much of the estate became (for more material relevant to the above see Chapter 13). The structure was ultimately removed to Blagdon Hall, Northumberland, and re-erected by the lake.[33]

The earliest remaining structure in the vale is the 'Camera of Adam de Jesmond', often known as King John's Palace, although no part of the building is thought to have been constructed at the time of King John. The building was probably merely a hunting lodge. However, it would have provided a point of curiosity for those walking in the grounds of Heaton Hall, even though there is no evidence of landscaping views or planting to enhance the building as a romantic ruin. There are many other features in the grounds of the estate, such as a windmill shown on a Buck engraving of 1743; the 1872 Ordnance Survey map shows 'Robin Sheep's Cave', which was said to be inhabited by a recluse. Heaton Hall now lost favour as a principal residence and the Ridleys moved to Blagdon Hall. The Heaton estate was sold off during the late nineteenth century and the mansion was demolished in the 1930s.

[30] Anon., *The Garden, Alnwick Castle*, vol. 13, part 20 (1881), pp.155–6.

[31] Faulkner and Lowery, *Lost Houses*, p. 21.

[32] J. Wallis, *The Natural History and Antiquities of Northumberland, etc.*, 2 vols (London, 1769), ii, p.249.

[33] Tyne & Wear Archive Service, MD/NC/26/9 8.12.1936.

Jesmond Dene: a woodland garden

Following the abandonment of Heaton Hall and the cessation of coal mining the mills were the only industry in evidence in Jesmond Dene. The Dene appears to have been adopted as a pleasant place for public walking by 1825 when it was visited by Robert Gilchrist: 'This valley can boast some of the finest scenery in the North of England, being most delightfully diversified with wood and water, forming some beautiful walks'.[34] Here Lord Armstrong built his house Jesmond Dean in 1835 and subsequently purchased land along the Dene. Many connections have been made between his childhood fascination for water and his talent as an engineer who used water primarily as a source of power. He grew up in the adjacent valley, Pandon Dene, before choosing to settle in and beautify Jesmond Dene, and there was a continuing similarity between the landscapes he knew as a child and those he created with Lady Armstrong later in life. The Armstrongs would also have undoubtedly have known of the growing vogue for 'woodland gardens' which were being created by industrialists in the suburbs of northern industrial towns. Significantly, Jesmond Dene was described in 1894 as 'the finest piece of ornamental planting about Newcastle, but it will vie with the best attempts in that way anywhere'[35] (Fig. 7.5). It was also the precursor for probably the most successful woodland garden in the country, at Cragside, Northumberland, which Lord and Lady Armstrong embarked upon c.1863.

The evolution of the 'woodland garden' occurred during the mid nineteenth century. However, the bones of the style came from the 'Picturesque' movement, which was at a peak at the end of the eighteenth century, when pleasure grounds were laid out at estates such as Castle Eden Dene in County Durham. The Picturesque made use of dramatic scenery and contrasted texture and vegetation, and played on the sense of wilderness, but was soon modified, Humphry Repton and others returning the garden to the main facade of the house. Despite this, the remnants of the Picturesque are very strong in these northern woodland gardens, as is reflected in an evocative quotation from Bulwer-Lytton's *Godolphin* (1865):

> The scene as they approached was wild and picturesque in the extreme. A wide and glassy lake lay stretched beneath them: on the opposite side stood the ruins. The large oriel windows, the Gothic arch, the broken, yet still majestic column, all embowned and mossed with age, were still spared, and now mirrored themselves in the waveless and silent tide. Fragments of stone lay around, for some considerable distance, and the whole was backed by hills, covered and gloomy with thick woods and pine and fir.[36]

The 'woodland garden' style thus continued to develop throughout the nineteenth century. The wild qualities of woodland gardens were often associated in the 1870s with the designer William Robinson, but other forms developed much earlier. As well as Jesmond Dene, there was in the North East Saltwell Park Dene,

---

34 *Jesmond Dene in 1825* (Newspaper Cuttings relating to Newcastle, vol. 2, p.59) (Newcastle City Library).
35 *Gardener's Chronicle* (1894), pp.748–51.
36 Cited in M. Waters, *The Garden in Victorian Literature* (Cambridge, 1988), p.78.

Figure 7.5. Jesmond Dene, Newcastle (photograph: Thomas Faulkner).

Gateshead, which was laid out by the highly successful stained-glass designer William Wailes during the 1850s; he almost certainly used Jesmond Dene as a model. The inspiration for woodland gardens also came from the flow of exotic trees and shrubs which were being introduced from abroad. In this context the typical North-Eastern topographic feature 'the dene' was of great value, offering both privacy and a dramatic terrain. Good examples of the inclusion of denes as part of pleasure grounds can be found at Whinney House in Gateshead and Allen Banks in Northumberland. Some denes were even renamed 'glens', as at the Valley Gardens, Saltburn, and Jesmond Dene. The steeper and craggier the sides of a dene, the better: in some cases the 'dene' was even embellished with artificial features such as rock-work crags, as at Whinney House, Gateshead.

Existing mature woodland was also advantageous as it provided immediate privacy. Tall trees such as beech and fastigiate species such as Lawson's Cypress also accentuated the depth of the dene. Much planting was dominated by the use of native species, particularly those with Scottish associations, such as birch, pine, heathers and bracken. A desire for recreating romantic Scottish landscape was stimulated by writers such as Sir Walter Scott, who, like Armstrong and Wailes, had formal gardens close to his house and a landscaped park with woodland plantations. The frequent use of Balmoral by the royal family also generated interest in romantic, wild landscape.

Polite public parks

By the time the Armstrongs donated Jesmond Dene to the citizens of Newcastle in 1883, and shortly afterwards the adjacent Armstrong Park (see Chapter 13), the patronising rhetoric associated with reforming the visitors to the early public parks had diminished. During the early days of public parks behaviour was strictly controlled. For example, soon after Peel Park, Salford, was opened in 1846 Joshua Major's design was changed,[37] to a large extent because of perceptions of the way the park should be used. Through this reworking the Public Parks Committee showed their true feelings about the threat which they felt was posed by the noisy and unruly behaviour of the very same visitors whom they sought to encourage; thus to counter that threat the area for sport was reduced and a series of new paths and flower-bed displays was provided to encourage sedate promenading.

The potential for unruly behaviour in parks was approached with customary Victorian zeal, with the result that copious lists of bye-laws, such as those prohibiting dancing or playing games on Sundays, were drawn up. At Peel Park, one bye-law dictated that 'All gambling and improper language is strictly prohibited; and no games or gymnastics permitted on Sundays.'[38] There was disquiet regarding preaching in the parks but the real concern was political rallying, as there was a great fear of the Chartists and insubordination on the part of the working classes. In 1846 a Manchester councillor, James Heywood, made a speech which soon moved from religion to his real concerns, politics and discipline: 'If this sort of thing were allowed, there would be public meetings in the park, and supposing Fergus O'Connor were to come on a Sunday, how could this prevent him from going to the park and getting up discussion about the Charter?'[39]

The drinking fountain was a significant feature in public parks. Clean water was important for two reasons. Firstly, enquiries into the health of the towns in the 1840s revealed that disease, especially cholera, was spread by poor water supplies. Provision of clean water supplies gave rise to great celebration. Secondly, drinking fountains praised the delights of water and promoted the value of temperance. A sundial at Albert Park in Middlesbrough (see Chapter 14) is inscribed 'First the moments, then the day, time by moments melts away', as a warning against idleness.

For public parks, traditional design principles lingered throughout the nineteenth century. The park lodge was a device which mimicked the entrance to an eighteenth-century landscaped estate. Having entered the park via ornamental gates the visitor was reminded by the lodge that the park was attended by staff and that they had entered a special place which demanded particular standards of behaviour. As at other public parks, a terrace was constructed at Heaton Park, Newcastle, to imitate the front of a grand house, where people could promenade and feel encouraged to behave in a decorous manner. It also acted as a focal point to the lower section of the park, overlooking a lake which has now gone. This terrace was actually located in the former kitchen garden and here visitors

37 H. Conway, *People's Parks: the Design and Development of Victorian Parks in Britain* (Cambridge, 1991), p.229.
38 H. Conway, 'The Manchester Salford Parks: their Design and Development', *Journal of Garden History*, 5:3 (1985), p.244.
39 Cited in T. Wyborn, 'Parks for the People: the Development of Public Parks in Victorian Manchester', *Manchester History Review*, 9 (1995), p.10.

were at one time able to buy grapes from the glasshouses which remained from the days of the Hall.[40]

Overall, the Ouseburn valley changed from being an area exploited for its ground resources to one where two affluent families, the White Ridleys and the Armstrongs, attempted to recreate its former verdant qualities. In this context James Horsley's sentimental poem of c.1890, entitled 'Jesmond Dene', is particularly noteworthy

> Thou fair lovely dene, with thy rippling burn,
> Surpassing in beauty at every turn,
> Thy forest of verdure in serried ranks,
> Thy meandering walks and thy flowery banks,
> Say, where shall Elysian glades be found
> To rival thy valley, oh Jesumound?
> Oh for a Wordsworth! Oh for a Scott!
> To give thee a voice, thou beautiful spot.[41]

These lines are perhaps a representation of the ideals taken to the landscape today by those seeking a rural idyll in the midst of a dense conurbation. Now the landscape has returned to being naturalistic in many places and there is little sense of either the exclusion associated with private parks or the demarcation characteristic of public ones. Fortunately, landscape is a transient medium and can change to absorb the aspirations of the community of the time.

Acknowledgements

I am grateful to friends in the Northumbria Gardens Trust, in particular Harry Beamish and John Pendlebury. I am also grateful to staff at the Beamish North of England Open Air Museum (County Durham), Durham County Record Office, Durham University Library Special Collections, Northumberland County Record Office, Tyne & Wear Archives, Newcastle Central Library (Local History Section) and the Literary and Philosophical Society Library, Newcastle.

---

[40] 26.7.1880: Tyne & Wear Archive Service, Newcastle City Council Parks Committee Minutes, D/NC/144/1.

[41] See J. Horsley, *Lays of Jesmond and Tyneside Songs and Poems* (Newcastle upon Tyne, 1891), p.4.

PART THREE

LIVING IN THE LANDSCAPE

8

Houses and Landscape in Early Industrial County Durham

ADRIAN GREEN

During the seventeenth and eighteenth centuries the landscape of northern County Durham was transformed by the mining and movement of coal. Intertwined with the collieries and wagon-ways were newly hedged fields, as farms were enclosed to feed the coal workforce and customary tenants were deprived of land in the process. While those who prospered from commercial opportunities built substantial houses, the majority experienced fragile employment and frequent mobility, and lived on the margins of collieries, agricultural land and established villages. These new sites of settlement formed the pattern of industrial housing that has characterised the area through to the present. Usually regarded as a creation of the nineteenth century, northern County Durham's modern landscape of mining villages actually originated in the seventeenth century.

Workers' housing ranged from temporary shelters to terraced cottages, in locations usually determined by their employers or where the more settled inhabitants allowed residence. Middling houses were themselves rebuilt to signal substance in the community at locations that further marked out a process of social polarisation. Meanwhile, the residences of the genteel elite had an ambiguous relationship with the landscape that created their prosperity. This essay explores some of the ways in which houses were integral to landscape change, and argues that the location of houses in the landscape was fundamental to the experience of social relations. For the built form of houses was an expression of the social position of the household within the house and offered contemporaries an immediate sense of the relative prosperity or poverty of a community. Yet responses to houses in the landscape are rarely documented; they were part of an implicit awareness of the material world that can be made explicit through attention to the social and spatial relations between houses.

Seventeenth- and early-eighteenth-century descriptions of Tyneside's landscape, usually written by tourists from southern England, are notably silent on housing outside the towns. They invariably dwelt instead upon its extraordinary industrial character, describing the profusion of coal pits, wagon-ways and salt pans, and the polluted atmosphere they generated. Approaching Newcastle from the west in the 1690s, Celia Fiennes found 'this country all about is full of this Coale the sulphur of it taints the aire and it smells strongly to strangers; upon a high hill 2 mile from Newcastle I could see all about the country which was full of coale pitts'.[1] The language of 'country' equates very nearly to our sense of the term landscape, and was used to demarcate contrasts in the landscape.[2] Such contrasts could be drawn at a local or a national scale, and Tyneside's industrial reputation led some to imagine its landscape as a world away from southern England. William Ellis famously declared in the mid seventeenth century that 'England's a perfect World! Has Indies too!/Correct your Maps: Newcastle is Peru.'[3] This conveys the coal trade's importance for the national economy, but simultaneously presents it as colonial, as the peripheries of the national polity were often regarded in the later seventeenth century.[4] The reality, however, was very different from the colonial situation. The resemblance of County Durham's landscape to southern England seems to have surprised Fiennes: 'Thence [from Newcastle towards Chester-le-Street] I proceeded a most pleasant gravell road on the ridge of the hill and had the whole country in view' (a view approximate to the sweep of the Wear lowlands seen from the Angel of the North today); 'the whole country looks like a fruitfull woody place and seems to equal most countys in England.'[5]

Travelling in the opposite direction a generation later, Daniel Defoe described the road from Chester-le-Street to Newcastle as giving 'a view of the inexhausted store of coals and coal pits', for 'in this country we see the prodigious heaps, I might say mountains, of coals, which are dug up at every pit, and how many of those pits there are'. For Defoe, the most important aspect of County Durham's landscape lay in its economic significance for the nation; for 'when we are at London, and see the prodigious fleets of ships which come constantly in with coals for this encreasing city, we are apt to wonder whence they come'.[6] Defoe stressed the population of London but omitted to pay any attention to the population who produced the coal. He does, however, recognise coal's regional significance, identifying at Newcastle the 'two articles of trade which are particularly occasioned by the coals', the glass-houses and salt pans:

> the first are at the town it self, the last are at Shields, seven miles below the town. It is a prodigious quantity of coals which those salt works consume; and the fires make such a smoke, that we saw it ascend in clouds over the hills, four miles before we came to Durham [from the south], which is at least sixteen miles from the place.[7]

As Fiennes and Defoe remind us, coal infused the atmosphere of the region.

[1] C. Morris (ed.), *The Illustrated Journeys of Celia Fiennes 1685–c.1712* (Stroud, 1982), p.176.
[2] A. Everitt, 'Country, County and Town: Patterns of Regional Evolution in England', *Transactions of the Royal Historical Society*, 5th ser., 29 (1979), reprinted in P. Borsay (ed.), *The Eighteenth-Century Town: A Reader in English Urban History 1688–1820* (London, 1990), pp.83–115, esp. p.86.
[3] See W. Ellis, *News from Newcastle* (London, 1651).
[4] M.G.H. Pittock, *Inventing and Resisting Britain: Cultural Identities in Britain and Ireland, 1685–1789* (Basingstoke, 1997), p.54. See also M. Hechter, *Internal Colonialism: The Celtic Fringe in British National Development, 1536–1966* (Berkeley and Los Angeles, 1975).
[5] Morris, *Celia Fiennes*, p.178.
[6] D. Defoe, *A Tour Through the Whole Island of Great Britain, 1724–26*, 2 vols (edn pub. London, 1966), ii, p.250.
[7] Ibid., p.251.

Although some commentators compared this northern landscape to the colonies of the New World, colonial settlements themselves were invariably seeking to create a more pristine landscape. Philadelphia was designed by William Penn in the late seventeenth century as a 'greene country towne' that would form the nucleus of a planned landscape across the Quaker-founded colony of Pennsylvania, recreating the English countryside on a grid plan. Philadelphia was to combine the virtues of the countryside with the administrative and economic roles of the town by fashioning a city out of 100-acre rectilinear farm-plots. In practice, commercial imperatives and a preference for closer residential propinquity created a concentration of housing around the port, but still within the security of a grid plan.[8] The very ordered nature of settlement planning in colonial landscapes raises the question of why the industrial landscape of Durham lacks such order or apparent planning. In north-west England, after all, the trade in coal and salt gave rise in the mid–late seventeenth century to the new industrial port town of Whitehaven, developed on a grid plan by the Lowther family.[9] Mining settlements in North-East England have long been regarded as a form of 'colony', but the reason they do not resemble colonial settlements in America is that they developed in a landscape thick with pre-existing rights to property and access. Moreover, the relationship between and attitudes of natives and newcomers were the reverse of the colonial situation, as the incoming migrants were forced to dwell where the settled indigenous inhabitants would tolerate them.

Philadelphia, County Durham

County Durham has its own Philadelphia, a mining settlement established in the eighteenth century below the hilltop village of Newbottle, in the parish of Houghton-le-Spring. It was supposedly named after the American city during the War of Independence between 1776 and 1783, and it is presumed to declare a sympathy with colonial independence, though there is no firm evidence for this. If true, it would invert the more usual eighteenth-century practice of naming ships, collieries and mining settlements after naval victories.[10] The name may indicate a Quaker connection, though while there were plentiful links between Durham and Pennsylvania in the eighteenth century, there is again no actual evidence. The earliest reference I have been able to locate dates from 1785, when Thomas Cummin of Philadelphia, yeoman, entered into a mortgage agreement with Ralph Meggeson of Houghton-le-Spring, butcher.[11] Philadelphia may have originated as a farm; its location away from the main settlement of Newbottle suggests that it was established after the enclosure of the town fields

---

8   S. Doughty-Fries, *The Urban Idea in Colonial America* (Philadelphia, 1977), pp.79–107.

9   See S. Collier with S. Pearson, *Whitehaven 1660–1800* (London, 1991).

10   V. Watts, *A Dictionary of County Durham Place-Names* (Nottingham, 2002), p.xix; E.F.M. Prince, 'Coal-mining Names in the North-East of England', *Nomina*, 7 (1983), pp.97–101.

11   Durham County Record Office (hereafter DCRO), D/El 15/32. Mortgage for a cottage and orchard in Great Chilton; deeds to the same property (DCRO D/El 15/30 & 31) show the Cummin family were resident at Great Chilton in 1729 and 1759.

in 1691.[12] The name itself may thus derive from a field called Philadelphia, 'a common type of name for a field distant from the farm-house'.[13] As mining expanded in the eighteenth century, Philadelphia formed the nucleus for a settlement of labourers' cottages. Colliers were certainly needed to work the new pits known to have been started in 1719, when 'the costs of "working", that is, of getting a new pit at Newbottle were put at 3s 6d a score', and in 1774, when on 10 August there 'commenced to sink a pit at Newbottle from the surface to the Main Coal Seam'.[14] By 1796, a 'Thomas Cumins' was described as 'of Newbottle', which suggests that the Cummins had moved uphill to the middling village of Newbottle, away from the labourers' settlement.[15]

The township of Newbottle experienced a considerable increase in population between the seventeenth and nineteenth centuries. In the 1666 Hearth Tax, Newbottle contained sixty-eight households representing a total population of around 300.[16] Thirty-one households paid the tax, with thirty-seven exempt. Of the chargeable households, the two largest had four and three hearths (indicating middling status houses, with heated parlour or bedchamber in addition to fires in the kitchen and main living room of the hall) and a further seven had two hearths (probably heating a second ground-floor room in addition to the hall, where the cooking still took place), while the remaining twenty-two had only one fireplace (with presumably one or two other unheated rooms). The smallest of these tax-paying households would not have been much more elaborately housed than the thirty-seven single-hearth households exempted from the tax.[17] The Hearth Tax relates to the township of Newbottle (some 1,454 acres), and may include dispersed settlement in addition to the village itself. Some of the inhabitants would have been employed in mining, but the most transitory of these are unlikely to have entered the administrative record.[18] By 1801 the recorded population of the township had risen to 970, with 1,224 in 1811. The trebling of the population since 1691 relates to mining employment, and only a part of the expanded population was accommodated in the original village of Newbottle.

Robert Surtees described the township in his *History of Durham* (1816):

---

[12] E. Mackenzie and M. Ross, *An Historical, Topographical and Descriptive View of the County Palatine of Durham*, 2 vols (Newcastle upon Tyne, 1834), i, p.356. There was a farm in the centre of Philadelphia until the twentieth century. The principal names in the enclosure agreement of 1691 were Wilson, Watson, Chilton and Byers, all of whom appear among the larger householders in the 1666 Hearth Tax.

[13] Watts, *Durham Place-Names*, p.94.

[14] E. Hughes, *North Country Life in the Eighteenth Century: The North-East 1700–1750* (Oxford, 1952), pp.250–51; Durham Mining Museum website, http://www.dmm.org.uk/colliery/n025.htm, accessed viewed 22 October 2009.

[15] DCRO D/El 15/33.

[16] A multiplier of 4.3 persons per household gives a population total of 292 (T. Arkell, 'Multiplying Factors for Estimating Population Totals from the Hearth Tax', *Local Population Studies*, 28 (1982)); A. Green, Elizabeth Parkinson and Margaret Spufford, *Durham Hearth Tax Assessment Lady Day 1666* (British Record Society, Index Library 119, Hearth Tax Series Vol. IV, 2006), pp.57–8 and 147.

[17] A quarter of heads of household were widows (seven charged and ten exempt), all of whom had only one hearth.

[18] A. Green, 'The Durham Hearth Tax: Community Politics and Social Relations', in P.S. Barnwell and M. Airs (eds), *Houses and the Hearth Tax: the later Stuart House and Society* (Council for British Archaeology Research Report 150, 2006), pp.144–54.

A little to the north of Newbottle, below the brow of the hill, lies Philadelphia-Row, one of those settlements provided by the coal-owners for their workmen, who live here as a distinct class in society, almost entirely separated from the agricultural part of the community. These colonies form at every point the strongest contrast to the varied and picturesque appearance of the genuine village – consisting, in general, of long uniform lines of low brick buildings, running along each side of a public road, black with coal dust.[19]

The pastoral ideal of virtue residing in the agricultural countryside that underpinned Penn's plans for Philadelphia, Pennsylvania, was lacking in Philadelphia, County Durham. Yet Surtees suggests that morality was not absent, for

> Even here Flora asserts her rights; the kailgarth [a boarded pig-sty] is frequently set with a profusion of Spring-flowers; and from May to December a Pitman seldom appears at Church without a possy of pinks and gillyflowers, or a sprig of mint or Southern-wood in his breast. The single pink has acquired the name of the pitman's pink.[20]

Surtees may idealise the 'genuine village', but his representation of the landscape marks a new interest in the living conditions of the working population which contrasts with earlier commentators' emphasis on the infrastructure of the coal trade. This was part of a wider concern over housing conditions, and their moral effects, in the early nineteenth century.[21] Surtees makes the connection between the mining settlements and the neglect of housing in the manufacturing towns: 'Though strictly *sui generis*, they bear some resemblances to the last outlets of a large Manufacturing Town – "Here our Reformers come not; none object/To paths polluted, or upbraid neglect;/None care that ashy heaps at doors are cast,/That coal-dust flies along the blinding blast"'.[22]

Philadelphia's pitmen were employed in the 'Peggy' or 'Dolly' pits, named as the Margaret, established in the eighteenth century, and the Dorothea, sunk between 1811 and 1816. With this new pit the census population peaked at 2,306 in 1821, a level not reached again before 1861.[23] A street scene in Philadelphia is depicted in a painting by Robert Young (Fig. 8.1).[24] This shows a view of workers' housing in 1899, by which date some of the 'long, uniform lines of low buildings'[25] present in the early nineteenth century had been rebuilt into two-

---

[19]   R. Surtees, *The History and Antiquities of the County Palatine of Durham*, 4 vols (London, 1816–40), i, p.180.

[20]   Ibid.

[21]   For example, J. Walsham, *Three Reports on the State of the Dwellings of the Labouring Classes in Cumberland, Durham and Westmoreland* (London, 1840). See also A. Green, 'Heartless and Unhomely? Dwellings of the Poor in East Anglia and North-East England', in J. McEwan and P. Sharpe (eds), *Accommodating Poverty: The Households of the Poor in England, c.1650–1850* (Basingstoke, forthcoming).

[22]   Surtees, *History*, i, p.180.

[23]   N. Emery, *Banners of the Durham Coalfield* (Stroud, 1998), p.202; the Newbottle township collieries were owned by the Nesham family until sold to the Earl of Durham in 1819. W. Page (ed.), *The Victoria History of the County of Durham*, 3 vols (London, 1905–28), ii, p.270: census records 2,674 in 1861, climbing to 5,742 in 1901.

[24]   Also illustrated in J. Ayres, *Two Hundred Years of English Naïve Art 1700–1900* (Alexandria, Virginia, 1996), pp.138–9.

[25]   Surtees's 1816 description is followed (or plagiarised) by Mackenzie and Ross, *Historical, Topographical and Descriptive View*, i, p.357.

Figure 8.1. R. Young, *Street Scene, Philadelphia, County Durham*, 1899, oil on canvas, 47.5 × 77.5 cm (Beamish: The North of England Open Air Museum).

or one-and-a-half storey houses. There is a late-nineteenth-century brick-built end terrace on the far left, presumably occupied by a higher income family, its status marked out by the embellishment of the doorcase. Its pediment is wittily 'broken' in the painting, signifying the fragility of the household's economy and the community's social order. The older stone cottages behind indicate the survival of earlier workers' housing. Such terraced cottages were known as 'rows'[26] from the late seventeenth century, and were themselves occupied by the more securely paid members of the workforce. These Philadelphia rows may date from the eighteenth century. The cottages on the right have one and a half storeys in stone, with the orange pantile roofs typical of County Durham's east coast. The bricked-up cart entrance to the left of this row implies a rebuilding of non-domestic buildings, possibly in agricultural use originally. Ironically, the fate of many such cottages in the twentieth century was their conversion into outbuildings. The modernisation of these stone cottages is represented by the addition of brick 'netties' (lavatories) projecting into the street as the pigsty or bakehouse oven did hitherto ('Add to each mansion a kailgarth, a boarded pig-sty, which frequently obstructs the entrance, and a bakehouse or oven across the public pathway – "Where here and there convenient bricks are laid,/ And door-side heaps afford their dubious aid" – and the domestic economy of the Pitman's dwelling is complete'[27]). The row of cottages leading away to the colliery at the centre of the painting was clearly of one storey originally, with a second storey added in a different stone. A similar row of houses survives at Philadelphia (Fig. 8.2). The stonework of these house-fronts indicates a row of one-storey cottages no more than one room wide and one and a half rooms deep, later raised to two storeys and much rebuilt in brick to the rear. Young's painting documents the addition of brick chimneys; the six flues would equate to three

---

26 For more on this see Chapter 9 (eds).
27 Surtees, *History*, i, p.180.

Figure 8.2. Colliery workers' cottages at Philadelphia Row, Co. Durham (author's photograph).

hearths per household in 1899, but when the cottages were originally built they would have had only one heated room.

In contrast to the modest cottages at Philadelphia Row, several substantial eighteenth-century houses still stand in the 'genuine village' of Newbottle. The village probably took form in the twelfth century, when Church landlords established nucleated settlements, invariably arranged around open greens and surrounded by strip-farmed open fields, across lowland County Durham.[28] Dispersed settlement outside the nucleated villages was relatively rare between the twelfth and seventeenth centuries, after which time enclosure encouraged the foundation of new farms amid their own hedged fields and the influx of mining workers necessitated an expansion in housing. It seems that established residents of middling status were reluctant to tolerate these mobile, and often transitory, incomers in their own immediate neighbourhoods. In Newbottle township geology helped to keep the colliery population apart from the agricultural part of the community, for whereas Philadelphia is low-lying, Newbottle village stands on a ridge of high ground, an area of magnesian limestone not mined for coal till the mid nineteenth century. The village was thus located above and beyond the area exploited for coal, and is unlikely to have been inhabited by mining families. In common with many of the older village settlements in this part of the county, it was at least partly reserved for middling households – Levine and Wrightson noted their residence in Whickham town.[29] These sorts of houses are described in newspaper advertisements, and it is notable that middling residents

[28]   See B.K. Roberts, *The Green Villages of County Durham: A study in Historical Geography* (Durham Local History Publication No. 12, 1977).
[29]   D. Levine and K. Wrightson, *The Making of an Industrial Society: Whickham 1560–1765* (Oxford, 1991), p.165.

Figure 8.3. An eighteenth-century house in Newbottle village, Co.
Durham: Newbottle House, c.1720, now the Working Men's Club
(author's photograph).

frequently supplemented their income with tenant houses such as 'a very good
Dwelling House, containing eight Fire Rooms, four Garrets, with a Garden,
Stable, Brew-House, Cellar, Stack-yard, Barn and Backside, with three other
Tenant Houses, all freehold' in Whickham.[30]

   The eighteenth-century houses remaining on Newbottle's village green testify
to the prosperity and genteel status of households in the village. Newbottle House
(Fig. 8.3), built in c.1720, was of three storeys in stone, with the hallmarks of
eighteenth-century polite architecture – a symmetrical facade of five bays, stone

---

[30] *Newcastle Courant*, 7 February 1730.

dressings and a parapet to disguise the roof. Its later use as the Working Men's Club reflects the relatively late working-class character of Newbottle village. Along the green, and built in brick at around the same date as Newbottle House, is Storey House, a dwelling of two storeys with panelled rooms inside. Dial House, c.1730, is built from the local limestone, with a pantile roof, and has a fine staircase inside – another marker of status for those who passed over the threshold.[31] The nomenclature 'House' is significant here, differentiating these houses from their cottage neighbours. Several of these houses stood on the northern side of the green, overlooking the mines and miners' housing in the area of Philadelphia, towards New Herrington. This would have been a dramatic prospect: 'The view, at night, from the west part of the village is peculiarly grand and striking, as the whole surrounding country seems in a blaze from the immense fires burning at the mouths of the numerous pits.'[32]

Workers' housing

The stone cottages at Philadelphia are an unusual survival: most such pre-1800 buildings have been replaced or incorporated into later buildings. The survival rate of pre-1700 buildings in northern County Durham is about 1 per cent, and this mostly relates to the very largest houses.[33] Surviving buildings elsewhere indicate that the late seventeenth century witnessed significant rebuilding of cottages as the value of wages rose.[34] In County Durham, it was the better-paid skilled workers in secure industrial employment who were most likely to have occupied rebuilt cottages. At Shotley Bridge, 'in close proximity to where the first sword factory stood', a terrace of two-storey cottages on Wood Street (now demolished) was built for the sword cutlers from Solingen in Germany. Two houses had stone door lintels inscribed in German, expressing a commitment to meticulous care in work and referring to Deutschland and Vaterland, with one dated 1691.[35] Two storeys marked out the household's economic status, while the inscriptions bore witness to their identity. The symbolism of houses in the landscape meant that residential segregation by social group extended to the stratified workforce of the collieries. Those in managerial occupations, significant in the operation of the coal trade from the seventeenth century, and

---

31 N. Pevsner and E. Williamson, *The Buildings of England: County Durham* (Harmondsworth, 1983), pp.332–3; also noted are Cellar Hill House, Houghton Road, c.1700, altered 1770, and eighteenth-century stone and brick farm buildings at East Farm.

32 Mackenzie and Ross, *Historical, Topographical and Descriptive View*, i, p.357.

33 A. Green, 'Houses and Households in County Durham and Newcastle upon Tyne, c.1570–1730' (unpublished PhD thesis, University of Durham, 2000), pp.98–113.

34 A point first made by M. Spufford, *The Great Reclothing of Rural England: Petty Chapmen and their Wares in the Seventeenth Century* (Cambridge, 1984) pp.1–3, citing R. Leech, *Early Industrial Housing: The Trinity area of Frome* (London, 1981).

35 Pevsner and Williamson, *County Durham*, p.409; Page, *Victoria History of Durham*, ii, p.37, 'Des Herren segen machet Reich ohn alle Sorg wan du zughleich in deinem stand Treuw und Flesig Bist und duest was Du Befohlen ist' 1691; another may have read 'Deutschland ist unsuer Vatterland Soligen ist die Stadt Gehasset Der Herr behüte deinen Ausgang und Eingang'. See also D. Richardson, *The Swordmakers of Shotley Bridge* (Northern History booklets 37, Newcastle upon Tyne, 1973), pp.24–5, 36–7 and passim; D. Vernon, *Thread of Iron: A Definitive History of Shotley Bridge and Consett* (Knebworth, 2003), p.102.

the higher-paid operatives, often dwelt in a particular location. Such residential segregation is familiar for the nineteenth century. In Newbottle township the hamlet of Bunker Hill was described in the 1830s as containing 'some good houses, inhabited by different directors and superintendents of the adjoining coal-works'.[36] It is seldom recognised that such social segregation has its origins in the later seventeenth century; Robert Lee has demonstrated that the pattern of social distancing in the landscape between middle-class and collier communities was repeated in the nineteenth century, and shows that even then there was limited awareness of the seventeenth- and eighteenth-century antecedents.[37]

Skilled workers were certainly better accommodated than the majority of the workforce, the most poorly paid and irregularly employed of whom occupied lodgings in other households or 'hovels' erected near the collieries. Leases record the obligation of the coal-owner to provide tied housing for the pitmen and a special coal allowance for domestic use. According to Hughes, the 'obligation of providing "hovels" or dwelling-houses for the pitmen as new pits were opened up rested from the first with the coal owner. Indeed, in new areas, it was customary for the owner or lessee to give an allowance "for the pitmen's lodging till houses can be built for them".'[38]

Sir Henry Liddell's lease of Urpeth colliery in 1712 was to include '40s. damage for heap room yearly, and to make ample satisfaction for wayleaves and all spoil ground for building hovels, stables and cottages and all other necessarys for ye Colliery'.[39] This implies that the workers were housed around the spoil heaps, which took priority in the efficient movement of coal and its waste. The lease also distinguishes between 'hovels' and 'cottages'. Whereas 'hovel' was a seventeenth-century term for a poorly constructed habitation, cottages implied a somewhat more stable level of income and social standing, although both were occupied by households with only a single hearth. The 'hovels' of the coalfield were probably temporary structures, given that individual coal workings were usually open for a limited period; the poorest-paid members of the colliery workforce were subject to transitory employment and might migrate across the whole of the coalfield in the course of their working lives.[40] Short-lived colliery cottages may have been constructed using similar techniques to those known from excavation for seventeenth-century America, where posts rammed into the earth obviated the need for foundations.[41]

Accommodation was also provided for agricultural workers. Younger farm servants usually 'lived in', often enjoying more secure food and shelter in the house of their employer than they were able to attain in lodgings, or

[36] Mackenzie and Ross, *Historical, Topographical and Descriptive View*, i, p.357.
[37] R. Lee, 'A Shock for Bishop Pudsey: Social Change and Regional Identity in the Diocese of Durham, 1820–1920', in A. Green and A.J. Pollard (eds), *Regional Identities in North-East England, 1300–2000* (Woodbridge, 2007), pp.93–110.
[38] Hughes, *North Country Life*, p.257.
[39] Ibid.; see also, Levine and Wrightson, *Whickham*, pp.189–92 and 209.
[40] Levine and Wrightson, *Whickham*, pp.191–2. See also Green, 'Heartless and Unhomely?'.
[41] C. Carson, N.F. Barka, W.M. Kelso, G.W. Stone and D. Upton, 'Impermanent Architecture in the Southern American Colonies', *Winterthur Portfolio*, 16 (1982), pp.135–92.

even perhaps for their own household after marriage.[42] Tied housing for adult workers with families was therefore an attractive benefit of employment. In 1725 the *Newcastle Courant* carried a notice for the lease of 'Cross-Fines, nigh Houghton-le-Spring', 'well hedg'd, with a dwelling-house thereon, and all Out houses convenient'; the workers lived in 'six Cottage Houses in good Repair in Houghton aforesaid'.[43] Significantly, the agricultural labourers were provided with cottage houses in the medieval village of Houghton-le-Spring, a parish centre dominated by its church and rectory. Houghton's associations to the Church were further enhanced by the occupation of Houghton Hall by a clerical-gentry family, the Huttons, and the lordship of the manor being held by the bishop.[44] The agricultural part of the community was preserved in the centre of the parish, contrasting with the pitmen on its fringes in Newbottle township. Yet their social and economic lives were not so far apart, and the provision of tied housing for farm workers may have been a product of competition for labour: agricultural wages were usually lower than those available in industrial employment, and competition for reliable labour encouraged the provision of such benefits for farm workers, with farmers bearing the cost of maintaining cottages. Housing 'in good repair' enabled farmers to attract better-quality workers, for well-constructed houses were not only a perquisite but also a prerequisite of respectability in the community. Farm houses themselves were routinely advertised in the newspapers as 'in Tenantable Repair'.

Newspaper advertisements also record that tied housing was provided for salt-pan workers in the form of terraced houses, such as 'A Row or Onset of Houses, at the East End of South Shields'.[45] Descriptions of houses advertised with the salt pans show that owners dwelt in a 'mansion house' or 'seat house' distinct from the steward's house and salters' housing. Many of the salt pans were advertised for sale by women; this was partly a case of widows selling up, but also demonstrating the engagement of genteel women in the industrial economy. Mrs Jane Shipperdson of South Shields had 'Six Salt-Pans, with several Tenants-Houses and Seat-house';[46] Mrs Margaret Moore sold 'THE Seat-House of two salt-Pans at the upper End of South Shields'.[47] Some owners were resident at Shields, but others lived in (or moved to) the genteel parts of Durham or Newcastle: Mrs Johnson of Durham advertised 'Six Salt-Pans at South Shields, with a Mansion-House, and other Houses'.[48] Mrs Elizabeth Emmerson, living at her house in Pilgrim Street in Newcastle, had in North Shields 'To be SOLD, between this and Christmas next, A Good House, with

[42] A. Kussmaul, *Servants in Husbandry in Early Modern England* (Cambridge, 1981), pp.41–2, 117 and 124; see also K.D.M. Snell, *Annals of the Labouring Poor: Social Change and Agrarian England, 1660–1900* (Cambridge, 1985), and on labourers' 'dependency' more generally, K. Wrightson, *Earthly Necessities: Economic Lives in Early Modern Britain, 1470–1750* (London, 2000), pp.307–30.

[43] *Newcastle Courant*, 30 January 1725.

[44] W. Hutchinson, *The History and Antiquities of the County Palatine of Durham*, 3 vols (Newcastle upon Tyne and London, 1785–94), ii, pp.539–40; Surtees, *History*, i, pp.147–8.

[45] *Newcastle Courant*, 24 May 1729.

[46] *Newcastle Courant*, 20 February 1725.

[47] *Newcastle Courant*, 3 February 1728.

[48] *Newcastle Courant*, 6 July 1723.

two Salt Pans, Graineries and Salters Houses'.[49] The women cited here enjoyed a rentier income and engaged in leisure activities, with gardens and bowling greens, as at the lower end of South Shields: 'A Great many Tenements, with Coble-landings convenient for the Fishery, a Muck-Key, two gardens [and] a Bowling-Green'.[50] Although the location and appearance of housing in South Shields doubtless reflected the status of its occupants – not least through the new urban-industrial landscape of terraced housing – the juxtaposition of bowling green and muck-key cautions against over-simplifying the leisured as separate from the working landscape.

Gibside revisited

Gibside, in Whickham parish, is justly celebrated as an elaborate eighteenth-century landscape park (see Fig. 0.6, p.14, and Chapters 5 and 7). It was created by George Bowes, who inherited the estate in 1722, and, from 1743, with his second wife Mary Gilbert.[51] The park lay at the centre of Bowes's empire and was the administrative hub of his capitalistic enterprises – farms, coal pits, paper mill and wagon-ways carrying both coal and lead were all situated immediately around and even within the park. The landscaped park was conceived as a series of walks, with structures arranged as focal points, resting places and entertainment spaces, and the whole was centred on the Grand Walk, framing views of the Palladian Chapel and Column to British Liberty at either end. The Column – erected in the 1750s, and 'a work of great magnificence ... above 140 feet high', as the coal owner Edward Montagu described it to his wife Elizabeth[52] – dominates the Derwent Valley, and is visible as far as the north bank of the Tyne. This raises the question of what meanings the monument was given by those outside the park. Even though its Whig conception of British Liberty may have been commensurate with the pitmen's capacity to moderate the conditions of their dependency – a reflection of their bargaining power as a highly skilled workforce, with the capacity to strike – it is difficult to escape the conclusion that the Column was a symbol of subordination.[53] Perhaps, however, the notion of shared British liberties was in force when – in unrecorded responses to the Column's phallic profile – humour was deployed to make the inequalities of wealth and power easier to bear. While it is inevitably easier to reconstruct the

---

[49] *Newcastle Courant*, 18 November 1727.

[50] *Newcastle Courant*, 7 November 1724.

[51] M. Wills, *Gibside and the Bowes Family* (Chichester, 1995). Bowes's wife was actively involved: in 1748 she 'Paid Mr Garret for 6 of his Plans for building Farm houses' (Wills, *Gibside*, p.42).

[52] Ibid., p.48.

[53] Levine and Wrightson, *Whickham*, pp.375–427, provides a careful analysis of the politics of the eighteenth-century coalfield; A. Wood, 'Custom, Identity and Resistance: English Free Miners and Their Law, c.1550–1800', in P. Griffiths, A. Fox and S. Hindle (eds), *The Experience of Authority in Early Modern England* (Basingstoke, 1996), pp.249–85, examines the politics of a rather different mining community. Wood also emphasises the protective self-distancing of elite houses and parks, making the important point that 'many of the descriptions offered by gentry outsiders of mining communities reveal not only a sense of class hostility towards what they perceived to be unruly industrial workers; they are also the account of *outsiders* to those communities' (p.255).

views of the elite, this may in itself enable us to reflect more carefully upon the attitudes and experiences of those below them.

Located on the hill above Bowes's Column, the Banqueting House, built in the 1740s,[54] provides extensive views beyond Gibside Park. Views of the industrial landscape were an integral part of the experience of Gibside, and the genteel elite were fascinated by its wonders. Mrs Montagu wrote jokingly to her literary friend Elizabeth Carter of 'the delectable *agrément* of a coal mine'.[55] The Bowes family were proud of their industrial achievements: Causey Arch, constructed to carry a wagon-way from the Wortley Montagu collieries at Causey and Tanfield to staithes on the Tyne, was George Bowes's first major architectural commission, and evoked comparisons with the achievements of ancient Rome. On the opening of The Great Western Way in 1721, Bowes wrote: 'Last Munday we begun to lead down ye new Waggon-way, which is ye beginning of my profitt: it is a work of such great importance and crosses so many Mountains and Vales, which are all levelled that I can compare it to nothing more properly than to ye Via Appia'.[56] The drive into Gibside ran close to the Western Way. The proximity of genteel passengers to this wagon-way is usually regarded by historians as an unfortunate intrusion on Gibside's polite space, but it is more convincing to suggest that Bowes was pleased to show off its engineering and cargo. Shortly after the completion of the Great Western Way, Gibside village was removed to make way for the landscaping of the park, indicating a desire for distance from the workers themselves. In 1739 the Western Way was replaced by the New Western Way, which took a route away from the estate on the western side of the river Derwent. But within the Gibside grounds in the eighteenth century there were still a paper mill, forge and coal pits.[57] Views outwards from the park, framed by tree-planting, were seemingly designed to take in the industrial landscape, most of which was owned by the Bowes family and their business partners. The colliery settlements and tenant farms were inter-visible with the wooded park and its structures, particularly The Column to Liberty and the Banqueting House. This was the landscape of social relations aptly caught in Levine and Wrightson's epigram, 'Sooty Faces and Elysian Shades'.[58]

Gibside was not unique in interweaving the industrial and the genteel in the landscape. The medieval castle of Lumley, remodelled by the architect Sir John Vanbrugh in the 1720s, faces the coal town of Chester-le-Street across the valley. Defoe described Lumley Castle as 'pleasantly seated in a fine park',

---

54 Daniel Garrett designed both the Banqueting House (which is 'Gothick') and the Column to British Liberty, the latter structure being completed after Garrett's death by James Paine (eds).

55 *Letters from Mrs Elizabeth Carter, to Mrs Montagu, between the Years 1755 and 1800*, 3 vols (London, 1817), i, p.346, cited in P. Langford, *Public Life and the Propertied Englishman, 1689–1798* (Oxford, 1991), p.62. For the relationship of these women to the Bowes family, see A. Green, '"A Clumsey Countrey Girl": The Material and Print Culture of Betty Bowes', in H. Berry and J. Gregory (eds), *Creating and Consuming Culture in North-East England, 1660–1830* (Aldershot, 2004), pp.72–97.

56 Hughes, *North Country Life*, pp.153–4.

57 Wills, *Gibside*, p.1; DCRO D/St/P6 1/2, 3 & 5; Tyne & Wear Archives 3415/CK5/183; J. Gibson, 'Plan of the collieries on the rivers Tyne and Wear' (1788) shows the routes of wagon-ways around the gentry parks, reprinted in Levine and Wrightson, *Whickham*, p.64.

58 Levine and Wrightson, *Whickham*, pp.274–5, the phrases are drawn from Hutchinson's *History and Antiquities*, ii, pp.447–51.

which, 'besides the pleasantness of it, has [a] much better thing to recommend it, namely that it is full of excellent veins of the best coal in the country'.[59] Landscape parks were a deliberate statement of conspicuous consumption, the wealth of their owners being displayed in their ability to remove land from cultivation,[60] the former strip farming symbolised by the retention of ridge and furrow under grass – a feature of Lumley's park. Yet the presence of mine workings in Lumley Park, as at Gibside, was an equally emphatic statement of wealth. North of the Tyne, Seaton Delaval, the mansion built by Vanbrugh in 1719–26, stood a short ride from Seaton Sluice, a haven audaciously re-engineered in 1761–4 to create a much-admired harbour for the Delavals' coal, salt and glass enterprises.[61] The Delavals were as proud of this engineering feat as the Bowes' were of their wagon-ways; yet both families seem to have been aware of the ultimate vulnerability of their position in a newly industrial society. Seaton Delaval Hall stands on a fortified platform with ditches and bastions. In 1727, William Etty, clerk of works to Vanbrugh at Seaton Delaval, sent designs for 'bastions' to George Bowes. As Robert Williams asks: 'Did Etty think Bowes was the kind of magnate who might one day find himself in serious need of a fortified home?'[62] Etty's plans for Gibside were not implemented, and the Bowes family made considerable efforts to placate the poor through charity.[63] We simply do not know for certain whether insurrection was ever on the industrial population's minds, and while their theoretical capacity to rebel often haunted the elites it is unrealistic to think that working families would jeopardise having a roof over their heads.[64]

The landscape park has been regarded as the epitome of gentility and Englishness. But we should not allow this enduring set of meanings to suppress the significance of the industrial in 'genteel' northern landscapes. Proposals to carry out open-cast mining in the Derwent valley were objected to in parliament in July 2005 by the Labour MP David Anderson, who highlighted 'visual pollution' and the impact on Gibside – 'an absolute gem of a place ... in the shadow of the proposed site'. Despite referring to his father's generation of miners in the 1930s as having been 'treated like slaves', Anderson did not mention that Gibside (now a National Trust property) was created two centuries earlier from the profits of mining. Anderson made a cogent case for both the North East

[59] Defoe, *Tour*, ii, p.249; on Chester-le-Street's socio-economic composition, see C. Issa, 'Obligation and Choice: Aspects of Family and Kinship in Seventeenth-Century County Durham' (unpublished PhD, University of St Andrews, 1986).

[60] R. Williams, *The Country and the City* (London, 1973), pp.120–26; T. Williamson and L. Bellamy, *Property and Landscape: A Social History of Land Ownership in the English Countryside* (London, 1987), pp.130–56.

[61] Northumberland County Record Office 650/E/1 and 650/F1 & 2; N. Pevsner et al., *The Buildings of England: Northumberland* (London, 1992), pp.560–65.

[62] R. Williams, 'Fortified Gardens', in C. Ridgway and R. Williams (eds), *Sir John Vanburgh and Landscape Architecture in Baroque England* (Stroud, 2000), p.69.

[63] Wills, *Gibside*, p.14; e.g. DCRO D/St/E5/7/63, which details annual distributions to the poor, 1747–71, by Mrs Mary Bowes.

[64] See J.M. Ellis, 'Urban Conflict and Popular Violence: the Guildhall riots of 1740 in Newcastle-upon-Tyne', *International Review of Social History*, 25 (1980), pp.332–49 and idem, 'A Dynamic Society: Social Relations in Newcastle-upon-Tyne, 1660–1760', in P. Clark (ed.), *The Transformation of English Towns, 1600–1800* (1984), pp.190–227.

and the Derwent valley to 'move on': 'We have turned a corner in the north-east of England, we look to new opportunities and developments to embrace a new millennium, and we have more respect for our environment than we were ever allowed in the past.'[65] And yet one could equally argue that the resumption of mining in view of Gibside would make for a landscape entirely in keeping with the area's heritage, which might even be turned to advantage in promoting public understanding of the historical depth and complexity of social relations in northern industrial landscapes.

Conclusion

Levine and Wrightson have criticised historians for perpetuating the nineteenth-century view that the pitmen were a 'race apart', too distant from the civilising influences of their social superiors to live in more than brute ignorance before the arrival of religious and political reformers.[66] Attention to the landscape context of social relations reveals that while social stratification had a strong spatial aspect in early industrial County Durham, its landscape and society were characterised by visible inter-relationships rather than blind polarities. And yet the residential patterning of this landscape undermined the contemporary ideal of neighbourliness binding communities together. As Keith Wrightson has written, '"Neighbourliness" was one of the key words of early modern social relations – a critically important social ideal', including vertical social ties linking the separate social groups of areas of residential propinquity.[67] That was the norm. But in the industrialising society of northern County Durham, 'it might well be argued that long before 1750 Whickham was not one community but several overlapping communities, and that relations between its inhabitants were conducted not within "*the* neighbourhood" but within several neighbourhoods.'[68] Philadelphia means brotherly love, but the place name represented more of a promised land than a reality of mutual aid among neighbours.[69]

In early industrial County Durham, the location of houses demonstrates considerable social distancing in the seventeenth and eighteenth centuries. This was at its most dramatic where the houses and parks of the grand stood in guarded proximity to the settlements of industrial workers. While the industrial infrastructure was celebrated throughout the eighteenth century, the workers themselves seem to have been literally overlooked. Elizabeth Montagu in 1758 described the mining communities on Tyneside as 'an anthill swarming with black creatures no better than savages'.[70] Being overlooked in both senses might be compatible with interpretations which presuppose the power of the gaze and

---

65 House of Commons Hansard Debates, 21 July 2005, http://www.publications.parliament.uk/pa/cm200506/cmhansrd/vo050721/debtext/50721–35.htm, accessed 22 October 2009.

66 Levine and Wrightson, *Whickham*, pp.274–8.

67 K. Wrightson, 'The Politics of the Parish in Early Modern England', in Griffiths, Fox and Hindle (eds), *Experience of Authority*, pp.10–46, quoting p.18.

68 Levine and Wrightson, *Whickham*, pp.279–95 and 340–45, quoting pp.340–41.

69 Mobility and poverty at Philadelphia are highlighted by the presence of paupers from other parishes: e.g. DCRO EP/Lam 7/27a, Peter Nicholson received 2s in 1822 and 1823 from Lamesley Chapelry Overseers of the Poor.

70 P.M. Horsley, *Eighteenth-Century Newcastle* (Newcastle upon Tyne, 1971), p.238.

a panoptic role for elite structures in view of dependent populations; indeed, this would explain why the coal owners chose to reside within sight of their industry.[71] Equally significant for the tensions that ultimately held this society together was the pattern of separation between middling and working populations. The Hearth Tax records reveal that certain communities in the later seventeenth century contained particular clusters of high-status households headed by persons privileged by the designation Mr or Mrs. Most other communities were characterised by smaller houses and poorer households.[72] Even within the same village, middling houses stood apart. This pattern remained basically unaltered through to the nineteenth century. Geographical distance was circumscribed, however, by the over-riding imperative to accommodate labour. The fact that many village greens in County Durham were infilled by workers' housing, progressively rebuilt into substantial cottages, suggests that the middling members of these communities acquiesced to the housing of those who worked the land, fetched fish from the sea, evaporated salt from sea water and mined or moved coal and lead. This does not mean that communities were cohesive. A house implied a household in seventeenth- and eighteenth-century England, and the term 'household' defined the basic social unit, as householder and housewife denoted adult status in the community. Those who did not occupy a house, but dwelt in rows of cottages, were logically excluded from the established social order, though they formed communities and a culture of their own.

Acknowledgement

I would like to thank Keith Wrightson for his encouragement and support; my debt to his work will be obvious.

---

[71] See, for example, M.P. Leone, 'A Historical Archaeology of Capitalism', *American Anthropologist*, 97:2 (1995), pp.251–68; M.P. Leone and S. Hurry, 'Seeing: The Power of Town Planning in the Chesapeake', *Historical Archaeology*, 32:4 (1998), pp.34–62.

[72] Green et al., *Durham Hearth Tax*, pp.lxix–lxxii.

9

'The Raws':
Housing the Durham Pitman in the Nineteenth Century

WINIFRED STOKES

The 1953 volume on *The Buildings of England: County Durham*, by Nikolaus Pevsner, draws attention to the ubiquity of colliery workings in the view from Penshaw Hill, near Gateshead, but ignores the rows of colliery houses along-side them. Indeed, the only implied reference to these rows is in the Introduc-tion, where the author notes the survival of woods and fields near 'the tips, the furnaces and the mean housing';[1] condescension perhaps permissible in an indi-vidual seeking buildings of architectural interest. Yet this housing was as much a part of the North-Eastern landscape as the collieries themselves and in many places has survived them, although the rows that remain tend to be mainly, if not exclusively, those built near to the end of the nineteenth century and in the period up to the First World War. These were rows built with some attention to public health regulations and structurally capable of modification to meet the requirements of the later twentieth and early twenty-first centuries.

An eighteenth-century source refers to North-Eastern miners' dwellings as 'hovels', which seems to imply wooden, impermanent structures.[2] What is clear, however, is that although it may have been of doubtful quality, by the time of the 1831–2 strikes in the Tyneside and Wearside coalfields much colliery housing was under the direct control of the colliery owners and its supply had become part of the miners' contract of employment, the annual 'bond'.[3] By the middle of the nineteenth century it has been estimated that a large proportion, even the majority, of miners in the North East were living, usually rent-free, in dwellings owned and often built by the various colliery companies, a situation not repli-cated to the same extent in other coalfields. During the succeeding decades, in an increasingly competitive labour market, housing provision and the quality of

---

[1] N. Pevsner, *The Buildings of England: County Durham* (Harmondsworth, 1953), p.11.

[2] E. Hughes, *North Country Life in the Eighteenth Century: The North-East 1700–1750* (Oxford, 1952), p.257, quoting Sir Henry Liddell on housing provision at Urpeth colliery in 1712. In the early nineteenth century the word 'hovel' was defined as 'a mean low habitation, a shed' (J. Barclay, *Dictionary of the English Language* (Bungay, 1812)).

[3] For coverage of the issues surrounding the miners' 'bond' see R. Colls, *The Pitmen of the Northern Coalfield* (Manchester, 1987), pp.74–100.

that housing became important elements in managerial strategies for recruiting, retaining and disciplining the workforce.[4]

Housing the pitmen in compact rows close to the colliery not only enabled the 'caller' to fulfil his task efficiently, thereby assisting punctuality, but also offered some degree of supervision of the miners' social life on the part of the immediate management – the overmen and 'keekers' who were frequently housed in somewhat superior accommodation further down the same row. It also offered the sanction of eviction for dissidence. As the situation described above indicates, mining had a hierarchical structure. Those subject to the bond regulation and its concomitant housing provision were the 'hewers' and 'putters', the men who 'got' the coal and those who brought it to the surface, men whose wage contracts were based on productivity. Ancillary workers lived where they could and, even if in colliery housing, usually paid rent.

Since contemporary observers were as uninterested as Pevsner in the external appearance of the colliery rows it is difficult to envisage them as they appeared at the time. Descriptions are rare, pictorial representations even more so. Even the admirable T.H. Hair, while giving exact detail on pithead installations, offers only the scantiest notion of any adjacent housing.[5] Where the pitmen's dwellings are alluded to, it is as in Pevsner, as 'mean' housing – 'mean' in the sense of cheap or shabby, devoid of architectural interest, or as the 'insanitary' dwellings described in public health inspectors' reports, dwellings liable, in the twentieth century, to be demolished under the terms of slum clearance acts.[6] More recently, as the realities of coal extraction in the Durham coalfield are fading from living memory, the rows have become objects of nostalgia, as fondly remembered centres of communitarian values, part of a way of life that has slipped into history or been recreated by the 'heritage industry'.

There is probably some validity in all these perceptions. In general, mid-nineteenth-century colliery owners were not willing to consider architectural niceties to put a roof over the heads of what was, given the initially annual and subsequently monthly nature of the contracts of employment, quite likely to be a transient workforce. The provision of housing involved a considerable capital outlay over and above that of sinking a new pit, but the skilled 'hewers' and 'putters' had to be housed or they would go elsewhere, and the more solidly built the rows the cheaper the upkeep. The recurrent incidence of cholera and fevers of various sorts and the provisions of successive Public Health Acts from 1848 onwards forced colliery owners dependent on the physical well-being of their workforce to pay more attention to water supply, drainage and sanitation. Although the relative isolation of the colliery rows meant that numerically the deaths from epidemic diseases were rarely such as to merit official intervention,

[4]   R. Church, *The History of the British Coal Industry*, 5 vols (Oxford, 1986), iii, pp.277–82.
[5]   T.H. Hair, *Views of the Collieries of Northumberland and Durham* (first pub. 1844, repub. Newcastle upon Tyne, 1987); here the picture of Waldridge colliery facing p.36 does show a shadowy row of cottages in the background but without any discernible detail.
[6]   J. Seeley's unpublished Durham University MA thesis 'Coal Mining Villages of Northumberland and Durham: a Study of Sanitary Conditions and Social Facilities 1870–1880' (1973), available in Newcastle upon Tyne Central Library's Local Studies section, provides valuable information on these aspects of colliery housing.

nevertheless the fact that much of the documentation available to historians has emanated from officials appointed under the terms of these Public Health Acts, or from social commentators, has perhaps made for too black an overall picture; while, similarly, the nostalgic memories of open doors and mutual support and the cosy interiors of rows such as that preserved at the Beamish Open Air Museum, a fairly late example, gloss over the undoubted hardships experienced in even the best housing provided.[7]

The evidence of how the nineteenth-century pit rows appeared to 'non-official' contemporary observers is scanty indeed. J.R. Leifchild, writing in the early 1850s when cholera was rife, gives a general description of houses built in double rows with the front doors facing each other over an unpaved space, a long ash pit and dunghill outside the back of the houses and a pigsty by each back door.[8] Unsurprisingly, he is preoccupied by the lack of sanitary provision and never describes a specific location. As the first Ordnance Survey maps[9] demonstrate, the double row in which the approaching observer would see only the backs of the houses was commonplace, but so also were other sites described by Leifchild where the rows were built in a triangle, an arrangement that in his view facilitated better sanitation.

A much more visually useful though somewhat later contemporary source is that provided by a series of articles on 'Our Colliery Villages', which appeared in the *Newcastle Weekly Chronicle* over a period of some nine months starting from the autumn of 1872. The *Chronicle*, owned by the radical Joseph Cowen and at this date edited by the equally radical W.E. Adams, had supported the miners for over a decade in their pressure for extended safety legislation and more equitable treatment in industrial disputes. In addition, it was in the early 1870s backing their claim to voting rights under the terms of the 1867 Parliamentary Reform Act, rights which risked being denied them because of their non-rate-paying status. There are several allusions to this issue in the articles, although the avowed purpose of these reports is to put before colliery owners the conditions in which many of their workers were living, to praise those owners who were providing 'respectable' housing and amenities and, by implication, to 'name and shame' those who were neglecting such provision. The articles carry no indication as to the identity of the investigative journalist, and where several villages are dealt with at the same time the extent of the coverage of particular rows can be minimal or non-existent. However, at their best the descriptions do provide the element of contemporary perception lacking in other sources. They also provide unwitting evidence of norms for working-class housing at that date. 'Model' housing offers a parlour, a kitchen and a pantry downstairs and two bedrooms up, a piped water supply with proper drainage into a local sewer, a garden and a separate yard with coal-house and earth closet. However, in the

---

7   The row now rebuilt at Beamish formed part of a 'model' estate built at Hetton-le-Hole in the 1870s following an adverse public health report on the local prevalence of 'fever' (Seeley, 'Coal Mining Villages', p.288).

8   J.R. Leifchild, *Our Coal and Our Coal Pits* (first pub.1853, repub. London, 1968), p.190.

9   The first Ordnance Survey was produced between 1856 and 1859. It should be noted that the date of the survey (in this case 1856) of any particular area was not necessarily the date of publication and that subsequent reprints did sometimes contain additions.

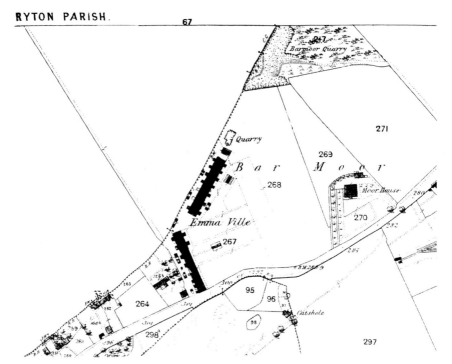

Figure 9.1. Emmaville, Co. Durham: detail of Ordnance Survey map of 'Ryton Parish', c.1856. The main road indicated is the Hexham turnpike.

early 1870s such housing was usually projected rather than actual. Rows with some sort of regular water supply, some sort of privy arrangement with regular clearing of ash pits, and with drainage gutters that at least led to sewers or into streams or open ground were clearly considered perfectly acceptable.[10] As in the case of Leifchild, the reporter pays little attention to structural details unless the dwellings are visibly collapsing or notably dilapidated.

The 1850s and 60s were decades of great expansion in the Durham coalfield, an expansion stimulated by the growth of coal- and coke-consuming industrial complexes on Tyneside, Wearside and Teesside. Housing provision had always lagged behind industrial development and most of the mining villages at this time were made up of hastily erected buildings. The *Chronicle* articles are particularly useful in noting what already existed and what was projected or in the process of being built. Used in conjunction with the first Ordnance Survey maps, they provide a means of approximately dating the construction of particular rows. A further source for dating early housing is the decennial

---

[10] *Newcastle Weekly Chronicle* (*NWC*), 5 Oct 1872. The series starts with Seghill in south Northumberland: 'All colliery villages fortunately do not rest upon the same low level of wretchedness'. At Hetton, Francis St, the row preserved at Beamish, has not yet been built but the reporter examines its prototype, Barrington St, the first of what is 'intended to be a model colliery settlement' (*NWC*, 18 Jan 1873). The articles relating to County Durham have been transcribed by A.E. Shield (typescript copy available in the Durham County Record Office).

census which, while offering no visual dimension, gives a clear indication of an influx of labour and some sort of provision in new locations during the periods 1841–51 and 1851–61. On the other hand, the survival of information about housing construction in coal company papers, particularly for the mid-century period, is largely a matter of chance (a number of companies failed or amalgamated in the financial crisis of the late 1840s). Even when specifications appear to have been laid down, there is no guarantee that they were adhered to either by the building contractors or by the coal companies themselves when finance became tighter.[11]

The two examples considered in detail in this chapter relate to different parts of the coalfield, emerge from somewhat different industrial contexts, and were chosen unashamedly on the basis of availability of information. They are the Stella Coal Company's Emmaville in the north of the county and Pease and Partners' Roddymoor and Grahamsley in the south west.

The Stella Coal Company archive in the Durham County Record Office[12] includes detailed plans and specifications for several types of housing, to be erected on an open hillside on the northern outskirts of the historic village of Ryton-on-Tyne following the Company's sinking of a new pit, the Emma, in 1845. The earliest houses for which plans are available were built between 1854 and 1856 and are clearly visible on the first Ordnance Survey map (see Fig. 9.1). In the Company's files there are the builders' accounts, which seem to indicate that the specifications were indeed followed to the letter, and lists of the earliest occupants. Some slightly later constructions built to the same plans as those in Fig. 9.3, below, can still be seen, much modified, at Townley Row, where a long terrace of the original back-to-back one-room houses has been divided into units of four to provide squat but spacious modern dwellings.

Most of the collieries in the area were long established; the Coal Company itself, with a shifting number of partners, had been running the enterprise successfully for over twenty years. These first rows for which the plans are available were clearly custom-built to attract a workforce to the most recently sunk pit. Curiously, Emmaville seems to have escaped the attention of the *Chronicle* reporter, possibly because it was on the doorstep of the newspaper's proprietor Joseph Cowen, whose fortune was derived from the local brickworks. Although the original rows were inhabited into the twentieth century, there do not seem to be any photographs of them.

There are no surviving plans for the building of the rows at Roddymoor and Grahamsley, unless some exist in private hands, but unlike Emmaville these are covered in the *Chronicle* articles. The present writer was brought up in the area and has not only edited the memoirs of a pitman who lived in one of the rows, but has also had access to diaries which describe his family's life there and to

[11] For example, the housing specifications offered by the developers of Whitworth colliery in 1840, which included an individual oven and copper for each cottage as well as a water supply from the colliery engine, were certainly not adhered to when the company ran into financial difficulties in the following year, although some basic housing was provided. See R.S. Abley, *Whitworth Park Colliery 1836–1855* (Spennymoor, 1991).

[12] Durham County Record Office NCB1/SC/1024–7 and SC/2009.

Figure 9.2. Roddymoor, Co. Durham, c.1937 (photograph: James Green).

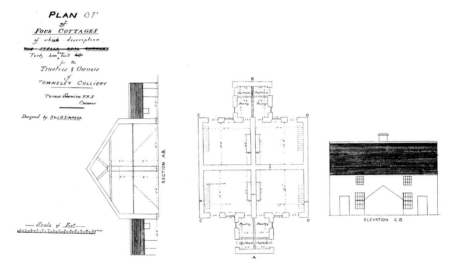

Figure 9.3. 'Plan of Four Cottages' for the Stella Coal Company at Emmaville, Co. Durham, of two-storey, back-to-back type; mid-1850s (reproduced by kind permission of Durham County Record Office, ref. no. NCB1/SC1003/7; with acknowledgement to P.R. Wiggans).

a photograph of several of the rows taken by a member of that family[13] before the slum clearances, involving partial demolition, of 1937–8 (see Fig. 9.2). High Row, the taller buildings to the left of the photograph, still survives, although the houses are much modified and extended, now being designated High Terrace.

---

[13]   See W. Stokes (ed.), Henry Green, *Memoirs of a Primitive Methodist* (Durham, 1998) and W. Stokes, 'A Durham Miner' and 'A Durham Miner's Wife', in *Bulletin of the Durham County Local History Society*, 58 (Autumn 1998) and 63 (Autumn 2001), which use material taken from the diaries of Henry Green and his son. Henry's son James was a keen amateur photographer and it is his photograph of the rows that is reproduced as Fig. 9.2.

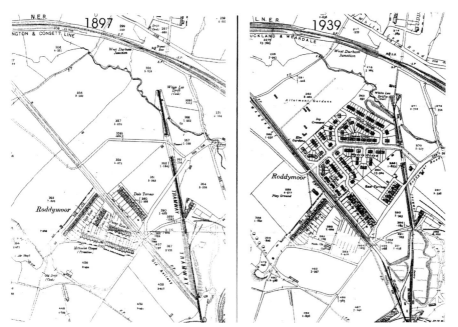

Figure 9.4. Detail of Ordnance Survey map of 1897 showing the Roddymoor Rows after the building of Dale Terrace, with ditto of 1939 showing the same area, now with only High Row, Dale Terrace remaining (with acknowledgement to P.R. Wiggans).

The four rows at Roddymoor are clearly visible on the first Ordnance Survey map but according to the 1861 census at that date contained only eighteen families. By 1871 this number had risen to seventy, even though on the evidence of the 1897 map (see Fig. 9.4) very little new building had taken place. The 1861 figure is possibly a case of census error or enumerator negligence, or it may be that two or more of the rows, at that date unnamed, had been covered by a different enumerator under a different heading.

Even without direct photographic evidence the Stella Coal Company plans and specifications and the surviving rows offer a good idea of the external appearance of the two types of solid but basic dwellings erected in the mid 1850s (see Fig. 9.3). The single room cottages were built back to back in fours, with protruding pantries and coal-houses attached to the external walls of each pair and a loft room reached by an open ladder. They were solidly built of stone, probably quarried locally at Barmoor (although this is not specified), and roofed with Welsh slate, while the woodwork was specified to be of high-quality American or Memel deal 'free from sap shakes loose knots and other defects'; sash windows with internal shutters provided lighting. There was provision for one two-seater privy per three cottages, presumably each back-to-back pair counting as one cottage, and a water conduit draining into an adjoining field – although the source of the water is not indicated. There was also provision for them all to have pigsties. There are similar specifications for the two-roomed cottages. The Ordnance Survey map of 1897 shows thirty-two of the back-to-back houses in one row with two sets of four at an angle to the first row, and extended by ten two-room non-back-to-back cottages of the second type. The front elevation suggests that the overall appearance of the rows from the fields opposite would correspond to that of many of the other rows described approvingly by the *Chronicle* reporter as 'exceedingly neat and as like to one another as a line of soldiers'.[14]

The Roddymoor and Grahamsley rows must have been built at about the same time. The Ordnance Survey map of the area shows a ring of small pits serving the rapidly developing coke works at Bankfoot. Most of these pits, and the coke works, belonged to Pease and Partners, the Darlington-based Quaker industrialists whose backing for the Stockton and Darlington railway had opened up the south Durham coalfield – although their interests in this area dated back only to the mid 1840s. The coke works supplied the Teesside iron industry which, in 1873, at the time of the *Chronicle* reporter's visit, was at the height of its productivity. By then the reporter estimated that there were in the area a dozen collieries serving over a thousand beehive-type coke ovens. With the exception of Billy Row to the north, which was an ancient township, nearly all the housing described in his three successive articles on Peases West, Grahamsley and Billy Row, Stanley and Woolley, and Sunniside and Roddymoor had been built within the past twenty-five years. The only possible exceptions are those dwellings marked on the map as Wood Cottages, which probably antedated the Company's acquisition of what was then called East Roddymoor Colliery in 1846. As the name implies, these early houses were built of wood with only the gables of brick. The reporter notes that because they had apparently been built hastily with unseasoned timber the wood was shrinking from the gables and the doors were warped. However, internally 'these unprepossessing cottages have every sign of snugness'[15] (this was in June in good weather!) with plenty of garden space and pigsties at the front.

Behind these rows was better housing including the 'pretty cottage' occupied by the Peases' temperance missionary.[16] All these settlements were built on the south side of the steep ridge that ends at Tow Law, a sheltered and sunny site. Interestingly, the reporter makes no comment on the characteristic smell of the coke works, which had been remarked upon adversely twenty years previously.[17] According to the 1871 census these houses were already known as Temperance Terrace and under that name the row still survives. The houses to the north of Temperance Terrace in New Grahamsley, described by the reporter as 'solid high spacious neat dwellings with every convenience required for comfortable domestic life',[18] disappeared in the late 1930s. As at Emmaville the houses in Temperance Terrace were stone-built with the characteristic protruding coal-

[14] *NWC*, 22 February 1873.
[15] *NWC*, 28 June 1873.
[16] Ibid. Stanley and Woolley were dealt with in the issue of 5 July and Sunniside and Roddymoor in that of 12 July.
[17] By T.W. Rammell in his *Report to the General Board of Health on a Preliminary Enquiry into the township of Crook and Billy Row* (London, 1854). His report was a response to an outbreak of cholera in the non-Pease owned older housing in the area.
[18] Note 15.

Figure 9.5. Existing view of Institute Terrace, between Grahamsley and Billy Row, Co. Durham (author's photograph).

house and pantry on the access road side. This permitted the delivery of coal and the clearance of night soil, often by the same cart, at regular intervals. Unlike either of the Emmaville rows, these houses have gables with windows overlooking their long gardens.

The reporter was informed of plans for an even better housing development between Grahamsley and Billy Row. These dwellings were to have a parlour, a kitchen with a kitchen range – earlier rows had a communal oven – an indoor tap in the pantry with water supplied at a price from the reservoir at Waskerley in Weardale by the Weardale and Shildon Water Company (a Pease subsidiary), a garden and an enclosed yard with an earth closet. This row was built between 1871 and 1881 and because of the building of a Miners' Institute at its eastern end became known as Institute Terrace (Fig. 9.5). However, even as early as 1881 most of the occupants were not 'hewers' or 'putters' and, as the reporter noted, these houses were from the outset intended for rented tenancy. The change in nomenclature from 'row' for pitmen's houses to 'terrace' for those structures not designed specifically as miners' dwellings is interesting.

Passing through the hilltop villages of Stanley, Woolley and Sunnyside, which also mainly housed workers from Pease-owned collieries, the *Chronicle* reporter notes that some of the houses are built entirely of white silica brick that glistens in the summer sunshine, while Temperance and Institute Terraces, although stone-built, incorporate silica-brick surrounds to windows and door-ways and silica-brick corner angles. The Peases had their own brick and fire-clay works beside the coke ovens at Bankfoot and, as at Emmaville, there was a local

Figure 9.6. Existing view of Dale Terrace, Roddymoor, Co. Durham (author's photograph).

quarry. The reporter approached the Roddymoor Rows from the north, walking down the open hillside along one of the mineral railways that delivered coal from the various pits to the coke ovens. His initial impression was favourable. 'The village enjoys a fine expanding triangle of playground and clothes hanging space over and above its proper proportion of garden', although, he continues, 'most of the houses are less comfortable to dwell in than pleasant to look at. The rooms are small – the two-roomed houses are cramped and coffin like.'[19] However, he was told that new rows were being planned on the same lines as those at Grahamsley. In fact only one such row, Dale Terrace (Fig. 9.6), seems to have been completed (this is the row at the back right of the photograph shown in Fig. 9.2, with gables similar to those at Temperance Terrace). Dale Terrace, like Institute Terrace (see Fig. 9.5, above), was for 'independent letting' rather than free colliery housing.

By the time that the *Chronicle* reporter visited Roddymoor the rows had been named as High Row, Chapel Row, Pump Row and Cross Row; Chapel Row, the row facing the camera on the photograph (Fig. 9.2), was so called because in the intervening years the Peases had provided a preaching room there, Pump Row because this was the source of the local water supply – probably initially from a colliery engine. The Green family, to whose papers the present writer was given access, moved into No. 36 Chapel Row in 1890. At an earlier date they had apparently lived briefly in High Row and it is a measure of the peripatetic nature of the Durham miner's existence that Henry Green claimed to have lived in no less than twenty-two different houses since moving to the North East from rural Norfolk in 1871.

This possibly calls into question the notion of the rows and the mining villages of which they formed a part as being integrated communities, at least at the time of the *Chronicle* articles and during the previous decades. It is true that Henry Green's moves seem to have been within a fairly limited radius, always

[19] Ibid.

retaining contact with those members of his own family who had moved north at roughly the same time and with other immigrant workers from the same part of Norfolk. A similar pattern emerges among miners coming in from Wales and Staffordshire. Another social bond was derived from membership of the Primitive Methodist connexion. Of Henry Green's known domiciles all but one fell within the Crook Primitive Methodist circuit, in which he had built up a reputation as a powerful lay preacher. Manifestly it would be dangerous to date the emergence of the pit row community on the basis of the evidence of one family. However, there do seem to be indications in other sources and from personal reminiscences that the intermarried mutually supportive colliery communities based on the rows were only beginning to emerge at the end of the nineteenth century, when the industry itself was undergoing a period of consolidation and the second generation of the immigrant population was beginning to put down roots.

Yet even among transient inhabitants there had to be some degree of community. There were shared baking facilities, shared clothes-hanging space, shared chores like the gutter-clearing celebrated in the miner-poet Tommy Armstrong's *Row in the Gutter*, an essential piece of communal activity also referred to in the *Chronicle* articles. Armstrong, a working miner whose poems were closely based on his experience of pit and domestic life, depicts a situation alluded to in the *Chronicle* reporter's article on the Hetton rows: 'a gutter behind the houses which must be kept clean or somebody is down on somebody else'[20] and which in this case descends from argument to outrageous physical violence. Equally outrageous is the better-known 'Wor' Geordie's lost his Penka', in which the increasingly wild efforts of the inhabitants of the row to dislodge a child's marble from the conduit running between the houses results in the destruction of the whole street.[21] But these were women's activities and it is arguable that the early community of the row was that of the wives and children who spent the majority of their time there. The men had the alternative communities of work, chapel, allotment, sport and public house. The children played and the women worked largely within the confines of the 'raws' and it was they rather than the miners whose terms of service had put them there who experienced both the benefits and the discomforts of the rows and who are rightly celebrated in popular dialect songs of the period.

Architecturally unremarkable, frequently insanitary, but home to the majority of the population of the Durham coalfield, the colliery rows were strung out across the county's countryside in a seemingly haphazard way, their existence justified only by the presence of the pits they served. The economics of their construction determined their shape and endowed them with a certain spartan symmetry. For the best part of a century they constituted the archetypal vernacular architecture of the North East.

---

[20] *NWC*, 18 January 1873.
[21] A gentler treatment of the role of the rows as a children's playground is the anonymous 'Up the Raw doon the Raw', which contains the graphic description of a child who has been playing in the coal dust-filled back lane as 'double japanned'.

10

Crathorne Hall: The Making of an Edwardian Landscape

HILARY J. GRAINGER

It is not perhaps generally realised how markedly the local aspect of the land should influence the buildings that are set upon it. We are more accustomed to look at Sir Ernest George for houses inspired by an earlier stage in the development of English building than is represented in Crathorne Hall.[1]

In his article 'Crathorne Hall: Yorkshire – The Seat of Mr. Lionel Dugdale', published in 1911 as part of the *Country Life* magazine series 'Country Homes and Gardens – Old and New', architectural editor Lawrence Weaver (1876–1930) pursued two themes. First, that the style of the house, which 'may be said to derive its inspiration from the times of Wren',[2] marked something of a departure for its architect Sir Ernest George; and, second, that the reason for this might well be attributed to the influence of the local landscape, characterised by Weaver as 'a large bleak country just south of Yarm-on-Tees, on the Durham border'.[3] An exploration of the reflexive relationship between the style of the house, its garden and its northern landscape, suggested by Weaver, together with some consideration of the context of the article itself, form the basis of this chapter.

Country Life, first published in 1897 with the intention of presenting a vision of all aspects of the countryside to a general, but predominantly urban-based readership, was 'to become the manual of gentrification for the late Victorian and Edwardian middle classes. It was launched at a crucial period in the formation of the attitudes and ideas which were to dominate British society well into the twentieth century.'[4] Its well-researched articles accompanied by high-quality photographs not only documented extant country houses with impressive historical accuracy but also presented them as unified works of art, involving architecture, landscape, gardens and interiors. This chimed with a growing demand on the part of those readers seeking historically correct information with which

---

1   L. Weaver, 'Country Homes and Gardens – Old and New: Crathorne Hall, Yorkshire: The Seat of Mr Lionel Dugdale', *Country Life*, 29 (April 1911), pp.598–604, p.598. The building is now a hotel (eds).

2   Ibid., p.601.

3   Ibid., p.598.

4   R. Strong, *Country Life 1897–1997: The English Arcadia* (London, 1996), p.29.

to inform their country-house designs and restorations. In the words of Henry Avray Tipping (1855–1933), who was to become one of the most prolific contributors to *Country Life*, it was a case of 'good seed falling on fertile soil'.[5]

The early articles forming the series 'Country Homes and Gardens' made clear from the outset the authors' admiration for the old, restored properties considered to embody social continuity by forming a living connection with an idealised past. However, when Lawrence Weaver joined as architectural editor in 1910, he chose to direct attention towards the work of leading contemporary architects. By 1916 *Country Life* was thought to have succeeded 'in being educative without being pedantic, informing, yet attractive'.[6]

Crathorne Hall joined designs by E.S. Prior (1852–1932), Philip Webb (1831–1915), W.R. Lethaby (1857–1931), Sir Reginald Blomfield (1856–1942), Sir E. Guy Dawber (1861–1938), Ernest Newton (1856–1922) and Sir Robert Lorimer (1864–1929) in becoming the subject of one of a series of articles published between 1910 and 1911. Despite their lack of extensive pedigrees, these new houses by contemporary architects were regarded as 'keeping the faith'.

Crathorne Hall (now, incidentally, a hotel) has a special place not only in the development of its architect but also in the history of the English country house. Designed by Ernest George & Yeates for James Lionel Dugdale (1862–1941) and built by George Trollope & Sons between December 1903 and June 1906, it was reputed to be the largest house built in England during the reign of Edward VII, containing as it did 115 rooms, 41 bedrooms, 7 bathrooms and 30 different types of room requiring 14 different categories of servant. Yet it was built during a period of social and economic change in which the passing of the old aristocratic order and collapsing agricultural economics were eroding the pre-eminence of the country house as a social institution. The agricultural depression of the 1870s had weakened the historical bond between house, farm, estate and village, together with the land and workforce that supported it, and, by 1910, it was clear from an editorial in *Country Life* that this had resulted in many of the great estates being broken up:

> the impoverished owners of land were in a very large number of cases unable to keep up the houses and estates to which they had become accustomed. Hundreds were left empty and allowed to fall into half ruinous condition. Others were let to sporting tenants and other strangers. A complete revolution was brought about in rural England.[7]

Those who belonged to a 'conspectus of Edwardian writing' nowadays known as the *Condition of England* genre, so named after C.F.G. Masterman's book, published in 1909, were expressing 'an apprehension of trouble and change'[8] and suggesting that the Edwardian country house was 'in crisis' and harbouring

---

[5] H.A. Tipping, writing in *Country Life* in 1916, quoted in J. Cornforth, *The Search for a Style: 'Country Life' and Architecture 1879–1935* (London, 1988), p.56.

[6] Quoted in J. Musson, *The English Country House: From the Archives of Country Life* (London, 1999), p.48.

[7] Quoted in Strong, *Country Life*, pp. 51–2.

[8] A. Saint, '"An Early Day in a Fine October": the Fugitive Edwardian House', in M. Airs (ed.), *The Edwardian Great House* (Oxford, 2000), p.12.

the seeds of its own decline. In his novel *Tono-Bungay* (1909), H.G. Wells uses the fictional house Bladesover as a metaphor for 'the broad slow decay of the great social organism of England'.[9]

> The great houses stand in the parks still, the cottages cluster respectfully on their borders, touching their eaves with their creepers, the English country-side – you can range through Kent to Bladesover northward and see – persists obstinately in looking what it was. It is like an early day in a fine October. The hand of change rests on it all, unfelt, unseen; resting for a while, as it were half reluctantly, before it grips and ends the thing forever. One frost and the whole face of things will be bare, links snap, patience end, our fine foliage of pretences lie glowing in the mire.[10]

The landowners who survived the economic depression and political changes alluded to in the *Country Life* editorial of 1910 were those with incomes from manufacturing, industry, the City or urban rents. James Lionel Dugdale emanated from the first group. His family had long been associated with the cotton manufacturing industry in Lancashire, his great-grandfather Nathaniel (1761–1816) having founded the Lowerhouse Mill, near Burnley, in 1813. The firm expanded into spinning, weaving and calico printing and by the mid 1840s Dugdales had become one of the largest and most prosperous cotton manufac-turers in Lancashire, with several interests in the USA and India. By 1868, the firm was in the hands of Nathaniel's grandsons, John and James Tertius, and, although they withdrew from foreign commitments during the 1870s, Lower-house Mill nevertheless remained one of the largest cotton factories in England. In January 1880, a year before his death, John Dugdale sold his shares to his brother, leaving James Tertius sole owner of the firm.

In 1844, at the age of twenty-one, John Dugdale had purchased the 'manor of Crathorne' in North Yorkshire at auction. The previous owners of the estate had lived at Crathorne, one of the prettiest and most sheltered points along the river Leven, for five centuries and had taken the name Crathorne in the late fourteenth century. Dugdale reputedly bought the estate for the partridge shooting and trout fishing, never choosing to live there permanently. When he married fifteen years later, he and his wife Charlotte (d. 1891) lived instead at Irwell Bank, Pendleton, Eccles, Lancashire, presumably regarding Crathorne as a country retreat – an escape from the smoky atmosphere created and perpetu-ated by the mill chimney. It was for the same reason that his brother James bought Sezincote, near Moreton-in-Marsh, Gloucestershire, in 1884.

None of the Dugdale family had engaged in any notable building, contenting themselves with substantial but unostentatious houses. Lowerhouse village, their philanthropic development dating from the 1830s and 1840s, was likewise executed largely in a decent, unexceptional Lancashire vernacular. John Dugdale followed family tradition in showing no interest in replacing the existing manor house at Crathorne, which was described as 'small and plain'. After his death in 1881 the estate passed to his only son James Lionel, who had no involve-

---

9   J. Hammond, 'Introduction', in H.G. Wells, *Tono-Bungay* (London 1994), p.xxxiv.
10 Wells, *Tono-Bungay*, pp.8–9.

ment in the family business, but who clearly had architectural ambitions for Crathorne Hall. Educated at Eton, Lionel married Maud Violet Woodruff and was described as 'landowner' when, in 1903, at the age of forty-one, he set about rebuilding the house with the intention of its being a principal residence, the original presumably now deemed inadequate for its new purpose, both in terms of size and design.

In the wake of the agricultural depression those owners who were in a position to do so 'transformed their country houses into houses in the country'[11] and, where landed families had more than one house on the estate, they moved into the smaller. Dugdale, however, was clearly in a position to rebuild and in so doing demonstrated his commitment to a particular way of life. The new Crathorne Hall was intended to form the focus of an agricultural estate and, as such, perpetuated a social order which acknowledged the country house as a social institution involving far more than the house itself, but as one that embraced the offices, home farm, outbuildings, lodges, gardens and the wider ranges of the estate and village. The role that Dugdale envisaged for himself in the country must have determined to some large extent the style and type of country house that he wanted to build. The present Lord Crathorne maintains that:

> the size of the house perhaps reflected Lionel Dugdale's wife, Violet's supposed ambitions to launch her son into politics and her daughter into an advantageous marriage. If these were her wishes she succeeded as her daughter Beryl, married the earl of Rothes at Crathorne in 1926 and her son, Thomas Lionel (1897–1977) became a Conservative MP for the Richmondshire Division in 1929. Seven years later Thomas married Nancy Tennant who was a talented painter, some of whose works hang in the Hall.[12]

Crathorne Hall was therefore intended in its entirety to create an 'Edwardian landscape', one which provided a setting for entertaining on a large and lavish scale, facilitated by twenty-six live-in servants. It was furnished with a number of modern labour-saving devices, while at the same time 'keeping the faith' in terms of its style, planning and landscaping. It could be seen therefore as representing a final blaze of light in that autumnal, vespertine interlude described so hauntingly by Wells.

The choice of architect would prove crucial for Dugdale. At a local level, there were few architects building country houses in the North Riding in the early 1900s on the scale planned for Crathorne Hall. One possibility open to Dugdale would have been York-based Walter Henry Brierley (1862–1929), then architect to the North Riding County Council. His domestic work, creditable though it was, tended towards the smaller country house, although Brierley had attained a degree of international recognition when two illustrations and a plan of 'The Close' at Northallerton (1895) appeared in the influential *Das Englische Haus*, published in 1904–5 by the German architectural commentator Hermann

---

[11]   Ibid., *Tono-Bungay*, pp.8–9.
[12]   Lord Crathorne, 'A Short History of Crathorne Hall' (unpublished). Thomas Dugdale was created a baronet in 1945 and a peer in 1959. He sat in the House of Lords as the first Lord Crathorne (*Oxford Dictionary of National Biography*, Oxford, 2004).

Muthesius.[13] Brierley was also known for additions and alterations to earlier houses and for restoration work which included the rebuilding of the Jacobean Welburn Hall, Kirkdale, after a fire in 1890. In 1926 he 'massively and successfully' enlarged Easthorpe Hall, a house designed originally by James Carr for the third Lord Grimthorpe.[14] However, given Dugdale's ambitions for Crathorne, it is quite understandable that he should have looked beyond the local level to architects of established national reputation, to the likes of Sir Edwin Lutyens, (1869–1944), Reginald Blomfield, E. Guy Dawber, Ernest Newton, Arnold Mitchell (1864–1944) and finally to Ernest George (1839–1922).[15] In commissioning George, who in 1903 was sixty-four, Dugdale was turning to one of the most respected national architects of the day; some foreknowledge of his work is thus central to an understanding of the final design of Crathorne Hall and the subtleties of its relationship with the landscape in which it stood.

By 1903 George had established a high public profile and was widely acknowledged as one of the most successful late Victorian architects. Awarded the Royal Institute of British Architects Gold Medal in 1896, he went on to serve as President of the Institute from 1908 until 1910 and was knighted in 1911. He was also an etcher and watercolourist of considerable ability and E. Guy Dawber, one of his many pupils, claimed that George was 'in some way without rival and might justifiably be ranked among the best architectural draughtsmen of the day'.[16] It was undoubtedly the case that his distinctive Royal Academy drawings, executed in pen and sepia wash, were always awaited eagerly by the architectural profession and the public alike.

George worked with three partners during his long career – Thomas Vaughan (1836–1875), Harold A. Peto (1854–1933) and Alfred B. Yeates (1867–1944) – and though his work included commercial, ecclesiastical and public buildings, he was principally a domestic architect, enjoying spectacular success throughout the 1870s and 1880s. Commissions ranged from the picturesque Queen Anne-style premises for Thomas Goode & Co. in South Audley Street, London (1875–6), to the Ossington Coffee Palace, Newark-on-Trent, Nottinghamshire (1881–2), interior schemes for Claridge's Hotel, London (1897), and the design of Golders Green Crematorium (1902). It was, however, the houses in Harrington and Collingham Gardens, Kensington, London (1880–88), which undoubtedly established George and Peto's reputation as domestic architects. These superbly conceived designs represent the extreme point of late Victorian individualism and were inspired by the old Flemish and German town houses sketched and painted so evocatively by George on his frequent tours. Muthesius declared these houses to be 'among the finest examples of domestic architecture

13 H. Muthesius, *The English House*, ed. D. Sharp, translated by J. Seligman (London, 1979), p.112.

14 For many years the house was attributed to John Carr, but more recent scholars have suggested Thomas Atkinson as an architect. Brierley's enlargements dating from 1926 suggest that he might have looked at Crathorne Hall, since there are some faint echoes in terms of the chimneys and the canted bay introduced by George and Yeates in the service wing.

15 For a full account of George's life and work, see H.J. Grainger, 'The Architecture of Sir Ernest George and his Partners c.1860–1922' (unpublished PhD thesis, University of Leeds, 1985).

16 E. Guy Dawber, 'Preface to the Catalogue of a Memorial Exhibition of Watercolours by the late Ernest George RA', held at the Fine Art Society, 148 New Bond Street, London W1, March 1923, no. 616.

to be seen in London'.[17] Special interest attaches to No. 39 Harrington Gardens, built for the dramatist W.S. Gilbert.

Country houses, considered to be George's métier, formed the backbone of the practice, not surprisingly, since he designed over three dozen and altered, restored and added to many others. His preference for domestic work was clear: 'To those of us who deal little with public buildings it is no mean thing to build Homes about the country, if our endeavours secure they are well built, pleasant to live in, and comely.'[18] He worked in a range of styles – Queen Anne, Elizabethan, Jacobean, Tudor, neo-Georgian – and also in a more understated vernacular manner particularly influential to the next generation. All his domestic work reflected a deep understanding of the English tradition, but his informed and intelligent eclecticism also embraced foreign, particularly Northern European, exemplars, which he studied on regular sketching tours.

To stylistic variety and integrity George added sound and practical planning. He had an intuitive command of domestic requirements and 'understood the mechanism of life as it was lived in great households',[19] Muthesius maintaining that 'his plans are among the best achievements of contemporary architecture. They have a consistent clarity and simplicity which is pleasing.'[20] George's outstanding gift lay in his ability to design houses giving the impression of having been lived in by many generations, in which the charm of 'olden days' was combined with modern conveniences. His designs were thoroughly English in construction and planning and this was significant, given that many of his clients were new men who nevertheless wanted to live in big houses surrounded by plenty of land with all the feudal trappings. His work, nevertheless, appealed to clients drawn from a wide social spectrum and it was not only the landed gentry but also the professions, trade and industry and the middle classes who flocked to his fashionable West End London offices. George, according to Guy Dawber, was 'immensely versed in all the many dresses buildings could assume and he never had the least difficulty in getting them right; he had admirable taste and feeling.'[21] But, regardless of his chosen idiom, his work was 'personal and as easily recognised as if it were signed with a conspicuous autograph'.[22] By preference George was drawn, doubtless by his innate romanticism, to the worthy dwelling houses, the Tudor, Elizabethan and Jacobean mansions of the fifteenth, sixteenth and seventeenth centuries, dubbed by J.W. Gleeson-White, editor of *The Studio* magazine, as 'the palaces of merchant princes'.[23] By the same token, George realised that clients had their own preferences:

---

[17]   Muthesius, *The English House*, p.34

[18]   E. George, 'The Opening Address', *Journal of the Royal Institute of British Architects*, 3rd series, 16 (November 1909), p.9.

[19]   D. Braddell, 'Sir Ernest George', *Dictionary of National Biography, 1922–1930* (London, 1937), p.335.

[20]   Muthesius, *The English House*, p.36.

[21]   J.W. Gleeson-White, 'The Revival of English Domestic Architecture IV: The work of Mr Ernest George', *Studio* (1896), p.33.

[22]   J.W. Gleeson-White, 'The Revival of English Domestic Architecture III: The work of Mr Ernest George', *Studio* (1896), p.147.

[23]   Ibid.

While to one the dignity of columned portico, classic proportion, and breadth of treatment of appeal, another, in whom the romantic element is strong, finds formality chilling; he will be happier in panelled rooms with their long mullioned windows. There will still be Horace Walpoles and Walter Scotts as well as Greek Revivalists.[24]

For the most part George and his partners catered for the Walter Scotts and generally adhered to Elizabethan and Jacobean precedents, but also for the Walpoles in so far as his houses were often for collectors where interior decoration was important. Certain qualities and principles underscored all George's domestic work, regardless of size or elaboration: composition, proportion, massing, breadth and simplicity, quality of materials and craftsmanship and, of particular importance, sensitivity to site. This was evidenced by his well-published drawings in which his employment of soft sepia pen-and-ink technique was eminently suited to capture the visual and physical qualities of English domestic architecture. Such qualities, namely a concern for texture, colour, scale, detail and the character of the site and place, formed an authentic part of George's work.

While George's understanding of the role that indigenous materials and local building practices might play in the assimilation of houses into the English landscape was most conspicuous in his smaller domestic work, it was also evident in his larger country houses – Batsford Park, Moreton-in-Marsh, Gloucestershire (1888–93), for A.B. Freeman-Mitford, later Lord Redesdale, being a particularly good example. At first sight it looks disarmingly like a genuine Tudor manor house. Described as 'Cotswold-Elizabethan' and 'a clever working up of the Dorset-Tudor Gothic style',[25] it was built of local mellow grey Broughton stone. Its style, however, was based less upon the very grand sixteenth-century houses than on the more modest contemporary houses for the gentry: Chastleton House rather than Montacute. The house has an air of austerity, especially to the north, where the gable walls were left almost completely windowless and blank. George ignored the opportunity for elaborate parapets and chimneys offered by Tudor precedents. This well-judged reticence can be placed in the wider context of a contemporary move towards classicism. George's intention was summed up in *The Architect* as being 'to treat the symmetrical Tudor house in a broad Classical and dignified way, after the manner of an old building of the period, avoiding all the prettiness and fanciful features'.[26] But it may be also the case that the austerity of Batsford owes something to George's sense of the locality in which he was working. Although there are few direct references to the distinctive Cotswold vernacular, other than the cottage-scaled porch on the west front, the architecture and the landscape of the Cotswolds are austere and George appears to have responded to this in the broader treatment of the house. Guy Dawber, who acted as clerk of works at Batsford, claimed that George's houses 'seemed to fit the site, to grow out of the ground, and his great artistic sense

[24] George, 'The Opening Address', p.3.
[25] M. Girouard, *The Victorian Country House* (New Haven and London, 1979), p.396.
[26] *Architect* (1 June 1888), p.315.

enabled him to see them as a completed whole, whilst he was planning them.'[27] This level of sensitivity in designing a large country house which takes account of the locality in which it is to be set must have proved irresistible to Dugdale.

George had worked only twice before in Yorkshire, designing a Jacobean-style vicarage in Amotherby in 1889 and restoring and making additions to Monk Fryston Hall near Leeds, an Elizabethan house owned by the Hemsworth family and damaged by fire in 1897. For his earlier country houses George had invariably remained faithful to early Renaissance – Batsford serving as a fine example – and, indeed, by 1900 he was widely acknowledged as being its chief protagonist. Crathorne Hall (1903–6) and Eynsham Hall, Witney, Oxfordshire, begun the following year (1904–8), were George's last two great country houses. While Eynsham, built for James Francis Mason, typified George's 'Elizabethan manner', and was reminiscent of English seventeenth-century precedents such as Holland House, Kensington, and Bramshill House, Hampshire, Crathorne marked something of a departure for its architect. So why then did George choose to abandon early Renaissance in favour of a style which, as Weaver pointed out, derived 'its inspiration from the times of Wren'?

Avray Tipping had reflected in March 1916 that each country house selected for inclusion in *Country Life* had 'been so treated as to show some merit, teach some lesson, and exercise some influence on the taste of the day'.[28] The 'lesson' embodied in Weaver's article on Crathorne Hall concerned the power of land-scape. George's debt to Wren, however, afforded the prompt for Weaver to endorse the growing appreciation of an architectural figure Weaver considered had much to offer contemporary thought and taste. Taking first the issue of land-scape, Weaver was quick to acknowledge the character of this region, a point reiterated by Nikolaus Pevsner some fifty-five years later when he argued that 'The North Riding of Yorkshire, more than many counties, needs some general remarks on landscape and architectural character in advance of the detailed survey.'[29] Acknowledgement of Weaver's own interests is important here. His *Small Country Houses of Today* was published in 1911, the same year as the *Country Life* article, and goes some way to explaining why he found the reso-lution of architecture and landscape so compelling at Crathorne Hall. Weaver promoted Arts and Crafts ideals in his book, noting formative factors affecting the site, soil, views, altitude, protection, slope, contour and neighbourhood as helping to determine the setting of a house. And it was this notion of the house as product of the landscape that formed the introduction to his article:

> It is in a large, bleak country just south of Yarm-on-Tees, on the Durham border that Mr Ernest George ARA and his partner Mr. Alfred Yeates, have built for Mr. Lionel Dugdale the house which forms the subject of the accom-panying pictures. Although the land does not stand high – for it is towards the north of the Vale of York, which finds its outlet to the sea at Tees Mouth – and the moors of the North Riding and the Cleveland Hills are somewhere away

[27] E. Guy Dawber, 'The Late Sir Ernest George RA', *The Builder*, 123 (15 December 1922), p.903.

[28] H.A. Tipping, 'The Country Homes of England: As Revealed in a Thousand Numbers of Country Life', *Country Life* (4 March 1916), quoted in J. Musson, *The English Country House*, p.11.

[29] N. Pevsner, *The Buildings of England: Yorkshire: The North Riding* (Harmondsworth, 1966), p.20.

towards the south east, the scenery does not lack that grim expansive flavour that we taste so intimately in a Brontë novel. It is not perhaps generally realised how markedly the local aspect of the land should influence the buildings that are set upon it.[30]

Weaver well knew that George had 'taken the Elizabethans to heart', but, as he argued, 'their sway is more sensitively felt in more smiling country than the North Riding affords', pointing out that:

the whole history of building in Yorkshire is an example of the influence on design, not only of local characteristics, but also of the strength and hardness of the Yorkshire temperament. The more seductive prettiness of Elizabethan and Jacobean art never reached in the North that efflorescence which we see in the Midlands and in the south.[31]

He concluded:

Mr. George, then, was wise to speak at Crathorne the language of the country, and out of his simple and straightforward planning of the house, there has grown an architectural expression, which is not only the result of the adoption of late seventeenth century motifs, but also a tribute to Yorkshire traditions.[32]

But, as will be seen, the relationship is arguably even subtler than Weaver suggests; the particular location of the house is removed slightly from the 'grim' expansiveness of its wider location. In 1903 the *Building News* announced that the 'house will occupy a beautiful site among the hills in the North Riding and will have a terraced garden between it and a winding river'.[33] The river in question is the Leven, a tributary of the Tees, which runs through a wooded valley stretching from just east of Yarm, south through Middleton-on-Leven, through Crathorne and east to Hutton Rudby, Stokesley and Great Ayton and beyond to Kirkdale Moor. The beauty of the site had been acknowledged as early as 1844, when the author of the auction catalogue waxed:

to a lover of the picturesque it affords facilities for the erection of a mansion seldom, if ever, exceeded, combining the richest, with the most sublime varieties of nature. The varied and beautiful wooded vale of the romantic River Leven in the foreground, and the majestic Cleveland Hills in the distance.[34]

It was to be sixty years before the 'mansion' was built, but the setting is indeed spectacular and is still unspoilt today. Legend holds that George and Dugdale stalked the proposed area with a pair of stepladders in order to secure the most propitious site (see Fig. 10.1). The new house did not disappoint, *The Builder* reporting in 1910 on the Royal Academy Architectural Exhibition that:

the designs for domestic buildings exhibited this year show an increasing appreciation of the necessity for a skilful wedding of the actual building with its surroundings, too much neglected during the last century, and undoubtedly

---

30 Weaver, 'Country Homes', p.598.
31 Ibid.
32 Ibid.
33 *Building News*, 84 (15 May 1903), p.681.
34 Auction catalogue (1844) in the possession of Lord Crathorne.

Figure 10.1. Crathorne Hall, Yarm-on-Tees, by Ernest George & Yeates, 1903–6: view of the south-facing garden front from the river Leven (author's photograph).

display a marked feeling for the picturesque as a whole … One of the most noticeable is the drawing of Crathorne Hall, Yorks … a drawing that renders in an attractive way a design in which the simplest means are successful in achieving an effect of undoubted dignity.[35]

The Dugdales must also have been pleased to read Weaver's view that Crathorne Hall took its place 'pleasantly and naturally in the long lineage of English Domestic Architecture … It relies for its effect on an unaffected study of the character and requirements of a Country House.'[36] It is not known whether Dugdale expressed any opinions about the style, but what is known is that George always treated a client with respect in this matter, counselling his students wisely not to vaunt their knowledge, 'but let your scheme seem to emanate from him … You cannot have all your own way, and your pet schemes may often be frustrated. After all, it is not your house that you build, though you are allowed the fun of shaping it'.[37]

In moving towards seventeenth-century sources, George was acknowledging the broadly classical style of the locality, which in turn had responded over the years to the landscape. Here, in the North East, Renaissance motifs had 'survived unexpectedly long' and 'were combined with Palladian fronts'.[38] Local examples included seventeenth- and eighteenth-century houses: Stillington Hall, north of York; Easthorpe Hall, Amotherby, dating from the late eighteenth

[35] *The Builder*, 98 (21 May 1910), p.576.
[36] Weaver, 'Country Homes', p.604.
[37] E. George, 'Address to Students', *Journal of the Royal Institute of British Architects* (5 February 1910), p.282.
[38] C. Aslet, *The Last Country Houses* (New Haven and London, 1985), p.131.

century; Wiganthorpe Hall; and most famously Stanwick Park, a seventeenth-century house remodelled in Palladian style in about 1740 and owned by the first Duke of Northumberland. Nor was George the first Victorian domestic architect to be prompted by the locality; architectural precedent had undoubtedly exerted its influence over his distinguished older contemporary Philip Webb. Webb's Rounton Grange, designed for Sir Lothian Bell in 1871, was a tall and striking tower house just two miles south of Crathorne. Its form was the result of Bell wishing to preserve mature trees on the site. However, it was 'somewhat inspired by North Country and Scottish pele-towers, but there was more than a hint of Vanbrugh (whom Webb admired) in the busy and massive skyline of gables and chimneystacks'.[39] Webb's acknowledgement of the locality is hardly unexpected, given his respect for indigenous building practices and the employment of local materials. But, as has already been explained, George was also sensitive to such matters.

Meanwhile, having explored the impact of the landscape, Weaver then turned his attention to the ensuing style, explaining that Crathorne 'relies for its effect on an unaffected study of the character and requirements of a country house, and an architectural statement of them in the straightforward language which we owe to the last half of the seventeenth century'.[40] By the early 1900s English Renaissance had become overwhelmingly popular with country-house architects who were interested in historical precedent. For big country houses the sturdy, full-blown style of the mid seventeenth century, exemplified by Wren, was preferred – Reginald Blomfield being a leading practitioner. For smaller country houses, architects and clients tended towards the quieter neo-Georgian, based on eighteenth- rather than seventeenth-century precedents. George was not completely unmoved by the contemporary vogue for neo-Georgian, having made sensitive additions and alterations to two Georgian houses – Colworth House, Sharnbrook, in Bedfordshire (1894–95), and Shockerwick House, Bathford, in Somerset (1896 and 1907), originally by John Woolfe and John Palmer respectively. George's own design for a smaller house, Holwell in Hertfordshire (1900), echoes the style, but at Crathorne Hall George was making a much bolder statement that went beyond the vagaries of architectural fashion by taking into account landscape and tradition.

Blomfield, writing in 1897, believed Wren to be 'the greatest architect this country possessed, perhaps our one architect of commanding genius ... the most English of all English architects',[41] and in Weaver's view, a suitable national precedent. Weaver therefore invoked Wren's principles of beauty, firmness and convenience to form the framework for his discussion of the exterior of Crathorne. Indeed, Weaver devotes more than half of the text of his article to an encomium on Wren who, he claimed, argued for an air of uniformity, sobriety and balance, but counselled the creation of a marked difference between front,

---

[39] E. Waterson and P. Meadows, *Lost Houses of York and the North Riding* (York, 1990; 2nd edn 1998), p.34.
[40] Weaver, 'Country Homes', p.604.
[41] Quoted in A. Service, *Edwardian Architecture: a Handbook of Building Design in Britain, 1890–1914* (London, 1977), p.62.

Figure 10.2. Crathorne Hall, Yarm-on-Tees, by Ernest George & Yeates, 1903–6: the entrance porch from the forecourt (author's photograph).

back and side elevations of buildings – while warning that too much variety was the mother of confusion. George, according to Weaver, had absorbed the spirit of Wren and as a result had struck the perfect balance.

Set in acres of parkland, Crathorne Hall is approached from the west by a winding drive. Although records show there to have been an original house on the estate, there is no evidence to suggest that the surrounding area had been landscaped. It would appear that James Lionel Dugdale laid out the grounds in the early 1900s. The large courtyard to the north is entered through a stone boundary wall from the west, so that the majestic grandeur of the north front is not immediately apparent. The style, as we have seen, is broadly classical, with an imposing south front. While a general feeling of symmetry is apparent in both north and south elevations, on closer examination the north elevation is less symmetrical. Here George created an interesting and original courtyard in which the eastern wing, containing the billiard room, projected forward to form one side of the service court, while to the west a lower wing formed the boudoir. The grouping of this entrance front is simple and dignified, with its towers flanking the low, massive central porch.

The twin bell towers in the inner angles of the forecourt, with concave-shaped roofs surmounted by lanterns (see Fig. 10.2), while contributing to the well-judged note of distinction, are reminiscent of those employed by George to more overtly picturesque advantage at Dunley Hill, Effingham, Surrey (1886), and Cawston Manor, Norfolk (1896). The south elevation shows complete symmetry, with a projecting central classical portico on a rusticated base flanked by two-storeyed projecting bays (Fig. 10.3). The symmetry is maintained to a degree in the recessed service wing. It was becoming apparent in the early 1900s that the classical style could retreat into a dull, lifeless pastiche if handled insensitively. George argued that houses must be designed to make a living connection with the past and this was more than a matter of style; it was a question of understanding and interpreting history: 'The question of style is a minor matter, for the artist's hand will be evident in the work, whatever the treatment he affects or the vogue of his time.'[42] Weaver endorsed George's success in this respect at Crathorne:

> the building has an unaffected and reasonable air which does not derive merely from a close study of style. Sheer scholarship in architecture does not commonly produce very noticeable results; it may serve merely to recall the man who knew fifteen languages but failed to express an idea in any one of them.[43]

The subtlety of George's handling of style finds an interesting parallel in the landscape itself. Just as the picturesque wooded landscape of the Leven at Crathorne mitigated the 'harshness' of the North Yorkshire landscape, then so too the picturesque details employed by George relieved any possible austerity arising from his employment of a broadly classical vocabulary. As Weaver noted:

[42] E. George, 'Address to Students', p.225.
[43] Weaver, 'Country Homes', p.601.

Figure 10.3. Crathorne Hall, Yarm-on-Tees, by Ernest George & Yeates, 1903–6: the south, garden front (author's photograph).

the earlier manner to which he [George] is more accustomed has left its mark on the building. The pinnacles at the corners of the south balconies, the great mantelpiece in the dining room and the treatment of the heraldic beasts which guard the way down to the sunken garden all evidence his more usual preoccupations.[44]

George had long been interested in landscape gardening. His partner Harold Ainsworth Peto (1854–1933), aesthete, architect and landscape gardener, had laid out a number of important formal gardens around the turn of the century, including those at Buscot Park, Oxfordshire, and at his own home, Iford Manor, Wiltshire, which he bought in 1899. It was described by his close friend Avray Tipping, in *Country Life*, as being 'a museum of art and architecture, a garden of delight and beauty, a happy valley of rural England'.[45]

In 1902, the year before work began at Crathorne, George was working with Peto at Wayford Manor, Somerset, making additions to an Elizabethan house while Peto laid out the gardens. The results were an endorsement of the values being upheld and promoted by *Country Life* at the time. George was also a friend of William Robinson (1838–1935), the indefatigable and outspoken gardening writer and horticulturist, with whom he had collaborated on various projects, most recently on the designs for the gardens at North Mymms, Hertfordshire, where George and Peto were making additions and alterations for the banker Walter H. Burns in 1893–8. Here George and Robinson assimilated the details of the site and related the garden to the environment of the house, laying out an enclosed formal garden with walls, pavilions and gates designed by George.[46] The close relationship between house, garden and wider landscape were characteristic of George; his houses were linked, seemingly effortlessly, to surrounding gardens using terraces and sometimes staircases constructed from local materials. Glencot, Wells, Somerset, designed in 1887, was a good example, where the use of local mellow Doulting stone served to weld the house to the surrounding landscape.[47] At Crathorne, the rich cream-coloured Swainby stone, taken from the Shraw End Quarry near Whitby, invested the house with local authenticity. George once again employed garden terrace walls to anchor the property to its surroundings. Beyond, he designed lodges and a stable block, as well as the garden pavilions, gates and ornaments close to the house.

The grounds immediately surrounding Crathorne Hall were landscaped. On the north side, opposite to the main entrance, was 'the Glade', a long broad grassed walk bordered by trees. To the west was a hedged rose garden (now removed) and, to the south, the main gardens and now lawn. There was also a formal paved garden in front of the south front of the servants' wing, which created a rather intimate, sheltered space (see Fig. 10.4). Stone alcoves jutted out from the ground floor to form small, sheltered sitting-out places supporting

---

[44] Ibid.
[45] Quoted in Tipping, p.158. Iford Manor was the subject of two articles in *Country Life* in 1907 (22), p.450, and 1922 (52), p.242, both by Tipping. The gardens were discussed in *Country Life* in 1907 (22), pp.242 and 272, and (94), p.907.
[46] See Grainger, 'Sir Ernest George', vol. ii, pp.578–9.
[47] Ibid., pp.556–7.

Figure 10.4. Crathorne Hall, Yarm-on-Tees, by Ernest George & Yeates, 1903–6: the formal garden in front of the servants' wing, south front (author's photograph).

bay windows in the floor above. The wall on the east side of the garden formed a boundary between the gardens and the parkland beyond. Not that the gardens were purely ornamental, since in 1905 glasshouses were erected by W. Richardson & Co. at a cost of £918 15s 0d, presumably to cultivate produce as well as flowers.

In his prize-winning Oxford essay of 1907, 'The National Character of English Architecture', Geoffrey Scott, later a contributor to *Country Life*, spoke of the English manor house as being 'made from the quarries of its own hills and merging itself into the lines of them; quiet with the repose which comes of a deliberate and fitting growth'.[48] George, too, believed that contemporary vagaries of style should not supplant the importance of 'Tradition' in domestic architecture, irrespective of its scale, arguing that 'Its stronghold; the love for the time-honoured buildings, the associations with them, their texture and mellowness instinctively appeal to us.'[49] George was an inspired choice of architect, being well placed to understand and interpret the workings of a large country house and to provide an imposing design, while at the same time showing sensitivity towards context. At Crathorne Hall George furnished his client with a house which respected the locality and which offered, on the one hand, an authentic link with tradition and, on the other, the modern conveniences necessary to fulfill the social ambitions of an Edwardian country-house owner. For Weaver, who was interested in the relationship between houses, gardens and the wider landscape and for whom a sense of place was important, nowhere were these concerns more eloquently expressed than at Crathorne Hall. He was wise indeed to suggest to readers that 'It is not perhaps realised how markedly the local aspect of the land should influence the buildings that are set upon it.'[50]

[48] Quoted in Tipping, p.7.

[49] E. George, 'Address to Students', *Journal of the Royal Institute of British Architects* (7 November 1908), p.4.

[50] Weaver, 'Country Homes', p.598

PART FOUR

URBAN LANDSCAPES

11

From Defensive Moat to Romantic Landscape: The Riverbanks of the Durham Peninsula

MARTIN ROBERTS

The classic view of Durham Cathedral and Castle rising above the wooded gorge of the river Wear, despite its chocolate-box familiarity, is a great deception. Its visual message, which seems to contrast the natural world against the man-made, nature against history, leaf against stone, is misleading. The riverbanks, rich in history, are also shaped by man. Their development is a layered and changing landscape, a palimpsest that has shifted with the fortunes of the city above them. Today the riverbanks at Durham are an essential part of the visual character of the city: they provide the memorable setting for the castle and cathedral, while their extensive woodland softens and frames many picturesque viewpoints. They are also, to use that rather hackneyed planning phase, 'a green lung in the heart of the city', a place of contemplation and quiet reflection.

Such a place would have been unrecognisable in fifteenth- or sixteenth-century Durham. The peninsula was a border fortress and the medieval river and its banks served as a castle moat, a working quarry, an industrial power source and a convenient repository for the human effluent of the entire town. It was treeless, busy with people, noisy and odorous. By the seventeenth century the gradual evaporation of the military function of the peninsula (a process detectable from the late medieval period onwards) was all but complete. Its riverbank quarries were largely exhausted too. The river was no longer a moat and became instead the focus of a new appreciation of the peninsular landscape. Formal walks appeared outside the castle walls for the first time and, by the middle of the eighteenth century, the southern and eastern slopes cascaded with terraced gardens descending from the bailey houses.

On the western slopes beneath the castle and cathedral the first tree-planting appears at the same time, a gradual process completed only in the nineteenth century, when the public footpath network was developed and improved. What resulted was a sylvan, picturesque landscape in which to set the great medieval buildings; a landscape part accidental, part deliberate and consciously planned. So it remains today, essentially an 'urban parkland', to give it current nomenclature, developed with new public art, improved footpaths and still a vital component in the life of a busy cathedral and university city.

As this chapter will describe, the predominantly wooded landscape of the

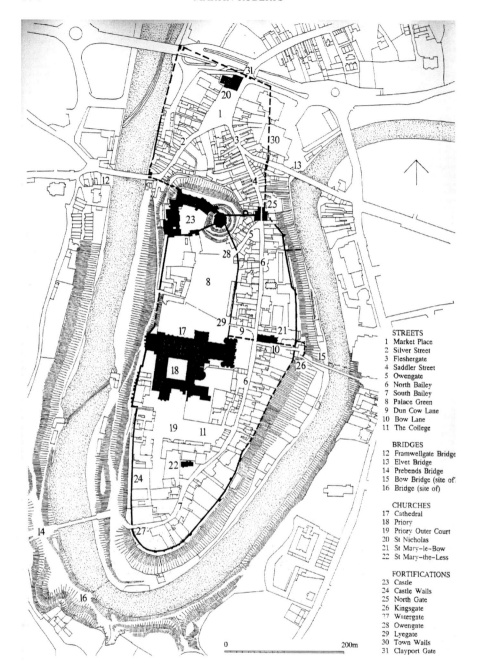

STREETS
1 Market Place
2 Silver Street
3 Fleshergate
4 Saddler Street
5 Owengate
6 North Bailey
7 South Bailey
8 Palace Green
9 Dun Cow Lane
10 Bow Lane
11 The College

BRIDGES
12 Framwellgate Bridge
13 Elvet Bridge
14 Prebends Bridge
15 Bow Bridge (site of)
16 Bridge (site of)

CHURCHES
17 Cathedral
18 Priory
19 Priory Outer Court
20 St Nicholas
21 St Mary-le-Bow
22 St Mary-the-Less

FORTIFICATIONS
23 Castle
24 Castle Walls
25 North Gate
26 Kingsgate
27 Watergate
28 Owengate
29 Lyegate
30 Town Walls
31 Clayport Gate

0   200m

Figure 11.1. Durham: the peninsula and the medieval defences (author's drawing from M. Roberts, *Durham: 1000 Years of History*, 1994, p.49). The Durham peninsula with the castle and cathedral set within the castle walls. North of the castle is the early-fourteenth-century addition of the town walls around the market place.

Durham peninsula, so easy on the eye, disguises a pattern of development as complex and subtle as that of the city it serves.

The border fortress, 995–1550

The meandering course of the river Wear developed in the period after the last Ice Age when the old river valley had been choked with glacial deposits. As the glaciers receded the river had to re-excavate its old course and, where this was blocked, it carved out a new route and cut deep into the underlying sandstone, so creating the peninsula. The sides of the gorge would have been steep, near-vertical cliffs, as still survive behind St Oswald's Church.[1] In 995 the monks of the Community of St Cuthbert settled on the peninsula at Durham and finally laid the body of their saint to rest in a little church 'of boughs of trees'.[2] The Community did not stumble on the site by accident, as the embellished historical accounts describe, still less as a result of any saintly intervention. The settlement was a planned event of major political importance in Anglo-Saxon Northumbria and before the monks arrived the site would have been well prepared and fortified.

In choosing the site, the natural defences provided by the loop of the river Wear in its deep gorge would have been of the greatest importance to the Anglo-Saxons. Only the neck of the peninsula needed substantial fortification to complete the defences at Durham: the 'hill-island'. The site of the medieval castle along this northern neck would have been fortified and the timber palisade work carried around the lip of the entire peninsula to the south.[3] The coming of the Normans brought major rebuilding in stone with the establishment of the castle and the castle walls following the line of the earlier defences. First and foremost the river and its banks served a defensive function and, from the earliest occupation, it was essential to keep the banks below the castle walls free from all vegetation to ensure an open view for the garrison[4] (Fig. 11.1).

The construction of the Anglo-Saxon cathedral, and the later and more extensive Norman building campaigns, required vast quantities of local stone, and the exposed sandstone on the cliff sides of the river gorge enabled easy and accessible quarrying. This would have occurred first on the peninsula itself; later, particularly after the construction of Framwellgate Bridge, the left bank opposite the peninsula would have been quarried, where operations were not constrained by the buildings above.[5] Only at St Oswald's did the early church and churchyard prevent quarrying, thus preserving the original gorge cliffs.

---

1 T. Johnson, 'The Durham Banks', in *Friends of Durham Cathedral Annual Report* (1991), pp.30–35.
2 *Symeon, A History of the Church in Durham*, trans. J. Stephenson (Llanerch, 1988), p.56.
3 M. Leyland, 'Origin and Development of Durham Castle', in D. Rollason, M. Harvey and M. Prestwich (eds), *Anglo-Norman Durham 1093–1193* (Woodbridge, 1994), pp.404–24.
4 There are a number of topographical illustrations of the treeless riverbanks at Durham, of which three of the best are paintings in the collection at Durham Castle. A number of early- to mid-eighteenth-century views are illustrated in P.R. Andrew, *Durham Cathedral: Artists and Images* (Durham, 1993), pp.11–15.
5 K. Dunham and G.A.L. Johnson, 'The Site and Stones of Durham', in *Friends of Durham Cathedral Annual Report* (1984–5), p.19.

The medieval period witnessed the transformation of the gorge into the more gently banked profile that survives today. The banks would still have been predominantly treeless, for defensive reasons on the peninsula side and because of active quarrying on the opposite bank. Quarries were owned by the cathedral priory and by individual citizens of the town. Most were concentrated on the south and west sides of the peninsula below South Street, where the priory's sacrist had a quarry, now identified as The Dell near Prebends' Bridge.[6] In 1478 'Thilstone', a fissile stone used for paving and probably roofing, was quarried here. The almoner at the priory also had a quarry nearby as well as in Elvet, presumably near Palmers Close. John de Ulkyliston had a private quarry in South Street in 1314, while the Great Quarry stretched along the banks below the present South Street houses.[7] Quarrying continued into the post-medieval period, though on a much reduced scale, and Bishop Cosin's rebuilding of the castle after 1660 made use of stone from Broken Walls quarry, just below the castle's western defences.[8] In the early eighteenth century small-scale quarrying was still taking place.[9] Eventually, the exhaustion of easily won stone, the limitations of quarrying beneath the developing town and improved transport bringing other sources of stone into the city led to the final abandonment of the quarries.

During the medieval period the river Wear was also a convenient means of disposing of Durham's sewage. Both the castle and the cathedral priory have surviving garderobes and reredorters (individual and communal toilets) that discharged on to the banks and so ultimately into the river. No doubt most of the town's citizens with reasonable access to the banks or the bridges would have discharged their effluent in this way. Interestingly, the townspeople who lived by the Milneburn (which flowed from Flass Vale, along the line of North Road and into the Wear) were fined for erecting privies over it, but no such constraints were imposed with regard to the Wear itself – it was an open sewer.[10] Not surprisingly then, the river was rarely used as a ready source of drinking water. There were many wells around the town and the priory was served by a piped supply across the river onto the peninsula.[11]

---

[6] M. Bonney, *Lordship and the Urban Community: Durham and its Overlords 1250–1540* (Cambridge, 1990), p.102.

[7] Ibid., pp.156 and 166.

[8] G. Ornsby (ed.), *The Correspondence of John Cosin D.D. Lord Bishop of Durham, together with Other Papers Illustrative of his Life and Times: Part Two*, Surtees Society, 55 (1872) (Appendix XIV); 'Series of Agreements relating to the Restoration effected by Bishop Cosin in the Castles of Durham and Auckland', for Durham Castle hall porch 1663 (no. 4, p.369).

[9] Dean and Chapter Act Books record stone extraction on the riverbanks in November 1706 and August 1711.

[10] Bonney, *Lordship*, p.51.

[11] The Priory Account Rolls [Surtees Society, 99, 100 and 103 (1898 and 1900)] detail many references to the repair of the medieval water supply to the peninsula – a lead pipe running from the higher ground at Bellasis (modern Durham School area) and Elvet Moor further west, into the outer court of the monastery, now the College. This same water supply was frequently repaired after the Dissolution, notably by both Bishop Cosin and the Dean and Chapter between 1660 and 1665, when the huge sum of £335 16s was spent relaying the supply pipe; see Ornsby, *The Correspondence of John Cosin* (Appendix XXIV), p.380.

After the arrival of the Community of St Cuthbert on the peninsula it is likely that there was the need to cross the river to reach the settlements that grew up on the opposite banks. To the west, the Old Borough of Crossgate/South Street/Milburngate was on the old north–south route, a major trading link in the area. To the east, in Elvet the settlement around St Oswald's may even pre-date 995, in what later was to become the Barony of Elvet based on New (then Old) Elvet.[12] Crossing to these neighbouring settlements was by ford and ferry; the first bridge was not built until around 1120, when Bishop Flambard constructed Framwellgate Bridge. This was rebuilt after a flood (c.1400) by Bishop Langley, with towers and gates, and was widened in the mid nineteenth century.[13]

Elvet Bridge was built at some time during Bishop du Puiset's episcopacy (1153–95) and, like Flambard's bridge, served to link the peninsula to the new urban development, in this case the bishop's new borough of Elvet at Old (then New) Elvet. The bridge was probably rebuilt in the thirteenth century, repaired later in the medieval period and widened in the early nineteenth century.[14] It supported two chantry chapels in medieval times and considerable commercial activity was concentrated at the bridgeheads. Together, the two bridges established the east–west axis through the Market Place that has been maintained to the present day.

There was a late medieval bridge linking the area of Kingsgate and Bow Lane to Water Lane in Elvet called Bow Bridge, but little else is known about it.[15] This link was restored, after a somewhat extended delay of over 500 years, by the construction of the award-winning Kingsgate Bridge in 1964, built in concrete to the designs of Ove Arup. At the southern end of the peninsula the medieval monks of the priory gained access to their mill, orchard and fishponds in Crossgate by ferry.[16] In 1574 the Dean and Chapter, newly established in 1541 after the dissolution of the cathedral priory, and successor in title to its vast estates, improved matters with the construction of a permanent footbridge in stone and timber.[17] The need for constant repairs to its timber superstructure led to its being rebuilt with stone arches in 1696.[18] However, this bridge was swept away in the 1771 flood and replaced with a temporary bridge until the new Prebends' Bridge was completed in 1777 to the designs of George Nicholson.[19] The southern abutment of the 1574 bridge survives south of the present bridge (see Fig. 11.1).

The medieval city boasted eight mills, a product of its complex borough development and the requirements of the boroughs' overlords, the bishop, priory

---

12 See Bonney, *Lordship*, pp.12 and 47–9, for a summary of Durham's borough development.

13 W. Page (ed.), *The Victoria History of the County of Durham*, 3 vols (London, 1905–28), iii, p.64.

14 R. Surtees, *The History and Antiquities of the County Palatine of Durham*, 4 vols (London, 1816–40), iv, p.56.

15 Bonney, *Lordship*, p.152.

16 Page (ed.), *Victoria History of Durham*, iii, p.64.

17 Surtees, *History*, iv, p.51.

18 Dean and Chapter Act Books record the decision to build stone arches between the stone abutments (April 1695), timber supply for the arches' centering (November 1695) and the installation of the water pipe in the completed bridge (August 1696).

19 Page (ed.), *Victoria History of Durham*, iii, p.47. The timber supply for the post-1771 flood temporary bridge is noted in the Dean and Chapter Act Books for 1772 (pp.117r and 121).

and Kepier Hospital, that their tenants grind their corn in each borough's own mill.[20] To the north, beyond the peninsular castle, which embraced the cathedral and priory, lay the Bishop's Borough, centred on the Market Place. The priory controlled most of the other boroughs: the Old Borough to the west, and the two Elvet boroughs to the east and south (Borough and Barony). Still further east, St Giles Borough was controlled by Kepier Hospital. As a consequence, there were three mills between the two medieval bridges, situated either end of the river weir below the cathedral. On the peninsula side the priory built two corn mills for its own use, the Lead Mill and later, in about 1416, the Jesus Mill. One was converted by this time to use as a fulling mill, but later reverted to grinding corn. Both were rebuilt in about 1509.[21] The mills were later combined in one building and now stand as the Fulling Mill Archaeological Museum. On the opposite side of the river the South Street Mill, owned by the priory, began life as a fulling mill, but by 1462 was grinding corn for the tenants of Elvet Barony when their old mill silted up. It had two water wheels.[22] Interestingly, Durham, for a number of reasons, never developed much in the way of water-borne trade; the construction of the town's three weirs on the river Wear was certainly one obstacle to this.[23]

The regular visits to South Street mill by the people of Crossgate, as well as nearby quarry workings, would have made the riverbanks a relatively noisy place. The monks at prayer in their priory suffered considerable disturbance from the townspeople using the bishop's own riverbanks on the peninsula below them. In the early sixteenth century the bishop gave the banks to the priory so they might better be able to control their use – and abuse.[24] With that went all the fishing rights around the peninsula.

Before leaving the medieval period, it is worth speculating on one inter-relationship needing further study.[25] The castle at Durham, as has already been said, was not just the motte and inner bailey: it was the whole peninsula, and the river was its natural moat. Only the northern neck of land required substantial fortification. That impassable moat was always effective, provided that the river ran deep and strong, and that it was not bridged or otherwise obstructed. The early Norman city was accessible only by fords on its western and eastern sides. Bishop Flambard's Framwellgate Bridge of c.1120 provided easy access for all, from traders in the town to pilgrims to the cathedral. Conversely, of course, it could also aid those who might attack the town, and therefore it needed fortifi-cation with gate-towers. The increased population of both the peninsula citadel and the surrounding town would have needed a steady supply of flour for bread. To meet this demand, as we have seen, water-powered mills with weirs were

[20] Bonney, *Lordship*, pp.54–8.

[21] Ibid., p.54.

[22] Ibid.

[23] C. Morris (ed.), *The Illustrated Journeys of Celia Fiennes 1685–c.1712* (Stroud, 1982), p.180. Fiennes visited Durham in 1698.

[24] Page, *Victoria History of Durham*, iii, p.27.

[25] The implications behind a planned, integrated relationship between Durham's river-moat, mills, weirs and bridges is further discussed in M. Roberts, *Durham: A Thousand Years of History* (Stroud, 2003), pp.47–8.

provided. The weirs not only provided power to the mills but also ensured a constant supply of the deep water in the river, essential for military security. But these benefits would have resulted in the flooding of the old fords – hence the need to build a bridge.

There is clearly an inter-relationship between river-moat, ford, mill, weir and bridge that needs examining. It is far from clear whether these urban developments were separate, or conceived as a co-ordinated project. In all this we should not ignore the role of Rannalf Flambard, a builder-bishop whose work in twelfth-century Durham demonstrates a holistic view of what we would call today town planning. Without firmer evidence little more can be said, but certainly it was the constant and impassable flow of water around the peninsula that was the essential prerequisite for the defence of the citadel. The success of the medieval river-moat is best illustrated by the great military threat to the peninsula in the early fourteenth century, when the Scottish king Robert Bruce attacked the city on three occasions. There is documentary and physical evidence to show that the city responded with refortification and strengthening of its northern defences.[26] By contrast, along its peninsula walls nothing was done. No towers were added and there was nothing comparable to the substantial circuit of town walls, gates and towers built a little earlier at nearby Newcastle upon Tyne. This absence must testify to the effectiveness of the river as an impassable moat, a military importance that was beginning to wane towards the end of the medieval period.

'Middle Shire', c.1550–1750

The period in Durham's history between the Reformation and the Restoration marked the gradual shift away from the old medieval order to the new. Final unification with Scotland a generation later, in 1707, completed the region's transformation from 'Border to Middle Shire'.[27] In Durham, the dominant duopoly of the bishop and the dean began to decline, civic powers developed and a new era of prosperity began. The arrival of Bishop John Cosin in 1660 also brought a dynamic personality to the city to spearhead the physical improvements needed after the depredations of the Civil War and Commonwealth period. Cosin began work on repairing and improving his accommodation in Durham Castle.[28] After the major building works were complete, it is clear that he turned his attention to the gardens, one of which made a small but significant impact on the riverbanks (see below). Moreover, Cosin's castle improvements recognise the final abandonment of its military role. Nothing symbolised this change of attitude better than the downgrading of the medieval defences and the ingenious introduction of new

---

26 M. Johnson, 'The Great North Gate of Durham Castle', *Transactions of the Architectural and Archaeological Society of Durham and Northumberland*, 4 (1978), pp.108–9.

27 The title of this section is taken, appropriately I hope, from S.J. Watts with Susan J. Watts, *From Border to Middle Shire: Northumberland 1586–1625* (Leicester, 1975).

28 Cosin's building and landscaping works can be identified in both his contracts with his craftsmen, and with the extracts from his day book, printed in Ornsby, *The Correspondence of John Cosin* (Appendix XIII), 'Extracts from Bishop Cosin's Household Book 1665–67', pp.332–56 and (Appendix XIV), 'Series of Agreements relating to the Restoration effected by Bishop Cosin in the Castles of Durham and Auckland', pp.356–82.

Figure 11.2. Durham Castle and Cathedral in the early eighteenth century (detail of painting attributed to Samuel and Nathaniel Buck, reproduced by kind permission of Durham University). This portion of a large *grisaille* painting of the western panorama of the city depicts the riverbanks shorn of vegetation with, directly below the cathedral's central tower and north transept, the crenellated terrace of Bishop's Walk with its espaliered fruit trees, probably the first garden outside the medieval castle walls. Rising centrally above it is the brick belvedere with its well-lit upper room.

gardens within the redundant earthworks. In 1664 Cosin introduced a magnificent fountain into the open courtyard and a year later widened the barbican that led to it.[29] Between 1665 and 1666 he levelled the partially filled moat and turned William the Conqueror's motte into a terraced rose garden.[30]

One final garden, called the Bishop's Walk, is most important to the present study. It is delightfully recorded in early-eighteenth-century paintings, complete, it would seem, with promenading bishops. Sadly it is poorly represented in the documents.[31] It lay south-west of the castle, below and outside the castle wall. A long terrace walk with formal planting was set out here, bounded by crenellated brick walls with stone dressings. Rising above it was a tall octagonal tower with a well-lit upper chamber, an early belvedere, aligned on Cosin's new library and looking out over the river below. Were these the 'battlement' and

---

[29] Ibid. (Appendix XIV), for the fountain (no.18, p.373) and barbican widening (no. 23, p.379).
[30] Ibid. (Appendix XIII), pp.338 et seq.
[31] The existence of this belvedere building is known only in three early-eighteenth-century topographical paintings held in Durham Castle, in the ownership of University College. The building appears to have vanished by the middle of the eighteenth century.

Figure 11.3. Prebends' Walk, Durham, today. Prebends' Walk of c.1680 is still maintained as a terraced garden, its retaining wall (right) later carved with distances by a nineteenth-century cathedral mason to aid the fitness regime of one of the canons who daily dragged a garden roller along its lawn (author's photograph).

'mount' referred to in the bishop's accounts in 1667?[32] The vestiges remain of the enclosing walls; the site of the tower is acknowledged by the angled projection of the castle wall. The collective evidence of the library alignment, the choice of English garden wall bond brickwork, much used by Cosin's builders elsewhere, and the scale of his castle garden works strongly suggest that this first garden outside the castle walls was Cosin's work (Fig. 11.2).

Cosin's work in the castle was no doubt an exemplar and a catalyst for the improvement of much of the city. The condition of the prebendal houses in the College was, after the Interregnum, no better than that of the castle, to judge by the renovation and rebuilding undertaken during the late seventeenth and early eighteenth centuries. Formal gardens would be laid out in imitation of the bishop's work and the Prebends' Walk of c.1680 was constructed outside a length of the medieval castle walls that had collapsed.[33] This is a more substantial engineering work than the Bishop's Walk, wider and longer, and built off steeper ground, and incorporates relieving arches along its length, probably to concentrate its support on solid rock rather than on sand gullies. Its panorama is now lost in the woodland canopy that overwhelms the fine grassed terrace[34] (Fig. 11.3).

---

32 Ornsby, *The Correspondence of John Cosin* (Appendix XIII), p.348 (June 1667).
33 The Dean and Chapter Act Book for 1728 (p.208v) records the enclosure of 'the waste' on the river-banks, also noting the construction of Prebends' Walk 'about 40 years ago'.
34 The continued use of the Walk by the Cathedral Prebends into the nineteenth century is nicely

The essential ingredients of these early riverbanks gardens – a long terraced walk, a sloping site beneath and an outward prospect over flowing water – link the Bishop's and Prebends' Walks back to John Heath IV's new garden at Old Durham, just outside the city.[35] This garden, under construction before the Civil War, was the local exemplar for the peninsula gardens that followed. Before he moved from the city to Old Durham, Heath lived in the buildings now occupied by Hatfield College in North Bailey. The unusual position of these buildings, against the castle wall, not along the bailey, demands far more research than it has received to date. From Bok's 'South East Prospect' of the city it is clear that there was a substantial tower house here by the late seventeenth century.[36] The ability to view the riverbanks directly from the house, rather than from the end of a level rear garden, was a unique situation for a house on the bailey. Given Heath's gardening prowess at Old Durham, he might have pioneered an early terraced garden on the bailey. The existing flat terrace below the castle wall was present in the 1850s. Might it have been a much earlier creation?[37]

Bok's 'South East Prospect' of the city was drawn from Whinney Hill, and probably dates from about 1665. The illustration suggests that at this time the banks were still bare, with trees only on the St Oswald's side. In 1696 St Cuthbert's Well was constructed below the castle's western slopes, perhaps around an existing spring, providing at that time more of a useful urban amenity than the landscape feature it was later to become.[38] At about the same time the intrepid traveller Celia Fiennes visited Durham and remarked that the 'walks are very pleasant by the riverside'.[39] Significantly, there is no mention of trees.

The turn of the eighteenth century is a convenient place to discuss the development of private bailey gardens on the peninsula banks. The limited incursion of Bishop's and Prebends' Walks outside the castle walls and onto the riverbanks has been described, and the possibility of an early garden at Hatfield College has been considered. How did the gardens of North and South Bailey houses develop beyond their castle wall boundaries? There were always 'closes' below the castle wall even in medieval times; these were probably walled or fenced areas of flatter ground on the east and south sides of the peninsula, accessible through the Watergate postern at the end of South Bailey – land where some cultivation could be carried out. The formation of direct links between upper rear bailey gardens and the correspondingly narrow plots below the castle wall, which were

commemorated by a series of carved distances stones cut into the parapet copings. This was apparently done by the cathedral masons at the request of one of the canons, who obtained his daily exercise by dragging a garden roller specific distances along the length of the garden (Roger Norris, pers. comm.).

35   A. Allen and M. Roberts, 'Excavations at Old Durham Gardens 1989–92', *Transactions of the Architectural and Archaeological Society of Durham and Northumberland*, 10 (1994), pp.69–92.

36   V. Bok, *The Prospect of Durham from the South East*, Bodleian Library, Gough Collection, shelfmark Gough Maps 7, fol. 2b. The analysis of this panorama has been undertaken by the present author; see M. Roberts, 'The Prospect of Durham from the South East: A Late-Seventeenth-Century Panorama of the City', *Bulletin of the Durham County Local History Society*, 67 (Autumn 2003), pp.7–27.

37   Ordnance Survey first edition (1857), 1:500 scale.

38   T. Johnson, 'St Cuthbert's Well and the Galilee Well', in *Friends of Durham Cathedral Annual Report* (1990), pp.36–8.

39   Morris, *Celia Fiennes*, p.179.

extensions of the burgage plots within the walls, might be broadly said to have taken place in the period 1660–1750.

Bok's illustration is frustratingly accurate in not showing the full extent of the east slope of the peninsula, as it was screened by the outer banks and the trees behind St Oswald's church. How trustworthy, then, is the very detailed engraving from the same spot by Buck, of c.1723?[40] Here the gardens are shown less in tight burgage plot width strips; rather, they are combined into larger parcels of land, some being open terraces, some orchards. Did Buck move to a new position in order to gain this detail or did he imagine what the gardens might have looked like? Certainly by the mid eighteenth century a number of southern panoramas of the city all display the same sweeping apron of narrow terraced riverbank gardens, admired by their owners from gazebos and belvederes atop the castle walls[41] (Fig. 11.4). This process of extension probably took place along the whole length of the bailey; however, this can only be an assumption given the scarcity of contemporary illustrations of the peninsula from the east and the artistic license in which some illustrators chose to indulge.

'The pure and tranquil stream': 1750 to the present day

Over the following century, from 1750 to 1850, the bailey riverbank gardens situated along what Hutchinson called 'the pure and tranquil stream'[42] remained in cultivation but underwent further transformations, as shown in the wonderfully detailed Ordnance Survey first edition maps of 1857 that provide such rich material for analysis.[43] They also pose many questions, however.[44] For example, how were the gardens south of Bow Lane (modern St Chad's College) actually used? The layout of paths indicates part-private and part-communal areas within the narrow but interlinked gardens. The maps provide considerable detail. They reveal the formality of many of the gardens, which were focused on ponds, fountains or statuary, with paths leading through the castle wall to bank-side

---

40 S. Buck, 'The South East Prospect of the City of Durham from Maiden Castle Hill', drawn c.1728 for *A Prospect of Britain*. The actual vantage point for the panorama is Whinney Hill.

41 Andrew, *Durham Cathedral*, pp.11–15; see also S. and N. Buck 'The South West Prospect of the City of Durham' (1745).

42 W. Hutchinson, *The History and Antiquities of the County Palatine of Durham*, 3 vols (Newcastle upon Tyne and London, 1785–94), ii, p.317.

43 By analysing the maps to identify garden curtilages, linking steps and gateways through the castle wall to lower gardens, it is possible to establish individual property boundaries with their complex history of garden extension, amalgamation, truncation and dislocation.

44 At the time of presenting the paper that was the forerunner of this chapter to the 'Northern Landscapes' conference at Northumbria University in September 2000, there was little structured research into the Bailey Gardens. Since then, the Durham Riverbanks Gardens Project has advanced to its next stage towards implementation, with the production of a feasibility study. Essential to that study was one involving a deeper understanding of the history of the gardens and this has been undertaken by Fiona Green, a noted garden historian and a considerable authority on the planned landscapes of the North East of England. Ms Green (see also Chapter 7 – eds) has generously offered all her work to be absorbed into this published chapter, and the present author has taken advantage of this to check the general truth of the narrative set out here. However, the research on the Bailey Gardens demands separate publication elsewhere, with due acknowledgement to the researcher, and it is to be hoped that the City of Durham Council, who commissioned the work, will allow its publication for a much wider readership in due course.

Figure 11.4. South view of Durham, c.1750 (artist unknown). An anonymous engraving showing the sweep of the lower garden terraces around the southern end of the peninsula. Prebends' Walk is visible below the western towers of the cathedral with the Water Gate in the castle wall giving access to the old Prebends' Bridge, which was swept away in the flood of 1771. Note the adaptation of turrets on the castle wall to garden gazebos. (Despite its unknown author or provenance, this closely detailed engraving can be roughly dated to the middle of the eighteenth century.)

icehouses set in more wooded areas. Informal flowerbeds are also shown. The most notable example of the bailey gardens in 1857 was the great garden of the Bowes family house (No. 4, South Bailey); this was the result of extensive amalgamation of lower garden plots to create a space worthy of landscape gardening on a grand scale. The broad and long terraced walk (now the Principal's Walk of St John's College) overlooks narrow paths cutting down diagonally across the slope towards the river's edge.

The effect of this expansion was to deny many bailey householders the chance of enjoying the lower slopes, their predecessors having presumably sold, leased or sub-let their land to the acquisitive Bowes family. This was a problem faced by the Shipperdsons who, probably in the early nineteenth century (c.1820–30), found that their lower garden formed the southern end of the great Bowes terrace. They therefore appear to have created a path across the end of their neighbour's upper garden along the top of the castle wall which then descends into their own generous grounds, a dislocated plot some distance from their house. These grounds they beautified with informal planting, an icehouse with an Egyptian or Mycenean-style tomb-portal and a gardener's cottage designed as a classical Greek temple (the erroneously named 'Count's House'), possibly from a design by the Durham-based architect Ignatius Bonomi.[45] The informality of their planting was by this time reflecting the broader naturalistic woodland planting of the riverbanks, and the story of that wider landscape should now resume (Fig. 11.5).

By about 1750 the garden developments on the east side of the peninsula had not been matched on the west, where there were no conventional residential plots, only the sweeping banks below the cathedral and castle. Here was a barren landscape ripe for improvement.[46] The cathedral prebend, Dr Joseph Spence, an accomplished garden designer and advocate of the new informality of landscape design, may have been one of the first to begin these improvements to the riverbanks, which included paths and tree-planting, during his residency (1754–68).[47] Certainly by 1780, Sullivan, surveying the riverbanks,

---

[45] The curious life of Count Joseph Boruwlaski is best told in a short account by T.M. Heron, *The Little Count* (Durham, 1986). This celebrated Polish dwarf lived on South Bailey and also on a house that stood on the riverbanks close to the end of the old pre-1771 Prebends' Bridge. It was demolished in about 1850 but the close proximity of the Shipperdsons' little Doric Temple in their lower garden meant that this soon acquired the name 'The Count's House' in the absence of his actual home. Bonomi's authorship of the building is not documented but stylistically it fits with his work, and he was a tenant of the Shipperdsons at 10 South Bailey before moving to 6 North Bailey (C.R. Hudleston, 'Eighteenth and Nineteenth Century Residents of the South Bailey (Durham)', *Transactions of the Architectural and Archaeological Society of Durham and Northumberland*, 2, parts 3 and 4 (1962), p.247–55).

[46] Andrew, *Durham Cathedral*, which illustrates two of the three topographical paintings showing treeless riverbanks which are on display in Durham Castle. Two of them are also illustrated in R. Brigstock, *Durham Castle: Fortress, Palace, College* (Durham, 2007), pp.46 and 111.

[47] There is only a single reference in the Chapter Acts books to a meeting at which Spence was in attendance, when path improvements from St Oswald's to Prebends' Bridge were agreed. We have no record of whether Spence spoke in favour of this, though it would seem likely he did. Professor Michael Tooley, a noted garden historian and Durham academic, told the present author that he believed Spence was responsible for instigating the tree planting below the Cathedral, but no documentary evidence has yet been produced to support this view.

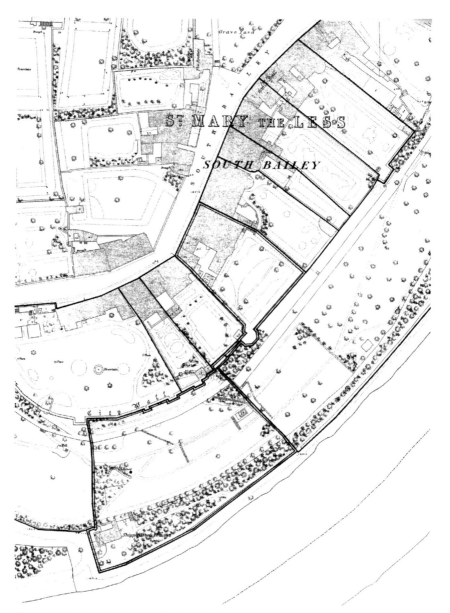

Figure 11.5. The highly detailed 1:500 Ordnance Survey first edition town map of Durham (1857), showing the southern end of South Bailey, with its houses and their upper and lower gardens either side of the castle wall. Property boundaries have been highlighted, notably the Shipperdsons' house at No. 9 South Bailey (double lined), showing how the great lower garden of the Bowes house (southern half shown), probably a mid-eighteenth-century creation, prevented the Shipperdsons' expansion in the early nineteenth century. As a result, they had to negotiate a narrow dog-leg access with neighbours along the castle wall to a new dislocated lower garden complete with ice house and Doric temple summer house, then named Shipperdson's Cottage but now known as the Count's House, both structures of c.1820–30.

noted that 'the good people (of Durham) have not been inattentive to their improvement.'[48]

The eighteenth-century 'improvers' in Durham saw in the riverbanks many of the components that create the classic romantic landscape. The site had dramatic topography, a sheet of water framed by an ancient bridge, and was overlooked by great historic monuments, with their abandoned defences and shattered shrine, all highly evocative of past times. The scope for melancholy contemplation of the great history of Durham, now gone – its immense Norman monuments, St Cuthbert's pilgrimage and the border citadel – was considerable. This landscape lacked only the trees to soften and unite those elements and the paths from which to admire the landscape, stopping at composed panoramas or moving along past rocky springs, secluded dells and rushing weirs. The necessary work here – tree-planting and path-making – was therefore a far easier task than was faced by other contemporary landscape designers elsewhere, who had to import water, create the topography and usually build the ruins or temples too. Young trees begin to appear on engravings of the period around 1775, which implies planting ten to twenty years earlier[49] (Fig. 11.6). However, even in 1846, when Billings was drawing Durham Cathedral, the tree canopy is still light and the planting gener-ously spaced.[50] On the eastern peninsula side there were pockets of trees in 1750 but here the more gentle slopes below the castle walls were cultivated for gardens up to the mid nineteenth century. Their subsequent change to woodland is more as a result of abandonment than deliberate intent.

It is worth noting that the Great Flood of 1771 may have uprooted several young trees on the immediate banks of the river, although the majority of the new planting was higher up the slope away from danger. That flood also led to the building of the present Prebends' Bridge, its predecessor having been swept away in the torrent. Whatever practical considerations led to a new site for the new bridge, its position in the landscape garden of the riverbanks was perfect. It offered the eighteenth-century visitor an unrivalled, and seemingly quite delib-erate, panorama.[51] Above the Arcadian Fulling Mill, shrouded in woodland and washed by the river Wear, rose the ancient cathedral – the whole composition being closed with a distant view of Framwellgate Bridge.

Into the emerging wooded landscape of the riverbanks appropriate features were introduced during the eighteenth and early nineteenth centuries. The Count's House has been mentioned above, and this building was supplemented by a

48 R.J. Sullivan, *Observations during a Tour through parts of England, Scotland and Wales in a Series of Letters* (London, 1780), p.47.
49 S.H. Grimm, 'Topographical Drawings in Pencil and Ink, in Various Counties in England, for Sir Richard Kaye' (late eighteenth century), British Library Ref. Add 15538. County Durham. Grimm sketched the riverbanks from a number of positions in the city, c.1780, showing young trees of about twenty years' growth on the banks below the cathedral.
50 R.W. Billings, *Illustrations of the Architectural Antiquities of the County of Durham: Ecclesiastical, Castellated and Domestic* (London, 1846), frontispiece.
51 In the interest of objectivity, it is worth noting that, in an enjoyable site discussion between the present author and Mr Tom Hay several years ago, Mr Hay suggested that, following the collapse of the old Prebends' Bridge, the need to relocate the bridge away from its old site could have been dictated as much by an avoidance of fast currents in the river at the southern extremity of the peninsula as by any aesthetic considerations. Perhaps it was elements of both, but undoubtedly the new position offers substantial panoramas appropriate to the then-fashionable English landscape movement.

Figure 11.6. S.H. Grimm's (attributed) sketch of c.1775–80 of the Broken Walls footpath, below Durham Castle, looking north towards Framwellgate Bridge. This drawing, showing the young tree growth on the peninsula, is attributed to S.H. Grimm, but is not one of the many Durham drawings in his large portfolio in the British Library's Kaye Collection. It may be by Grimm's own hand, or else is a contemporary copy of one of his drawings, many of which were redrawn at a later date.

number of well-heads and springs that were all identified as points of interest on the perambulation. The whole scene could be contemplated from the gardens and gazebos of the bailey houses, set above the castle walls and towers. These ancient walls were yet another feature in the landscape and, if they lacked a suitably medieval appearance, they were embellished with new battlements.[52] This appreciation of the romantic landscape in Durham was never better, if excessively, expressed than in Hutchinson's *History of County Durham*, published in 1787. Quoting Thomas Pennant, author and friend of the garden designer Thomas Wright, he says of the riverbanks (starting at St Oswald's, where the landscape was probably more mature than on the west side): 'they are covered with wood, through which are cut numbers of walks, contrived with judgement, and happy in the most beautiful and solemn scenery. They impend over the water, and receive most venerable improvement from the Castle and ancient Cathedral, which tower far above'.[53] Hutchinson himself continues:

the banks are steep and clothed with forest trees; in several parts the rocks break forth, where venerable oaks are suspended: The river, with a pure and

---

[52] The detailed analysis of the castle wall, in those lengths above the Bailey Gardens, has been undertaken by Richard Annis as part of the Durham Riverbanks Gardens Feasibility Study commissioned by the City of Durham Council (unpublished).

[53] Hutchinson, *History and Antiquities*, ii, p.316.

tranquil stream, glides at the bottom of the hill, reflecting the noble objects which crown her banks: Here the opening valley pours forth a rivulet, and there the solemn dell, with nature's wildest beauties, yawns with broken rocks, which yield the living fountain from their lips, whilst each brow is crowded with bending oaks, whose naked talons and twisted arms rival each other in grotesque figure. You see the towers of the cathedral rising sublimely from the wood, and lifting their solemn battlements to the clouds; and beyond those the turrets of the castle, on their rocky base; whilst on the other hand, the houses of South Street are stretched along the summits of hanging gardens. In front is an elegant new bridge of three arches, through the bows of which, at the first distance, are seen a fine canal of still water, with a mill; at the second distance, ... This prospect, perhaps, is not to be equalled in the environs of any city in the known world. [54]

By the mid nineteenth century, with the growing maturity of the tree canopy, the essential transformation of the riverbanks from defensive moat to one of our most treasured romantic landscapes was complete.

In 1857 orchard planting survived below South Street and also below Hatfield College in North Bailey, whose upper terrace may represent an early garden outside the walls.[55] Also visible on the 1857 plans are two cleared allées through the trees, one below St Cuthbert's Well and the other, more mysteriously, below Windy Gap. Is it possible that the latter may have been cleared to enable an ancient 'Beating the Bounds' ceremony up the banks? In the later nineteenth century Canon Tristram and the Rev. H.S.A. Fox carried out more plantings and further extended the network of walks along the banks for the benefit of local people.[56] Tree-planting during this period included that of both native and non-native species. Beech, oak, horse chestnut, sycamore, birch and willow are still dominant on the banks. Other species introduced include holly, hornbeam, lime, cherry, sweet chestnut, yew and some conifers. During the nineteenth century rhododendrons, bamboo and other exotic species were also introduced, and have survived.[57]

The riverbanks in Durham, though developing in the eighteenth and nineteenth centuries as informal landscaped woodland, were never much removed from the city in which they lay. Industry was never far away. Coal had been worked near to the Wear gorge from at least the latter years of the seventeenth century and probably earlier. Over succeeding centuries collieries under Bow School and Elvet Banks were able to work to between 15 and 20m below river level to extract from the rich 1m-thick Hutton coal seam.[58] From 1823 to 1908 the Elvet Landscape Colliery was working shafts under the present University Library and further west.[59] A circle of masonry marks the old pumping shaft

54 Ibid., p.317.
55 Ordnance Survey first edition.
56 Canon Tristram's influence is noted in Fiona Green's research and was also highlighted to the author by Michael Tooley, who cited Tristram's letter to the *Durham Advertiser* on 16 February 1906 imploring the public to protect the plants and animals on the banks. Tristram's biography has been set down by F.S. Bodenheimer in the *Durham University Journal* (June 1957).
57 Johnson, 'The Durham Banks', p.32.
58 Ibid., p.31.
59 Ibid.

behind the Anchorage. No extraction of coal ever took place under the peninsula itself. In 1985 a brick-arched tunnel, visible at the western end of Prebends' Bridge, was opened up. It was probably a water level, used to draw off water that was seeping into nearby coal mines.[60] Brief mention should also be made of one of the city's largest buildings, although it has not survived. This was a huge cotton mill on the south side of St Oswald's churchyard, built in 1796 and burnt to the ground in 1804. Its gable retaining wall still survives on the riverbanks.[61]

Since the Ordnance Survey first edition map was produced in 1857 the major change in the riverbanks' landscape has been the abandonment of the bailey gardens and orchards to naturalised woodland. By the early years of the twentieth century the bailey houses had been transformed to predominantly institutional ownership, with all but one of the properties coming under control of the University or one of its two independent colleges, St John's and St Chad's. The Dean and Chapter estate, as successors to the medieval cathedral priory, has remained unaltered. The Dean and Chapter's management of most of the riverbanks has in recent years extended to the siting of a number of sculptures by their artists-in-residence. During the period 1986–7 Colin Wilbourn sited two such works. These are a logical development of the riverbanks' landscape history; *The Upper Room* in particular was a brilliantly imaginative composition of thirteen elm trunks carved with a representation of the Last Supper. However, this sculpture was always intended to be temporary, and so it proved to be. Despite generating considerable public affection, it suffered from the natural processes of timber decay, leading to its recent removal. On the outer banks near Prebends' Bridge another sculptor, Richard Cole (in 1992–3), reassembled and pierced the old stonework of the north-east pinnacle of the Nine Altars to frame a view of the cathedral. The care and conservation of the precious landscape of the Durham riverbanks has been set out in a Management Plan (2001), an important partnership agreement between owners and local authorities.[62] The wider significance of the riverbanks' landscape has now been formally acknowledged in the recently published *Durham Cathedral and Castle World Heritage Site Management Plan* not only as a setting to the cathedral and castle, but as an historic landscape in its own right.[63]

Conclusion

The choice of the riverbanks at Durham as a subject to illustrate the theme of 'Northern Landscapes' arguably relates well to the sub-title of this book: 'Representations and Realities'. The popular visual *representation* of the riverbanks has always implied that its landscape, of solid wooded banks, was an acci-

[60] P.G. Woodward, 'Stalactites and Stalagmites in the River Banks', in *Friends of Durham Cathedral Annual Report* (1984–5), pp.22–4.

[61] I. Atkinson and R. Norris, 'The Account of the Messrs Salvin's Cotton Mill', *Transactions of the Architectural and Archaeological Society of Durham and Northumberland*, new series, 6 (1982), pp.1–3.

[62] City of Durham Council, *City of Durham Riverbanks Management Plan* (2001).

[63] C. Blandford Associates, *Durham Cathedral and Castle World Heritage Site Management Plan* (2006).

dent of nature, a purely vegetative counterbalance to the 'real' history that was set out in the buildings on the peninsula above, and the essential characteristics of that representation – 'leaf against stone' – remain powerful and seductive images. Any historical analysis of the peninsula does, however, confirm that the *reality* of the development of the riverbanks is a strong reflection of Durham's history and its changing role over the centuries.

The Durham riverbanks served first as a moat to the peninsular fortress that protected St Cuthbert's Shrine. The effectiveness of this natural barrier can be gauged by the modesty of the walled fortifications that stood above them. Only at the neck of the peninsula were heavily fortified walls, towers and gates needed. In maintaining a deep flowing river around the castle, building weirs with their attendant mills and bridges, the early Norman bishops showed considerable sophistication in their defence of the city. When Durham's pivotal role in the defence of England's northern border gradually evaporated during the sixteenth and seventeenth centuries the redundant earthworks of the castle and the treeless slopes of the riverbanks were transformed and their defensive walls were breached. It was now safe to look out beyond the high-walled peninsula and see a larger landscape. Defensive earthworks were remodelled to recreational use. Direct English parallels are not easy to identify,[64] but the sixteenth-century reworking of the terraced slopes of Raglan Castle in Gwent, executed between 1549 and 1589, for example, was echoed later by the terraced walks of Durham Castle and the new Bishop's and Prebends' Walks out beyond the castle walls into the riverbanks. In France the similar abandonment of medieval defensive earthworks led to the establishment of broad tree-lined boulevards below many circuits of town walls. However, where France maintained the formality of its landscape tradition well into the eighteenth century, in England a growing awareness of the beauty of the natural landscape developed into a new approach to garden design, inspired, paradoxically, by continental artists.

Durham's natural landscape of the river gorge, supplemented by the great peninsular monuments of the castle and cathedral, offered wonderful gifts in the eighteenth century to those responsible for the maintenance and improvement of the riverbanks. Walks provided vital movement through the landscape, creating new views and framing new pictures of ancient buildings in a natural setting. Rural landowners throughout the country were seeking similar improvements to their estates. In Yorkshire, for example, visitors to Thomas Duncombe III's estate at Rievaulx were taken along a high wooded terrace, newly laid out in 1750, to look down, in periodic glimpses, at the ruins of the great Cistercian abbey. At Studley Royal, in the same county, the Aislabie family completed their landscape garden and brought their visitors around the natural bend of the Skell valley to confront them with the magnificent climax of the ruins of Fountains Abbey. Closer to Durham, the Carr family at Cocken concluded their perambulation around the estate with a framed view of the similarly ruined Finchale

---

64 Nick Owen has kindly noted, in answer to a search for English parallels, that the Norman motte at Moccas Park, Herefordshire, had a summerhouse built on it and a lake around it as part of eighteenth-century landscaping works, and that the moat of the medieval Bishop's Palace at Lichfield Cathedral was modified to create garden terraces in the 1680s.

Priory. In Durham, by judicious tree planting, the careful laying-out of paths and the aesthetic judgements made in the resiting of Prebends' Bridge, visitors were offered those same experiences right in the heart of the city. With a deftness of touch that can be misleading, the riverbanks of Durham have been modelled and remodelled over the centuries, so creating a planned man-made landscape of subtlety and complexity, always worthy of continuing study.

12

The Darlington Landscape

GILLIAN COOKSON

Darlington has been, and is still, a town of many aspects, and a town largely untypical of the North East. An Anglo-Saxon settlement, a medieval bishop's borough, a thriving market town of the early modern period – it was all these before the famous railway and a revolutionary nineteenth-century iron age. With this swift expansion came close-packed workers' terraces, a fine Victorian middle-class west end and redevelopment of the central area. Growth continued apace, the town emerging relatively unscathed even from the inter-war depression which ravaged much of the region. A broad-based economy, in which markets and passing trade from the Great North Road have been consistent features, has underpinned the town's prosperity for centuries. Even in the heyday of railways, iron and engineering, Darlington, never entirely dependent upon heavy industry, was markedly less vulnerable than neighbouring towns to the forces of recession.[1]

Through periods of reinvention, rebuilding has generally taken the form of infilling, addition and evolution rather than wholesale redevelopment, so that within the modern town are exposed layers of its history. Admittedly there is nothing now to be seen of the Anglo-Saxon settlement, presumed to have been near to a pre-Conquest burial ground, one of the largest and richest found north of the Tees, discovered off Bondgate.[2] Anglo-Saxon sculptures have been found around St Cuthbert's church, Darlington's sole surviving medieval building,[3] and there is archaeological evidence of an earlier, possibly Anglo-Saxon, church in the market area.[4] Certainly there was a church in Darlington long before Bishop du Puiset refounded St Cuthbert's in c.1192.[5]

---

1   For the economic history of Darlington, see G. Cookson (ed.), *Victoria County History of County Durham*, iv, *Darlington* (Woodbridge, 2005) (hereafter *VCH Durham*, iv). The town's landscape history is explored in G. Cookson, *The Townscape of Darlington* (Woodbridge, 2003).

2   R. Miket and M. Pocock, 'An Anglo-Saxon cemetery at Greenbank, Darlington', *Medieval Archaeology*, 20 (1976), pp.62–74. For the town's early landscape, see C.M. Newman, 'Darlington before 1600', in Cookson, *Townscape*, pp.3–39.

3   R. Cramp, *Corpus of Anglo-Saxon Stone Sculpture*, 7 vols (Oxford, 1984–2006), i, pp.62–3.

4   M. Adams, 'Darlington Market Place: Archaeological Excavations, 1994', report in Durham SMR, 4000, 4812.

5   E. Wooler and A.C. Boyde, *Historic Darlington* (London, 1913), pp.75–6; H.D. Pritchett, *The Story of the Church of St Cuthbert, Darlington* (Darlington, 1965), p.12; P.F. Ryder, 'St Cuthbert, Darlington: An Archaeological Assessment', report in Durham Diocesan Office, DAC section (1997), pp.14–15.

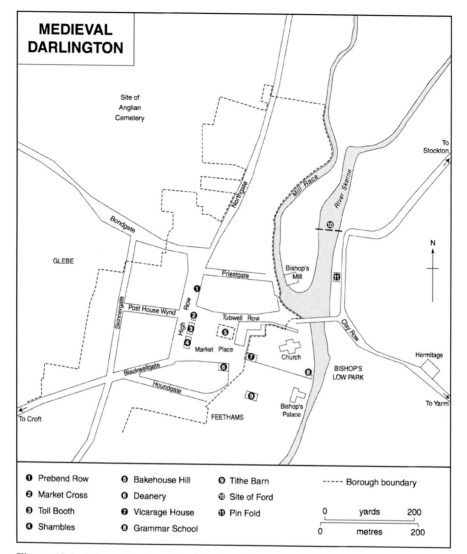

Figure 12.1. Schematic plan of medieval Darlington.

The borough of Darlington, with its dyeworks, mill and common bakehouse, is mentioned first in Boldon Book, c.1183.[6] Du Puiset, who was probably responsible for setting out the borough within his copyhold vill of Bondgate, is thought to have also built the bishop's palace, or manor house, in about 1164.[7] The palace was the focal point of an ecclesiastical complex including St Cuthbert's church; a medieval vicarage and later, fifteenth-century, deanery; a tithe barn; and a grammar school probably of sixteenth-century date, all of which were situated on land, mainly copyhold, just to the south east of the clearly defined rows of the twelfth-century borough. At the centre of the borough was a rectangular market place surrounded on three sides by freehold burgage plots, with main roads heading in all directions, one of them south across the river Skerne via a bridge which was at latest fourteenth-century[8] (see Fig. 12.1). There was a market cross by 1313,[9] and a tollbooth, focal point of the market place and of local administration, which was demolished and rebuilt during the episcopate of Thomas Langley (1406–37).[10] This new two-storey structure contained a courthouse, a dozen shops or workshops, the town gaol and the granary.[11] The settlement of Bondgate was a typical vill arrangement, with two rows of plots facing each other across a green which narrowed into the lane leading to Cockerton.[12] By the late 1530s, Darlington, its outstanding features already dating back several centuries, was recognised by the Tudor antiquary John Leland as 'the best market town in the bishopric, saving Durham'.[13]

Over the river to the east, partly incorporated into the borough, was Clay Row, at the south end of which stood the Hermitage, adjoining the bishop's Low and High Parks. Other than those in Clay Row, most houses of the town were on the narrow-fronted rectangular burgage plots of the borough, or on copyhold land in the street of Bondgate itself.[14] Darlington's medieval street pattern survives pretty much intact to this day. Behind High Row, or Borough Row, with its vista of the whole market place, vennels – the largest of which was Wynd, now Post House Wynd – led to the back road of the borough, Skinnergate, which adjoined the open fields of the glebe. The area between High Row and Skinnergate became packed with cottages, workshops, stables and outbuildings as pressure on space increased. These – presumably mainly wooden – structures fell victim to a 'most fierce and terrible fire' in 1585, said to have consumed

6   W. Greenwell (ed.), *Boldon Buke: A Survey of the Possessions of the See of Durham made by Order of Bishop Hugh Pudsey, 1183* (Surtees Soc., 25, 1852), p.17; W. Page (ed.), *The Victoria History of the County of Durham*, 3 vols (London, 1905–28), i, pp.259–341; D. Austin (ed.), *Boldon Book: Northumberland and Durham* (Chichester, 1982).
7   Greenwell (ed.), *Boldon Buke*, p.17; Page, *Victoria History of Durham*, i, pp.308, 339.
8   Cookson, *Townscape*, pp.12, 18–19.
9   T.D. Hardy (ed.), *Registrum Palatinum Dunelmense* (Rolls Ser., 1882–5) ii, pp.205, 662–3.
10 Durham Univ. Lib. ASC, CCB B/48/2 (188788).
11 Durham SMR, 1514; N. Sunderland, *Tudor Darlington*, 2 parts (Durham, 1974), i, p.7.
12 Cookson, *Townscape*, pp.12–15.
13 L. Toulmin Smith (ed.), *The Itinerary of John Leland in or about the Years 1535–1543*, i (London, 1907), p.69.
14 Cookson, *Townscape*, pp.34–7.

Figure 12.2. View of Darlington from the south east (engraving by John Bailey, c.1760).

273 houses, including the best of the town, in just two hours.[15] Although damage seems to have been confined to part of the borough – the ecclesiastical buildings, relatively isolated at the bottom corner of the market place, survived, as evidently did much copyhold property – the fire made 800 people homeless and destroyed many livelihoods, including inns and hostelries.[16]

Some rebuilding was soon under way, notably of the prestigious frontages on High Row, but the town endured long-lasting ill effects from the fire. It appears that Darlington had not fully recovered its former size almost a century later.[17] Matters were not helped by a series of poor harvests in the 1620s and privations suffered during Scottish incursions, civil war and plague during the 1640s.[18] But the town's staple industries thrived. Leather – which succeeded woollen cloth as the main manufactured product – and, increasingly, linen and worsted spinning and weaving were supplemented by a variety of other trades and services, consistent with the town's growing importance as the market centre of a large

[15] *Lamentable N[ewes] from the Towne of Darnton in the Bishopricke of Durham* (1585) (copy in BL); N. Sunderland, *A History of Darlington* (Darlington, 1967), pp.35–6; Sunderland, *Tudor Darlington*, i, p.13.

[16] TNA: PRO, SP 12/275/44; *Lamentable N[ewes] from the Towne of Darnton*, pp.5–6.

[17] TNA: PRO, E 179/106/28; A.G. Green, 'Houses and Households in Co. Durham and Newcastle, c.1570–1730' (unpublished PhD thesis, University of Durham, 2000), p.87, also pp.67, 75.

[18] *Cal S.P. Dom.* 1640–1, 127, 201; 1644, 130; 1644–5, 329.

hinterland, and as a post town on the Great North Road.[19] The seventeenth century saw the establishment of a number of inns and large houses fronting the market place. The deanery, which after the Reformation fell into lay occupation, became a private residence – it was later subdivided – while the bishop's palace, restored by Bishop Cosin in 1668, was converted into the town's poorhouse.[20]

Through the eighteenth century came a sharp increase in population, though the town barely extended beyond the bounds of its late medieval development (see Fig. 12.2). A local census of 1767, probably slightly overestimating, counted 3,280 people spread between 885 households.[21] The additional population was accommodated in the increasingly crowded area behind High Row, and in unhealthy yards stretching from Northgate towards the Skerne, where factories and textile workshops also grew up near the site of the medieval corn mill, which by 1800 was largely converted to leather and worsted use. The concentration of new structures and more people, mainly within the freehold plots of the borough, seems not to have deterred the town's wealthiest citizens from building themselves prestigious houses in the central area during the late eighteenth century. George Allan of Blackwell Grange had his town house in Houndgate; the bailiff of Darlington, Henry Ornsby, lived off Horsemarket; there were five large Pease residences, including ones at Houndgate, Feethams – near the bishop's palace – and Northgate; and the other leading Quaker family, the linen-manufacturing Backhouses, had properties in Northgate.[22]

Many of these fine houses were to fall into commercial use during the iron and engineering boom of the mid nineteenth century, as industrialists moved their families away from an increasingly insanitary and polluted town into suburban villas and mansions. This trend can first be discerned c.1780, with the building of Polam Hall and West Lodge on the fringes of the central area. Both of these houses were soon rebuilt and extended by members of the Backhouse family. Other new and larger properties followed, mainly to the west and south of the town. The Peases, Quaker worsted manufacturers, developed their own mansions from the 1830s, at first along Northgate, while the next generation moved to grander premises with extensive grounds beyond the town's west end.[23]

As late as 1850 Darlington's suburbs amounted to little more than a belt of mansions in their own grounds and a handful of small middle-class housing developments off Coniscliffe Lane and along Northgate, these few set against a background of unspoilt agricultural acres (see Fig. 12.3). In the town itself there had been moves to improve public buildings, with a new town hall replacing the dilapidated tollbooth in 1808, the shambles rebuilt in 1815, and a dispen-

19 See *VCH Durham*, iv, on Darlington trades and industries.
20 W.H.D. Longstaffe, *The History and Antiquities of the Parish of Darlington* (Darlington, 1854), p.153; see also W. Hutchinson, *The History and Antiquities of the County Palatine of Durham*, 3 vols (Newcastle upon Tyne and London, 1785–94), iii, p.189.
21 Darlington Lib., E810024034; E800004006; North Yorkshire County Record Office, ZDG (A) IV/7; c.f. Longstaffe, *Darlington*, p.299.
22 Durham County Record Office, D/Ki 31; Cookson, *Townscape*, p.57.
23 Cookson, *Townscape*, pp.64–5, 86–91; V. Chapman, *Rural Darlington: Farm, Mansion and Suburb* (Durham, 1975), pp.37–49; N. Pevsner, rev. E. Williamson, *The Buildings of England: County Durham* (London, 1985 edn), pp.151–4.

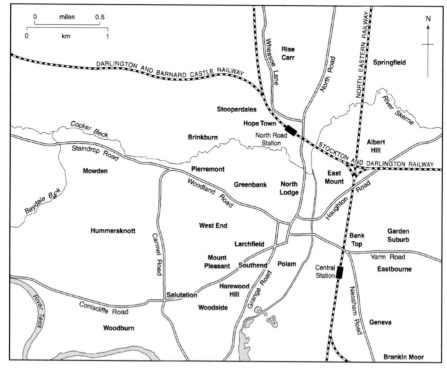

Figure 12.3. The suburbs of Darlington, c.1830.

sary and lock-up added to the market-place facilities.[24] The former bishop's palace, long in use as the poorhouse, was bought by the town in 1808 and much extended.[25] With an expansion of St Cuthbert's churchyard in 1813, the grammar school moved to a new building further south, where it was joined in 1824 by an adjacent national school.[26] The Friends' meeting-house in Skinnergate, a building of c.1760, whose members held a growing influence in town affairs, was substantially altered in the early years of the nineteenth century and refronted in 1839.[27] The imposing Bondgate Methodist church was built in Saltyard in 1812, on a corner of the glebe land bought from the lay rector the earl of Darlington, of the Vane family, later raised to dukes of Cleveland.[28]

---

[24] Durham County Record Office, D/Ki 317, 61; F. Mewburn, *The Larchfield Diary* (London, 1876), p.5; H. Spencer, *Men that are Gone from the Households of Darlington* (Darlington, 1862), p.167; W.J. Mountford, 'Biographical and Historical Notes on Bygone Darlington', typescript in Darlington Lib. (c.1912), p.10; *Parson and White's Dir. Northumbs. and Durham* (1827) i, p.241; Longstaffe, *Darlington*, pp.317–18; Teesside Archives, U/OME 4/10; Durham County Record Office, D/Ki 313, p.106.

[25] Longstaffe, *Darlington*, p.188; Spencer, *Men that are Gone*, pp.259–60; Durham County Record Office, D/Ki 313, p.106; Barclays Bank Archives, 388/730.

[26] Spencer, *Men that are Gone*, pp.244, 258.

[27] Pevsner and Williamson, *County Durham*, p.144; Spencer, *Men that are Gone*, pp.452–3.

[28] Pevsner and Williamson, *County Durham*, pp.143–4; Spencer, *Men that are Gone*, pp.429–30.

Pressure of increasing population – 4,670 people recorded in the township in 1801 had become 5,750 by 1821 and 8,574 a decade later – did not bring a commensurate rise in housing. There were only two building schemes of this era which had any sense of the systematic about them. The first was that in the Commercial Street district, where Bondgate meets Northgate, from about 1820.[29] It is unclear who led the project, which may have amounted only to laying out streets with little infrastructure, the plots sold piecemeal. Although one, Albion Street, was described as 'once the most aristocratic street in the town ... quiet, reserved and very select' with posts barring the way to all cabs and carts at the Northgate end,[30] it was later noted that nearby 'between King Street and Queen Street, where the houses stood back-to-back, were open middens which served the houses on either side; into these middens went everything that wasn't wanted.'[31] In fact the Commercial Street development was a strange melange of impressive town houses, modest cottages, and commercial and public buildings, including a number of chapels and schools and a mechanics' institute.[32] The second significant housing scheme started with Park Street, on the bishop's Low Park, marshy land east of the Skerne, an area which over the following decades became crowded with working-class terraces in a more uniform style.[33]

The impact of the railway

Darlington's claim to historical fame, from which is derived the modern popular image of the town, rests in this decade. The Stockton and Darlington railway, opened in 1825, was the first to connect two towns and is considered a significant historical milestone. Yet as with most milestones, the birth of the railway, on closer inspection, turns out to have been a matter of great complexity in its roots, its execution and its effects.[34] This great symbol of the railway age might never have been thought of had more progress been made with a canal scheme, the subject of serious but intermittent discussions from the 1760s. The impetus for the canal came from merchants and manufacturers in the main Tees valley towns – Stockton, Yarm and Darlington – seeking to ease transportation problems which limited trade and prevented the opening of the Auckland coalfield, for the Tees was not navigable above Stockton. Though detailed plans were drawn for a canal, which would have skirted the southern edge of Darlington town, the idea was several times taken up and then dropped on the grounds of cost. Only in 1818 was it finally decided to proceed instead with a railway, and not until almost the eve of the start of works was the scheme amended to take the line through the northern outskirts of Darlington, rather than bypass the town altogether.

29 Longstaffe, *Darlington*, p.311.
30 Mountford, 'Biographical and Historical Notes', p.164.
31 C.P. Nicholson, *Those Boys o' Bondgate* (Arbroath, 1949), p.78.
32 Longstaffe, *Darlington*, pp.249, 251; Spencer, *Men that are Gone*, p.449.
33 Cookson, *Townscape*, pp.70, 82–3.
34 These issues are discussed in detail in *VCH Durham*, iv; and see M.W. Kirby, *The Origins of Railway Enterprise: The Stockton and Darlington Railway, 1821–1863* (Cambridge, 1993).

While the Stockton and Darlington railway soon demonstrated its potential for coal transportation, and quickly became highly profitable, its full impact on the Darlington landscape and economy did not unfold for perhaps another thirty or forty years. In technological terms the line was far from revolutionary, building as it did on existing wagon-way practice used elsewhere in the North-East coalfield, so there was at first little indication of what was to come. Indeed, most traction was by horse, as steam locomotives proved unreliable, and it can be argued that the Stockton and Darlington's main contribution to modern railway development was as a testing ground for Timothy Hackworth's and the Stephensons' new locomotives in the late 1820s. Not until 1828 was it decided to phase out horse haulage, with horse-drawn wagons finally abolished from the main line as late as 1833, though continuing on branch lines to 1856. Few passengers were carried, railway management was subcontracted out, and a canal-type practice of allowing public rights of way on the line continued into the 1830s.[35]

The railway moved coal, lime and lead, none of which was extracted in or near Darlington, so that it had limited immediate effects upon the town, and those effects were economic rather than environmental. Ownership and control soon concentrated in the hands of a few Darlington Quaker promoters, notably the Pease family, who made healthy profits during the 1830s. The railway's immediate benefits to other inhabitants included an easier traffic in manufactured goods and the slashing of coal prices, both of which certainly helped other local trades.[36] But Darlington, already a prosperous town with a broad-based economy, was not a railway town in the sense of a Crewe or a Swindon: not for another several decades did railways and railway engineering become major employers of labour, and they never did provide workers' housing on any scale. In fact, before 1840, the Stockton and Darlington railway, extended in 1830 to Joseph Pease's new 'Port Darlington' near the mouth of the Tees (see Chapter 14), had far greater consequences for Stockton – which it killed as a coal port – and Middlesbrough, which it made.

In Darlington, where most industries – textile factories, breweries, foundries, and brick, tile and tan yards – were centrally situated, the railway was unusual in its location half a mile north of the town. A cluster of activity grew around the North Road station and its short branch line to coal depots near the Northgate bridge.[37] There was a railway hotel,[38] and then the first, and until the 1850s only, major engineering works in the town, established by a local Quaker iron-founder and railway subcontractor, Alfred Kitching.[39] A little later came a lime depot and goods station, a worsted factory and gasworks, a few railway company houses and cottages with gardens, and then speculators' terraced houses nearby which formed the embryonic industrial suburb of Hope Town. These settlements remained, for a time, physically separate from the town centre.[40]

---

35   Kirby, *Origins*, pp.3, 67, 90–91, 94.
36   *Parson and White's Dir. Northumbs. and Durham* (1827) i, p.244; *Pigot's Dir. Durham, Northumbs. and Yorks.* (1834), p.11.
37   Darlington Lib., E810026864.
38   Durham County Record Office, D/Ho/F 123/2; Darlington Lib., E810033877.
39   See *VCH Durham*, iv.
40   Darlington Lib., E810041663; OS Map 1:2500, Durham LV.6 (1858 edn).

Such development was as nothing, though, by comparison with the forces unleashed upon Darlington's physical and industrial landscape by the construction of the north–south York and Newcastle Railway. In 1841 the Darlington to York section of the Great North of England Railway opened, later amalgamating with Hudson's 1842 Newcastle and Darlington Junction Railway.[41] This new line ran higher than and slightly east of the town centre – close enough to avoid the need for a new central station, far enough away to spare Darlington the destructive upheaval experienced by many Victorian towns when railways tore through their heart. A station was built at Bank Top by 1842, on the site of the present main station, along with coal depots and a large railway shed nearby.[42] Streets of houses soon appeared all around,[43] and Bank Top was described in 1854 as a new town in its own right.[44]

Darlington's iron age

Though dramatic enough, the building of Bank Top was only the start of the town's transformation. The key to Darlington's next phase of expansion lay a short distance to the north, where the new railway crossed the Stockton and Darlington line. Although miles from any sources of minerals, the town was about to experience its own 'iron age'. The railway network which Darlington promoters had played such a pivotal role in establishing – Joseph Pease and others had been as active in the GNER as in the earlier line – was both a means and an end, a supplier and a consumer, in this new phase. While Middlesbrough lost its role as a coal port – minerals could travel south more easily by rail – and was forced to find a new function in iron manufacture, the Stockton and Darlington line was far from redundant, transporting iron and coal to Darlington and taking finished goods in all directions. Many of these goods were themselves destined for the railways, for, as a network spread across Britain, Europe and beyond, the market for rails, locomotives, rolling stock and all manner of specialist accessories was booming.

The iron industry arrived in Darlington in 1854 and within a decade there were four firms, between them representing each stage of iron production. The Darlington Forge Co., established in 1854, produced castings and forgings for railways; the South Durham Iron Co. occupied a six-acre site from 1855, where it made pig iron; Barningham's Darlington Iron Co., a manufacturer of iron rails, set up in 1859; and the Skerne Ironworks, iron founders and bridge builders, started as Pease, Hutchinson and Ledward in 1864. All were located near the junction of the two railways, where sidings could run into the plants, on farmland formerly known as Nestfield. The Quakers who had promoted and managed the railways were closely involved in some of the ironworks, and in the company set up to develop Nestfield, reborn as Albert Hill; the area was soon built up with terraced housing, churches, schools and Darlington's highest

41   Kirby, *Origins*, chapter 5.
42   Darlington Lib., E810033813; *Newcastle Courant*, 17 July 1840.
43   OS Map 1:2500, Durham LV.10 (1858 edn).
44   Longstaffe, *Darlington*, p.248.

concentration of public houses and beer shops. By 1875 the four iron businesses employed about 3,500 men and boys out of a total male population of around 15,300, many of these workers having migrated from south Wales, the Midlands and, especially, Ireland.[45]

With the working out of the Tyne valley's thin ironstone seams and the systematic exploitation of Cleveland ironstone from 1850, the North East, specifically the Tees valley, rose to be the biggest iron-producing district in the world by the mid 1860s. The heyday of local iron-making was the 1860s and 1870s, although even then the trade was vulnerable to economic fluctuations, such as the post-Crimean War slump, which hit a low in 1860.[46] Darlington in 1878 had 288 puddling furnaces out of a total in the region of 2,136, but by then was losing ground to Middlesbrough and was in absolute decline by the mid 1880s.[47] The South Durham Iron Co. had closed by 1881, the year the Darlington Iron Co. also failed, although the latter, reconstituted, struggled on into the 1890s. The Skerne Company closed in 1875, reopened and finally shut in 1882, but leaving something of a legacy in the shape of the Cleveland Bridge company, founded upon bridge-building expertise developed at the Skerne works. The only one of the original iron companies to survive long-term was the Darlington Forge, which endured an inter-war mothballing before finally succumbing to economic forces in the late 1960s.[48]

Fortunately for Darlington's enduring prosperity, engineering compensated for the declining iron trade. The railway company's engineering workshops moved from Shildon in 1862, attracted by a more convenient location on the network, and were soon the largest employer in town. Kitching diversified into permanent way equipment and his business eventually became the Whessoe Company. Others secured their futures by finding specialist niches: Thomas Summerson in crossings, switches and sidings for railways, the Darlington Forge as marine engineers and Cleveland Bridge in bridge-building. As engineering factories grew larger, the flat land, good communications and vacated premises of failed firms attracted businesses into Darlington, the most illustrious arrival being Robert Stephenson & Co., who came from Newcastle in 1899. In 1913, nine of the ten largest employers in Darlington were engineers. Of the North Eastern Railway Co.'s 4,526 Darlington-based staff, 2,366 were in its mechanical departments; then came the Darlington Forge with 1,300 workers; Robert Stephenson (1,000); Rise Carr Rolling Mills (800); Cleveland Bridge (600); and the Whessoe Company (600). Eight others employed between 100 and 500.[49] The vast sheds and workshops of these companies covered many acres of land at Albert Hill and in the North Road and Whessoe Lane areas, and to a lesser extent at Bank Top.

[45] B.J. Barber, 'The Economic and Urban Development of Darlington, 1800–1914' (unpublished MA thesis, University of Leicester, 1969), p.17; Darlington Lib., E810048646.
[46] J.K. Harrison, 'The Production of Pig Iron in North-East England, 1577–1865', in C.A. Hempstead (ed.), Cleveland Iron and Steel (Redcar, 1979), pp.49, 64.
[47] Barber, 'Development of Darlington', p.17.
[48] For a full account of Darlington's iron and engineering industries, see Durham VCH, iv.
[49] Durham County Record Office, Da/DM/7/27/7; Darlington Lib., E810029687.

Because much of its engineering industry was specialised, Darlington escaped the inter-war recession relatively lightly. In particular, the North Road workshops' relationship to the railway provided a degree of stability. During the build-up to war in 1939, 38 per cent of the town's workforce was employed in engineering.[50] Post-war, there was a surge of investment and an engineering boom,[51] followed by collapse in the 1960s. In 1964, Darlington's last locomotive was produced, as both the Robert Stephenson and the North Road workshops closed.[52]

Urban and suburban growth

The iron and engineering factories which dominated the northern and eastern suburbs of Darlington for more than a century have all but disappeared. Many former industrial sites have been rebuilt with housing and, of the mighty North Road railway workshops, only the factory clock remains, attached incongruously to a supermarket which now occupies the land. The housing and other infrastructure which was constructed during Darlington's Victorian boom has survived much better. The town's housing stock more than doubled in 20 years, from about 2,000 houses in 1851 to almost 5,000 in 1871; during that same period the population grew from 11,582 to 27,729. Rapid growth continued, and there were 42,195 people and nearly 9,000 houses in 1901.

Much of the new working-class housing was north of the town, near to the main places of employment, including Albert Hill and the areas on either side of the North Road. Some local industrialists promoted housing schemes, but there was no company housing as such. One of the more unusual projects was at Eastbourne, off Yarm Road, where a freehold land society laid out streets and offered 144 plots for sale. The prime movers in this, some of the same group involved in developing Albert Hill, were mainly Liberal Quakers intent on extending the electorate to respectable working-class men through the ownership of freehold property. The plots of land at Eastbourne were also large enough to enable some food to be grown, providing a measure of independence. The scheme was slow to move, with only a few houses built during the 1850s – the varied style of housing there bears testimony to its gradual and individual building over the following decades.[53] Eastbourne's failings were its distance from major workplaces and the reality that house ownership, even at a cut price – the Eastbourne scheme was cheap, but not charitable, the promoters aiming to cover costs at least – was beyond the means of most workers.

Much more significant was the development of the glebe land, which had been in the hands of the Vane family since the seventeenth century. The opening-up of the west end by the Cleveland estate started with the construction of Duke Street leading out of Skinnergate, with working-class streets hidden behind the

---

50 TNA: PRO, BT 64/3120.
51 Durham County Record Office, D/Whes 14/47.
52 G.W. May, *British Industry and Commerce: 5, Teesside* (c.1965), p.20.
53 Darlington Building Society, abstract of title of John Harris and Michael Middleton, 1851; Darlington Lib., E810030517, E810030539 and E810028164; M. Chase, 'Out of Radicalism: the mid-Victorian Freehold Land Movement', *English Historical Review*, 106 (1991), pp.319–45; OS Map 1:10,560, Durham LV (1858 edn).

facades of shops. A little further out, Stanhope Road was laid out with a small park overlooked by the new Queen Elizabeth Grammar School and alongside it the Ladies' Training College. From this point west was built exclusively good-quality housing aimed at the professional classes. Cleveland's agents laid out streets and sold plots, individually or in small groups, with strict covenants on the style and standard of houses. The west end was the site of much of the town's new housing after 1870, and continued to be developed, out as far as Carmel Road, until the 1930s.[54]

With the establishment of the Darlington Local Board of Health in 1850 had come improvements in building standards and in the town's environment, especially of the market area. While housing continued to intensify in the central yards and wynds, the trend was towards developing new streets and public buildings, in keeping with Darlington's increased size and status. Pease's Priestgate textile factory, once considered vast, began to pale in comparison to the new constructions.[55] The Mechanics' Institute moved to impressive new premises in Skinnergate in 1854;[56] a police station was built in Northgate in 1866–7, and the county court building in Coniscliffe Road at around the same time;[57] the eminent architect Alfred Waterhouse built a new bank on High Row for Back-houses. Waterhouse's clerk of works there, George Gordon Hoskins, settled in Darlington and became the town's pre-eminent Victorian architect, responsible for, among other things, the Queen Elizabeth Grammar School (1875–6), the Greenbank Hospital (1885), Edward Pease Free Library (1884), the rebuilding of the King's Head (1890–93) and Red Lion Hotel, Priestgate (1903), the technical college in Northgate (1894) and the Hippodrome theatre, Clay Row (1904).[58] Darlington bridge, called St Cuthbert's bridge to distinguish it from a series of new bridges along the Skerne, was rebuilt in 1895 under the supervision of the county engineer.[59] Most striking of all in terms of the townscape, and an enduring symbol of the town and of the era, was Waterhouse's new town hall, incorporating the present market buildings, which was built in 1861–4.[60]

A project mooted barely thirty years later to replace this town hall with new municipal buildings along Horsemarket and Feethams proceeded to an architectural competition but was abandoned in the face of fierce opposition from a consortium which instead organised the rebuilding of Central Hall.[61] In the 1930s another attempt was made to consolidate various local government departments on one site, including one plan which would have built across the

---

[54] Cookson, *Townscape*, pp.92–5.

[55] Spencer, *Men that are Gone*, p.271.

[56] Longstaffe, *Darlington*, pp.cvii–cviii.

[57] Darlington Lib., E810032485–518; E810032519; Pevsner and Williamson, *County Durham*, p.148.

[58] V. Chapman, 'George Gordon Hoskins, J.P., F.R.I.B.A.: a Darlington Architect and his Work, 1864–1907. Part 1: Hoskins and his Darlington Buildings', *Durham Archaeological Journal*, 4 (1988), pp.64–8. See G.R. Potts, 'The Architects of Nineteenth-Century Darlington', in Cookson, *Townscape*, chapter 4.

[59] Inf. on bridge; Darlington Lib., Wooler cuttings book 2, pp.22, 68.

[60] Pevsner and Williamson, *County Durham*, p.145.

[61] Darlington Lib., E810034281; E810036074; E810043913–15; E810009621–4; E810033179–87; Wooler cuttings book no. 2, p.77; *Northern Echo*, 6 March 1894; Chapman, 'George Gordon Hoskins', p.65.

whole central market area, including both banks of the Skerne.[62] The bishop's palace, deanery and other medieval structures near to St Cuthbert's church had already fallen victim to late Victorian developments, but Darlington's medieval street pattern escaped obliteration when the inter-war project was scrapped, perhaps on the grounds of cost or aesthetics. The outbreak of war brought an end to such schemes.[63] Not until 1970 was a new town hall finally completed, on Feethams, beyond the south-eastern corner of the market place, its car park covering the site of the bishop's palace. This was envisaged as the first phase of a much larger central redevelopment scheme which would have seen civic buildings on the market square, a covered market and new 'civic square' on Feethams, shopping malls and a multi-storey car park.[64] Known as the Shepherd plan, this provoked a storm of local protest and was eventually abandoned, marking the salvation of one of the town's finest Georgian houses, Bennet House, the even older Pease house and other dwellings and inns in Horsemarket, as well as the Central Hall, covered market and Waterhouse's old town hall.[65]

Suburban growth during the twentieth century followed a more predictable pattern. Streets of terraced housing connected the town centre with the outer settlements of Bank Top, Albert Hill and Hope Town, while the Brinkburn Road area to the north west was filled with dozens of new roads of working-class housing. On Yarm Road came a small garden suburb, starting in 1912.[66] The first slum clearances came between the wars, starting in the Park Street and Clay Row areas near the Skerne. Displaced residents moved out to Darlington's first council estates, at Cockerton and Geneva Road. The rate of council-house construction, though, lagged far behind that of the private sector. Beyond the still-developing Cleveland estate of the west end, the land around Hummersknott and other nineteenth-century Quaker villas beyond Carmel Road was sold for development in the 1920s. Several other Quaker mansions, which by then were falling to institutional use as schools and offices, also had their grounds taken for housing.[67] After 1945 came acres of new housing, much of it semi-detached, on the agricultural land which had surrounded the built-up area. The intensity of twentieth-century development was ameliorated by the large number of public parks, cemeteries and recreation grounds which had been established from the mid nineteenth century and which continued to be given priority, thanks to far-sighted council policies recognising a need for public open spaces.[68]

After years of lobbying by the borough council from the 1920s the Great North Road, which, especially on market days, brought gridlock to the town centre, was in 1965 diverted onto a bypass west of the town. Soon after this came a new inner ring road. Since then, major developments in the central area,

62 Darlington Lib., E810033119–20.
63 Darlington Lib., E810006352; E810033466; E810033520–1; E810032945–7; Durham County Record Office, D/DL/1/105–6.
64 'Design in Detail: New Town Hall, Darlington, Co. Durham', *Building* (19 March 1971), pp.79–86; Pevsner and Williamson, *County Durham*, pp.144–5.
65 Darlington Lib., Market Place Conservation Group report; *Northern Echo*, 27 November 2002.
66 Cookson, *Townscape*, pp.99–102.
67 Ibid., pp.152–6.
68 Ibid., pp.97–9, 145–7.

notably the Dolphin leisure centre and the Cornmill shopping mall, have been accommodated within the old street pattern, so that despite the loss of significant landmarks such as the Borough Road power station and Pease's worsted factory in Priestgate, Darlington has retained much of its historical integrity.[69]

But change continues, and sometimes with unexpected consequences. In 2004, during site preparation for a new distribution depot near the A1 at Faverdale – for Darlington's location on the Great North Road still delivers considerable economic benefits – a much older, hitherto unsuspected chapter of the town's history has been revealed. Less than a mile from what had been thought the first settlement, of Anglo-Saxons in Bondgate, builders discovered signs of an earlier encampment. Archaeological investigations continue, but it appears that Faverdale had a Roman fort, possibly only a temporary construction, alongside a number of Iron Age huts. Darlington's first Iron Age is now a chapter waiting to be written.

Acknowledgement

The author would like to acknowledge the work of her colleague on the *Victoria County History of Durham*, Dr Christine Newman, from which is derived the account of Darlington's development to 1600.

---

[69] Ibid., pp.140–41, 143–5, 162–3.

13

Urban Landscapes of Newcastle upon Tyne

THOMAS FAULKNER

The concept of 'urban landscape' is commonly understood in at least two fairly well-defined ways. Perhaps the more straightforward of these involves the idea of landscapes within an urban situation. This definition would include parks and gardens, as well as those areas of designed landscape around or between buildings, which, in recent times, will almost certainly have required the services of a landscape architect. The landscape architect, in fact, is an increasingly important professional whose ever-widening remit may now include planning not only the location of buildings, roads and walkways, but also the arrangement of flowers, shrubs and trees.

More generally, however, 'urban landscape' can also mean the totality of a town or city's appearance and topography, seen both in height and width and involving its layout, buildings, public spaces and streets. These elements are of course conditioned by the natural terrain upon which the structures that give character to this 'landscape' (or 'townscape') are built. But, interestingly, they can also be seen as a metaphor for the forms of natural landscape, with its hills and valleys, ridges and plateaux, eminences, heights, depressions and declivities. Thus, for example, it is possible to think of streets as being like rivers, with side streets forming their 'tributaries'. Similarly, if buildings can be 'read' as trees, then an urban square becomes a clearing in the forest. A cathedral tower or spire may make us think of a mountain or rocky prominence.

This chapter deals with 'urban landscapes' of Newcastle upon Tyne, mainly during the period c.1700–1900, when a still almost medieval town was transformed into a major commercial and industrial metropolis with its traditional status as a regional capital substantially enhanced. The emphasis here is mainly on 'urban landscapes' as defined as 'landscapes within an urban situation': that is, involving parks, gardens and other open spaces. Indeed, Newcastle prides itself on containing, pro rata, an unusually high proportion of such spaces, including designated public parks.

Yet this is not to imply that the city is less than richly endowed in the other, more general sense of the term, and the undoubted topographical richness of Newcastle was emerging as early as the later Middle Ages, when the town's basic character had become strongly established. Newcastle was not really a planned medieval town, even though it had been 'planted' by the Normans, but was walled, and now presented an irregular, horseshoe-like layout on the north bank of the Tyne; this was crossed by one bridge, probably on an earlier, Roman alignment. The Town Moor, a very large area of inalienable grazing land owned by the Freemen of Newcastle and still present today, lay outside the walls to the north and west, while on all sides was already the visible evidence of coal mining. The town's centre of both population and commercial activity was near the quayside, from which ran narrow alleys, or 'chares', of which a few traces still remain, while the (still-existing) principal streets, Pilgrim, Newgate and Westgate Streets, ran north, north west and west respectively. The haphazard awkwardness of all this, especially the steep and tortuous entrance into Newcastle from the bridge, later prompted the Georgians to construct Mosley Street (1784–6), and then the still very steep Dean Street (c.1787–9), giving better access from the quayside.

The Nunnery of St Bartholomew and, to the east, an adjacent Franciscan friary were situated between Newgate and Pilgrim Streets. After the Dissolution this substantial combined site – so important, as we shall see, for the later development of the town – was sold. On the part occupied by the friary a large mansion, the 'Newe House' (later Anderson Place), was built by the merchant Robert Anderson from about 1580, possibly using salvaged material from the earlier building. Meanwhile, on the south bank of the river was Gateshead, always a much less substantial settlement, that was evolving, ribbon-like, on each side of the Great North Road, and to a lesser extent along the river bank.

In fact, at the present time it is from the southern, or Gateshead, side of the Tyne that the richness and excitement of central Newcastle's 'urban landscape' – in the second, more general sense as defined above – can most readily be perceived. From this position one sees, for example, the neo-classical Moot Hall, with the old Castle Keep to the left, and the Vermont Hotel (originally an early-twentieth-century office building) behind and above. These structures are in turn surmounted by the tower and spire of St Nicholas's Cathedral. Further back, and higher, are a number of modern office blocks. This cliff-like panorama, revealing as it does layer upon layer of visible structure and history, seems to be composed of strata; as the historian and topographer Eneas Mackenzie commented in the 1820s, 'the lower parts of the town seem to have been embanked from the river'.[1] Indeed, it was this precipitousness that gave the town the defensive potential that was so crucial to its development. Overall, too, 'Newcastle is essentially a hilly town',[2] as the late-nineteenth-century novelist and historian R.J. Charleton pithily observed, although even by his time this aspect had become a little less dramatic as a result of the smoothing out of hill-tops and the culverting and filling-in of several steep lateral valleys or 'denes' (see below).

Newcastle had originated around a Roman fort and river crossing (at the most eastward convenient point) near the eastern end of Hadrian's Wall. There had been an Anglo-Saxon settlement here but after centuries of obscurity the

---

[1] E. Mackenzie, *A Descriptive and Historical Account of the Town and County of Newcastle upon Tyne*, 2 vols (Newcastle upon Tyne, 1827), i, pp.157–8.

[2] R.J. Charleton, *A History of Newcastle upon Tyne* (London, c.1885), p.17.

town's strategic position, particularly as a bastion against the Scots, was recognised anew by the Normans with the building and rebuilding of its Castle Keep. The site chosen was much the same as that which the Romans had used and was virtually impregnable. Set in a small area enclosed by walls – later much enlarged – it also had crucial flank protection provided by the aforementioned deep ravines of small tributaries flowing into the Tyne (now mostly filled in). The most important of these watercourses were, from west to east, the Skinner Burn, the Lort Burn and the Pandon Burn. There was also, less than a mile further to the east of the Pandon Burn, the still-existing and much larger Ouseburn.

The Skinner Burn formerly marked the western boundary of Newcastle. It rose in the 'Spring Gardens' in Gallowgate and near the top of Bath Lane, so-called because of its Public Baths (1781), then flowed past an area of open ground known as the Forth and then the old Infirmary – all these sites are discussed later in this chapter – and into the Tyne at the bottom of Forth Banks. This latter location would have been outside the town's medieval walls and is not far from the present Redheugh Bridge. By the late nineteenth century this burn had disappeared, but its existence is commemorated in the name 'Skinner Burn Road'. The Lort Burn ran down to the Tyne through the middle of the old walled town. The present High Bridge Street marks the site of a bridge that once crossed it. Speed's Map (1610) shows, or appears to show, it more or less bisecting Robert Anderson's property between Newgate Street and Pilgrim Streets and flowing behind his new mansion house. The late-eighteenth-century historian John Brand tells us that Anderson 'filled up the dene' and converted the area 'into a very pleasant field'.[3] However, it is likely that here he is referring to a still smaller burn, the Lamb Burn (a tributary of the Lort) which evidently bisected the Nun's Field – that is, the western part of Anderson's property.[4] In any event, by the late eighteenth century the Lort Burn had become dirty and insanitary and was beginning to be filled in. On its site were now built, firstly, Dean Street, then a new Butcher Market to the north (1808) and later, in the 1830s, Grey Street. The Pandon Burn lay (largely) outside the town walls, on their eastern side. The former village of Pandon, or 'Pampeden', had once been a separate entity, possibly walled, around the area where the burn joined the Tyne. Rising north of the town, the burn flowed under the Barras Bridge, north of the wall, and then curved eastwards, following a serpentine course before entering the old town near the Pandon Gate. Its valley (the 'Pandon Dene') was deeply wooded (Fig. 13.1).

It is now time to return to the subject of Newcastle's 'urban landscape' in the other sense, indicated above, of 'landscapes within an urban situation'. In this context it is worth noting that, during the eighteenth and even the early nineteenth century, Newcastle still largely retained its essentially medieval, constricted site. Many of its houses were 'very ancient and mean',[5] while communication

3   J. Brand, *The History and Antiquities of Newcastle upon Tyne*, 2 vols (London, 1789), i, p.233.
4   See also T. Wake, 'Isaac Thompson's Plan of Newcastle upon Tyne, 1746', *Archaeologia Aeliana*, 4th ser., 14 (1937), p.116.
5   H. Bourne, *The History of Newcastle upon Tyne, or, the Ancient and Present State of that Town* (Newcastle upon Tyne, 1736), p.53.

Figure 13.1. Pandon Dene, Newcastle upon Tyne, now removed; an early-nineteenth-century engraving showing the new bridge of 1810–11 (© Tyne and Wear Museums Service).

routes were generally inadequate and parts of the town, especially around the quayside, were seriously congested. However, late in life the architect John Dobson, recalling the Newcastle of his youth around 1800, described its immediate vicinity as 'surrounded with pleasant and romantic walks'. In addition, he went on, 'the banks of the Tyne, from Newcastle to Shields ... were well covered with magnificent hanging woods, enriched with flowering shrubs to the water's edge, presenting to the youthful mind a picture little short of Paradise.'[6] Similarly, present-day suburbs such as Benton, Benwell, Elswick, Fenham, Gosforth, Heaton and Jesmond were then rural villages encircling the still compact town of Newcastle itself. Particular beauty spots included Benwell, 'overshadowed by noble trees',[7] and Elswick, both on its western side. Elswick was 'a place ... much frequented by the town's people, for its pleasing walk and rural entertainment';[8] it also offered attractive views of Newcastle, Gateshead and the Tyne.[9] One regular visitor was the artist Thomas Bewick, who walked there every morning 'to drink whey, or buttermilk'.[10]

[6]   J. Dobson, *Presidential Address to the Northern Architectural Association* (April 1859), reprinted in L. Wilkes, *John Dobson: Architect and Landscape Gardener* (Stocksfield, 1980), p.104.

[7]   'Benwell, Miscellaneous Articles' (Newcastle City Library), vol. i, p.43.

[8]   Bourne, *History of Newcastle*, p.146.

[9]   The topographer P. Russell observed that from Elswick 'The admired pinnacle of St. Nicholas's steeple of Newcastle, the artificial ruin on the hill at Biker, the church and town of Gateshead, all contribute to form a most pleasing prospect to the east.' (P. Russell et al., *England Displayed, being a New, Complete, and Accurate Survey of the Kingdom of England, etc.*, 2 vols (London, 1769), ii, p.215).

[10] T. Bewick, *A Memoir of Thomas Bewick written by himself* (written 1822–8, first published 1862; ed., with an Introduction, by I. Bain, London, 1975), p.184.

These villages were ultimately swallowed up by the relentness expansion of Newcastle, especially during the boom years of both industrial and residential (mainly terraced) development between about 1880 and 1914. For the moment, however, in or near all of these villages were numerous mansions of the local gentry and aristocracy, mostly now lost, which were invariably set in substantial gardens or landscaped parks. Good examples were Benton Hall, Benwell Hall, Elswick Hall and Heaton Hall. The last-named, 'an elegant mansion, ornamented with plantations in a good taste',[11] was the nearer country seat of Sir Matthew White Ridley, also of Blagdon Hall, Northumberland. Heaton Hall occupied an elevated position, its attractive wooded park containing a splendid circular temple and sweeping down to the Ouseburn valley below[12] (see Chapter 7 and Fig. 7.4, p.117). Around 1780 the Hall had been remodelled in castellated style by the local architect William Newton, before which time Sir Matthew's father had extended his property by purchasing land as far as the 'Shields Turnpike', the forerunner of the route delineated by the present City Road, Byker Bank and Shields Road. Near to this he built an eye-catcher, consisting of a group of mock ruins, at Byker Hill (approximately on the site of the present Denmark Street).

Also worthy of note were the grounds of a still-existing house, Benwell Tower (now known as Benwell Towers), on the north side of Benwell Lane. This was substantially remodelled and enlarged in Tudor-Gothic style by Dobson from 1830. After later service as a bishop's residence, it became a public house and latterly a television centre. Nearly a century before Dobson's reconstruction no less a figure than Lancelot 'Capability' Brown was almost certainly consulted in work done for Benwell Tower's then owners, the Shaftoes.[13] There is little or no physical evidence today of Brown's possible involvement here, although the mansion is still surrounded by the residue of an attractively wooded, if much truncated, estate. However, nineteenth-century Ordnance Survey maps show to the east of the house a substantial park with clumps of trees in the style of Brown and – perhaps indicating the later, more 'picturesque' involvement of Dobson – a wooded 'rookery' behind the Tower to the north and west. We also know that at this time there was in front of the mansion a lawn, another Dobsonian feature, separated from the park by a ha-ha[14] (presumably eighteenth-century in date and just possibly constructed by Brown).

Meanwhile, the Town Moor, saved from enclosure or urban development through its ownership by the Freemen of Newcastle and subsequently further protected by a specific Act of Parliament of 1774, was now used for horse racing, a grandstand being built on its north side in 1800. Earlier, new roads across the Moor included one from Barras Bridge to 'the north end of the Cow-Causeway' (1747), one dating to 1748–9 running north from Newcastle to Morpeth (a turnpike) and another turnpike from Gallowgate to the West Cow Gate (1753). (For the position of the Moor in relation to the centre of Newcastle and also the

---

[11] W. Hutchinson, *A View of Northumberland, with an Excursion to the Abbey of Mailross in Scotland,* 2 vols (Newcastle upon Tyne, 1776–8), ii, p.365.
[12] Heaton Hall was demolished in 1933. Its site was that of the present housing in Shaftesbury Grove.
[13] P. Willis, 'Capability Brown in Northumberland', reprinted from *Garden History,* 9:2 (1981), p.163.
[14] Article in *The Northern Daily Express,* 3 May 1882, in 'Benwell, Miscellaneous Articles', vol. ii, p.112.

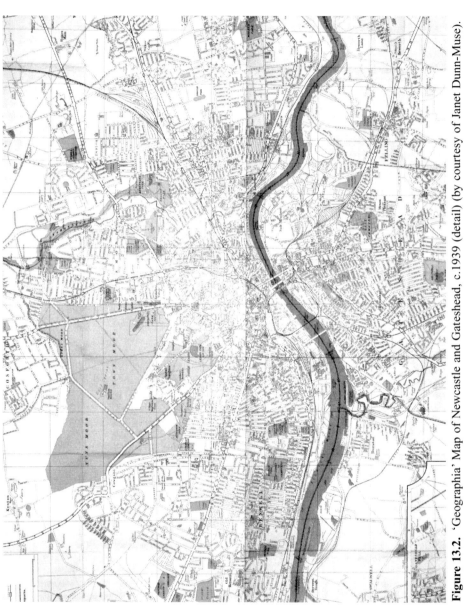

Figure 13.2. 'Geographia' Map of Newcastle and Gateshead, c.1939 (detail) (by courtesy of Janet Dunn-Muse).

location of other sites, including public parks, mentioned in this chapter, see Fig. 13.2.) In addition to the unique amenity of the Moor, inner Newcastle still possessed in the eighteenth century and subsequently a remarkable concentration of gardens and public open spaces, both within and just outside the still-surviving but soon-to-be-demolished walls. Even if, paradoxically, this may have actually exacerbated the circulation problems mentioned earlier, it still led the evangelist John Wesley to comment of the town that he knew of 'no place in Great Britain comparable to it for pleasantness'.[15]

Thus, for example, the public could stroll in the attractive Forth Walk, a little to the south west of Westgate Street, while, nearby, even the new Infirmary, designed in Palladian style by Daniel Garrett in 1751, had impressive landscaped grounds. These had been laid out by William Joyce, a Gateshead nurseryman and surveyor who was sufficiently well regarded to be employed in a similar capacity by George Bowes at Gibside and by Sir Walter Blackett at Wallington Hall, Northumberland.[16] To judge from engravings, the effect was akin to that of a country house, with lawns sweeping down from the Infirmary itself and with judiciously placed groups of trees (Fig. 13.3); later, as shown on nineteenth-century maps, there were also serpentine walks and a fountain.

The Forth Walk itself surrounded a square, walled piece of land (the Forth) at the top of Forth Banks. This 'mighty pretty place, exceeding by much any common place of pleasure about the town'[17] contained a tavern, a bowling green and a tree-lined path. It had been a place of recreation since at least the seventeenth century.[18] So too had been the Shield Field, a much plainer but still popular open space just to the west of the Pandon Burn, on the other side of town, which may at one time have hosted horse racing.[19] The whole area of the Forth was at this time still semi-rural. From it 'the Maiden's Walk crossed a bridge over the Skinner Burn ... and proceeded through a grove to the fields of Elswick'.[20] Other places of recreation in Newcastle included Garth Heads, a large area to the west of the Keelmen's Hospital, not far from the river and just outside the western portion of the wall, and the Spital Field, popular with the boys of the nearby Grammar School, then occupying the former Hospital of St Mary the Virgin in Westgate Street. The Grammar School itself possessed a delightful walled garden with lawns (Fig. 13.4). Newcastle's most important pleasure gardens were the Spring Gardens, 'a fine grass field, ornamented with

15 Wesley's *Journal*, 4 June 1759, in N. Curnock (ed.), *The Journal of the Rev. John Wesley, A.M.*, 8 vols (London, 1909), iv, p.323. Wesley said further that 'Certainly, if I did not believe there was another world, I should spend all my summers here.'

16 See M. Wills, *Gibside and the Bowes Family* (Chichester, 1995), pp.23–4, and J. Cornforth, G. Jackson-Stops and S. Pettit, *Wallington* (London, 1976), p.25. Joyce also constructed the turnpike road from Newcastle to Morpeth, mentioned above, as well as the Durham turnpike road (*Newcastle Advertiser*, 28 March 1789).

17 Bourne, *History of Newcastle*, p.146.

18 It is recorded that in 1680 a wall was constructed and trees imported from Holland were planted by the Corporation (see Brand, *History and Antiquities*, i, p.418), while Mackenzie refers to recent municipal renovation and replanting in his day (Mackenzie, *Descriptive and Historical Account*, ii, p.714).

19 After c.1738 this ground became for a time private property, much to the annoyance of the local population (Brand, *History and Antiquities*, i, pp.441–2). It is now entirely built over.

20 Wake, 'Isaac Thompson's Plan', p.118.

Figure 13.3. The Infirmary, Newcastle upon Tyne, by Daniel Garrett, 1751, now demolished; an eighteenth-century engraving (by courtesy of Dr Jeremy Gregory).

trees' and 'used as a place of genteel resort, where the gay and fashionable were entertained in tents, and amused with music, singing, &c.'[21] During the later eighteenth century the music played here included that of the major local composer and musician Charles Avison (1709–1770). The nearby Public Baths of 1781 (now demolished) were also pleasantly situated in a grove, with 'tastefully formed' walks and shrubs.[22]

There was also the Carliol Croft, an important area of ground which lay between the rear gardens of the houses on the east side of Pilgrim Street – it was accessible from this street – and the town wall. Here, the eighteenth-century historian Henry Bourne tells us, was 'a very agreeable walk, generally frequented in a summer's evening by the gentry of this part of the town; the prospect of the gardens, some of which are exceeding curious, affording a good deal of pleasure'.[23] Yet another, very small, burn, the Eric (or Erick) Burn, joining the Pandon Burn near Manor Chare, marked the rear boundary of these gardens, although this was arched over well before the 1820s. The deep, wooded banks of the Pandon Burn itself – 'a sweet rural place indeed'[24] – also provided scope for pleasurable perambulation (see Fig. 13.1). The route from the Pandon Dene bridge (constructed later, in 1810–11) up to Barras Bridge, flanked by neat tradesmen's gardens with summer houses, was especially attractive. So too were

[21] Mackenzie, *Descriptive and Historical Account*, i, p.191. The gardens opened in 1763.
[22] T. Oliver, *A New Picture of Newcastle upon Tyne, etc.* (Newcastle upon Tyne, 1831; facsimile edition, Newcastle upon Tyne, 1970), p.76.
[23] Bourne, *History of Newcastle*, p.81. The gardens of the Pilgrim Street houses to which Bourne refers were long and thin, probably indicating an earlier burgage plot arrangement.
[24] J. Harvey, *A Sentimental Tour through Newcastle by a Young Lady* (n.d. but catalogued in Library of the Literary and Philosophical Society of Newcastle upon Tyne as 1794; acc. no. 855 n 167), p.29.

Figure 13.4. *View of part of the Ancient Church of St Mary's Hospital, converted into a Grammar School* (engraving produced for J. Brand, *The History and Antiquities of Newcastle upon Tyne*, 1789).

the banks of the Ouseburn, especially near Heaton, where there were numerous corn (later flint) mills.

Private gardens abounded, especially behind the western side of Percy Street and on either side of Northumberland Street, north of the town wall. This was also the case around Gallowgate, just outside the northernmost portion of the wall, and, still further north, near Barras Bridge. Beyond Barras Bridge itself were several large nursery gardens. On the other side of town the rather exclusive Westgate Street was particularly well provided with gardens; the most noteworthy of these was the semi-formal Vicarage Garden, the western part of which became the site of the Assembly Rooms (1774–6). The now-demolished Mansion House, built near the riverside in 1691, had a spacious terraced garden, while the Barber-Surgeons' Hall, in the Manors, stood before a gracious prospect comprising 'a fine square, divided into four areas or grass-plats, surrounded with gravel walks, each of which is adorned with a statue'.[25] (The statues were of the medical luminaries Aesculapius, Hippocrates, Galen and Paracelsus.) This latter building adjoined two hospitals, the Holy Jesus, or Town's Hospital, and another that came to be known as Sir Walter Blackett's Hospital. All these buildings, of which only the Holy Jesus Hospital survives, fronted a pleasant field with walks. The ancient Black Friars, to the west of Newgate Street but within the town wall, was one of the few surviving structures from what once had been Newcastle's many religious foundations, having been taken over by a number of the town's trades and companies in the sixteenth century. Eighteenth-century maps and engravings show it still surrounded by orchards and

---

[25] Bourne, *History of Newcastle*, p.137.

Figure 13.5. Black Friars, Newcastle upon Tyne (engraving published by S. Hooper, 1784).

gardens (Fig. 13.5), although by 1830 these had disappeared except for a small area north of Stowell Street that had become a bowling green. Needless to say, this profusion of verdant, open space – much of it accessible to the public – contrasted markedly with the congestion, dirt and grime of many of the oldest parts of town, especially those near the quayside, such as Sandhill.

Meanwhile, the largest and most important private garden in Newcastle was undoubtedly that of Anderson Place. This house, as we have seen, had been built by Robert Anderson on the site of a Franciscan friary. Anderson also owned the adjacent 'Nun's Field' site, to the west, so that the dwelling was surrounded by a very large quantity of ground. In 1675 Anderson Place was bought by Sir William Blackett, who shortly afterwards added wings to the house and laid out a large formal garden, clearly visible in Kip and Knyff's early-eighteenth-century engraving (Fig. 13.6). Bourne, writing in the 1730s, gives a precise description:

> That part of it which faces the street is thrown into walks and grass-plots, beautified with images and beset with trees, which afford a very pleasing shade: the other part of the ground, on the west side of it, is all a garden, exceedingly neat, and curiously adorned with statues, and several other curiosities.[26]

We can only speculate as to who might have designed this layout, with its regular rows of small trees and shrubs, formal beds, parterres and paths at right angles reinforcing (for the most part) the main axes of the house. However,

[26] Ibid., p.85.

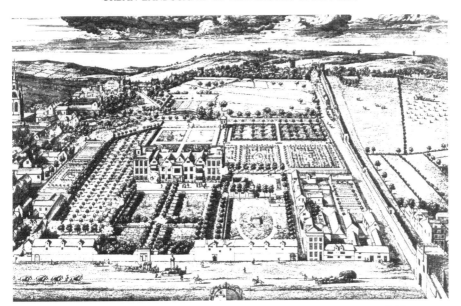

Figure 13.6. Anderson Place, off Pilgrim Street (seen in the foreground of this illustration), Newcastle upon Tyne (engraving by J. Kip and L. Knyff, c.1715).

this garden was so typical of its period – even though very few of this type now survive – that it could probably have been laid out by any competent local gardener or nurseryman working from standard patterns, as influenced by French and Dutch models. Moreover, impressive though it was, the Anderson Place layout was less fashionable and elaborate than such contemporary counterparts as the garden at nearby Blagdon Hall, Northumberland (now removed) – perhaps because it may well have been partly based on an Elizabethan garden already in place. Thus, for example, Kip and Knyff's engraving shows the area in front of Anderson Place itself to have been comparatively plain and, contrary to Bourne's description, without parterres, statuary or water features, while the three little summer houses at the back (one would have expected to find a fourth) could well have been part of an earlier garden. The most puzzling feature of the layout is the non-alignment of the main garden axes at the front and back of the house. Unless the engraving is very inaccurate, which is unlikely (although in some later impressions this feature is less marked), it would appear that the rear 'centre' of the house had been moved at some point and the front and rear gardens not co-ordinated.[27]

As is well known, the whole Anderson Place site ultimately fell victim to the builder and entrepreneur Richard Grainger's celebrated if rather ruthless redevelopment of central Newcastle of c.1834–40. Grainger purchased Anderson Place in July 1834 – it was demolished soon afterwards – having already presented to the Council a scheme involving a major new street (now

---

[27] In this analysis I have been greatly assisted by the expert commentary of the garden historian Robin Whalley, formerly of Bath Spa University.

Grey Street) running from Dean Street to the eastern end of Blackett Street. The new street was to have four lateral streets linking eastwards with Pilgrim Street and westwards to what is now upper Grainger Street, the last-named being one of a quadrilateral of streets containing a new market planned by Grainger. The most northerly of these was to become Clayton Street, connecting with Grainger's earlier Eldon Square development. This architecturally coherent arrangement was essentially the scheme as carried out. The construction of Grey Street in particular necessitated the demolition of the recently built Butcher Market of 1808; at the same time the remaining open section of the Lort Burn (which had become a sewer) was filled in. The burn in fact provided a convenient foundation for Grey Street – hence the street's slightly curving, as well as descending, line – while also allowing advantage to be taken of the natural features of the terrain to create an intentionally picturesque effect.[28] By this time, too, the demolition of the old town walls, in the interests of expansion and better traffic flow, was largely complete.

It is difficult to form an entirely accurate assessment of the state of the land acquired by Grainger prior to its redevelopment. Grainger himself, perhaps anxious to justify his activities, emphasised the previously poor condition of this 'horrible' site which according to him was let to cowkeepers and other tradesmen, and the enormous effort he had expended in levelling the ground.[29] It may be that he was exaggerating this state of affairs and may in any case have been referring only to the 'Nun's Field' element of the site. This must have deteriorated from the pleasant, parkland condition depicted in Kip and Knyff's engraving and later described by Bourne, for it seems that even in the early 1830s the more immediate surroundings of Anderson Place itself were still reasonably attractive. Eighteenth-century maps, including Beilby's of 1788, show the actual Anderson Place layout as substantially intact, as does the map by Cole & Roper, produced for *The Beauties of England and Wales* series in 1808.

Interestingly, however, Thomas Oliver's well-known 1830 Map of Newcastle, while showing formal gardens remaining behind Anderson Place, appears to indicate a reduced, and more informal, wooded area in front of the house, a situation corroborated by contemporary engravings of the site depicting mature trees; the narrow avenue of small trees or shrubs leading up to the centre of the house (shown in Fig. 13.6) seems to have disappeared. Yet, perhaps confusingly, we know that as late as 1827 there still existed a 'walk up the middle avenue, with the trees on each side' that was to have been 'carefully preserved' as part of a contemporary, unexecuted redevelopment scheme by Dobson.[30] One can only assume that this avenue was a more widely spaced one, possibly a mature evolution of part of Sir William Blackett's original planting and aligning with his lateral additions to the house.

[28] 'An Accurate Ground Plan and Description of Mr. Grainger's Improvements', *Newcastle Journal*, 24 October 1835.

[29] *Report of the Cholera Commissioners* (1854), pp.353 et seq.

[30] See T.E. Faulkner and A. Greg, *John Dobson: Architect of the North East* (Newcastle upon Tyne, 2001), p.45, and Mackenzie, *Descriptive and Historical Account*, i, pp.200–201.

In any event, with the exception of the Town Moor, by the mid nineteenth century most of the open spaces detailed above had been, or were soon to be, built on. For example, in addition to Grainger's redevelopments, the Carliol Croft was purchased in 1823 for the construction of Dobson's Newcastle Gaol,[31] while the historic Hospital of St Mary the Virgin (see Fig. 13.4) was now demolished for the widening of Neville Street in 1845. In the same year the Forth was appropriated for the construction of Central Station (also designed by Dobson). Before long, too, the once-attractive Infirmary had become completely surrounded by urban development and railway works.[32] The loss of these open spaces did not go entirely unnoticed. 'Where were our Orator Patriots when these places of recreation were taken from us? Did the toiling thousands not then require fresh air?' clamoured a pamphleteer in 1869.[33]

Admittedly, the comparatively modern residential area west of Pandon Dene and north of New Bridge Street was still fairly pleasant at this time. The terraced houses in Ellison Place had attractive gardens, while other private gardens in this vicinity included those of two large detached villas (again designed by Dobson), David Cram's residence at the end of Ellison Place (c.1825) and the contemporary Picton House. Both of these gardens led down to the dene and, like many nineteenth-century villa gardens in Newcastle, contained trees and shrubs, perhaps with a few architectural features, all traversed by winding paths in the now-fashionable 'gardenesque' style popularised by the eminent horticultural writer J.C. Loudon. Nearby, a cricket ground was situated between Ellison Place and Northumberland Street. This in turn was overlooked by the Northumberland Street Baths, a domed building of 1837–9, yet another Dobson design and set amid wooded grounds again leading down to the dene. It is also worth noting that, in this area, as late as c.1900, gardens still lay to the east of the wooded precinct of St Thomas's church and south of the (now-demolished) Lovaine Place and Lovaine Crescent; this was before the eastwards extension of St Mary's Place and the building of the present City Hall and Baths.

However, the lowest stretches of the Pandon Dene, near the Tyne, were now beginning to become insanitary. Before long the whole course of the burn was filled in, mainly for railway, warehouse and residential development. This was done at intervals between about 1842 and 1886, and largely with material obtained from the levelling of nearby higher ground. The area of Byker Hill, referred to earlier, was still semi-rural in the 1860s (at this time Byker was 'a pleasant village'[34]). It still afforded excellent views of Heaton Hall, 'seen to great advantage in the distance surrounded with beautiful ornamental grounds',[35] but by the 1890s had been for the most part levelled and built over. The Ouseburn,

---

[31] The Newcastle Gaol was completed in 1828; it was demolished c.1929.

[32] After the opening of the new Royal Victoria Infirmary in 1906 it ceased to be a hospital, although it was not finally demolished until 1954. For more on the Infirmary see F.J.W. Miller, 'The Infirmary on the Forth, Newcastle upon Tyne, 1753–1906', *Archaeologia Aeliana*, 5th ser., 14 (1986), pp.143–65.

[33] R.C. Watson, *The Corporation and the Town Moor, etc.* (Newcastle upon Tyne, 1869), p.20. Although sceptical about the intentions of the 'parks movement', Watson did favour the creation of a public park in the west end. Yet he was firmly opposed to any alterations being made to the Town Moor.

[34] 'Byker Bank Improvements', letter to *The Newcastle Daily Journal*, 6 March 1862.

[35] Ibid.

to the east, was now diverted and culverted in part of its lower course between 1907 and 1911. In addition, much of its lower valley began to be filled in after 1904, although the work was haphazard and was still taking place, often via the tipping of rubbish, fifty years later.[36] A little earlier a tributary of the Ouseburn, the Sandyford Burn, flowing under the picturesque bridge known as Lambert's Leap, had also been filled in.

Newcastle was now increasingly built up and congested. Indeed, despite the splendour of Grainger's schemes of improvement, the town had become notorious for the insanitary conditions endured by many of its inhabitants. Cholera epidemics were frequent and a report of 1861 referred to Newcastle's 'narrow, dark and filthy entries', 'undrained chares', 'ill paved streets' and 'badly kept roads'.[37] The Tyne as described by Dobson was now heavily polluted by industry. Not surprisingly, there was by now considerable agitation for the provision of public, or 'people's', parks, which by the 1860s were present in London and most large provincial towns, although not in Newcastle. In 1845 a Dr Reid proposed the setting-aside of land for public use on both the east and west sides of town[38] and in 1857 a petition to the Council signed by nearly 3,000 working men called for the establishment of a public park on the Elswick Estate.[39] Five years later there were demands for land, then readily available, to be purchased for a 'people's park' in Byker.[40]

But parks of this kind were very slow to be provided in Newcastle, which in this regard even lagged behind its rival Sunderland. Paradoxically, one major impediment to such developments in Newcastle was the existence of the Town Moor itself. Many of those in authority argued that the Moor was one of the finest public parks in the country and therefore new ones were unnecessary. It was even suggested that working people could use some of the new urban cemeteries, being laid out during the 1850s, for their recreational walks.[41] Counter-arguments included those that the Moor was bare and in poor condition and had few if any paths. Therefore, it was only suitable for riding on and so beneficial mainly to the better-off. It was also comparatively inaccessible to the growing industrial communities of the east and west ends.

The history of the formation of public, or 'people's', parks in Newcastle is a long and convoluted one and within the limits of the present chapter only a summary of the major developments can be provided. Initially, despite widespread opposition, official proposals (dating from 1861–2) centred on improving the Moor itself with walks, drives and rides, and creating a continuous park from

---

[36] See A. Morgan, *Bygone Lower Ouseburn* (Newcastle upon Tyne, 1995), illustrations 1, 2.

[37] Cited in R. Thorne, L. Walker, et al., unpublished *Notes for Victorian Society Northumbrian Conference* (1981), p.11.

[38] S. Middlebrook, *Newcastle upon Tyne, Its Growth and Achievement* (1950; 2nd edn, East Ardsley, 1968), pp.274–5.

[39] See *Proceedings of the Newcastle Council*, 23 September 1857, pp.344–5.

[40] 'Byker Bank Improvements'.

[41] A good example of such a cemetery is All Saints', Jesmond Road, with buildings in neo-Gothic style by the architect John Green jnr. Dating from 1855–6, it was one of a number of municipal cemeteries built between 1855 and 1858 in what were then the outer suburbs of Newcastle. Other examples include St Andrew's (Tankerville Terrace, Jesmond), St John's (Elswick Road) and St Nicholas's (Wingrove Avenue, Fenham).

Castle Leazes to Brandling Village out of the south-east part of it. The chief supporters of these proposals, and of the 'parks movement' in general, were Council members Charles Frederick Hamond and William Lockey Harle, while the name of no less a figure than Sir Joseph Paxton was mooted as a possible designer. However, little was done until 1868, when a scheme for landscaping and beautifying the Town Moor by the eminent ornithologist and occasional landscape designer John Hancock (1808–1890) was laid before the Council by Harle. Based on an earlier plan by Hancock of 1863, it was produced in a full lithographed version by the Borough Engineer and Surveyor John Fulton in January 1869[42] (Fig. 13.7).

This scheme proposed a series of roads across the Moor, extending from Spital Tongues to Cowgate and crossed by Grandstand Road. The Moor itself would have been extensively planted with trees, especially around its edges, and in irregular belts extending to Castle Leazes. In the latter area a road, flanked by trees, would have extended to St Thomas's Terrace before curving round to cut northwards through the vicinity of Claremont Place into a more formal 'ornamental park' created in the south-east corner of the Moor. This, incorporating the area of the 'bull park' (now subsumed within the present Exhibition Park), would have included shrubberies, paths, both winding and straight, and several ornamental lakes created out of a number of existing small reservoirs. Hancock himself described his overall scheme – so different in its expansiveness from his more characteristically 'gardenesque' work for Lord and Lady Armstrong at Cragside, Northumberland, and at Jesmond Dene (see below) – as a 'home park'. He stated:

> I propose to construct a drive and promenade around the margins ... planting trees and shrubs by the sides of the roads and also planting clumps in the open to provide shelter for the herbage and cattle. A very fine effect might be produced in this way, the eye being carried over the whole expanse as one great continuous park for the health and recreation of the people at large.[43]

The scheme was rejected, partly because of cost, although it was resubmitted in slightly modified form by Hancock himself on two occasions in 1871, again unsuccessfully. Apart from the comparatively small ornamental area, the plan would have created something much too like a Georgian landscape park for the taste of the mid-Victorians and in any case many people remained reluctant to make substantial alterations to the Moor as a whole. Moreover, supporters of the 'parks movement' were now concentrating their efforts on the creation of two separate parks, both from land occupied by the Moor – one at Castle Leazes and the other in the area of the 'bull park'. As a result, a new park at Castle Leazes (the present Leazes Park) finally opened, in December 1873, as a typically Victorian layout with wooded areas, paths, an ornamental lake with an island, a cottage, a tea-room and a bowling green. It was designed in conjunction with John Fulton by John Laing, formerly Steward to Lord Armstrong, and

---

[42] A copy, reproduced here as Fig. 13.7, is held in the Local Studies Section of Newcastle City Library.
[43] See *Proceedings of the Newcastle Council*, 1 February 1871, p.186.

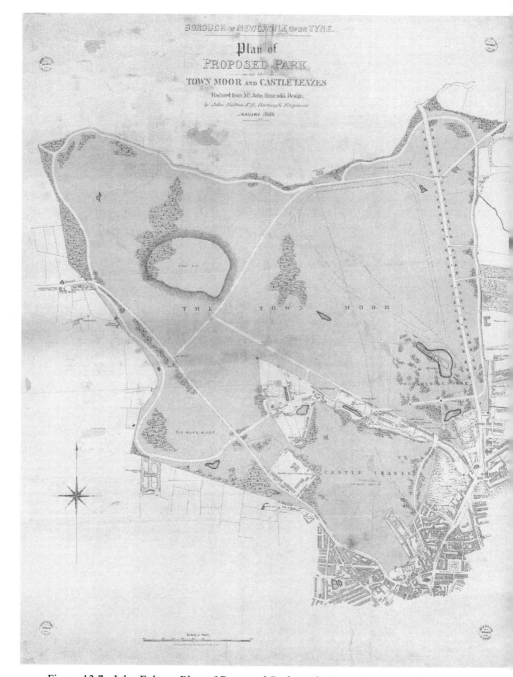

Figure 13.7. John Fulton, *Plan of Proposed Park on the Town Moor and Castle Leazes, reduced from Mr. John Hancock's designs, etc.*, 1869 (© Newcastle City Libraries and Arts).

was extended in 1875.[44] Two years later there were even proposals to construct a municipal art gallery in the park, to the designs of the Assistant Borough Engineer J.A. Bryson, but these came to nothing.[45]

In 1878 a municipal decision was taken, despite the usual opposition regarding cost, to purchase for conversion into parks the former Heaton Hall and Elswick Hall estates, in the east and west of the city respectively. During the 1870s there had been more deputations to the Council on the subject of 'people's' parks, with reference to the possibility of purchasing the Heaton and, particularly, the Elswick estates; and unfavourable comparisons were increasingly being made with the provision of parks by such cities as Birmingham, Glasgow, Manchester, Liverpool and Leeds. Ultimately, six prominent local citizens, including Joseph Cowen, Thomas Hodgkin and W.H. Stephenson, bought the Elswick estate in 1873 'and retained it in their hands for a period of six years until the Corporation saw fit to purchase it for the purpose of a public park',[46] in fact ultimately selling it at a loss. A drinking fountain in the present Elswick Park, erected in 1881, commemorates their philanthropy.

Heaton Park had been created in 1878–80. At the same time the adjacent Armstrong Park was added to it, following the donation to the city of a major area of land by Lord Armstrong, who made this more accessible to the residents of Jesmond by the additional presentation of Armstrong Bridge in 1878. This is a spectacular wrought-iron structure spanning the Ouseburn valley at a maximum height of 19.8m. Meanwhile, on the other side of the city, Thomas Hodgkin's generosity was again in evidence when he donated the substantial wooded gardens of his residence, Benwell Dene House, sloping attractively down towards the Tyne, for use as a public park. This was named Hodgkin Park and formally opened in 1899; it was extended in 1907–8. Despite additions such as terraces, bowling greens and (laid out for the most part by the new Borough Engineer, A.M. Fowler) winding paths, all these public parks still retain, even today, much of their original Georgian landscape character.

Parks of a more formal character, from land previously occupied by the Moor, were laid out at Brandling Park (1878–80), at Fenham (the Nun's Moor Recreation Ground, of 1886–87) and, following prolonged debate, in the area of the 'bull park'. The 'bull park' was used as the site of the Jubilee Exhibition of 1887 and ultimately became Exhibition Park. However, the greatest prize of all came in 1883, when Lord Armstrong completed the sequence initiated with Heaton and Armstrong Parks by making a gift to the city of his own private park, Jesmond Dene, also accessed by the Armstrong Bridge and formally opened to the public by the Prince and Princess of Wales in August 1884. In contrast to its neighbours, this is a typically Victorian layout. It is densely wooded, with much additional planting of evergreens and numerous picturesque winding paths that take advantage of its steep and rugged terrain sloping down to the Ouseburn.

44 For more on the history and development of Leazes Park see D. Potter, 'The Early Years of Leazes Park, Newcastle', *The Victorian Society North East Group Newsletter*, 17–18 (August and October 1990), pp.2–3 and 3–5 respectively.

45 *Proceedings of the Newcastle Council, Record*, July 1877, pp.xii–xiii.

46 See *Proceedings of the Newcastle Council, Record*, April 1881, p.xiv.

A more detailed account of Jesmond Dene is given here in Chapter 7 (see also Fig. 7.5, p.120).

Lord and Lady Armstrong had acquired most of the Dene by about 1860, planting and landscaping it with bridges, waterfalls and winding paths. As in the case of the not-dissimilar grounds of their country house, Cragside, they were assisted in this by their friend John Hancock.[47] Perhaps not surprisingly, under the terms of his donation Lord Armstrong requested the Corporation 'not to alter the laying out of the grounds in a manner to render them more artificial than at present'.[48] A contemporary commentator noted approvingly of this sequence of parks (Heaton Park, Armstrong Park and Jesmond Dene) that:

> the three parks form one line of continuation, and will cover lengthways the best part of a mile and a half direct promenading, with a great variety of gardenesque features ... to impress the most indifferent observer of Nature's beauties. This park also offers the advantages of carriage-driving and riding ... the drives being spacious and macadamized.[49]

In conclusion, it can be stated that by the 1890s Newcastle once again possessed at least as much public open space as any comparable town or city in the country. Yet this proportion was substantially boosted by the inclusion of an amenity which dated from medieval times, the Town Moor, and, as we have seen, this was in reality neither as accessible nor as attractive to the majority of citizens as is often thought. Newcastle had also been late in creating public parks. This was because of a reluctance to spend money and, not least, because of a feeling that the presence of the Moor rendered new parks unnecessary, while the immediate memory of the city's formerly rich legacy of Georgian public open spaces, only recently removed, probably induced further complacency. Moreover, many of the new public parks created by the Corporation of Newcastle were simply carved out of the existing locality of the Moor, with comparatively little modification. Others were conversions of earlier landscaped estates (see, again, Chapter 7) – and even these were usually the result of private benefaction rather than of municipal enterprise. Arguably Newcastle has somewhat less reason for self-congratulation than is usually supposed.

Acknowledgement

The author would like to acknowledge the receipt of valuable advice and information from the local historian and photographer Dr Tom Yellowley, which has been of considerable assistance in the preparation of this chapter.

---

[47] See *Proceedings of the Newcastle Council*, 5 July 1871, p.409.
[48] See *Proceedings of the Newcastle Council*, 7 February 1883, p.107.
[49] *Weekly Chronicle*, 28 July 1894 (Hayler Newspaper Cuttings, vol. 3, p.10, Newcastle City Library).

14

To Hell, Utopia and Back Again:
Reflections on the Urban Landscape of Middlesbrough

LINDA POLLEY

Despite the acquisition of an unprepossessing image (see below), Middlesbrough is one of the most interesting conurbations in the North East. With its speculative origins, amplified by the singular speed at which it grew, it has long been identified as an archetype of nineteenth-century urban and industrial development. Population growth alone would identify it as such. After the town's establishment, in 1830, the original small rural community of a few hundred had grown to 5,463 by 1841 and to nearly 40,000 by 1871. But one has only to walk its streets to appreciate the importance of this period in the town's relatively short history, and in the making of its urban landscape. There are still enough rows of identical terraced houses left to show how the majority of Middlesbrough's working population lived; still enough streets laid out with uniform regularity to indicate the utilitarian grid that passed for town planning even towards the end of the century; and still (just) enough large public buildings left standing as indices of the town's past wealth and civic pride.[1]

In contrast, therefore, to the accumulative, 'organic' growth of most of its counterparts in the region, with their medieval origins, Middlesbrough started life as a speculative development, created virtually from new in 1830 by the Darlington banker Joseph Pease and a number of his Quaker associates (see Chapter 12). Pease was at the centre of an influential Quaker network of businessmen that dominated banking, manufacturing and iron-founding in this area and which in 1821 had obtained an act of parliament to build a railway from Stockton to Darlington, principally in order to facilitate the provision of cheaper coal. This railway opened in 1825. Trade grew rapidly and soon the promoters, realising that they needed to find a site for larger coal staithes and adjoining land for a new dormitory town, bought freehold land at 'Middlesbrough Farm'. Pease had been favourably impressed on his first visit to Middlesbrough, on 2 August 1828:

---

[1] Two historically meaningful Middlesbrough buildings have been demolished recently, not without dissent: the North Riding Infirmary (1864) on Newport Road, despite a vociferous public campaign against its removal; and the unlisted Cleveland Scientific Institute, originally the Methodist New Connexion Chapel (1882).

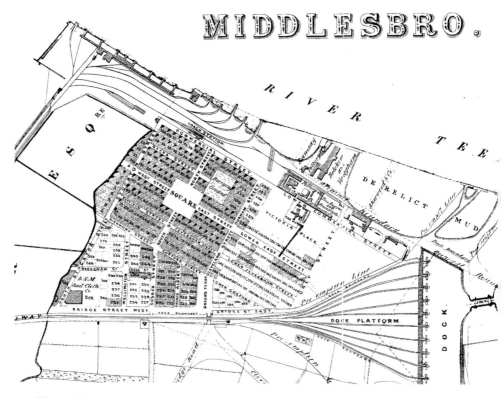

Figure 14.1. Detail from Middlesbrough in 1845, Owners of the Middlesbrough Estate (Teesside Archives Ref: U/OME/8/9).

I took a boat, and on entering the Teesmouth sailed up to Middlesbrough to take view of the proposed termination of the completed ending of the railway, and was very pleased with the place altogether ... Its adaptation far exceeded my anticipations. I was fancying the coming of a day when the bare fields we were then traversing would be covered with a busy multitude.[2]

A further act of parliament to extend the railway to Middlesbrough received Royal Assent in 1828, and the work was carried out within three years. The railway company also obtained powers to construct wharves, quays and staithes, and Middlesbrough soon became a large coal-shipping centre. Thus, early development of the south bank of the Tees was undertaken as an extension of the Stockton and Darlington Railway, to provide a point much closer to the mouth of the river from which to export coal brought from the Quaker-owned west Durham coalfields. Initially, therefore, Middlesbrough – originally called 'Port Darlington' – was a collection of coal 'drops' at the end of a railway line

2   Cited in W. Lillie, *History of Middlesbrough* (Middlesbrough, 1968), p.47.

running as close as possible to the river and, crucially, providing an opportunity for the speculative development of an entirely new town.

The Quakers' original plan for this, devised by Richard Otley, a land surveyor, consisted of a straightforward symmetrical grid with a church and market in a central square. This had four main streets radiating out to the cardinal points, named, logically, North, South, East and West Streets. A series of smaller streets ran east–west, bisecting the larger areas to form a grid pattern. High priority was given to the construction of St Hilda's parish church, opened in 1840, while other important new buildings included the Centenary Wesleyan Methodist chapel (1840), Richmond Street Primitive Methodist chapel (1841) and the Mechanics' Institute (1842). The first new school opened in 1843. The town's 123 building plots were spacious and the twelve main streets were wide, with every attempt being made to maintain 'respectability', but the uniform environment intended was almost immediately compromised by the choice of a convenient but low-lying riverside site. Damp was always one of the great problems of the town, followed by smoke and noise. In the 1850s it was reported that in all instances the drains were above the basements of the houses, and several of the lowest streets were subject to flooding since they were below the river's high-tide level.[3] 'None would have chosen the site if their first consideration had been people rather than coal'[4] (Fig. 14.1).

Yet Pease and his associates were not simply interested in coal staithes; instead they formed a company, comprising a consortium of Quaker businessmen known as the Owners of the Middlesbrough Estate, to develop the whole Middlesbrough area. Pease in particular sought investors and people to set up new businesses in the locality, such as his colleague the surveyor Richard Otley, who founded the highly regarded Middlesbrough Pottery Company in 1834, capitalising on the coal trade by importing clay as ballast in the returning boats. However, probably Pease's greatest achievement was to persuade the Newcastle-based industrialists Henry Bolckow and John Vaughan to set up an ironworks in the town in 1841, which initially consisted of a foundry and rolling mill for rolling rails and bars. The port at Middlesbrough was completed a year later and trade grew sharply for a time. Soon, however, it became cheaper to move coal by rail than by sea and the coal trade declined. In any case, by 1850 Middlesbrough was becoming primarily an iron town, thanks to the recent discovery of iron ore in the Cleveland Hills. At this time the town was still a compact, albeit increasingly dense, settlement which extended only slightly beyond its original layout and was surrounded by undeveloped countryside. However, a second and more intense phase of growth was soon initiated, leading to both severe overcrowding and a need for further expansion.

The earliest form of government in Middlesbrough was the Town Committee set up by the Middlesbrough Owners in the 1831 Deed of Covenant. A decade later the Middlesbrough Improvement Act was passed, enabling the local owners and occupiers of the town to make improvements such as paving, lighting, maintaining drains and sewers and establishing a market. The Bill allowed for the

3   C. Bell and R. Bell, *City Fathers* (London, 1969) p.137.
4   Ibid.

Figure 14.2. Middlesbrough's Old Town Hall, 1846; architect William Moffat
(author's photograph).

election of twelve Improvement Commissioners, who governed for just twelve
years, holding their last meeting on 7 April 1853. One of the issues debated
was the need for a civic building, the result being the Old Town Hall. Designed
by William Moffatt of Doncaster, this opened in 1846 and is one of the most
historically important, albeit sorely neglected, buildings still standing in the St
Hilda's area (Fig. 14.2).

By the time of its incorporation as a borough in 1853, Middlesbrough had
already experienced both sides of the capitalist coin. Initial development was
impressive, but the town had also seen how quickly speculative enterprise
could take the opposite course; in 1846 the historian J.W. Ord had perhaps been
rather premature in calling Middlesbrough 'one of the commercial prodigies of
the nineteenth century'.[5] Yet the desire for incorporation had itself implied an
increasing civic consciousness, an indication that Middlesbrough was aspiring
to the status of a more 'civilised' community and seeking recognition as such.
The Royal Charter of Incorporation, signed in 1853, vested authority in a mayor,
four aldermen and a town council. Four committees were appointed to deal with
finance, streets and lighting, watch and police, and sanitation, all indicative of
the complications a conurbation encounters when it had 'assumed all the char-

---

[5]   J.W. Ord (1846), cited in A. Briggs, *Victorian Cities* (Harmondsworth, 1968) p.244. For a good
     summary of Middlesbrough's early economic history see J.W. Kirby, *Men of Business and Politics:
     The Rise and Fall of the Quaker Pease Dynasty of North-East England, 1700–1943* (London, 1984).

acteristics of an industrial area'.[6] It appears that there was much improving to do; Middlesbrough had become in the early 1850s a town with urban problems, as well as possibilities.

In 1853, the estimated population of Middlesbrough was 9,332 and there was severe and unhealthy overcrowding in much of the developed area north of the railway line. Until the adoption of the Public Health Acts by the new Middlesbrough Corporation in 1855 there were no proper local building controls, and as early as 1846 there had been a certain amount of in-fill building within the grid plan. Narrow streets and courtyards continued to be added and, in some cases, rows of cottages along both sides of what had originally been quite large plots created a back-to-back arrangement. Not surprisingly, Middlesbrough had to withstand three separate attacks of cholera, in 1849, 1852–3 and 1854–5. The last and most virulent of these started, according to *The Darlington and Stockton Times*, in houses in Stockton Street,[7] of which the western boundary was a 'stell', or open drainage ditch.

The close juxtaposition of buildings dictated by the compact town plan meant that a profusion of residential, commercial and industrial premises were located side by side. In addition, a wide variety of residential accommodation was built close together, so that, as well as the narrow in-filled closes, there were by the early 1850s a number of larger houses on the periphery. For example, on the corner of Gosford and Cleveland Streets J.G. Holmes, one of the town's first shipbuilders, constructed a large house with elaborate gardens to the rear, while immediately opposite, on Cleveland Street, from about 1840 Henry Bolckow and John Vaughan lived in two large corner houses which were built in 1835. This relatively close proximity of inhabitants of diverse occupation, earnings and social standing was notable but inevitably short-lived.[8]

Middlesbrough's expansion is revealed by a study of the Ordnance Survey map of 1853, which shows how the town had started to extend beyond the original Pease plan. There were Bolckow & Vaughan's ironworks, situated on the aptly named Vulcan Street, various premises on Lower Commercial Street, some residential development on Lower East Street and further housing to the south west, but most of the town still remained north of the railway line. To the south of the line there was little more than the railway station itself (1847), the Station Hotel (1842), built when only a railway halt served the town, and, at some distance along what became Wilson Street, the Friends' Meeting House (1846).

As we have seen, the earlier period of house building had been controlled by the Owners of the Middlesbrough Estate, who were in sole possession of the available land. Now, during the 1860s, Thomas Hustler sold land for development that lay beyond the north-eastern boundary of the Estate. This is physi-

6   Lillie, *History*, p.159.
7   Cited in J.W. Leonard, 'Reaction to Cholera: Public and Private', *Cleveland and Teesside History Society Bulletin*, 38 (1980), p.9.
8   L. Polley, 'Housing the Community, 1830–1914', Chapter 7 in A. Pollard (ed.), *Middlesbrough Town and Community 1830–1950* (Stroud, 1996), p.157. The site of Holmes's house became the site of the National Provincial Bank (1871–2), while Bolckow and Vaughan's houses have been combined as Cleveland House; Queen's Terrace is still extant, although used as office accommodation.

cally manifested in the rather awkward coming-together of the Middlesbrough Owners' east–west pattern of roads and streets and the diagonal grid of Newport and Cannon Wards. Much of the town's still-existing row or terraced housing was constructed under local bye-laws during the 1880s and 90s. It exhibits the solid uniformity of the type, much more impressive in the aggregate than when considered alone, despite the subsequent deterioration of Middlesbrough's physical fabric.

Inevitably, migration of the more wealthy and influential had long since started. Some, like Henry Bolckow and John Vaughan, moved to outlying villages. These two iron-masters both evacuated from Cleveland Street to Marton, with Bolckow building Marton Hall from 1853 and Vaughan occupying Gunnergate Hall in 1858. For those who could not aspire to residences of that magnitude the southern reaches of the town offered a practical and healthy location from which to commute, and by the end of the century Middlesbrough boasted a number of increasingly grandiose residential suburbs (see below). The size, shape and experience of living in the town now changed out of all proportion. As it sprawled to the south, its original spacious centre was quickly turned into an unhealthy, overcrowded and neglected slum. Those who could afford to moved out into whichever suburban neighbourhood was appropriate to their means and social status. The railway line effectively cut off (if only psychologically) the rapidly deteriorating old town from a rapidly developing newer one, encouraging the 'over the border' epithet still current today.

In 1850, the discovery of iron ore in the Cleveland Hills had prompted Bolckow and Vaughan to open the first blast furnaces in Middlesbrough. Twelve years later there were forty-two blast furnaces in the town and by 1855 production of pig iron exceeded 84,000 tons and, by 1860, 500,000 tons.[9] There was also a dramatic growth in other trades, such as shipbuilding, and the discovery of a substantial bed of rock salt made by a number of iron-workers while boring in the 1870s led in due course to the formation of a major chemical industry. Similarly, as the town expanded during the 1860s and 70s it also developed socially and culturally, evolving a more complex infrastructure of shops, services and public amenities. Social institutions, clubs and activities that originated at this time included the new Mechanics' Institute in Durham Street (1859), the Masonic Hall on Marton Road (1861) and the Athenaeum (later the Literary and Philosophical Society) on Linthorpe Road (1864).

The rapid growth of the town and its incorporation led in 1873 to proposals for the building of a new Town Hall. Two architectural competitions were held. The first, in 1875, was abandoned but the second, in 1882, went ahead and was adjudicated by Alfred Waterhouse, one of the leading architects of the time.[10] The result was the present Town Hall and Municipal Buildings in Corporation Road (1883–9), the masterwork of the prolific Darlington architect G.G. Hoskins (1837–1911; see Chapter 12). The complex is in a thirteenth-century

---

[9] G.A. North, *Teesside's Economic Heritage* (Middlesbrough, 1975), p.20.
[10] Waterhouse's family were Quakers and cotton brokers. His plans for a Friends' Meeting House in Liverpool (not built) brought him to the attention of the Society of Friends professionally and socially. He married Elizabeth Hodgkin, which sealed the North-East Quaker connection.

French Gothic style, faced in local grey stone, with roofs of Westmorland slate. It is very much in the manner of Waterhouse himself (Hoskins had acted as clerk of works for Waterhouse on several projects early in his career) and owes an obvious debt not only to his great Manchester Town Hall (1868–77) but also to an earlier unexecuted design by him for a town hall in Middlesbrough, prepared for the first, abortive competition. Middlesbrough Town Hall's main front to Corporation Road, with its central gable and rose window, is a symmetrical composition, the central location of the great hall itself being clearly marked by the eight large windows on the principal floor. Between six of these are carved figures of Music, Literature, Painting and Commerce, while at either end of the range are French-style pavilion roofs with iron cresting. The Municipal Buildings, extending back along what was once Russell Street, have bands of carved ornament between the main storeys and at parapet level, topped by tall pitched and pavilion roofs.

Another splendid Victorian addition to Middlesbrough's urban landscape was Albert Park, received in 1868 as the gift of Henry Bolckow, the town's foremost iron-master and first mayor. It had been laid out, with a combination of informality and axiality typical of the contemporary 'gardenesque' style, by William Barratt, a horticulturalist and nurseryman from Wakefield, probably with the assistance of John Dunning, Middlesbrough's Borough Engineer. The park plan shows a cross-axis of paths that meet centrally at a *ronde pointe* (now the site of a fountain), carefully relating to the park's entrances. The original gates to the main entrance on Linthorpe Road, of which the whereabouts are now unknown, were made by Walker's Victoria Foundry of York and purchased by Bolckow from the city's Yorkshire Fine Art and Industrial Exhibition of 1866. A contemporary description recorded that the park:

> contains a fine avenue of Wellingtonias, planted by Mr. Bolckow and his friends … a handsome lake has been formed at one end of the park, and a bowling green and a cricket ground have also been provided. A circular plot in the centre is reserved for statuary; and on three sides of the park land is reserved for villas of approved design, in front of which is a macadamised road for carriages.[11]

The town also deserves to be better known for its once-attractive and substantial suburban development. Probably it would be were it not for the scale of recent destruction, as ring roads, redevelopment and the commercial and industrial reuse of many suburban villas have taken a heavy toll. Moreover, Middlesbrough's suburbs did not contain the rich or the upwardly mobile for very long. The scale of the town itself was never large, and perhaps the effect of its 'newness' was difficult to shrug off. Cultural institutions never really established themselves and arguably there was too little time for the development of the kind of urban elite which could support a permanent culture of wealth within the town.

---

[11] White's *Directory of the City of York, the Boroughs … Towns … and Principal Villages in the North Riding of Yorkshire* (Sheffield, 1867), p.554.

Of Middlesbrough's four major suburbs – Southfield Villas (developed from 1853), North Park Road, with its 'Park Villas' (from 1866), Grove Hill (from the early 1870s) and Linthorpe, also developed from the early 1870s onwards – only Linthorpe survives reasonably unspoiled. This is doubtless due to its location, its smaller-scale housing and its consequent present-day desirability. Perhaps significantly, Linthorpe was also the first of the Middlesbrough suburbs to be reliant on public transport, whereas its older and more prestigious counterparts were designed primarily for 'carriage folk'. It was also envisaged as a self-contained 'village community' in its own right, well supplied with shops and services. By contrast, Grove Hill seemed to outlive its purely residential purpose comparatively quickly and is no longer extant, although a certain number of its houses remain; Southfield Villas and North Park Road are similarly devastated.

The development of Southfield Villas began in June 1853, when the Middlesbrough Owners signed an agreement to sell ten plots of land to a 'Villa Building Society' for £100 each. These were situated on the southern-most boundary of the town and were quickly developed. The location chosen for the new suburb was about a mile from the railway line and along the main southbound thoroughfare, Linthorpe Road. The line of the new villa road had been the southern boundary of 'Middlesbrough Farm', and at that time would have seemed exclusive and remote from the town. All the sites seem to have been owned by the people actually intending to occupy these suburban villas, who formed a building society in order to do so. Indeed, the residents of the new suburb were local figures of considerable power and influence, mostly involved in the iron business and in public life,[12] and no doubt their enterprise seemed a sound investment. The houses at Southfield Villas were relatively large, three- and four-bedroomed family homes, two of which had the added status of being detached. There is no doubt that 'villas', with the associated image of grand and relaxed country living – by the middle of the nineteenth century a connection appropriated by the urban middle classes – were what was wanted, rather than mere houses. It was J.C. Loudon's *Encyclopaedia of Cottage, Farm and Villa Architecture and Furniture* (1833) that did most to popularise the semi-detached villa type chosen for Southfield Villas and which later became so much a part of suburban development nationally.

These sturdy, symmetrical brick-built dwellings, embellished with fashionable, classical architectural elements, also had bay windows, by this time an essential feature of the middle-class home. Although some of the villas remain, they have been altered almost beyond the point of recognition. However, the distinctive local brick that was used can be seen on parts of the surviving buildings and (until its demolition a few years ago) there was decorative cast-iron cresting on the end house on the corner of Woodlands Road, giving the more Italianate look that later became dominant in Middlesbrough. The original villas appear to have been designed by builders or surveyors, as opposed to architects, but, from the 1860s onwards, various local architects became involved.

---

[12] For nineteenth-century residents of Southfield Villas, their occupations and their local political achievements, see L. Polley, *The Other Middlesbrough: A Study of Three 19th Century Suburbs* (Middlesbrough, 1993), pp.20–21.

Southfield Villas remained a desirable neighbourhood for about twenty years. However, the Borough Surveyor C.E. Latham's plan of Middlesbrough of 1874 shows southward development closing the gap and thereby lessening exclusivity. Residents began to buy from the Middlesbrough Owners parcels of land behind the villas. This 'buffer zone' was in most instances used to provide a private back garden or, occasionally, stables and accommodation for servants. The 1874 plan also shows the laying-out of West Terrace, Woodlands Terrace and East Terrace at the eastern end of Southfield Villas. John Dunning may have had a hand in this, for in July 1866 he had drawn up a 'Plan of Villa Sites on the Middlesbrough Estate' for the Middlesbrough Owners. This shows an ambitious layout of four rows of nine buildings each, with entry from either Southfield or Borough Roads. There is no indication of the type of houses intended – they may well have been terraced – but in any case the scheme was never completed. Woodlands Terrace became Woodlands Road and, although some large houses were built there, plots appear to have been developed separately rather than as part of one scheme.

Southfield Villas was eventually engulfed as development followed the main thoroughfare of Linthorpe Road, and, although the Ordnance Survey map of 1895 shows the villas as still possessing large gardens, they no longer boasted unrestricted views to the south. By contrast, on the north side of the development there is something of a 'green belt' and here the villas are protected by the presence of the Grammar School (1876) and two houses with very large gardens on Woodlands Road. In addition, land between Southfield Road and Borough Road remained undeveloped, even though by this time the upper echelons of Middlesbrough society had long been looking to live elsewhere.

With the rapid encircling of Southfield Villas, it is no surprise to find that Albert Park itself was viewed as another location which could ensure a green and leafy vista for prospective residents, as well as an ideal landscape within which suburban houses could be viewed from afar. Moreover, the circular drive around the park linked directly to Marton Road at the north-east corner and could therefore facilitate visiting, via a pleasant and highly visible route. Thus by 1868 four very large, three-storey semi-detached 'Park Villas', designed by local architect William Lofthouse, looked out impressively across the park to the south. Two were built for Henry Bolckow himself. Although designed to create a unified whole, the two sets of semi-detached 'villas' were different enough internally and externally to appeal to middle-class notions of both individuality and conformity. Their main entrances were originally at the east and west ends rather than on the park fronts.

By 1875 six 'villas of approved design' had been completed adjacent to the park. These comprised Lofthouse's and two more near its entrance on Linthorpe Road: Hilda House, designed by local architect William Duncan in 1874 for Thomas Hutchinson, an ironmaster, and Bon Accord Lodge, built for David Douall Wilson, a local builder, alderman and mayor of Middlesbrough, in 1876. Both are now demolished. Hilda House was a detached, three-storey house of brick with stone dressings, with an elevated terrace and centrally placed main entrance with a Gothic arch above. A surviving house on the other side of North Park Road, on the corner of what eventually became Belk Street, was designed

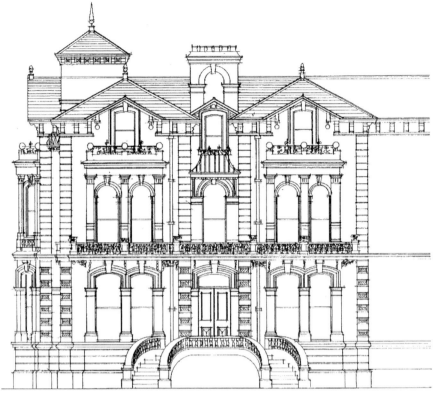

Garden Elevation

Figure 14.3. A 'French Chateau'-style villa: 'Ravenscroft', Grove Hill, Middlesbrough, 1878 (architect William Blessley), demolished. Redrawn from plans submitted for planning consent (L. Polley, *The Other Middlesbrough: A Study of Three 19th Century Suburbs*, 1993).

in 1876 by local architect John Hunter for the businessman William T. Keay. It has a double-bay-window front elevation with steps up to a porticoed front door, and is in a recognisable Middlesbrough style, with steeply pitched slate roofs, a certain amount of decorative stonework and that peculiar combination of Gothic above and Romanesque below that characterises many of the town's larger buildings. Nearby, Albert, Grosvenor, Park and Imeson Terraces had been laid out for development by 1875. They were never developed to the extent anticipated by the Middlesbrough Owners Plan, but for the most part those houses that were built still remain. The area expanded little after about 1885, the scale and continuing popularity of Albert Park saving it from intensive development; its surroundings are therefore comparatively easy to imagine in their suburban heyday.

Meanwhile, the Borough Surveyor's plan of 1874 also shows building plots laid out for middle-class housing in Grove Hill and on the Crescent in New Linthorpe, although at this time very few of the plots had been built on.

Both schemes were intended to take advantage of the possibilities offered by extending existing arterial routes (Linthorpe and Marton Roads) into the surrounding countryside. By 1874, too, the commercial focus and public face of Middlesbrough had shifted away from the original old town to the area of the railway station and the Exchange (1866–8). At its northern terminus, Marton Road led into Exchange Place, thus serving as one of the main routes to and from this central meeting place. By about 1870, as the town expanded, Marton Road became quite built up. Similarly, Linthorpe Road offered the potential for further growth through its importance as the main road south, and then by the accumulative positioning of the cemetery, Southfield Villas, Albert Park and all the in-fill building in between.

Along Marton Road a variety of housing was built. Small terraced houses for better-off working-class citizens and larger terraced housing for the upwardly mobile were juxtaposed with quite large semi-detached and detached houses. Along its southern reaches large detached residences, surrounded by very large gardens, were built from about 1864. This district, eventually known as Grove Hill, included the largest and most expensive houses ever built in Middlesbrough. Preferred architectural styles included Gothic, Italian Renaissance and even 'French Chateau' (Fig. 14.3). One surviving house, Park View, now used as office accommodation, was occupied in 1867 by George Neasham, an ironworks manager. It is a relatively unspoilt example of mid-Victorian suburban building, making good use of 'off the peg' architectural ornament.[13] By the 1880s Grove Hill had become a very specific area marked by a toll gate on the west side of Marton Road, emphasising the neighbourhood's separation and exclusivity. Up to the turn of the century it continued to be added to by the wealthiest of the Middlesbrough citizenry who had decided not to leave the town for country and county circles, a Grove Hill address retaining its 'snob value' until at least the First World War.

Middlesbrough also possesses some remarkable engineering landmarks that further punctuate any perceived monotony in the townscape. Examples include the Newport Lifting Bridge, opened in 1934, and the Transporter Bridge, both designed to facilitate the movement of shipping on the Tees. The Transporter Bridge is the more delicate of the two, with its tall, graceful, pylon-like towers and span of 174m. Opened in 1911, it was designed by the French engineer Ferdinand Arnodin (consulting engineer: C.G. Imbault) and replaced an earlier and long-established ferry service across the river to Port Clarence. Prior to its building, the ancient inland ports of Stockton and Yarm had provided the only bridge crossings within the area of the Tees estuary. The Transporter Bridge, the largest bridge of its type still operating worldwide, is often regarded as a symbol of Middlesbrough, and its iconic status has been recently enhanced by winter floodlighting. The steel truss structure, fabricated by Sir William Arrol

---

[13]   To the south was Cleveland Lodge, built for and occupied by Thomas Vaughan until the death of his father John in 1868, and the largest and most extravagantly landscaped house on Marton Road, while important later houses, all similarly indicative of the considerable architectural pretensions of the area, included Highfield (by Ross & Lamb, 1873, now the Highfield Hotel), Ravenscroft (by William Blessley, 1878, now demolished, see Fig. 14.3) and Southend (by I. Mitchell Bottomley, 1890, latterly a nursing home but now also demolished).

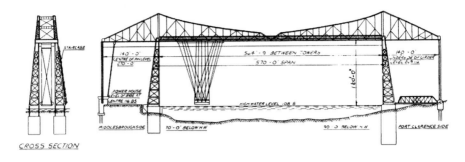

CROSS SECTION

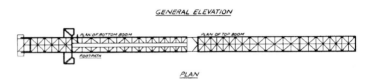

GENERAL ELEVATION

PLAN

Figure 14.4. General Elevation and Plan of the Transporter Bridge at Middlesbrough (D. Pattenden, *The History of the River Tees in Maps*, 3rd edn, 2001).

and Company Ltd, of Glasgow, consists of two cantilevered 'halves', rather like cranes, joining in the centre. From a travelling frame or carriage, supported on this structure, the passenger 'gondola', or car, is suspended by steel cables and propels a platform-like section of the roadway from one bank of the river to the other[14] (Fig. 14.4).

Throughout this period of expansion, the most significant long-term trend for Middlesbrough's seemingly buoyant economy was the worldwide increase in the demand for steel. But, with the Cleveland ores being unsuitable for steel production, ore had to be imported and the town found itself converting to the steel industry just when the economic conditions became unfavourable. The beginning of the twentieth century saw a world depression and a fall in the demand for steel. Even such enterprises as the local firm Dorman Long's construction of the Sydney Harbour Bridge – which alone required the production of 51,000 tons of steel – and Newcastle's Tyne Bridge, opened in 1928, were not enough to withstand poor economic conditions. The 1930s saw a new emphasis on the coke industry, with the building of the Cleveland Works in 1936 and a new mill which concentrated on light sections and bars.

By 1931 Middlesbrough had a population of 139,000 living in 29,000 houses. The economy became depressed and unemployment rose to a peak of 18,000 in 1933. This represented a proportion of 30 per cent, more than twice the national average.[15] In the 1930s great efforts were made to encourage businesses of all types to relocate to the region, with the formation of the Tees Development

14   For more on the Transporter Bridge see D. Pattenden, *The History of the River Tees in Maps* (3rd edn, Middlesbrough, 2001).
15   North, *Teesside*, p.74.

Board and the North East Development Board in 1930 and 1934 respectively. However, Teesside's failure to secure Special Area status in 1934 exacerbated the region's problems and added a further sense of urgency to finding a solution. A thirty-one-page *Daily Telegraph* supplement entitled 'Tees-side and its Industries', published in December 1935, actively promoted the area to potential investors,[16] but an upturn of the local economy occurred only as a result of impending war. After the Second World War those iron and steel works that remained became concentrated at Lackenby and Redcar, to the east of Middlesbrough. In 1951 49 per cent of the town's working population was still employed in the steel industry. However, by 1961 the figure had fallen to only 15 per cent and since this time there has been further contraction in heavy manufacturing jobs. As recently as the year 2000 it was still pertinent to observe that 'The old industrial Teesside of "fire and horror" has been replaced by a different vision of hell – a working town without work.'[17]

In view of all this, it is far from contentious to suggest that Middlesbrough has had a major 'image problem' for some time. Few, if any architectural historians have studied the town, despite the general revival of interest in Victorian architecture. Nikolaus Pevsner so loftily dismissed the worth of any buildings outside the centre of Middlesbrough that one wonders whether he visited the town at all. At the end of a 'perambulation' that started in the old Market Place and ended at Corporation Road, he wrote: 'Here endeth this report on the centre of Middlesbrough. The big-townish appearance goes only skin deep. Everywhere, looking out of the few main streets, are the interminable rows of two-storeyed cottages, and outside the centre hardly anything calls for perambulating.'[18]

Not surprisingly, the town has always felt the need to justify and explain itself. Indeed, one could argue that Middlesbrough has been involved in the 'image business' right from the start. Joseph Pease's prospectus and Richard Otley's plan promoted and depicted a civilised and brightly imagined future settlement – not exactly Utopia, but a well-ordered and regulated environment for anyone adventurous enough to accept the challenge of living there. Moreover, in the nineteenth century everyone in Middlesbrough was an immigrant, and had invested more than just money in their removal to this new and untried town – an industrial enclave within an agricultural landscape, which inevitably created a problematic cultural and economic dichotomy.

Thus people needed 'reasons to believe', and so 'myth-making was a central process in the shaping of Middlesbrough's early history',[19] contributing to the strong and continuing sense of community and place. W.E. Gladstone's calling the new town 'an infant, but an Infant Hercules'[20] is a good example of this, as is Lady Bell's less flattering reference to Middlesbrough's 'little brown houses'

---

16 'Teesside and its Industries', *Daily Telegraph*, 16 December 1935.
17 A. Croft, 'Fire and Horror: The Representation of Teesside in Fiction', in H.G. Klaus and S. Knight (eds), *British Industrial Fictions* (Cardiff, 2000), p.96.
18 N. Pevsner et al, *The Buildings of England: Yorkshire, The North Riding* (Harmondsworth, 1966), p.253.
19 A. Nicholson, 'Jacky and the Jubilee', in Pollard, *Middlesbrough Town*, p.52.
20 W.E. Gladstone on his visit to Middlesbrough, 9 October 1862.

in her book *At the Works* of 1907. This survey of the lives of the women whose husbands worked at Bell's ironworks has provided a lasting visual image of the town: 'there arise, hastily erected, instantly occupied, the rows and rows of little brown streets … day by day the little houses spring hurriedly into existence … the unending vista of street after street, all alike.'[21] Such images are still current today, perpetuated by their regular reappearance in newspapers and popular local histories.

However, Gladstone's 'Infant Hercules' was also one of many phrases used to promote the town's pride in its enterprise, financial success and municipal growth. As the nineteenth century progressed Middlesbrough acquired all the trappings of a burgeoning industrial town, not least its public buildings, and, in a town that had literally grown from nothing, buildings were always an important indication of status and achievement. The dissemination of images of these structures in journals such as *The Builder* and *The Illustrated London News* placed the town on a national stage, emphasising its youthful but serious demeanour, its technological innovation and its thriving and busy contribution to the world economy.

Yet in 1887 Middlesbrough was described as 'not an attractive town. Its position and surroundings, and its atmosphere heavy with the smoke and fumes of a hundred blast furnaces and hundreds of puddling furnaces are against that. Neither is it a well-built town.'[22] And by the end of the nineteenth century, after seventy years of neglect and industrial pollution, much of the town's earlier housing was unfit for human habitation and recognised as such. This aspect of Middlesbrough's history has been graphically captured in photographs, as in a series taken by the local Medical Officer of Health in the early 1900s, which provide haunting and unassailable evidence of the conditions in which some people were forced to live. Similar photographs taken in the 1940s and 50s indicate that these problems were not readily solved. These images have since achieved an iconic status through their disturbing depiction of an unimaginable existence, and through their repeated illustrative use.

For better or worse, Middlesbrough's identity is firmly rooted in its industry, its urban-ness, its novelty and its survival. The town has a relatively short history and its heritage is an industrial one. Consequently, much of its promotion or presentation has been based on a 'romantic' response to industry. What the novelist Arnold Bennett wrote about Tunstall in Staffordshire could just as easily apply to Middlesbrough:

> Nothing could be more prosaic than the huddled, red-brown streets; nothing more seemingly remote from romance. Yet be it said that romance is even here – the romance which, for those who have an eye to perceive it, ever dwells amid the seats of industrial manufacture, softening the coarseness, transfiguring the squalor, of these mighty alchemic operations.[23]

---

[21] F. Bell, *At the Works* (London, 1907), p.3
[22] *Daily Exchange*, 3 March 1887.
[23] A. Bennett, *Anna of the Five Towns* (1902; this edn, Harmondsworth, 1973), p.25.

Even in travel writer Douglas Goldring's damning view of the town in 1925, there is a hint of the romance inherent in Middlesbrough's 'alchemic operations':

> Until recently, so great was my ignorance, I had no idea such places really existed … And yet, even Middlesbrough, by accident as it were, has a kind of frightful loveliness which the eyes of a younger generation, trained by the Cubists, will be able to appreciate better than we can. Its miles and miles of ironworks, with their belching chimneys and enormous blast furnaces, their fantastic pipes and tubes and monstrous retorts, their sudden bursts of flame and rising columns of smoke – white brown or densest black – have a strange and dreadful beauty, *macabre* and terrifying. It is the only beauty, apart from the delicate outlines of its transporter bridge, that the town of Middlesbrough can boast. All else is mean with a meanness that has to be seen to be believed.[24]

A year later Harold Hood, a local printer and photographer, produced a vigorous response to Goldring's horrified critique in the form of a book containing photographs of every aspect of Middlesbrough life. Included are the Town Hall, Albert Park, the docks, the Exchange, the railway, blast furnaces, banks, the library, commercial and residential streets, the Dorman Museum, the cathedral, statues and heroic images of large-scale machinery.[25] On the other hand, Thomas Sharp's chapter 'Hell, Utopia and Middlesbrough' in his book *English Panorama* (1936) is a classic example of the 'country good, city bad' philosophy that was a quasi-official response to the squalid consequences of Victorian urban development as seen in towns like Middlesbrough, and which underpinned the approach inherent in so much inter-war planning. 'Towns in England,' wrote Sharp, 'are mean, squalid and squandering; they have neither form nor order, let alone beauty.'[26] Clearly referring to Middlesbrough, he stated that 'such were the new towns through which England gained half the world and lost her own soul.'[27] A later response is an article of 1945 by the artist John Piper, entitled 'Introduction to Middlesbrough'. Although in some ways wistfully romantic, it makes the post-war town seem a neglected and empty place. Walk in any direction from the station, he suggests, and 'the atmosphere of the years of forced and awkward growth will soon be felt; the background of Victorian compassion and cruelty, of aspiration fogged by commercialism that belong to this over-developed, half-decayed place.'[28]

Almost inevitably, therefore, the planner Max Lock's *The Middlesbrough Survey and Plan* (1945) included a carefully constructed series of 'before and after' photographs, drawings, models and plans. Lock had been appointed Town Planning Consultant to the Middlesbrough Corporation. His images made an apparently insurmountable case for wholesale demolition of the unhealthy and outmoded historical fabric and its replacement with a new, modern, scientifi-

---

[24] D. Goldring, *Gone Abroad, A Story of Travel, Chiefly in Italy and the Balearic Isles* (London, 1925), pp.234–35.
[25] See H. Hood (ed.), *Middlesbrough Industrial and Pictorial* (Middlesbrough, 1926).
[26] T. Sharp, *English Panorama* (London, 1936), p.12.
[27] Ibid., p.63.
[28] J. Piper, 'Introduction to Middlesbrough', *Cornhill Magazine*, 161:966 (1945), pp.432–3.

Figure 14.5. The Middlehaven (Middlesbrough) Master Plan, 2004, model. Architects Will Alsop Partnership (photograph © Tees Valley Regeneration).

cally planned urban environment. His scheme would have also entailed the demolition of the eastern range of the town's Municipal Buildings and, in order to create a more convincing town centre, the erection of several Le Corbusian office blocks terminating in a new council chamber. All this was in line with the idea of utopian reconstruction that lay at the root of much post-war urban redevelopment. However, very few of Lock's proposed alterations to Middlesbrough were implemented, and then only partially. It would appear that the mere act of commissioning a plan from a nationally recognised 'expert', together with the surrounding publicity and local promotion, was enough, providing local government with some sense of morale-boosting participation in a national programme of reconstruction.

Yet, despite all the unfavourable commentary, the sheer novelty of Middlesbrough's accelerated nineteenth-century growth, from almost nothing to 'a town which … commands the attention of statesmen',[29] cannot easily be disregarded. Even the article of 1887, cited earlier, describing the conurbation as 'not an attractive town', did continue as follows: 'But as it grows older the main thoroughfares are at least being improved. Here and there a fine public building is springing up, it boasts a good railway station, its shops are being enlarged: dotted all over the town are churches, chapels and schools with considerable architectural pretensions.'[30]

[29] L. Praed, *History of the Rise and Progress of Middlesbrough* (Middlesbrough, 1863), p.28.
[30] *Daily Exchange*, ibid.

One hundred and twenty years later Middlesbrough finds itself attempting to reconnect with its Victorian optimism in a practical and modern response to decades of economic depression and an accumulative 'bad press'. Middlehaven, an £18 million regeneration project currently underway north of the town centre, has been driven by needs similar to those of the 1930s, but comes couched in more recent terminology and in the form of more glamorous visual persuaders. In 2003, David Carr, English Partnerships' Area Director, spoke optimistically of the completed site's impact on public perception: 'The scope and ambition of the Middlehaven regeneration project creates the potential to change not only the waterfront and the under-used land adjoining it, but people's perceptions of Middlesbrough and the sub-region as a place for investment.'[31]

The arresting and certainly newsworthy riverside master plan (Fig. 14.5) is the work of architects Will Alsop Partnerships; the proposed mixed development promises to provide housing, offices, culture and leisure facilities, as well as a primary school and a new site for Middlesbrough College. Its impact on the existing town may well be a complete shift of emphasis to the north east, although the intention is that this will not be to the detriment of the existing centre. Consequently, in conjunction with the riverside project, a new regional art gallery (Middlesbrough Institute of Modern Art – MIMA, Fig. 14.6) has recently been created in an enlarged civic space. This lies on seemingly redundant territory right in the town centre and adjacent to the Victorian Town Hall, the early-twentieth-century Carnegie Central Library (1912) and the postmodern Court Buildings. Both the gallery, designed by the Dutch architect Erik van Egeraat, and the new green space, by Dutch landscapers West 8, have therefore had to make sense of a range of chronologically varied buildings – these are respected both in scale and materials – as well as the 'Bottle of Notes', an existing (1993) public sculpture by Claes Oldenburg and Coosje van Bruggen. In direct reference to Middlesbrough's industrial past, paths of oxidised steel cut across the grass, while a number of water features, some 'sumptuous public seating',[32] young trees and relocated statues of historical figures provide a third dimension to this very wide-open space.

MIMA's main facade fronts a three-storey glass 'box' and a full-height foyer, linking gallery and public square and through which the main staircase cuts diagonally up to galleries, archive and education rooms, a conservation studio and an outdoor observation platform. The building, which is intended to form the heart of the town's new cultural quarter, has had mixed reviews from the architectural press,[33] although most recognise what is involved in the 'regeneration game' and have been at pains to consider the building within its urban and cultural context:

---

[31] 'Regeneration Catalyst', *Outlook: The English Partnerships Magazine* ('Brownfield Revival' issue) (Spring 2003), p.10.

[32] H. Pearman, 'If that's Art, I'm a Dutchman: Erik van Egeraat's First Building and its Sisterhood of Regional Art Centres', *RIBA Journal* (February 2007), p.45.

[33] See, for example, Pearman, 'If that's Art' and 'You Don't Have to Have a Gehry to Change a Town', *Sunday Times*, 14 January, 2007; S. Bayley, 'How Boro Will Lose its 'Crap Town' Tag', *Observer*, 28 January 2007; S. Rose, 'Shine On', *Guardian*, 15 January 2007; I. Herbert, 'Introducing Mima, Middlesbrough's Moma', *Independent*, 27 January 2007.

Figure 14.6. The Middlesbrough Institute of Modern Art (MIMA), 2006–7; architect Erik van Egeraat (author's photograph).

Not only does it unify a disparate collection of buildings, it links up with a park beyond to create a useful new corridor of public space. There is still a plot next to MIMA for another new building, something to draw shoppers in, van Egeraat hopes. Footballers aside, Middlesbrough is still not a place that's flush with jobs or spending power, and it will be a while before any significant regeneration effects will be felt. But there is at least an abundance of optimism, and somewhere to channel it.[34]

As elsewhere, the local university finds itself another key player in the regeneration process, and over the last ten years has completed a range of steel and glass buildings to add to Middlesbrough's twenty-first-century urban 'mix'. In 1997 the University of Teesside's Learning and Resources Centre initiated the expansion and enhancement of this city-centre campus. Since then four more additions have reflected the growth in Middlesbrough's student population: the Centuria Building for the School of Health and Social Care (2000), the Olympia Building for Sports Science (2002), and the Phoenix and Athena Buildings for the School of Arts and Media (both 2007). The university's growth has also encouraged a peripheral 'buy to let' property boom. This has manifested itself most spectacularly in the complete renovation of a long-empty eight-storey

---

[34] Rose, 'Shine On'.

office block on Borough Road into relatively luxurious private student accommodation.

Modern, fashionable and expensive retail outlets have also begun to appear at the northern end of Linthorpe Road, taking advantage of redundant properties and an apparently vibrant retail culture. A number of tower blocks in the town centre have been revamped, and further north, near the railway station, a 'Heritage Quarter' of large Victorian commercial properties has been delineated and owners are offered grant funding in exchange for sympathetic restoration and repair. So, this particular North-Eastern landscape is again in the process of dramatic reshaping, the physical renaissance indicating (hopefully driving) a new sense of place for inhabitants and visitors alike.

If nothing else, these new and cosmetically improved buildings argue for an alternative modernity to the poorly constructed and badly ageing examples which, in this town, as elsewhere, had given Modernism a bad name. Middlesbrough appeared to have lost its way architecturally: the juxtaposition of neglected Victorian cheek by jowl with unimaginative Modern created a dispirited and dispiriting urban environment that seemed to provide physical proof of permanent disenchantment. Civic awareness and enthusiasm is presently being 'buffed up', along with the town itself, and although the transformation is far from complete, the town should once again become a source of pride to its inhabitants: not Hell, not Utopia, just Middlesbrough.

PART FIVE

PERCEPTIONS AND REPRESENTATIONS

15

Landscape, Taste and National Identity:
William Hutchinson's *View of Northumberland*
(1776–8)

HELEN BERRY

One of the key problems in addressing the idea of British identity is that there is no consensus about whether such a thing has ever existed. Historians such as David Rollinson have highlighted the slippage between the terms 'British' and 'English' as applied by contemporary observers of eighteenth-century society, a trend which continues even today.[1] Immediately after the Act of Union in 1707, the problem facing Britain, as Norman Davies has observed, was that the Union was not underpinned 'by history, by culture, or by popular enthusiasm'.[2] The challenge in the eighteenth century was to forge a common identity and purpose 'to create not just a British state, but a British nation'.[3] This chapter proposes that the county historian's role in the project of constructing a culturally unified nation was as a mediator of historical 'truth' about what it meant to be British through an exploration at the local level of the cultural and political inheritance of the Isles, what Jason Whittaker has called the 'matter of Britain'.[4] It proposes that the genre of county-history writing took on specific form and meaning in the eighteenth century, providing validation for a national political system after 1707 and a common identity in the face of perceived and actual external threats to British sovereignty. This was exemplified in the county histories of William Hutchinson, in particular his *View of Northumberland* (1776–78), the subject of which brings into especial focus the point of contact between English and Scottish cultures in this North-Eastern border county. Hutchinson's new contribution to the genre, as we shall see, was his introduction of the idea of the 'man of taste' as the standard-bearer for the good British subject. His county histories

---

[1] See D. Rollinson, 'Exploding England: the Dialectics of Mobility and Settlement in Early Modern England', *Social History*, 24:1 (1999), *passim*.

[2] N. Davies, *The Isles: A History* (London, 1999), p.696.

[3] Ibid. See also A. Janowitz, *England's Ruins: Poetic Purpose and the National Landscape* (Oxford, 1990), p.3.

[4] J. Whittaker, *William Blake and the Myths of Britain* (London and New York, 1999), see Introduction, pp.1–17 and *passim*.

both reflected and informed opinion on the meaning of local identity and land-scape within the context of British national culture.

In order fully to understand the county histories compiled during the late Georgian period we need to go back to the origins of the genre, which has its roots in the antiquarian writing of Tudor scholars.[5] English local histories were written as early as the fifteenth century by antiquaries such as William Worcester, and were part of a revival in the study of artefacts, history and liter-ature of ancient civilisations that is commonly associated with the European Renaissance.[6] County-wide surveys that formed a practical guide to each area, written by 'gentlemen writing for gentlemen', were also popular in the Eliza-bethan era; their common characteristics were a strong interest in topography, genealogy and antiquarianism. John Leland's projected *History and Antiquities of the Nation*, which remained incomplete at the author's death in 1552, and William Lambarde's *Perambulation of Kent* (1576) were two early examples.[7] These were followed more famously by William Camden, the most important antiquary of the late sixteenth century, and his *Britannia* (1586), a county-by-county description of Britain that was published originally in Latin and trans-lated into the vernacular in 1610. Camden's was the first comprehensive account of British history up to medieval times, with an encyclopaedia of English coun-ties and digressions 'upon all manner of curiosities'.[8] At approximately the same time the first comprehensive maps of English counties were produced by Christopher Saxton, whose achievements in cartography 'determined the visual image of England and of its constituent parts of over a century to come'.[9] In addition to their aesthetic or decorative merit, these maps served a utilitarian purpose as useful tools for central government, and a protection against foreign invasion: Saxton's work, for example, was sponsored by Thomas Seckford, a lawyer who was later surveyor to the court of Works and Liveries under the patronage of Lord Burghley, and his map of Devon marked out places of danger that were probable vantage-points for a foreign invader. Raphael Holinshed's *Chronicles* (1577 and 1587), which were famously used by Shakespeare as the main source for his history plays, also stimulated interest in Saxton's maps.[10]

English county histories produced in the sixteenth and seventeenth centuries were a response to the growing importance of the county as a political unit of administration at the local level.[11] The earliest county histories were in essence the stories of the local landed families, many of whom sponsored their publica-tion. The antiquarian interest of the Stuart gentry was a somewhat ambivalent indication of local identity, maintaining a symbolic status that did not neces-sarily find expression in economic reality or local social status.[12] The preoccupa-

---

5   See C. Currie and C. Lewis, *English County Histories: A Guide* (Stroud, 1994).
6   J. Simmons, *English County Historians* (Wakefield, 1978), p.4.
7   Whittaker, *William Blake*, pp.6–7.
8   Ibid.
9   V. Morgan, 'The Cartographic Image of 'The Country' in Early Modern England', *Transactions of the Royal Historical Society*, 5th ser., 29 (1979), p.133.
10 Ibid., pp.140–42.
11 L. Stone and J. F. Stone, *An Open Elite? England 1540–1880* (Oxford, 1986), p.27.
12 J. Broadway, 'William Dugdale and the Significance of County History in Early Stuart England', *Dugdale Society Occasional Papers*, 39 (1999), p.8.

tion and concerns of the gentry were reflected mainly because the new county histories were facilitated by gentlemen scholars and a group of professional surveyors who systematically compiled descriptive accounts of each county for the first time.[13] Thus the popular perception of England's geography was shaped during the early modern period by a visual and written culture that was delineated according to one of the key units of political administration: the county. John Speed's *Theatre of the Empire of Great Britain* (1611), in the immediate aftermath of the Union of the Crowns, was a volume of maps accompanying his *History of Great Britain*, and appealed to educated groups nationwide with an interest in antiquities and current affairs. Meanwhile, a new generation emerged in the seventeenth century whose life work consisted of surveying and mapping specific counties. The more famous early examples of these included Richard Carew's *Survey of Cornwall* (1602), and the *Description of Leicester* (1597–1604) by William Burton.[14] Many early works, such as Sampson Erdeswicke's *Survey of Staffordshire*, begun in 1593, remained unfinished at the time of the author's death and were unpublished for many decades, even centuries. Both Burton and Erdeswicke reflected the primary interest of their own sort, the gentry, in their preoccupation with genealogy.[15]

The first 'classic' county history is generally considered to be William Dugdale's *Antiquities of Warwickshire* (1656). This 800-page text drew upon public records, private papers, chronicles, genealogies and heraldry; it was a scholarly and comprehensive account that many subsequent writers on other counties sought to emulate. Dugdale's methodology was also representative of the practice of authors and antiquarians in that he enlisted the help of local gentry and professional groups in gathering material for his work. A close-knit circle of gentlemen historians working in the Midlands, many of whom were given personal encouragement by Dugdale, produced several accounts in the late seventeenth century that imitated the latter's *History of Warwickshire*; examples include Robert Thoroton's *Antiquities of Nottinghamshire* (1677) and Peter Leycester's survey of Cheshire, the *Historical Antiquities* (1673). The late seventeenth century also witnessed a growing interest in natural history that was reflected in these volumes. In 1658 Francis Willughby started to undertake the first systematic account of British natural history, the original guide to the flora and fauna of the Isles. This dovetailed with interest in antiquities and topography as 'part of the earth and landscape', and was a recurring feature of later-eighteenth-century county histories.[16] Robert Plot, the first Keeper of the Ashmolean Museum in Oxford, illustrated the main preoccupations of the late-seventeenth-century county historian when he gathered information for his *Natural History of Oxfordshire* (1677) by enquiring of a network of gentleman-scholars, 'Are there any ancient *Sepulchers* hereabout of Men of *Gigantick* stature, *Roman Generals* or *others* of ancient times? has there ever been any

---

13 Morgan, 'Cartographic Image', p.134.
14 Simmons, *English County Historians*, p.6.
15 Broadway, 'William Dugdale', pp.1–2.
16 S. Piggott, *Ruins in a Landscape: Essays in Antiquarianism* (Edinburgh, c.1976), p.102.

apparations hereabouts' or '*British*, *Roman*, *Saxon*, or *Danish* antiquities?'[17]
When Edmund Gibson, later bishop of London, sought to edit and enlarge
Camden's *Britannia* (published in 1685), he engaged two dozen scholars in a
network that extended throughout the Isles.[18]

The Act of Union in 1707 was a spur to the construction of new British
histories. This was not to say that previous authors of county history had not
been aware of the political dimensions of their endeavours. Camden's *Britannia*
had deliberately cast the Isles as a Roman province, thus reworking the Anglo-
centric approach of Tudor historians such as Leland, Harrison and Lambarde,
who had continued the tradition of Bede in regarding the English, rather than
the 'British', as God's chosen nation.[19] Dugdale was also aware of the political
and didactic potential of county histories (some gentry families, after all, had
tried to glorify their ancestry by sending him false information).[20] The parliamentary unification of the historically antagonistic English and Scottish nations
in 1707 demanded new perspectives on the cultural history of the two kingdoms.
A quest for the origins of 'authentic' British identity became rooted during
the eighteenth century in ideas of ethnicity that were closely associated both
with the interpretation of ancient history and the landscape itself. The 'Natural
History' approach to the writing of county histories after the Restoration set out
a precise 'scientific' account of 'land forms, geology, soil types, flora and fauna'
of Britain, compiled by members of the Royal Society such as John Aubrey
(1626–1697). Aubrey even described the natives of his home county, Wiltshire,
in proto-anthropological fashion, as 'aborigines', and catalogued them together
with the county's flora and fauna.[21]

The focus upon the relationship between the landscape and people was a new
approach to the subject of British ethnicity. Another was the growing interest
in the history of the ancient Britons and Anglo-Saxon culture. From at least the
1540s Anglo-Saxon records had been selectively used as religious polemic by
Protestant antiquarians to argue in favour of the Reformation,[22] while, in the late
seventeenth century, Aubrey was the first to associate the stone circles of Britain
with the druids. This theme was taken up by William Stukeley (1687–1765) in
his *Stonehenge* (1740) and *Avebury* (1743). Stukeley proposed that the druids
were the 'noble precursors to a British (even Anglican) religion', an 'authentic'
proof of British resistance to 'foreign' and corrupt forms of worship that supposedly pre-dated the arrival of Roman influence in the Isles.[23] Growing interest
in the mystical aspects of ancient druidic worship was just one indication that
the 'romanticisation of antiquarianism' had begun to influence the writing of
county history by the mid eighteenth century. In other genres of writing, such
as the Scottish verse epics by James Macpherson (in the guise of the third-

17 Ibid., p.108.
18 Whittaker, *William Blake*, p.7; Piggott, *Ruins*, p.111.
19 Whittaker, *William Blake*, p.6.
20 Ibid., p.5.
21 Rollinson, 'Exploding England', p.4.
22 C. Kidd, *British Identities before Nationalism: Ethnicity and Nationhood in the Atlantic World, 1600–
    1800* (Cambridge, 1999), p.107 and *passim*.
23 Whittaker, *William Blake*, p.11.

century poet Ossian), the 'medieval' lyric poems penned by Chatterton and the literary compilations of Thomas Percy in his *Reliques of Ancient English Poetry* (1765), the lure of antiquity and quest for the (often fabricated) roots of an ancient British nation were evident.[24] It is largely due to the increasing influence of romanticism that county histories of the eighteenth century have been unfavourably characterised as achieving neither the scholarship of Dugdale nor the scope of later, nineteenth-century county historians such as John Hodgson (1779–1845), whose voluminous *History of Northumberland* was expanded by successive generations of county historians up to 1940.[25] The eighteenth century witnessed a shift in emphasis from the 'rational' to the 'romantic', or 'from classical calm to barbarian excitement', reflected in a style of county history that Victorian commentators later found intolerably 'unscientific'.[26]

William Hutchinson was born in 1732, the son of a Durham attorney.[27] He was probably educated at Durham school, although there are no records to confirm this, and was articled to learn the profession of lawyer from his father. In 1756, he married into the lesser gentry: his wife, Elizabeth Marshall of Stockton, was descended from the ancient families of Ogle and Bertram, lords of Bothal. It is a mark of the man that on a visit to Bothal Castle some years after his marriage Hutchinson still relished his 'alliance with a lineal descendant of those illustrious families', and drew a sketch of the gatehouse in commemoration.[28] He settled at Barnard Castle, where he practised law and became clerk to successive county lieutenants. His legal practice scarcely occupied him, however, and, whether out of boredom or diversion, he took up antiquarianism and literary pursuits to 'supply the hours of leisure in between'.[29] He was helped in this endeavour by a fellow lawyer, George Allan of Darlington, who had made extensive collections for a history of County Durham.

Hutchinson's background thus fitted the model of a provincial gentleman with sufficient leisure and funds to pursue his antiquarian interests. His main preoccupations were highly reflective of the age in which he lived: his approach to local history was influenced by a strong interest in legendary stories of 'British' mythology, and he was dedicated to the study of another arcane subject: freemasonry. His earliest printed work was *The Hermitage, a British Story*, published in York and London in 1772, which ran to a second edition in 1775. Hutchinson continued to write purely fictional or imaginative texts that were strongly

---

[24] See P. Baines, "Our Annius": Antiquaries and Fraud in the Eighteenth Century', *British Journal for Eighteenth-Century Studies*, 20:1 (Spring 1997), pp.33–52; M.H. Pittock, *Inventing and Resisting Britain: Cultural Identities in Britain and Ireland, 1685–1789* (London, 1997), pp.153–5.

[25] C.M. Fraser, 'John Hodgson: County Historian', *Archaeologia Aeliana*, 5th ser., 25 (1996), pp.171–85.

[26] Piggott, *Ruins*, p.118. The *Victoria County History* project, established in 1899, is now available on-line. Omitted from the *VCH* series are Northumberland (which reflects the dominance of Hodgson's work in this county), Westmorland and the West Riding of Yorkshire. See C.P. Lewis, 'Particular Places: English Local History and the Victoria County History', *Geography*, 73 (October, 1988), pp.344–6; C. Elrington, 'The Victoria County History', *Local Historian*, 22:1 (February 1992), pp.128–37.

[27] For a detailed biography of Hutchinson, see J.C. Hodgson, 'William Hutchinson F.S.A., the Historian of Three Northern Counties', *Archaeologia Aeliana*, 3rd ser., 13 (1916), pp.166–83.

[28] Ibid., p.168.

[29] Ibid., p.169.

influenced by Romantic and Gothic themes at the same time as his county histories. His *Romance After the Manner of the Castle of Otranto* appeared in August 1773, the same year as his *Excursion to the Lakes of Westmorland and Cumberland*. His *View of Northumberland with an Excursion to the Abbey of Mailross in Scotland* was written in 1776 and published in Newcastle upon Tyne in 1778. Some of his most successful works were on freemasonry, a subject close to his heart. He was elected Fellow of the Society of Antiquaries of London in 1781 and published his *History and Antiquities of the County Palatine of Durham* in 1785, an ambitious undertaking that was helped considerably by George Allan's donation of extensive notes on the subject. Hutchinson continued the tradition of antiquarians who engaged the services of a network of correspondents in writing county histories. His *History of the County of Cumberland* also owed a considerable debt to the Carlisle printer, Francis Jollie. He diversified his literary endeavours with poems, drama and novels (many of which remained in manuscript form) on diverse subjects, such as the anti-slavery polemic *The Princess of Zanfara* (1789), which was performed with some success in provincial theatres, and the tragedy 'Pygmalion, King of Tyre'. He died in 1814.[30]

Hutchinson undertook his tour of Northumberland, upon which the *View of Northumberland* was based, in the summer of 1776, a year of dramatic political events. The continuing war in the colonies, which had started in the previous year, was brought to a head in July 1776 with the American Declaration of Independence. Domestic political affairs seemed no less turbulent, with the Wilkes crisis a recent memory, ongoing public disturbances against the enclosure movement and increasing agitation in parliament for tax reform.[31] There is no doubt that the inhabitants of the North East, particularly those in concentrated urban areas, had access to national and international news. The rapidly expanding town of Newcastle upon Tyne was flanked by other emergent commercial centres such as North Shields, South Shields, Sunderland and Gateshead, and led the way in providing a thriving indigenous print culture in the region that supported no fewer than three local newspapers in the eighteenth century.[32] Public debate on national affairs was also promoted through the foundation of debating societies in the north during the 1770s. The Philosophical Society in Newcastle, for example, was the venue for radical lectures on 'The Real Rights of Man' by the utopian activist Thomas Spence; in 1775, its members debated the questions 'Whether the national abuse thrown at the Scotch in most of our political writings, be not only illiberal but also impolitic' and 'Is the resistance of the Americans to taxation without representation, constitutional or unconstitutional?'[33]

---

[30] Ibid., p.175.

[31] See J. Gregory and J. Stevenson, *Britain in the Eighteenth Century, 1688–1820* (London, 2000), pp.348–9.

[32] D. Read, 'North of England Newspapers (c.1700–c.1900) and their Value to Historians', *Leeds Philosophical and Literary Society Proceedings*, 7 (1956–9), p.200; see also F. Manders, 'The History of the Newspaper Press in North East England', in P. Isaac (ed.), *The 'Fourth Estate' at Work in Northumberland and Durham* (Richmond, Surrey, 1999).

[33] H.T. Dickinson, 'Radical Politics in the North East of England in the Later Eighteenth Century', *Durham County Local History Society* (1979), pp.6–7.

The impact of the new Methodist movement was also beginning to be felt in the remoter rural areas: John and Charles Wesley had a particular affinity with the North East, and were extremely successful at establishing new chapels in parts of Northumberland that had previously been beyond the reach of the Anglican Communion.[34]

In this context of turbulent and unpredictable urban politics and cultural change Northumberland provided a fertile subject for historians and antiquarians, and the raw material for plentiful reflections on the course of British history. The geographical boundaries of the county were shaped by the natural features of the landscape: the river Tweed forming the (historically disputed) boundary with Scotland in the north, the North Sea to the east, the Pennines to the west and the river Tyne in the south. The county possessed a rich cultural legacy that afforded material and textual evidence of Roman occupation and successive invasions by the Danes and Saxons. It was the cradle of the early church in England, the home of the Lindisfarne Gospels and the chronicles of Bede. Although its population was growing in the eighteenth century Northumberland remained a largely rural county, combining rugged wilderness, dramatic coastal scenery and other stimuli to the romantic imagination, with a prodigious number of monastic ruins and medieval castles. To this was added a bloody history of centuries of warfare between the English and Scots, the sites of the famous battles of Otterburn and Flodden Field, and countless raids from both sides of the border. The connection between romanticism and the reworking of border history in the literary realm was to find full expression in the novels of Sir Walter Scott some thirty years later, but the potential had already been recognised by Hutchinson in the 1770s for an imaginative recreation of history not within the genre of the novel or ballad, but within the discourse of an antiquarian survey of the border counties.

The structure of Hutchinson's *View of Northumberland* takes the form of a 'tour' of the county based upon notes made by the author on a journey that started just north of Newcastle and proceeded along the coast to the Scottish border, with a diversion into Scotland to the abbey of Mailross, before the author headed south again to Newcastle. The last quarter of the eighteenth century witnessed the growing popularity of excursions and the emergence of a new genre of travel literature. Hutchinson's narrative takes the reader through the towns and villages of Northumberland sequentially, via imaginary telescopic 'views' of neighbouring estates owned by the county gentry, with brief accounts of the genealogy of each landowning family. Unlike those included by Dugdale and his emulators, the plates that accompanied Hutchinson's work were of a relatively poor quality, and there were no topographical maps. He focused on illustrating his primary interest – antiquities – with occasional views of country

---

34 John Wesley's first visit to preach in Newcastle was in May, 1742. His diaries document frequent visits to the town and neighbouring Northumberland in the ensuing years, notably his experience of the 'utmost consternation' in Newcastle at the arrival of the Pretender in Edinburgh in '45. Wesley toured Northumberland during the 1740s, preaching and providing encouragement to local Methodist 'classes', a journey which took him to Morpeth, Alnwick and Berwick as well as smaller villages such as Widdrington, Alnmouth, Tuggal, Biddick, Tanfield and Spen. See N. Curnock (ed.), *The Journal of the Rev. John Wesley*, 8 vols (London, 1909), iii, pp.13–14, 110–12, 140–41, 210, 362–6, 427–8.

estates and churches (by Bailey). The Introduction to the text of the *View of Northumberland* exposed the author's political interest in the putative effects of history and landscape upon its indigenous people. Hutchinson cited classical historians such as Tacitus, Herodian and Strabo on the subject of the 'British character',[35] choosing to appropriate their accounts of the independence and ferocity of 'Britons' in battle while glossing over the fact that they were, at that time, under occupation by the Romans. In addition, he listed the 'modern' (as opposed to classical) authors worthy of note: 'Rowland's Mona Antiqua, Stukeley, Borlase, Strutt, Dr Henry's History of Britain' as well as 'Hollinshead' and 'Spottiswood', while also acknowledging the more immediate influence of the author of *Antiquities, Historical and Monumental of the County of Cornwall* (1769), William Borlase.[36] Although the latter's concern was primarily the mineralogy of his native county of Cornwall, he was also interested in Arthurian legend and the legacy of the druids among the ancient Britons. Hutchinson regarded the druids as the original 'British' caste of priests, who maintained an oral culture 'to prevent schisms and divisions'.[37] Such unity was beloved of staunchly Anglican Tories, in contrast to the fragmentation the author witnessed in his own lifetime among nonconformist Protestant sects, particularly in the face of the new Methodist movement. Another example of Hutchinson's manipulation of ancient British history to suit contemporary preoccupations is his account of the gratitude allegedly shown by the Brigantes when the Saxons arrived in Britain after the Romans left in the fifth century, which has more than an echo of the situation regarding the Hanoverian succession. Hutchinson noted that there was historical precedent for the Britons, in times of trouble, to apply to Germanic princes for assistance. Thus the arrival of the Saxons was depicted as bringing a welcome Germanic cultural change.[38] The parallel between 'northern ravagers' and the anxiety over foreign invasion by the 'corrupt' and 'superstitious' influences of continental European Catholicism would have been clear to the eighteenth-century reader.[39] Elsewhere in the text, mention of the Reformation leaves the reader in no doubt of Hutchinson's concurrence with the orthodox Protestant account of the Reformation. The historian had a low opinion of medieval history as written by 'the superstitious pens of monastic writers'.[40]

While Hutchinson's approach to writing county history has been shown to have had certain conventional elements, the distinctive contribution he made was his self-styling as a 'man of taste' and the application of this idea to his subject. As early as 1712 Addison had attempted 'to lay down Rules how we may know whether we are possessed of [Taste], and how we may acquire that fine Taste of

---

[35] W. Hutchinson, *A View of Northumberland, with an Excursion to the Abbey of Mailross in Scotland*, 2 vols (Newcastle upon Tyne, 1776–8), i, p.ii.

[36] P.A.S. Pool and C. Thomas, 'Introduction to *Antiquities, Historical and Monumental, of the County of Cornwall* by William Borlase' (2nd edn, London, 1769).

[37] Hutchinson, *View of Northumberland*, i, p.iii.

[38] Ibid., p.xiii.

[39] Ibid., p.v

[40] Ibid., p.59.

Writing, which is so much talked of among the Polite World'.[41] In an era when commercial prosperity, European travel and colonial trade facilitated the availability of a wider range of goods than had hitherto been available in Britain, taste became the necessary prerequisite as the guiding principle behind consumption that marked out the connoisseur from the philistine. Taste also had moral dimensions. On a national scale it prevented a decline into luxury and dissipation that was inevitably a precursor to personal ruin and the collapse of good government.[42] It required a measure of restraint and an educated discernment between the 'rational' and the frivolous. Famously, in an epistle to Lord Burlington (1731), Pope satirised the idea of the false 'man of taste', the 'wealthy fool' whose lack of personal discernment led him to rely upon others to tell him the fashion in 'Pictures, Music, Meats: Something there is more needful than Expence,/And something previous ev'n to Taste – 'tis Sense.'[43]

Pope defines a 'true taste' as one where 'Expence' and 'Splendour' are married with usefulness – thus elegant 'Harbors' and 'public Ways' serve a commercial as well as a decorative function, an elegant 'broad arch' of a bridge must withstand a 'dang'rous Flood': 'These Honours, Peace to happy Britain brings/These are Imperial Works, and worthy Kings'.[44] The guiding principle for the man of taste was 'to follow Nature, even in works of mere Luxury and Elegance'.[45] It is this connection between taste and nature that was taken up by William Hutchinson, whose preoccupation in his interpretation of the landscape of Northumberland was to praise those parts that most pleased his sensibility. Hutchinson's account of his tour of Northumberland began at Hedley-on-the-Hill, where he paused to describe the view of the Tyne valley towards the north west and the estate of the Fenwicks at Bywell. Hutchinson's account of the changes and improvements he observed there set the tone for his journey, which combined antiquarian interest with an eagerness to give his opinion on the modernisation of country estates. For example, he described the view of Bywell as though it were a painting, noting the contrasting effect of light and darkness, and distinct landmarks.[46] Hutchinson's commentary upon the spread of estate improvement was similar to that of Arthur Young, whose tour of the north of England over a period of six months in 1770 had resulted in the publication of a travel journal that provided an assessment of the state of agriculture in a national context.[47] Young was less concerned than Hutchinson with the cultural landscape, yet even he could not resist commenting upon the spread of cultivated taste to the northern counties: 'Architecture, painting, sculpture, and the art of adorning grounds', noted Young, 'every where exhibit productions that speak a wealth, a refinement – a taste, which only great and luxurious nations can know.'[48] Near

41 *Spectator*, 409 (19 June 1712).
42 See J. Sekora, *Luxury: The Concept in Western Thought, Eden to Smollett* (Baltimore, 1977), *passim*.
43 A. Pope, *Epistles to Several Persons (Moral Essays)*, IV, 'Epistle to Burlington, edited by F.W. Bateson (first published London, 1731; reprinted London and New Haven, 1961), p.140.
44 Ibid., p.131.
45 Ibid.
46 Hutchinson, *View of Northumberland*, i, p.120.
47 A. Young, *A Six Months Tour Through the North of England*, 3 vols (London, 1770).
48 Ibid., i, p.xi.

Morpeth, he noted, farm houses were built of good brick and stone, and among the local people 'All drink tea.'[49]

Northumbrian gentlemen such as Sir John Hussey Delaval, whose improvements at Seaton Delaval and the Ford estates near the border with Scotland saved his family's ailing fortunes, exemplified Hutchinson's idea of the true champions of British liberty.[50] His evaluation of the rural economy of the North East provided an explicit commentary on the economic development of Britain in a national context. The changes that had recently taken place in the region through better communication links, agricultural improvement and increasing prosperity through trade were foremost in Hutchinson's mind.[51] In the North East, improved transport south to London, north to Edinburgh and westwards across the Pennines to Carlisle was made possible by new roads, not to mention the astonishing increase in the volume of the coastal shipping trade.[52] Northumberland provided for Hutchinson some of the best examples in the country of estates where true taste was manifest in that they combined modern aesthetics with utility – increasing both food production and employment in mining. Surprisingly, he seems deliberately to have avoided going into too much detail about the developing coal trade, the single most significant contribution made by the North East to the national economy, perhaps through lack of interest in (or distaste for) the subject. He compared the 'narrow, dirty, populous and noisy' streets of North Shields to Wapping, and preferred to reflect philosophically upon the 'genius of man' rather than to provide a detailed account of the nature of the trade that went on there.[53]

Hutchinson's idea of taste lay in three elements: contrast, variety and simplicity. Present for him in the peaceful view of a fertile valley were the past memories of 'reiving', or bloody conflict with the Scots. He contrasted his own time with the 'aera of 1580', when the 'inhabitants of Tyne' were 'obliged to guard their cattle every night, and to cultivate no more lands than in proportion to the places of defence they had to secure their crops; living in a state of perpetual warfare and jeopardy'. He thus dwelt not only upon the 'devastation and ruin, which marked the incursions of the Scots' but also upon the 'vassalage and misery of a feudal tenure; by which genius was kept in fetters, and industry was distinguished only by the name of slavery'. He celebrated the liberty of constitutional settlement in 'this opulent and beautiful county of Northumberland' and the spirit of the age of improvement: 'The ferocity of the inhabitants is subdued; traffic, arts, sciences, manufactories, and navigation, have taken place of the brutal warfare, which is extinguished; Cultivation, with all the comeliness of Plenty, laughs in the valleys; the streams are taught to labour in mechanic systems, to aid the manufacturer.'[54] However, wherever marks of taste and cultivation were found, the 'savage' wilderness of the 'natural' North-Eastern landscape and its unruly

---

[49] Ibid., iii, pp.30–34.
[50] F. Askham, *The Gay Delavals* (London, 1955), pp.95–7, 126 and *passim*.
[51] Hutchinson, *View of Northumberland*, i, p.131.
[52] See J. Ellis, 'The 'Black Indies': the Economic Development of Newcastle upon Tyne, c.1700–1840', in W. Lancaster and R. Colls (eds), *Newcastle upon Tyne: A Modern History* (Chichester, 2001).
[53] Hutchinson, *View of Northumberland*, ii, pp.356–7.
[54] Ibid, i, pp.133–4.

local people intruded. Further south, at Ravensworth Castle near Chester-le-Street, County Durham, the seat of the Liddells, which boasted a fashionable bow window, elegant stucco, and landscape paintings in the upper apartments '*in the stile of Pous[s]in*', was within sight to the east of Gateshead Fell, 'wild and shaken, with a multitude of hovels and cottages'.[55] Hutchinson's pleasure in discerning elevated taste where he found it was heightened by highlighting its unique aspect among 'wilderness', a delight in variety and contrast that was wholly in keeping with Pope's definition of the 'man of taste'.

Another mark of the man of taste that Hutchinson was keen to elicit was his ability to interpret signs and metaphors in the landscape, especially those evoked by ruins.[56] Stuart Piggott has highlighted how the ruin was emblematic of the pursuit of antiquarianism that was a popular and fashionable pastime for the gentry in eighteenth-century Britain.[57] For example, ruins in the landscape of Northumberland evoked the recent memory of Jacobite incursion. The confiscation of lands that resulted from the uprisings of 1715 and 1745 were within living memory at the time of Hutchinson's tour. Material evidence of the demise of powerful Catholic families who had supported the Jacobites had a totemic value in Hutchinson's portrayal of the course of history, and was a satisfying reminder to him of the righteousness of the Protestant cause. At Dilston, the former home of the earls of Derwentwater, Hutchinson and his travelling companion 'approached the mansion, now consisting of disconsolate and ragged ruins'.[58] The last earl had been executed for his part in the rebellion of 1715. The antiquarian recorded his imaginative reconstruction of every right-thinking British citizen who regarded such evidence of folly: 'He looks upon them as monuments of sepultured oppression, over which the olives of peace are woven by the hand of liberty.'[59] It was a sentiment that was echoed countless times across the nation, but which one Hutchinson showed could be witnessed with more immediacy in the Northumberland landscape.

Hutchinson explicitly contrasted the peace and prosperity of Northumberland under constitutional British government with its previous 'barbarian' status. Tyranny and feudalism had been eradicated and antagonisms across the border had been settled. Notably, it was not specifically the Scots *per se* who were characterised as barbarians in Hutchinson's account. His contempt was reserved instead for ordinary Northumbrians, locked in a 'spirit of darkness', who did not appreciate the cultural value of their native county. For example, when he reached Corbridge, Hutchinson reflected upon a piece of Roman silver plate that had been recently discovered by a local labourer. The artefact was not intact, however, since 'some ignorant poor people ... cut off the feet in such a vile barbarous manner, that they have broke two holes through the table, and a small piece off one of the corners too.'[60] Likewise, near the border with Scotland, he

---

55 W. Hutchinson, *The History and Antiquities of the County Palatine of Durham*, 3 vols (Newcastle and London, 1785–94), ii, p.417.
56 Janowitz, *England's Ruins, passim*.
57 Piggott, *Ruins*, pp.101–31 and *passim*.
58 Ibid., pp.170–71.
59 Hutchinson, *View of Northumberland*, i, pp.170–71.
60 Ibid., p.147.

noted that 'a stone boat or coffin' associated with the legend of St Cuthbert had been saved from the hands of a peasant who had 'devised to pickle pork in it, or thereout to feed his hogs'.[61] Unsurprisingly, Hutchinson found that the common people he encountered to the east of the Cheviots, as far north as Wooler, possessed 'a ferocity and uncultivated sullenness of mind', and 'scarce confess ... civilization enough to direct a stranger on his way'.[62] By contrast, he praised the Scottish practice, established in 1618, of providing a school in every parish, and the tight control that the kirk exercised over the morality and discipline of the people.[63] He also contrasted the barren and mountainous terrain north of Wooler with the cultivated and pleasant vale north of the border at Kelso, which was a credit to the taste of its Scottish landlords, the duke of Roxburgh and Sir John Douglas.[64] Thus the county history formulated by Hutchinson transformed British taste into a mark of distinction that was dedicated to the spirit of improvement and the possession and appreciation of 'cultural capital'.[65]

If we locate Hutchinson's work within a broader national context of antiquarian writing at this time, his *Northumberland* prefigured the work of John Throsby, whose *History and Antiquities of Leicester* (1791) was similarly concerned with evaluating the taste of the nobility and gentry in that county. Throsby's taste, like Hutchinson's, was typical of his age; what pleased him most was 'a handsome house, suitable planting, and a lake or stretch of water'.[66] However, the latter's adoption of a literary style attracted scorn from some influential critics who dismissed his efforts as trifling and an abuse of the antiquarian tradition. One such critic was John Nichols, the joint manager of *The Gentleman's Magazine*. Nichols, a powerful and well-connected member of the London literati, and one-time friend of Johnson, Gibbon, Wilkes and Horace Walpole, was later the author of the well-known *Literary Anecdotes of the Eighteenth Century* (1812–15). He was also a close friend of the antiquary Richard Gough, who published his *Bibliotheca Topographica Britannia* in eight quarto volumes between 1780 and 1790; it was a topographical miscellany that was based on the results of an elaborate questionnaire sent to all 'the nobility, gentlemen, clergy and others, of Great Britain and Ireland'.[67] Gough wrote anonymous critical reviews of Hutchinson's work in *The Gentleman's Magazine*, mocking the latter's pretension in taking upon himself the task of writing histories of all three northern-most English counties (including Cumberland, printed between 1794 and 1797), 'any one of which,' stated Gough, 'would have occupied the life of a genuine Antiquary'.[68] The crux of Gough's criticism was Hutchinson's approach to writing county history, which Gough branded scathingly as '*polite* topographical writing'.[69] By

[61] Ibid, ii, p.23.
[62] Ibid., i, pp.259–60.
[63] Ibid.
[64] Ibid., p.262.
[65] See P. Bourdieu, *Distinction: A Social Critique of the Judgement of Taste* (Cambridge, MA, 1984), *passim*.
[66] M.W. Barley and K.S.S. Train, 'Robert Thoroton', in Simmons, *English County Historians*, p.34.
[67] J. Simmons, Introduction to John Nichols, *History and Antiquities of the County of Leicester* (first published 1795–1815; reprinted Wakefield 1974), p.vi.
[68] *Gentleman's Magazine*, 63 (March 1793), pp.202–3.
[69] Ibid. (supplement for 1793), pp.1198–9.

way of illustration, Gough cited Hutchinson's descriptive account of the parish-
ioners of Cumwhitton in his *History of Cumberland*. The villagers, according to
Hutchinson, were unenlightened: they did not keep abreast of national politics,
they were effectively illiterate, and they shunned the polite habits that were
the mark of 'civilised' British society. The local newspaper, *The Cumberland
Pacquet*, was first seen in the village as late as 1792, some decades after its
neighbouring settlements; there was (to quote Hutchinson) 'No taste for science
or polite literature; books are regarded as puerile amusement', and tea-drinking
was generally despised. Gough ridiculed Hutchinson's preoccupation with his
subject's 'rusticity of manners' and reflected that he could not 'help thinking the
Cumwhittonites happy in the want of luxuries which gain so little ground among
them'.[70] In all, Gough characterised the work of Hutchinson and his Carlisle
publisher Francis Jollie as exemplars of 'the fashionable spirit of *book-making*'.
'To what source, but that of profit to the writer or publisher,' asked Gough,
'are we to ascribe the many tours, journeys, environs, picturesque beauties, and
the long *et caetera* of description and anecdote, which multiply upon us?'[71]
Thus, while some county historians like Throsby pursued Hutchinson's style,
others attempted to distance themselves from his work by locating it within the
more populist genres of travel literature and 'polite' fiction, a charge which was
intended to discredit the author and his work.

   In conclusion, if we survey the rich diversity of 'Northern Landscapes' that are
the subject of this book, a common theme is the awareness, as David Rollinson
has written, that landscapes are in themselves not immutable, but 'invented,
constructed and reconstructed' over time.[72] Just as the physical surface of the
land is shaped by human settlement, so the political and cultural meaning of the
imagined landscape is subject to constant change over time. An example of the
construction of imagined landscape through discourse, as we have witnessed in
the works of William Hutchinson, is the genre of antiquarian history writing.
One commentator observed that, far from being objective, these accounts were
'a deliberate construct, designed to fulfil specific ideological ... purposes'.[73]
From their earliest manifestations in the sixteenth century, the political function
of county histories was therefore more than just a 'simple expression of particu-
larist local patriotism'[74] but a specific attempt to construct an idea of nationhood
through local surveys of national importance.

   Historian Rosemary Sweet has argued in a modern landmark study that by
the middle of the eighteenth century leading antiquarians were establishing
'a clearer distance between themselves and "men of taste"' such as Horace
Walpole, eschewing connoisseurship since it presented aesthetic rather than

---

[70] Ibid., September 1793, pp.1198–9.
[71] Ibid.
[72] Rollinson, 'Exploding England', p.3.
[73] M. Winstanley, 'Researching a County History: Edwin Butterworth, Edward Baines and the *History
      of Lancashire* (1836)', *Northern History*, 32 (1996), p.152.
[74] Morgan, 'Cartographic Image', p.145. See also J. Black, *Maps and History: Constructing Images of
      the Past* (New Haven, 1997), pp.6–9.

historical reasons for valuing antiquities.[75] Hutchinson's approach was therefore at variance with the direction that was being pursued by his fellow-antiquarians: taste for him was a means of mediating history, landscape and culture, a quality which flowed freely across borders and was esteemed wherever he found traces of it evident in the design of a country house or the landscaping of a garden. He was equally critical of landowner and commoner, the English and the Scots, wherever he found that taste was wanting, and in this sense was instrumental in promoting a new notion of Britishness that was founded upon the exercise of civility and judgement and which transcended topographical and cultural boundaries. The fact that some were unhappy with Hutchinson's method illustrates how hotly the history of the Isles was contested in the eighteenth century. The antiquarians who rejected taste as a critical tool felt that they 'owned' the subject of county history; Hutchinson's insistence upon its importance exposed the practice of antiquarian history-writing as a significant and politically charged contribution to the discourses that shaped the 'matter of Britain'.

Acknowledgement

Research for this chapter was made possible as part of 'Nationalising Taste: National Identity and Local Culture in Eighteenth-Century England', a project funded by Northumbria University. I am deeply indebted to its Directors, Dr Jeremy Gregory and Dr Thomas Faulkner, with whom it has been my privilege to co-edit this book.

---

[75] R. Sweet, *Antiquaries: The Discovery of the Past in Eighteenth-Century Britain* (London and New York, 2004), p.11.

16

Thomas Bewick and the North-Eastern Landscape

HUGH DIXON

Thomas Bewick (1753–1828) spent his working life as a trade engraver in Newcastle upon Tyne. From this improbable background he gained a national, and later an international, reputation with his illustrated books. A generation after his death his daughter published his *Memoir*,[1] which, as the account of the life and times of a provincial craftsman of the Georgian era, has no parallel. Yet despite its recognition in the worlds of art and craft, his work is less well known to historians than it ought to be. Reasons for this are not hard to find and some are suggested here; but most of the early obstructions should not apply to a researcher in our times. Increasingly, the significance of Bewick's achievement in both illustration and writing is being recognised, and its historical potential is becoming understood.[2] His was the Georgian world. Bewick was seven when George III succeeded his grandfather, and he died two years before George IV and less than a decade before Queen Victoria came to the throne. In this wide-ranging set of studies of the North-Eastern landscape Thomas Bewick steps forward, a shrewd, observant, energetic and reliable witness to life in his strata of society in the second half of the Georgian era.

The essentials of Bewick's life are uncomplicated.[3] He spent most of his life in the Tyne valley. He was born at Cherryburn, near Mickley, on the south bank of the Tyne. This is about eleven miles from the middle of old Newcastle where, apart from a few months, he spent his adulthood. Yet within these narrow limits there were influences which shaped his interests and intensified his vision. Principal among those was the landscape itself and men's interaction with it. His father owned a small farm and also had a lease on a coal pit, a modest enterprise

[1] Thomas Bewick's *A Memoir of Thomas Bewick written by himself* was published in edited form by his daughter, Jane, in 1862; but for Bewick's full text see Iain Bain's edition of the *Memoir* (Oxford, 1975, paperback edition 1979), which includes his vital introduction, and notes and bibliography.

[2] See, for example, J. Uglow, *Nature's Engraver: A Life of Thomas Bewick* (London, 2006) (a splendidly readable account). Other valuable modern works include I. Bain (ed.), *The Watercolours and Drawings of Thomas Bewick and his Workshop Apprentices*, 2 vols (Winchester and Detroit, 1981) and I. Bain, *The Workshop of Thomas Bewick* (Newcastle upon Tyne, 1979, revised Winchester and Detroit, 1989).

[3] For a full chronology of Bewick's life see H. Dixon, 'Bewick Landmarks', in D. Gardner-Medwin (ed.), *Bewick Studies: Essays in Celebration of the 250th Anniversary of the Birth of Thomas Bewick 1753–1828* (Newcastle upon Tyne, 2003), pp.9–21.

which supplied the needs of local people. Before becoming a farmer's wife his mother had been a young housekeeper for the Rev. Christopher Gregson across the Tyne at Ovingham. She was sufficiently educated to assist the parson, who also kept a school, in hearing the boys' Latin exercises. Later Thomas attended the same school. So, although he grew up on the farm and, as the eldest of a family of seven, soon took his turn working with the animals, there were wider dimensions to young Thomas's life. The view of some nineteenth-century romantics that he was 'purely a son of nature'[4] cannot be sustained. Although the family was not wealthy it was far from destitute; the parents created a loving family circle but they also encouraged aspirations to achievement in the wider world. In later years the children would happily return to see their parents at the farm; and, indeed, Cherryburn remained a home and a focus for the Bewick family for almost two centuries.

Thomas's real love was the natural world. While busy on the farm or when wandering further afield on youthful adventures, he took a keen interest in what he saw. He came to understand how things grew; where animals and birds lived and what they ate; what changes to expect with the passing of the seasons; and the place of mankind in the landscape. He took particular pleasure in the Tyne and its tributaries, the flow of currents, the placid backwater, and the dangerous winter torrent. He became happily embroiled with the trials of the angler. He saw the hazards for the traveller. He watched the hunter and the hunted. He experienced the heat of summer, and in the winter's chill he grew to respect the resilience of animals and birds. He came, too, to understand the brutalities of nature and, chief among these, the casual cruelties of man towards the rest of the animal world. His exceptional combination of talents ensured that this fascination was far from passive; eventually it shaped his life. His penetrating and detailed observation was combined with an extraordinary visual memory, and he had both an ability and a desire to draw. His parents recognised these gifts and, when it came to choosing a career, Thomas was not set to work on the farm or down the pit but was apprenticed to Ralph Beilby, a young engraver from an artistic Newcastle family. Beilby proved 'the best master in the World, for learning Boys, for he obliged them to put their hands to every variety of Work',[5] and by the time Bewick completed his apprenticeship, in 1774, he had a command of all aspects of the engraver's trade.

Ralph Beilby also deserves the credit for recognising the particular branch of the trade in which Thomas had the greatest potential. He was quite aware of Thomas's picture-making abilities, and was quick to encourage its application to the printed page. From the first days of his apprenticeship Thomas was set to work on diagrams, some pictorial,[6] which were to be printed with text. As

---

4   The phrase comes from John James Audubon, who met Bewick as an old man and had a great respect for his work. Later authors exaggerated a lack of schooling, preferring to believe that Bewick was entirely self-taught. See J.J. Audubon, *Ornithological Biography* (Philadelphia, 1831); quoted by Iain Bain in his Introduction to the *Memoir*, p.xxv.

5   Bewick, *Memoir*, p.40.

6   Ibid. Bewick worked on diagrams for Charles Hutton's *Treatise on Mensuration*; the first part, published in 1768, included a view of the tower and spire of St Nicholas's Church, Newcastle, a feature which would appear in so many of Bewick's later works.

his engraving technique matured, he progressed to more elaborate decorations and to series of pictures for children's books, morals and fables. When Beilby finally shook his departing apprentice's hand and wished him well, he could congratulate himself on having provided a sound training. He can scarcely have imagined how extraordinary a career would arise from his firm foundations.

Returning to Cherryburn, Thomas worked on his own account for over a year. This was a happy time. He renewed his familiarity with the places of his boyhood and found that the fondness had not waned. He may have been living in the town but it had not changed him:

> For the first time in my life I felt myself at liberty ... This was a time of great enjoyment, for the charms of the country was highly relished by me, and after so long an almost absence from it, gave even that relish a zest, which I have not words to express.[7]

He may not have had words but he soon had pictures. This was the moment when he seems to have realised, as he revived cherished boyhood memories, that birds and animals, local characters, buildings, hayricks, walls and hedgerows, gates and bridges, pranks and mishaps by the river, everyday sights and sounds and even smells could all become the basis for his adult illustrations. He must have recognised that he already carried in his memory a formidable store of such images. And it is from this time, too, that Bewick's preference for full scenes becomes apparent. The first sustained attempts came in a series of fables printed by Thomas Saint in Newcastle.

In 1776, when just over a year out of his apprenticeship, Thomas received a premium from the Society for the Encouragement of Arts, Manufactures and Commerce for an illustration of a huntsman and an old hound for Saint's edition of *Gay's Fables*; with some pride he presented his mother with the sum of seven guineas. It is significant that the award was made when for the first time Bewick was not working to instruction but deciding on his own pictorial material *and* when he was living at Cherryburn.

With this achievement, and in the restlessness of youth, Thomas asserted his independence by making a long walking tour to Scotland,[8] which gave him a lifelong respect for the country and the hospitality of its people. Less happy was a stay of eight months in London.[9] Although he soon found work and a good circle of friends (many from Northumberland) he did not warm to southern manners and vanities, he disliked what he saw as rudeness and duplicity, and he was shocked by the extremes of wealth and wretched poverty. Despite the protestations of friends and offers of important commissions, he returned north.

Even so, his time in London had not been useless. He established a reputation for the quality of his work, gained some experience of business practice, and had an opportunity to exercise not just his craft but also his artistic imagination in the art of book illustration. Not least, as his later work shows, he became

---

[7] Ibid., p.59.

[8] P. Quinn, 'Thomas Bewick in Scotland', in 'Cherryburn Times' (the Journal of the Bewick Society), 5:6 (Summer 2009), pp.1–11.

[9] Bewick, *Memoir*, pp.69–76: 'I would even enlist for a Soldier – or go and herd sheep at five shillings a week as long as I lived, rather than be tied to live in London.'

aware of wider artistic developments in the metropolis. Either directly from paintings, or from the multitude of prints then available, he absorbed, possibly quite unconsciously, the fundamentals of classical landscape as they were then being transformed into the fashionable, relaxed, decorative Rococo manner. Perhaps as important as any of these aspects, however, was the self-assurance he acquired. He realised that his work was as good as any around and was in demand. His return to the north was not a retreat in the face of competition but a preference to work in the place where he felt at home. Nor did this result in his developing a provincial outlook; on the contrary, he had gained a sense of his own worth and, as soon became apparent, when he decided to set out on a project he was ready to set himself very wide horizons.

Back in Newcastle in 1777 he joined his former master, Ralph Beilby, in a partnership which was to last for twenty years. The requirements of his trade meant that he had to stay in town and, indeed, apart from moving his home across the Tyne to Gateshead in 1812, he worked in Newcastle for the rest of his life. Even so, he never lost his delight in the countryside. He enjoyed weekly walks to Cherryburn to see the family and, even after the death of his parents (both died in 1785), he still went to call on his youngest brother, William, who had taken over the farm. If visits became slightly less regular, it was because he had new responsibilities. In 1786 he married Isabella Elliot, a childhood friend from Ovingham; and, in due time, they were to have four children: a son, Robert, who became Thomas's partner in his later years, and three daughters, Jane, Isabella and Elizabeth, who eventually had their own important part to play in the Bewick story.

At work in Newcastle Thomas had taken as his first apprentice in 1777 his younger brother, John. The brothers, though seven years apart in age, seem to have got on well. Perhaps this was because they were very different. Thomas[10] was well-made and firmly grounded; John was slighter and more finely featured. Both could be good company but for Thomas it was more of an effort. After a wild youth, he became, especially in business matters, more staid, more absorbed with propriety, and more inclined to share what he regarded as the correctness of his own opinions. He had also a northern directness which could and did lead to confrontation. John, by contrast was more relaxed, easy-going and with a light-ness of touch in any company. He also seemed able to turn his hand to anything and to do it well: his father even found his mechanical ingenuity helpful at the pit. While Thomas was only an enthusiastic whistler, John played both flute and clarinet – but just for fun. At work he proved to be so talented as an engraver and so industrious that he was given his freedom after only five years. After a spell in the workshop as a journeyman he went to try his luck in London. Unlike Thomas he enjoyed life in the capital and, through application – principally illustrating children's books – soon established himself. Though far apart the brothers remained in touch. Thomas, anxious as ever, advised on pricing and

---

[10] For portraits of Bewick and other members of his family see J. Holmes, 'The Many Faces of Bewick', *Transactions of the Natural History Society of Northumbria*, 65:3 (March 2007), pp.135–224. Not the least unusual thing about Bewick was the demand for his portrait – drawings, paintings and sculpture; at least twenty-three were taken from life, and almost 100 versions survive.

not working for long hours for little reward. He was right to be concerned, for it soon became apparent that John had consumption. When he died aged only thirty-five in 1795, he left Thomas his books, blocks, some unfinished work (which Thomas completed) and, not least, the Bewick name re-established as a mark of excellence in the capital. Ever after Thomas was punctilious about crediting John's work[11] when it appeared alongside his own.

The firm of Beilby and Bewick, meanwhile, had confirmed its place as the leading engravers in Newcastle. They had a reputation for fine work and efficient service. Some of their apprentices became assistants, others set up their own businesses, and a few, including Luke Clennell and William Harvey, went on the achieve prominence in London. The business embraced all classes of engraving work,[12] from names on dog collars and coffin plates to business cards and bill headings, even to the finest bright work on silverware. It may seem surprising that national notice came through books. In this case, however, the provincial situation was not a disadvantage for, apart from London and the two university towns, Newcastle was at that time the largest centre for publishing in England. In 1784 Bewick had started to engrave the illustrations for the first of the works which would make his reputation. The scope of this first book was breathtaking, the more so for being the scheme of provincial craftsmen (Ralph Beilby was also involved and largely responsible for the text). Eventually published in 1790, *A General History of Quadrupeds*[13] was an attempt to catalogue and illustrate all the quadrupeds in the world! The boldness of the enterprise was acknowledged but it was the quality of the illustrations which made the book a huge success. It was followed in two volumes by *A History of British Birds* (1797 and 1804),[14] which is widely regarded as the highpoint of Bewick's engraving skill. In this case, after some dispute with Beilby, Bewick wrote the text, too. Later, after a period of illness, Bewick produced his own edition of *Aesop's Fables* (1818).[15] In this case, because of Bewick's frailty, much of the engraving was done by talented assistants; nevertheless, the guiding hand, the artistic vision and the social and moral content are all his. This is not the place to examine each of the books in detail but, taken together, they provide an extraordinarily comprehensive survey of the North-Eastern landscape of Bewick's time.

[11] For a full account of John's life and work see N. Tattersfield, *John Bewick, Engraver on Wood 1760–1795* (London, 2001).

[12] In this context see, for example, N. Tattersfield, *Bookplates by Beilby and Bewick, A Biographical Dictionary of Bookplates from the workshop of Ralph Beilby, Thomas Bewick and Robert Bewick 1760–1849* (London, 1999).

[13] [R. Beilby and T. Bewick] *A General History of Quadrupeds: The Figures engraved on wood by Thomas Bewick* (Newcastle upon Tyne, 1790, with further editions 1791, 1792, 1800, 1807, 1811, 1820, 1824).

[14] T. Bewick, *A History of British Birds*, vol. 1 containing the *History and Description of Land Birds* (Newcastle upon Tyne, 1797; further editions 1799, 1805, 1809, 1814); vol. 2 containing the History and Description of Water Birds (Newcastle upon Tyne, 1804; further editions 1805, 1809). Combined editions appeared in 1816, 1821, 1826 and 1832, while a special combined edition of the illustrations without text was published in 1817, limited to twenty-five copies. The last 'living' combined edition was published in 1847 by Bewick's son, Robert Elliot Bewick. There have been numerous selections and facsimiles since.

[15] T. Bewick, *The Fables of Aesop and others with designs on wood by Thomas Bewick* (Newcastle upon Tyne, 1818); a second edition appeared in 1823 which Bewick regarded as 'better printed and otherwise managed'.

Bewick's works occupy a momentous place in the history of book illustration. The earliest printed illustrations, made in the late fifteenth century, were woodcuts, but were soon almost entirely superseded by copper engravings, which created richer and subtler detail but were technically more difficult – and thus more expensive – to combine with printed text. Bewick was the first great master of wood engraving, which, by using harder wood and finer tools, combined something of the economy and convenience of woodcut with the precision and finesse of copper engraving, while also allowing text and pictures to be more easily printed together. His success ushered in a golden age of wood engraving, which remained the dominant method of illustration throughout most of the nineteenth century, until it was eventually overtaken by photomechanical techniques.

Bewick's skill lay in both the accuracy of his observation and his ability to transfer this to print. By polishing the end grain of slow-growing woods, particularly box and some fruitwoods, he created a very fine surface on which to engrave. He cut printing blocks with a subtlety of texture and depth which produced, when printed carefully, not only black and white but gradations of grey. Bewick, however, was very much more than a highly skilled craftsman. The sure hand and the acute eye were backed with an artist's vision:

> It is due to Mr Bewick's merits as an artist, to state, that his powers extend far beyond the mere delineation of the animal or feathered tribe. The landscape, which he occasionally introduces, as a relief to his principal figures, as well as his vignettes, invariably show the hand of a master; possessing a truth and nature that will bear the most rigid examination.[16]

Unfortunately it was Bewick's very skill which caused one of the barriers to his full appreciation. The combination of his minute technique and acute eyesight meant that occasionally he was able to produce images with detail which many struggle to see.

That was a practical difficulty. There was also a technical one; Bewick had to work very hard to get his printers to appreciate the importance of the detail of his blocks. If the printer was in too much of a hurry, or if the ink was too loaded, too dry or too thick, much of the detail could be lost. Often Bewick had to struggle to ensure that the finished work met his exacting standards. This in turn led to a further economic difficulty. Although printing the letterpress and illustrations together should have had economic advantages, the need to balance the two could be very time-consuming. With *Quadrupeds* running to more than 500 pages and the other books each to around 400, the whole operation became very expensive. Inevitably, the completed works found their way into the libraries of the select portion of society which could afford them, overwhelmingly, it seems, professionals and gentlemen. Not that the books were not a success; they proved to be very popular, and led to exchanges with correspondents from all over the country. New specimens were sent (and one of the less popular tasks

---

[16] E. Charnley in the catalogue of Bewick's works included in his edition of *Select Fables with cuts designed and engraved by Thomas and John Bewick and others previous to the year 1784* (Newcastle upon Tyne, 1820), p.xxiv.

in the Bewick shop must have been opening the morning post); all the books had revised and enlarged editions. And all were still in print when Bewick died.

Difficulties in studying Bewick have been largely set aside with technical improvements in recent decades. Sophisticated flat copying and magnifying techniques allow original images to be examined more thoroughly and to be duplicated. Many editions are now available in public collections and the best can be copied. Where original blocks survive in good condition they can be carefully reprinted, producing images which, with startling immediacy, demonstrate both the resilience of the technique and the subtlety of the best work. Not least, the availability of decent modern reproductions of Bewick's works means that, without paying antiquarian book prices, it is possible to own and study good Bewick images.

What do Thomas Bewick's works offer to the understanding of the landscape he knew? The texts of his illustrated books are a product of their time, relying heavily on previous works; and perhaps it is only when Bewick relies on his personal observation of birds that there is interest for the modern ornithologist. The illustrations, however, were a revelation. Unlike those in early woodcuts, the animals and birds were so detailed as to be immediately recognisable; they were made lively by their attitude at the moment Bewick chose to depict them and the setting in which he placed them. The wonder is that he managed to contain so much in such small images. Few of his illustrations exceed two inches by three, yet the sharpness of his eyesight and the accuracy of his engraving made it possible even in such small spaces to render subjects with full and informative backgrounds. Nor was he content with limiting the illustrations to the main subjects. He used the spaces left at the ends of pages to introduce more small pictures. Some early ones are just decoration; others were used to augment the text. Gradually these tailpieces became 'talepieces', with self-contained subjects quite unconnected with the text.[17] As Bewick recorded in the last edition of *British Birds* before his death, there was a particular purpose for his method of illustration:

> When I first undertook my labours in Natural History ... my strongest motive was to lead the minds of youth to the study of that delightful pursuit ... My writings were intended chiefly for youth; and the more readily to allure their pliable, though discursive, attention to the Great Truths of Creation, I illustrated them by figures delineated with all the fidelity and animation I was able to impart to mere woodcuts without colour; and as instruction is of little avail without constant cheerfulness and occasional amusement, I interspersed the more serious studies with Tale-pieces of gaiety and humour; yet even in these seldom without an endeavour to illustrate some truth, or point some moral; so uniting with my ardent wish to improve the rising generation, the exercise of my art and profession ...[18]

---

[17] For more see, for example, I. Bain (ed.), *Thomas Bewick's Vignettes, being tail-pieces principally for his General History of Quadrupeds and History of British Birds* (London, 1978) (the best gathering of Bewick's vignettes, finely printed and with a helpful introduction by the authority on the subject).

[18] In the Preface to the sixth edition of *A History of British Birds* (1826).

Figure 16.1. upper: T. Bewick, *The Rook* (from T. Bewick, *A History of British Birds*, i, Land Birds, 1797); lower: T. Bewick, *The Old Exchange* [*and Guildhall*], *Newcastle upon Tyne* (engraved in 1819, from title page of *Select Fables with cuts designed and engraved by Thomas and John Bewick, and Others*, previous to the year 1784, Newcastle, 1820, reprinted Newcastle, 1975). (Note: the illustrations in this chapter are enlarged by about a third from Bewick's originals.)

The revelation that his books were intended principally for youthful readers may seem surprising but it is worth remembering that many of the books which Thomas and his brother John had illustrated before had been for children. This might also account for the relative simplicity of the text. What soon became clear was that the excellence of the illustrations made the books attractive to a much wider readership. Bewick's more specific intentions are instructive because they can be related precisely to his depiction of landscape. He sought fidelity or accuracy, animation, cheerfulness, occasional amusement and pointers to truth and morality.

Bewick's achievement in accuracy was two-fold. If he chose to do so, he could depict animals, birds or scenes with buildings with absolute fidelity. His portrayals could be much enhanced by background but these he would arrange for pictorial effect rather than topographical accuracy. His *Rook* (Fig. 16.1, upper), for example, is shown not in motion but standing still on a rock; but is this just a convenient pose to show its character or is it offering more? Is Bewick suggesting that, in its elevated position, this might be the sentry? In the background the flock is feeding on a newly sown field though carefully avoiding the area around a scarecrow. To emphasise the gregarious nature of the rook he shows the sky full of them and relates their great serpentine flight to the tall trees which shelter the big house and the farm in the background. The scene could be many places in the North East. The field gate with the stile curving from the hinges to support the diagonal brace is typical of the Tyne valley but also occurs elsewhere. The big house, clearly the residence of a landowner, has two storeys and prominent chimneys; its importance is marked by the surrounding wall with a more elaborate gateway and a stable with an oddly shaped opening in its gable. Further away is a single-storey farmhouse, built in two sections (like Cherryburn) with typically steep-pitched thatched roof and neat rows of hayricks in the yard. All this is minutely but clearly drawn but it is almost certainly not an attempt to show a particular place. There is little evidence that Bewick carried a sketch book with him when he was in the countryside; but he could call on his store of visual memories in his picture-making. He understood the rise and fall of the land, the combination of hedges and stone walls, the natural woodlands along water courses and the woods planted as shelter belts. He knew the peculiarities of buildings – and of the people working about them. The consequent value of his pictures is that, without being topographical, they embody the essence of the local vernacular, the ways things were built and done around those parts.

When appropriate, and when he wished to do so, he could make his buildings entirely recognisable, especially those not far from his Newcastle workshop: the town walls, the medieval castle, the library at St Nicholas's church, the clock and sundial of the Keelmen's Hospital; and, further away, Tynemouth Priory, Durham Cathedral; even Windsor Castle and the dome of St Paul's in London are unmistakeable. The lantern spire of St Nicholas's church (Figs 16.2, middle and 16.3, bottom) is used again and again to establish location as well as providing vertical emphasis to skylines. Some pictures have special significance. Robert Trollope's remodelled Newcastle Guildhall (1655–58) was a vigorous example of provincial Baroque design. It was engraved by Bewick before 1784

Figure 16.2. top: T. Bewick, *The Runaway Cart* (tale-piece vignette from *A History of British Birds*, 1797); middle: T. Bewick, *The Race Horse* (from *A General History of Quadrupeds*, 1790); bottom: T. Bewick, *Stallion's Tail*.

(Fig. 16.1, lower), damaged by fire in 1791 and remodelled in 1794–96. Another engraving corroborates the accuracy of Bewick's picture but, as the two views are from different angles, each has information about a now-altered building.

There may be portrayals of other lost buildings (and Bewick's 'architectural landscape' certainly merits further research) but where he excelled was in capturing the general character of the world about him. Nowhere is this more vivid than on Tyneside. Walking between Newcastle and Cherryburn he became very familiar with the gradual industrialisation; his extraordinary eyesight and powers of retaining images enabled him to see and remember. Eventually, he left a record of changing scenes which most others would have taken for granted and found unremarkable. In Bewick's work the business of the Tyne comes vividly alive. The importance of coal is never far away. Horses strain at the 'gins', lowering pitmen and raising the coal. The staithes, or great jetties, line the river with angled coal chutes (Fig. 16.3, top). Coal boats clutter the river, loading or under sail, using the prevailing winds going downstream, but hauled or rowed back empty on the return journey from depositing loads onto the London coasters (Fig. 16.3, middle). Smoke trails from the cones of the glassworks and from factory chimneys and, further off, windmills punctuate the horizon (see Fig. 16.3, top, middle and bottom).

In his search for animation Bewick was no less successful. He was particularly adept at capturing the antics of children, whether building snowmen or 'riding' gravestones when pretending to be cavalry or simply playing with boats in a stream (Fig. 16.3, bottom). He could also catch them at less attractive and more hazardous moments (Figs 16.4, middle and 16.2, top). With a few deft touches, the tip of the head, the angle of the mouth, the bracing of limbs, he could show spite and fear.

Bewick's vivid picture of life in both the town and country along the Tyne valley was never far divorced from animals. For example, his depiction of horses distinguishes types but also develops their character and their relation with men by use of the background. The common cart horse appears solid and steady; and its dependability is emphasised by the background scene of the farmer returning from market asleep on the cart. The much smarter Arabian has its fine ancestry and privileged surroundings underlined by its setting in front of a handsome stable block. This has a clock and the architectural conceit of an oculus, a circular opening, in the gable which, as well as being stylish, may well have had a practical use as a pitching eye through which hay could be forked. In a typical tailpiece a traveller on horseback crosses a river, his hat tied on with a scarf; on the bank a reluctant dog barks in alarm, delaying the moment when it, too, must make the plunge. *The Race Horse*[19] (Fig. 16.2, middle), with its sleek coat, plaited mane and wide eyes, embodies the nervous tension of its type. The background is no less telling. A full race meeting is shown on Newcastle's Town Moor with starting post and rows of temporary stables. No less than three races are progressing in the distance, and even further away, on the highest point

[19] From *The Figures of Bewick's Quadrupeds* (2nd edn, Newcastle upon Tyne, 1824); reproduced in B. Cirker (ed.), *1800 Woodcuts by Thomas Bewick and his school* (New York, 1962), pl. 6; this book is a very useful gathering of many of Bewick's illustrations but also much that is not by Bewick.

Figure 16.3. top: T. Bewick, *Loading Coal on the Tyne*; middle: T. Bewick, *Newcastle Arms with the Tyne* (vignette from title page of *A History of British Birds*); bottom: T. Bewick, *Boys Playing at a Stream* (from *A History of British Birds*).

of ground, is a carriage drawn by horses. In this small space fourteen separate horses and over fifty people can be distinguished.

Bewick also wished to illustrate some truth and to make moral points, and it was in this that he was most penetrating. The truths and morals he showed stood for his time but also for all time. Bewick deplored war, especially when it was waged on behalf of what he regarded as tyranny. As a working tradesman, and one who took interest in the political discussions of his times, he was probably not in a position to express radical views (unlike his friend Thomas Spence, who got into trouble for doing so). He was able nevertheless to use his illustrations to provide messages, sometimes in code. When he disagreed with the treatment of animals – the docking of horses' tails, or the ill-treatment of performing bears, for example – he would show a gallows or gibbet on the skyline. With war he was a little more subtle. Two old comrades meet on a building site (Fig. 16.4, top). Their uniform jackets show that they served in the same regiment. One is now employed building a large house; the other, less fortunate, has returned from the wars with a wooden leg. There is a warmth in their attitudes and the handshake. Is this just the suggestion of hardships endured or glories shared? If so, was it worth it? Bewick is good at posing the questions but he leaves the answers to his readers. Has the soldier escaped from one kind of hard labour for another? Is it an accident that it is a large house being built, and possibly a wall to enclose it, too? The elaborate dovecote on the right shows that this is a gentleman's place; is he away fighting, too?

Sometimes the moral is clear. The boys tormenting a dog (Fig. 16.4, middle) may not know better but the man ought to be stopping them instead of standing by and enjoying the scene. The runaway cart (Fig. 16.2, top) is a wonderful mixture of action and danger. The boys have been playing in the cart and the horse has bolted; perhaps the dog's barking was the cause. The drawing of the wheel – an extraordinary depiction for its time – shows that the cart has gathered speed. One boy has already fallen and probably hurt himself. The others hang on shouting with fear. And why has it all happened? The carter with his tankard in his hand runs too late from the inn. Has he been distracted by the shapely girl? And is it an accident that the inn sign looks a little like a gallows?

In another tailpiece a small child is about to pull a stallion's tail (Fig. 16.2, bottom). The distraught mother, realising the danger, leaps down from a stile. But why has it happened? Is the girl in the bushes on the left with her sweetheart the nursemaid who ought to be looking after the child? Is it accidental, or emphasising a point, that a little further away there are two horses 'necking'? Is it really the mother who is to blame for giving responsibility to an unreliable person? And, above all, will the stallion, wide-eyed with irritation, actually kick?

Bewick peoples his social and moral landscape with many memorable figures. His sympathy is usually with the outsider: not the well-fed divine who ignores the beggar, but the lame and the blind, the tramp at the gate threatened by guard dogs, the cheeky poacher with his catch, the honest road-mender with his simple meal. He was matter-of-fact in his approach to those basic functions of life not often depicted by artists. He could be earthy but effective in depicting smells and noise. In an age when the acceptable presentation of bare bottoms was

Figure 16.4. top: T. Bewick, *Old Soldiers*; middle: T. Bewick, *Boys Tormenting a Dog*; bottom: T. Bewick (?), *Baby in Basket* (from T. Hugo, *Bewick's Woodcuts: Impressions of upwards of Two Thousand Woodblocks, etc.*, London, 1870).

limited to cherubs and goddesses, Bewick showed in one first edition a human rear elevation in a necessary house or 'netty' in mid-performance. The humour was enhanced by a startled pig below making a hasty withdrawal. It was not only the pig that was shocked. The picture must have been the cause of some comment (perhaps from Bewick's womenfolk). In the next edition the view was adjusted so that a couple of strategically placed planks restore a measure of modesty. The essential humour remained, and it can be paralleled in many other pictures.

Bewick could also be much more serious. His observation of cruelty to animals leaves little doubt about his own stance. He is forthright in showing the hanging of cats and dogs for amusement; nor does he shrink from the despair of the suicide. Sometimes his message is quite disguised, however. Here, in a little picture with the oval format Bewick and others used for depicting fables, is a baby, not in a proper cradle but in a shopping basket (Fig. 16.4, bottom); and why? Is it a front doorway or a pump? Probably the former. The child, with an arm raised, appears to be anxious. There is nobody else in sight. Can this be a child abandoned by a scared young mother? In her awful situation has she at least retained the presence of mind to place the child where it will be quickly discovered and comforted? Where does the blame lie?

From just before Bewick's own times, Hogarth's bluntly drawn and relatively cheaply produced satirical engravings established a tradition which combined humour with biting social and political comment; this was consolidated by Rowlandson and Gillray and later Cruikshank, Leech and others. Bewick had a gentler, more subtle approach, sometimes coded (as with his introduction of a gallows or gibbet to note his disapproval) but, when closely observed, it could be open to no less forceful interpretation.

Thomas Bewick, however, was not just a Newcastle engraver. He was very much a child of the Enlightenment, aware of learning possibilities and keen to take advantage of them. He had a consuming thirst for knowledge and, as his library[20] later showed, interests which were wide-ranging and of the moment. It was Napoleon who said that to understand a man one must know what was going on in the world when he was twenty: Napoleon's twentieth year witnessed the storming of the Bastille. Bewick, born twenty-six years earlier, was certainly stirred by the events of the French Revolution (and what reasonably well-informed townsman of the period would not have been?) but he viewed them from a maturity which had already taken stock of the blunderings which brought about the American revolution. His own twentieth year saw the stupidity of the government's reduction in the tea tariff everywhere except in the American colonies, and the reactions at Boston and Charleston which eventually led to the War of Independence. Bewick's own radicalism seems to have been as much social as actively political. Certainly, from the evidence of his own *Memoir* we know that he took part in the lively debates at Swarley's (or 'Swarelys') Club in

---

[20] See D. Gardner-Medwin, 'The Library of Thomas Bewick', in Gardner-Medwin, *Bewick Studies*, pp.51–72.

Newcastle[21] but his account, even if a little defensive, does not suggest that the conversations were seething with revolutionary zeal; on the contrary:

> This happy society was however, at length broken up, at a time when the War on behalf [of] despotism was raging & the Spy system was set afloat – some spies, and others of the same stamp contrived to get themselves introduced & to broach political questions, for the purpose of exciting debates & feeling the pulse of the company, which before had very seldom touched upon debates of this kind.[22]

Bewick showed disdain for the *agent provocateur* and hostility to war. He may not have been at the barricades himself but he certainly shared Wordsworth's youthful bliss at the bruising of the *ancien régime*. But his real enemy was ignorance: 'If there is a plurality of Devils, Ignorance must be their king. The wretchedness which ignorance has spread over the world is truly appalling. This is a king that should be deposed without loss of time.'[23]

His own efforts at self-improvement were prodigious, and described in his *Memoir* in a matter-of-fact way which does not quite escape a hint of justifiable pride. His naturally enquiring mind was helped by the Newcastle book trade, which, like so much else in the town, was thriving through the wealth brought by coal, engineering ingenuity and industry. Bewick's first-hand account of sharing learning opportunities with fellow apprentices is simple but moving. Visits, often early in the morning, to friends in printers' and bookbinders' workshops gave him access to books that were still being made. Gradually he gained wealthier friends who would lend or give him books. Nor, although he was remarkable in recording what happened, was he alone. He presents himself as part of a new industrial society which, without inclination to armed revolution, was excited by radical thinking, absorbed by opportunities for wider understanding and deeply involved in the intellectual and scientific processes which could lead to better education, increased fulfilment and healthier living as well as new prosperities. Bewick shows that the Enlightenment did not emerge only from the ranks of those privileged with the time to think, from study in private libraries, from elegant saloons bright with witty rhetoric and embroidered waistcoats and thick with wig powder. His is the first-hand account of one who found a way, or indeed many tortuous ways, of slaking a thirst for understanding. He was a country boy with an innate talent that took him not to the field or the pit, but to opportunities to focus his acute observation and lively intelligence on both the countryside he loved and the new provincial urban life of Newcastle.

While Bewick's earlier evidence is overwhelmingly in pictures, his lasting reputation was confirmed because of his writing. In his seventieth year he began writing a personal memoir. Its overt purpose was to inform his children of their

---

[21] Bewick writes 'Swarelys' and Bain edits as Swarley's, which is more correct but less Bewick. Swarley's was an informal debating gathering held at the Black Boy – now the Blackie Boy – Inn, in the Groat Market, Newcastle, with Christmas club and charitable subscriptions: 'the few rules were only verbal, which bound us together, & the first of these was this, that every member should behave with decorum like a Gentleman' (see Bewick, *Memoir*, pp.102–3).

[22] Ibid.

[23] Ibid., p.143.

family history and to set down an account of his own life. The writing continued for most of the remaining six years of his life. Eventually the work embraced not only Bewick's experiences and accounts of a wide range of his contemporaries, but his philosophy of life. If, as it does, his advice occasionally borders on sermonising, it reflects his character. As Iain Bain has written, the *Memoir*

> owes its reputation as a minor classic to two principal facts: first, that as a record of a north country childhood and a craftsman's life and work in the latter half of the eighteenth century it is unique, and secondly, that the achievement of its author as an artist-engraver on wood had no precedent and remains unequalled.[24]

The historical background to the writing of the *Memoir* is significant. The monarchy in Britain was very low in public esteem, and even its survival was a matter of latent debate. The old oft-deranged king had died only a few years earlier, and the performance of his sons presented at best an unedifying and unattractive spectacle – a debauched and dissipated monarchy presiding over a tired ruling class in which corruption and preferment were the norm. Revolution was in the air. When Bewick was a young man, as mentioned earlier, the American colonies had broken free on a tide of disgust and resentment at the lack of simple fairness of British administration. At the moment when his work began to achieve national recognition, the French had removed their king. By the time his main works were complete France had also seen the departure of their self-made emperor. Bewick expressed views which were widely shared among his contemporaries, especially those whose success had been the product of their own endeavours. Bewick would certainly have subscribed to Burns's refrain that 'Rank is but a guinea stamp, a man's a man for a' that.'

The publication of the *Memoir* was delayed by Bewick's children until 1862, a full generation after his death, and even then it was altered by his daughter to suit what she regarded as proper. Even in its modified form the book had a profound effect. John Ruskin, as the first Slade Professor of Fine Art at Oxford, in 1872 showed Bewick's work in his drawing school and could praise Bewick and Turner in the same breath.[25] He also recommended the *Memoir* with such enthusiasm to his students that one of them later brought out his own edition.[26] The later Victorians reassessed Bewick's work and produced substantial books.[27] Museum curators sought out his daughters, loyal guardians of his memory, and his original drawings, his blocks and his tools. Collections, private and public,

---

[24] I. Bain, Introduction to *Thomas Bewick: A Memoir* (Oxford, 1975), p.ix.

[25] See J. Ruskin, *Ariadne Florentina, Six Lectures on Wood and Metal Engraving given before the University of Oxford in the Michaelmas Term 1872* (Orpington and London, 1890).

[26] The student, Selwyn Image, remembered Ruskin showing his own copy 'somewhat untidily scored with pencil marks, as was his habit with books generally'. Image went on to become Slade Professor himself and, after retirement, wrote a perceptive and moving foreword to a new edition: S. Image, (ed.), *Memoir of Thomas Bewick written by himself 1822–1828* (London, 1924); the above reference to Ruskin is in the Introduction to this, p.v.

[27] See, for example, D.C. Thomson, *The Life and Works of Thomas Bewick, being an account of his career and achievements in art with a notice of the works of John Bewick* (London, 1882) and J. Boyd, *Bewick Gleanings, being impressions from copperplates and wood blocks engraved in Bewick's workshop* (Newcastle upon Tyne, 1886).

were assembled. A steady trickle of publications grew through the twentieth century to become a spate in our time.

The potential for understanding elements of the North-Eastern landscape within the work of Thomas Bewick has been either assumed with little examination or left unstudied. Landscape exists on the ground, or in pictorial form, or in the mind. For his times, his country and his reach in society, Bewick left evidence which is clear, unequivocal and wide-ranging. Bewick's illustrated books, admired since they first appeared, gave him some celebrity in his own lifetime. His *Memoir*, published a generation after his death, brought about a new interest and a widening respect which has continued to grow ever since. The attraction to his contemporaries of Bewick's observations lay in their accuracy and amusement. Two centuries later these qualities are still recognised; but so, too, is the wealth and rarity of the historical information they have to offer.

Tailpiece

Less than twenty years after Bewick's death came an endorsement from a young woman with particular views of the northern landscape:

> A small breakfast-room adjoined the drawing-room: I slipped in there. It contained a book-case: I soon possessed myself of a volume, taking care that it should be one stored with pictures. I mounted into the window seat: gathering up my feet, I sat cross-legged, like a Turk; and, having drawn the red moreen curtain nearly close, I was enshrined in double retirement.
>
> Folds of scarlet drapery shut in my view to the right hand; to the left were the clear panes of the glass, protecting, but not separating me from the drear November day. At intervals, while turning over the leaves of my book, I studied the aspect of that winter afternoon. Afar it offered a pale blank of mist and cloud; near, a scene of wet lawn and storm-beat shrub, with ceaseless rain sweeping away wildly before a long lamentable blast.
>
> I returned to my book – Bewick's *History of British Birds* … Each picture told a story; mysterious often to my undeveloped understanding and imperfect feelings, yet ever profoundly interesting … With Bewick on my knee, I was then happy: happy at least in my way. I feared nothing but interruption, and that came too soon.[28]

The lonely but comforted young woman was Jane Eyre.

---

[28] Charlotte Brontë, as 'Currer Bell', first published *Jane Eyre* in 1847 with, because of its instant popularity, a second edition in the same year; it has been in print ever since. This quotation is referenced from Blackwell's Shakespeare Head edition of 1931 (reprinted by Everyman's Library, London, 1991), pp.2–3.

17

The 'Haven' and the 'Grisly Rokkes': Mary Linskill's Dangerous Landscapes and the Making of Whitby

JAN HEWITT

We have become accustomed to 'heritage' descriptions like 'Brontë Country' or 'Thomas Hardy Country' shaping ideas of region by aligning them with canonical texts of English literature and, in the process, reinventing our ideas of both. But given the astonishing amount of regional fictional texts that appeared at all levels across Victorian print culture, one sometimes cannot help but ponder on the relationships between *minor* texts and constructions of place, particularly on the functions they may have performed or the significance they once had *outside* the context of a canonical English literary history that valorises some authors over others.

Popular cultural texts are of course now commonly incorporated into current discourses of regional heritage ('Heartbeat Country', 'Catherine Cookson Country'), so clearly, by their very everyday nature and appeal, they also have a part to play in the reproduction of imagined landscapes, places and regions. However, attempting to understand such relationships as part of an historical/ cultural dynamic, when once-accepted values and ideals have changed, is to attempt a form of archaeology that demands a particular type of interdisciplinary approach.

My discussion contributes towards such an approach by suggesting how representations of place and landscape in the work of one 'minor' late Victorian writer, Mary Linskill (1840–1891), impacted upon changing constructions of place and local identities in and around Whitby on the North Yorkshire coast in the later nineteenth century. Seen as part of a complex interchange of print and visual culture, Linskill's fictions dramatise a sense of 'encounter'[1] between inside and outside constituencies that shared an interest in the emergence of

---

[1] See P. Burke, *What is Cultural History?* (Cambridge, 2004), pp.116–19, and *Varieties of Cultural History* (Cambridge, 1997), chapter 12, esp. pp.201–12, for an overview of ideas of encounter theory. See also A.P. Cohen, *The Symbolic Construction of Community* (London, 1993). I am indebted to my colleague Tony Nicholson for wide-ranging and stimulating discussions about the place and role of encounter models in the construction of identities.

Whitby and its surroundings as a tourist destination. The idea of 'encounter' is significant not just because it mirrors Whitby's 'discovery' by writers, artists and tourists, but because it also indicates how local communities make *themselves* in the process as part of an area that, in its supposed simplicity, honesty and ruggedness, holds something of value for the modern world.

Mary Linskill came from Whitby. She took its coastal area as the setting for most of her novels and stories in the 1870s and 1880s, with the fishing town and growing seaside resort designated as 'Hild's Haven' or 'Port St Hilda' in her work. From the early *Tales of the North Riding* (1871) to the much-reviewed novels of the 1880s, *Between the Heather and the Northern Sea* (1884), *The Haven under the Hill* (1886) and *In Exchange for a Soul* (1887), the sufferings and rewards played out in relationships between her characters are projected as interdependent with the spaces in which they operate – the land and seascapes of the North Yorkshire coast. Their plots and characters reproduce familiar narratives of women's romance: a young husband's desperate search for his wife who has disappeared after a vengeful and mistaken trick played by a love-sick lady's maid; the love-triangle of male hero competed for by two female characters, where moral strength and purity of intent win out; or the tangles of a cross-class love match and subsequent elevation of its socially marginal female. These are melodramatic plots, but Linskill is no idle sensationalist. They are also Christian narratives, where redemption comes through suffering and is articulated through conventional courtship tropes. Clearly such fiction had a popular status in the late nineteenth and early twentieth centuries, as Linskill's work remained in print at least until the 1920s and, sporadically, beyond. Limited in appeal today, however, it has long been out of widespread circulation.[2]

Yet I will argue that Mary Linskill's fiction played its part in a discursively produced Whitby-based 'place myth'[3] which saw the region's hitherto bleaker and less hospitable aspects transformed as the gaze upon it became increasingly aligned with the concerns of the urban middle classes.[4] In her work such a gaze is represented through her inclusion of an artist figure as a major character. This male character recurs in many stories to act as an outside interpreter of local landscapes and people, one that must discover the unique aesthetic and spiritual power of the area, both for himself and for the reader. By making this figure's reading of place significant in narrative terms, he also stands as a powerful referent for the authority of the female writer. However, this highlighting of a visual reading also mirrors, and in Linskill's case arguably complicates, the effects of a wider gaze in journalism and art that was itself turned upon the Whitby area as it increasingly came to be seen as holding particular attractions.

---

[2] The writer and publisher Cordelia Stamp, of Whitby, has been instrumental in keeping Linskill's name and work in the public eye, both in Stamp's biography (which draws heavily on Linskill's fiction for its information) and in her reprints of a number of stories and novels in the early 1990s. Though out of print, at the time of writing they are still occasionally to be found.

[3] The concept comes from R. Shields, *Places on the Margins: Alternative Geographies of Modernity* (London, 1991), pp.47, 60–61.

[4] J. Urry, *Consuming Places* (London, 1995), pp.194–5. Urry shows how the place-myth is part of a complex discursive structure that generates the desire to visit, to gaze at and to 'know' a specific landscape, arguing that it is representative of the commodified tourist experience in modern society.

An early example of this artist-character is Paul Hesildene, the narrator of 'Taught by Adversity' in *Tales of the North Riding* (1871), who, searching for his wife and with dwindling resources, sets up in the seaside town of Danesborough, a scarcely disguised version of Scarborough with its 'Cliff Bridge; the Spa ... Saloon; ... and ... Oliver's Mount in the distance'.[5] However, Paul's efforts prove futile, both with his painting and his search, in this fashionable town with its promenades, concerts and aristocratic patrons, until the turning point when a friend persuades him to take lodgings in 'Longscaur Wyke', a tiny fishing community near to his own at 'Port St Hilda' – 'a capital place for a marine painter'[6] – where he can concentrate his work on this different, bleaker, type of coastline:

> It was a barren, bleak-looking spot. Four or five fishermen's cottages were perched upon unsafe looking shelves that jutted out from the side of the cliff ... At first this sterility struck me with a sense of dreariness ... As the days wore on I began to perceive that the scenery along this rugged part of the coast-line had strange and peculiar charms of its own.[7]

Here, his initial perceptions change and the paintings that emerge from this altered vision start to sell for considerable sums in the London galleries, triggering a chain of dramatic events that lead eventually to the restoration of his wife and family. Yet Paul's initial sense of the landscape's 'sterility' and 'dreariness' that gives way to the recognition of its 'strange and peculiar charms' replicates exactly the shift in perceptions that is registered in the town's print culture during the middle and later years of the nineteenth century.

Print culture within Whitby played a key role in developing a new framework of self-consciousness at this time. A significant spurt of local literary journals occurred in the 1820s and 1830s, when, far from celebrating rugged, romantic coastlines and moors, or the picturesque charms of this seagoing town, the predominant tone of early publications was self-consciously critical, even negative. By the 1830s, miscellanies such as *The Whitby Repository*, *The Whitby Magazine and Monthly Literary Journal* and *The Whitby Treasury* were, in their various ways, united in addressing concerns about their town's image in relation to the world outside. The *Repository*, for example, complains that 'in this refined and enlightened age' Whitby's inhabitants should be 'qualified to compete with those of other places ...'[8] but sincerely doubts that they are; the *Treasury* too, mindful of the value of visual impact, promotes itself as 'a Diorama of past scenes and a Camera of present ones' for 'the mental improvement of the town'.[9]

Taken as a whole, these papers reveal a sense of urgency among local intellectuals who saw the town as hopelessly stagnant and permeated by provincial

---

5   M. Linskill, 'Taught by Adversity' in *Tales of the North Riding* (1871; this edition, London, 1904), p.285.
6   Ibid., p.303.
7   Ibid., pp.312–13.
8   'On the Organisation of a Discussion Society', *Whitby Repository*, 2 (July 1833), pp.197–202 (Whitby Literary and Philosophical Society Archives).
9   'Address to the Reader', *Whitby Treasury*, 1:1 (6 January 1838), p.2 (Whitby Literary and Philosophical Society Archives).

philistinism. While clearly concerned to extol the town's beneficial aspects, their articles represent the area and its people as conservative, even backward, in relation to the rest of the country. At this point in the century journals like the *Repository* felt all too keenly the dynamic contrast between the rapidly growing industrial belts of Teesside and County Durham and their own town's economic and intellectual stagnation. With many of its industries already in decline, the community could easily feel itself a backwater and, alongside its worrying economic depression, consider itself an 'un-intellectual town'.[10] These journals, floated in an uncertain mood of missionary optimism with the express aim of stimulating ideas and information to enable Whitby to embrace the advantages of the modern world, were to be short-lived. Clearly it was not an easy agenda. One *Repository* article describes the visit to his native town of the celebrated marine painter George Chambers. The writer rails at the way local society responded to him with a strange mixture of 'barbarous curiosity' and philistine indifference:

> Alas! the minds of the Whitby people are so engrossed by the concerns of trade ... [that a] painting by the 'foremost man of all the world' would ... be only valued in proportion to the costliness of its frame ... The truth is there is here no sympathy for the arts.[11]

Though registering personal embarrassment at the essential vulgarity of Whitby culture, this writer is yet more concerned that Chambers, 'a fellow-townsman whom their Majesties are proudly pleased to patronise',[12] would leave with a jaundiced view of the town, and feared that its clumsy encounters with fashionable society would colour important outside perceptions.

Such early commentators make clear links between Whitby's physical environment and its intellectual condition. They are all too aware of the town's poor roads, its rank harbour and stinking quayside, seeing in such physical features the outward manifestations of an inner moral and intellectual decay. Though recognising that the coast 'abounds with rich subjects for the artist's pencil', the *Repository* also notes that Chambers (at this point in his short life an invalid who came to the town in the hope of recovering his health) 'nothing bettered but rather grew worse'.[13] Whitby's climate, position and natural flora are compared, unfavourably, with fashionable Scarborough, 'which has the advantage in this as well as other essential respects', and the contrast feels painful: where self-assured Scarborough 'reclines on a gentle slope ... inhaling the sea breeze modified by expansion', Whitby struggles to breathe a blighted air 'compressed by a narrow passage betwixt the cliffs [and] ... evidenced ... by the sickly appearance of its flowers and shrubs'.[14] Though such self-critical preoccupations would not entirely disappear throughout the century, with 'health' in particular

[10] Review of Whitby authors and periodicals, *Whitby Magazine and Monthly Literary Journal*, 2 (1828), pp.149–57 (Whitby Literary and Philosophical Society Archives).

[11] 'George Chambers Esq.', *Whitby Repository*, 3 (1833), p.152 (Whitby Literary and Philosophical Society Archives., pp.149–57).

[12] Ibid., p.151.

[13] Ibid., pp.149–50.

[14] Ibid., p.149.

a recurring focus for Whitby's relations with 'civilised' society, the dominant mood of this early period in the town is unmistakably dark and self-doubting.

The next few decades saw a remarkable change in perceptions. The arrival of the railway and new speculative developments from the 1840s and 1850s prompted rapid changes in visitor patterns. The decline of local industries – whaling, shipbuilding, alum and jet working – was counterbalanced by a burgeoning tourist growth as the railway entrepreneur George Hudson and others invested heavily in the West Cliff estate, building hotels, villas and lodging houses to cater for better-off visitors staying for the traditional month in the summer.[15] This was precisely the kind of modern development local commentators could only dream of during the dark decades of the 1820s and 1830s, but later visitors to the town were not coming just for plush railway carriages, sunny promenades and comfortable hotels, but to 'discover' for themselves what the exhibitions, journalism and literature were increasingly chronicling as a landscape and way of life preserved from the encroaches of modern industrialism and urbanisation.

Similarly, the arrival of artists, literati and other denizens of metropolitan life formed an intellectual vanguard from outside the area to generate and disseminate new images for an educated middle class seeking relief from a modern, urban world. Once seen as stagnant and provincial, Whitby was increasingly hailed as wonderfully unspoilt; its cramped alleys and dilapidated houses turned out to be delightfully picturesque; what had been vulgar and coarse was reframed as simple and unaffected. George du Maurier, commissioned by Smith, Elder & Co. to illustrate *Sylvia's Lovers* by Elizabeth Gaskell, whose 'Monkshaven' was based on the town, worked from photographs. Alongside the novel's descriptions they so excited his admiration that he regularly holidayed there, first in 1864 soon after completion of his commission, and then in the 1880s and 1890s, when it became a topos within his own work.[16] Indeed, the area was a favourite both with the *Punch* circle and with a wider metropolitan artistic *milieu*. By the 1870s and 1880s John Leech, James Russell Lowell, Henry James, Edward Burne-Jones, Linley Sambourne, George du Maurier and others were coming, in truth as much for the picturesque views of the harbour, the rocky coastlines and the surrounding moorland landscapes as for the holiday atmosphere so frequently alluded to in the pages of *Punch*.

That this was not simply a one-way dynamic can be seen in the local papers, which had their own interests in scrutinising such material as exhibition reports in the national and London press, and which communicated back to their readers that outside gaze directed upon them. Local perceptions also engaged in this shift as Whitby's people started to see *themselves* in relation to the more favourable external views. What its visitors thought, wrote and painted had an impact within the town itself as the local press reciprocated the gaze by circulating and responding internally to images generated of itself: by the 1880s, trawls of metropolitan and regional newspapers routinely highlighted evidence of how

---

15 A. White, 'The Victorian Development of Whitby as a Seaside Resort', *Local Historian*, 28:2 (May 1998), pp.78–93.

16 L. Ormond, *George du Maurier* (London, 1969), pp.148, 156, 481–3 and 492–7.

Whitby was viewed under such headings as 'Whitby as Strangers see it'. Linskill herself was part of the exchange, making a comment – albeit brief – about du Maurier's depictions of Whitby life in an article for *The Whitby Gazette*.[17] As, by this time, the *Gazette*'s owners were involved in the production of their own carefully inclusive *Horne's Guide to Whitby*, this is the point at which we might locate the emergence of a new regional self-consciousness soundly located in commercial activity – one much more positive in tone, where the individual qualities of local landscapes and people could become a source of pride rather than of dismay.

If, during Mary Linskill's early years, intellectual circles in the town had despaired of its provincialism, then within her lifetime this isolated corner of the country was rethinking itself. The process of shifting from negative to more positive perceptions created imaginative tensions and possibilities for a writer situated as she was. Born in 1840 in one of the crowded yards in the old part of Whitby alongside the harbour described in *The Haven under the Hill*, Linskill was first and foremost an *insider*, who came from a well-known local family. Yet she too had seen it from the outside, leaving the area in the 1860s to work in the Midlands and West Yorkshire, when she started to produce her tales and stories. Returning to Whitby around 1870, probably for financial reasons, she relied increasingly on her writing to provide an income for herself and her mother, especially after her father's death in 1874, which left them struggling under a precarious financial burden.[18] As she had had some success by that time, particularly with *Tales of the North Riding*, published in 1871 under the pseudonym 'Stephen Yorke,' the move to exploit growing interests in regionally based writing and provincial themes made sound financial sense.

Mary Linskill's North Yorkshire novels were directed primarily at an outside, educated, audience. The particular contours of place she evokes were shaped as much by the literary, artistic and moral codes of this wider readership as by her knowledge of local landscape and culture. If visiting artists and writers had discovered a 'new' romantic landscape, full of rugged beauty and spiritual power, Linskill was encouraged by their visions to create her own – part real, part imagined – with a distinctive moral and spiritual transformative power. We might think of her novels as regional melodramas whose moral landscapes are constructed by more realist modes of reference than conventional melodramatic codes generally allow. Densely allusive, they draw on a rich array of sources to construct a version of a literary national culture where a romantic 'northern-ness' is built up and given historical resonance.[19] Echoes of Whitby's founding

---

[17] Dated c.1885. This appears in a scrapbook of newspaper cuttings in the archives of the Whitby Literary and Philosophical Society; full reference not identified.

[18] For biographical details see Rev. D.A. Quinlan and A.F. Humble, *Mary Linskill: The Whitby Novelist* (Whitby, 1969); C. Stamp, *Mary Linskill* (Whitby, 1980); C. Stamp, 'Linskill, Mary Jane (1840–1891)', *Oxford Dictionary of National Biography* (Oxford, 2004).

[19] See P. Dodd, 'Englishness and the National Culture', in R. Colls and P. Dodd (eds), *Englishness: Politics and Culture 1880–1920* (London, 1986), pp.1–28; A. Howkins, 'The Discovery of Rural England', in Colls and Dodd, *Englishness*, pp.62–88; also I. Chambers, 'Narratives of Nationalism: Being "British"', in E. Carter, J. Donald and J. Squires (eds), *Space and Place: Theories of Identity and Location* (London, 1993) p.147.

narrative of the poet Caedmon lie behind the structure of *The Haven under the Hill*. Linskill's references (among others) are to Chaucer, Drayton and Scott, her social frameworks are drawn from Carlyle and Emerson, and quotations from Wordsworth and post-Romantic poetry, along with devotional writings from Bede and others, underline a combined emotional and spiritual significance. On to this essentially national cultural framework are grafted local stories, familiar to Linskill certainly but also, by the 1880s, to many of her holiday readers, who might read about them in miscellanies and guidebooks. Characters refer to the phantom 'Barguest', the 'Gabriel Hounds', or the legend of 'Beggar's Bridge'; the linguistic provenance of local topographies is embedded in names such as 'Northscaur Bay', 'Soulsgrif Bight', 'Skerne Dun' and 'Raithe Wyke'; and the region's widely recognisable associations with Viking and Norse settlement is re-presented in names such as 'Thorsgrif', 'Lodbrok Bay' and 'Oswaldthorpe'.

Despite such realist referents, Mary Linskill's northern landscapes are primarily moral landscapes. In 'Taught by Adversity' the fashionable setting of 'Danesborough' (Scarborough) does little to help Paul Hesildene. However, that of 'Longscaur Wyke', near Port St Hilda, facilitates resolution of the tale not through being 'safe' and conventionally attractive but precisely *because* it is mysterious, strange and rugged. In the tale, as a great sea storm rages, Paul is tormented by visions of his lost family and the nearness of his wife. Yet in this same storm, Paul's friend is drowned while out with the local fishermen. The implications are clear. This coastline offers a dangerous landscape that will not be subsumed into any cosy rural idyll. Far away from modern life and the uncertainties that threaten the family unit, it submits characters to extreme experiences that, endured, will heighten their moral sympathies and restore social harmony.

By the mid-1880s Linskill's tendency to heroicise this encounter between her land and seascapes and the figures within them is intensified by a neo-medievalism that both elevates her characters in their battles with the wild natural coastline and further aligns them with it. *Between the Heather and the Northern Sea* (1884) reworks a celebrated event that occurred near Whitby just three years prior to the novel's publication, when the local lifeboat was hauled overland through a hostile winter landscape in order to save a boat wrecked on an inaccessible piece of rocky coastline:

> The day and the deed will live, as brave deeds have lived in England always. The children of children yet unborn will tell of the cutting of the frozen and deeply drifted snow over hills and through hollows for six long miles; the painful dragging step by step, of the massively built boat, mounted on her own carriage, by men who wrought in silence, in utter obedience, in splendid willingness, with desperate resolve.[20]

Here the heroic register aligns local with national history, where the deed 'will live … in England always'. The lifeboatmen are medieval knights, 'brave sea-soldiers' who wear 'buoyant armour', carry 'pale blue lances' and are

---

[20] M. Linskill, *Between the Heather and the Northern Sea* (1884; this edition, Whitby, 1991), p.37. This novel was serialised in *Good Words* in 1884.

Figure 17.1. 'The Landslip at Whitby' (*The Graphic*, 21 January 1871, p.151) (by courtesy of Newcastle City Libraries and Arts)

'Chivalrous!'[21] in their battle with the stormy sea.[22] Yet this action also provides a dramatic start to the romantic narrative when its heroine, newly arrived from London with her father, is cut off by the tide while watching the event and is herself rescued by a local landowner. She is conscious only of a 'dark form dashing through the white whirl of spray', whereas he is reduced to his single 'strong arm', represented as a comparable human force pitting itself against the tremendous forces of nature, the 'fierce … drenching … blinding shock' that threatens to engulf her.[23] His actions are all but repeated later in the novel when the selfsame characters hover on a declaration of love, interrupted by a dramatic rock-fall:

> It seemed as if the very stones and the stems of the trees were cracking and rending asunder … Genevieve … only heard the riving, snapping, craunching sounds; … only felt … the shiver of earth, then, even while a strong arm was clasping her, almost flinging her outward from the path, there came the thunderous thud of falling rock.[24]

If this dangerous landscape is, therefore, one where a heroic masculinity is being acted out, it is also one in which the feminine, too, is being organised. These two key events – the tidal rescue and the rock-fall – take local features and stories as part of the courtship narrative, and are drawn together so that the

[21] Ibid., p.38.
[22] See also J. Hewitt, '"Such girls as you would hardly see anywhere else in England …": the "Regional Feminine" of Mary Linskill's Fiction', in C. Ehland (ed.), *Thinking Northern* (*Spatial Practices Series* (Amsterdam, 2008), for an argument that develops the gender aspects of this discussion in other ways.
[23] Linskill, *Between the Heather*, p.40.
[24] Ibid., p.92.

repeated motif of the strong manly arm naturalises the heroine's transition from girl to adult, ultimately to position her as a loved and loving wife.

Yet such alignment of gender ideals with geographical features of the North Yorkshire coast suggests wider issues. Erosion along this coastline was well documented throughout the period, catching the popular imagination in newspapers and illustrated magazines (see Fig. 17.1). In Linskill's fiction such emphasis on instability, on ground that constantly moves, changes and literally falls away from beneath the feet of its characters metaphorically dramatises the doubts and anxieties of modernity. This is a North Yorkshire setting constructed against the forces of modernity and the extent to which those forces highlight female independence must also be negotiated and its unacceptable aspects expunged. This occurs in *The Haven under the Hill* (1886),[25] where both the elements, of neo-medievalism and the instability of the northern landscape, are again brought into play. Most immediately, the forename of this novel's protagonist, Dorigen Gower, is from Chaucer's 'Frankleyn's Tale' and alludes to the 'good woman' who contemplates suicide rather than gainsay her 'trouthe'. Chaucer's Dorigen is caught between two men, the husband for whom she patiently waits while he is at sea and a young squire who wishes to be her lover. Throughout the tale she is obsessed with fears that her husband's ship will ground on the 'grisly rokkes blake'[26] yet the promises she makes to the squire to secure her husband's safety throw her into an impossible, and testing, moral dilemma. Edward Burne-Jones's painting *Dorigen of Bretagne Longing for the Safe Return of her Husband* (1871) offers a more contemporary representation to suggest the frustrations of a Victorian Dorigen whose sphere of action is reduced to the doubly confining frames of her room and window as she overlooks the 'rokkes' (Fig. 17.2). Intertextually, both emphasise the novel's landscapes as repeatedly and dramatically unstable, with equally overwhelming consequences for the characters caught up in them.

The moral framework of *The Haven under the Hill* is triggered when its alum-master hero rescues Dorigen – again in a landslip – to realise his love for her. As with the earlier novel, this first landslip episode proleptically foreshadows the later dramatic climax based on a verifiable event: that of a well-documented disaster of 1829 when the alum workings at Kettleness slipped into the sea.[27] In Linskill's fictionalised account it kills the wife of the alum-master as she leaves him to become an actress. The dangerous landscape here adjudicates between contrasting modes of female agency: that of the 'bad' woman, who leaves her children to be punished by a terrain she despises but cannot escape; and that of

---

[25] M. Linskill, *The Haven under the Hill* (1886; this edition, Whitby, 1991). This novel was serialised in *Good Words* in 1886.

[26] F.N. Robinson (ed.), Geoffrey Chaucer, *The Canterbury Tales* (Oxford, 1979), p.137.

[27] An article in *The Illustrated London News* about the destruction, by landslip, of the Victoria Iron and Cement Works at nearby Wreckhills ('Destruction of the Victoria Iron and Cement Works at Wreckhills', 24 April 1858, pp.415–16) notes this earlier disaster, where 'Warehouses, offices, dwelling-houses, and cottages, together with mine-heaps, machinery &c, to a large amount, were completely swallowed up', and comments how along 'the whole line of coast ... these landslips have been of such frequent occurrence as to excite but little notice'.

Figure 17.2. Sir Edward Burne-Jones, *Dorigen of Bretagne Longing for the Safe Return of her Husband*, 1871, gouache (courtesy of the Victoria and Albert Museum, London).

Dorigen who, as 'good' woman, shows her integrity by prioritising moral obligations and yet, independently, also follows a writing career.

Mary Linskill's landscapes then also suggest conflicted notions of authority in the 'escapee' woman writer who similarly prioritises moral obligations in her mission to marry her local loyalties with her wider literary ambitions. As an insider she may have attempted to represent the Whitby area in local terms, but she was still dependent on the approbation of that outside readership, which might all too easily slip into seeing it as the uncivilised, literally 'outlandish' place of earlier memory. Though initially she sought publication with metropolitan, 'quality' periodicals, such as *London Society, New Quarterly, The Athenaeum*, and *Blackwood's Magazine*,[28] it was the respectable if less prestigious *Good Words* that saw the publication of much of her work. Her novels were serialised, then followed up by book publication, a typical mode of production that has been seen as both addressing and constructing a domestic, middle-class and middle-brow readership with increasing time at its disposal.[29] This, we might note, was a constituency that was also simultaneously contributing to the changing visitor patterns of holiday places like Whitby.

[28] Quinlan and Humble, *Mary Linskill*, pp.13, 24.
[29] L.K. Hughes and M. Lund discuss in detail how the serial format is an essential factor in the way its readers created meaning in a wide range of Victorian texts in their *The Victorian Serial* (Charlottesville, 1991).

Writing as an 'insider' for an implied 'outside', metropolitan readership potentially inverts the conventional power basis of centre and margins to generate suggestive tensions in the later novels of the 1880s. Here, the inscription of local knowledge through characters, settings and narrators, where secrets of the landscape are unlocked as its histories, names and events are re-presented, makes Linskill's fiction act as a highly mediated guide to the area, a heightened version of the growing number of texts produced for the tourist market. In such writing the local, instead of being subordinated to metropolitan authority and blindly reproducing its assumptions, is elevated beyond the everyday concerns of provincial realism to offer a powerful referent of place along with its imagined and universalising fictional themes. Though personal recognition of place may heighten readerly pleasure, direct knowledge is not necessary as vicarious armchair visiting is accessible through the wider framework of print culture. In either case, the contours of place also become a significant space for identification and desire, for escape not just in physical terms but in moral, emotional and spiritual ones too.

The construction of Linskill's 'Hild's Haven' landscapes clearly contribute towards a Romantic-inspired Whitby place-myth, but any suggestion of a transcendent, spiritual, natural landscape is overlaid with significance that is specific to a broadly evangelically minded social and moral order. *Good Words* itself gained much of its reputation as an illustrated literary magazine designed specifically for family and Sunday reading where subject matter could encompass a variety of social concerns and popular scientific commentary alongside religious instruction and debate.[30] Over the period of Mary Linskill's career it increased its inclusion of biography, natural history and travel writing, marking that shift with editorial policies that increasingly emphasise geographical authenticity in the accompanying illustrations to her work. If 'Taught by Adversity' exemplifies an earlier fictionalisation of 'Danesborough', where references pin down precise geographical location, in 1871 that landscape is still subject to the workings of character and plot. By the mid 1880s the movement is surely going another way. In 1884, the illustrations for *Between the Heather and the Northern Sea* highlight its characters against landscapes that, possibly because of the metropolitan artist's unfamiliarity, are only loosely localised. Two years later, however, those for *The Haven under the Hill* subordinate its action to extremely detailed Whitby imagery, including, for example, the Church Stairs and the Abbey (Figs 17.3 and 17.4). As Mary Linskill became readily known as 'Miss Linskill, the Whitby novelist', so too her otherwise more ambiguous landscapes are fixed into place. It is a shift that suggests the extent to which 'authenticity' and iconic resonance became part of the experience of reading regional fiction, and marks external pressures to shape responses in terms of dominant expectations of place and region.

Issues of consumption and dissemination in contemporary reception of the novels also assist in the fidelity to readerly assumptions of 'authentic' place over and above the working-out of character and action. To one reviewer in

---

30 A. Sullivan (ed.), *British Literary Magazines: The Victorian and Edwardian Age, 1837–1913* (Westport, 1984), pp.145–9.

Figure 17.3. 'The Church Stairs', from Mary Linskill, *The Haven under the Hill*, in *Good Words* (1886), p.5.

The Academy, Linskill's *The Haven under the Hill* was a 'fine, healthy, breezy novel'[31] – a vindication of those earlier internally generated anxieties about the physical healthiness of Whitby now translated into the moral health of her work and its settings. To *The Sheffield Daily Telegraph* she was 'the novelist of the North', her characters 'portraits of Northern folk, as they who have lived among them will recognize, and her scenery is precisely what one recalls'.[32]

---

[31] Cited in Quinlan and Humble, *Mary Linskill*, p.39.
[32] Ibid., p.13.

Figure 17.4. 'And towering above all, the Abbey on the hill-top', from Mary Linskill, *The Haven under the Hill*, in *Good Words* (1886), p.513.

From a more aesthetic perspective, too, *The Spectator* praised *Between the Heather and the Northern Sea* for its 'shifting scenes of a great sea storm', its 'aspects of wild, high moorland; ... lonely, desolate and reedy marshes; ... rare bits of cornland, [and] sheltered orchard'[33] and, in its obituary in 1891, the *Manchester Examiner* went so far as to state that, had she lived, 'what Mr Hardy is to the West Country, Mary Linskill might have been to the North Riding of Yorkshire.'[34] Though expressing conventional respect, this still illustrates how far place and authenticity could act as markers for popular, and commercial, approbation.

Given that Whitby's own print culture was by this time well-attuned to pick up every detail of wider responses to the area, it is unsurprising that it should start to celebrate Linskill in similar terms and claim her work ever more securely for local and regional interests. In the later 1880s she contributed to the local press, and the annually produced *Horne's Guide to Whitby* carried a section on her life (and eventually death) alongside its other commentaries, advertisements and walks for visitors. It continued to do so until the early 1900s. After her death

[33] Ibid., p.39.
[34] Ibid. p.13.

in 1891 details of a memorial cross, constructed in her memory, were added. Beyond this, a deluge of regional guides and commentaries up until the 1920s cite her as one of a number of 'famous' Yorkshire men and women whose 'force-fulness and strength of character are dominant notes in their lives' and whose novels still 'charm lovers of the sea-coast and the moorlands'.[35] It is echoed in the characteristic rhetoric of Edwardian travel literature, as with Mrs Rodolph Stawell, who incorporates Linskill's title into a breathless description of a drive down the moorland coast to Whitby where one dips into 'one of the many green gorges that run down, "between the heather and the northern sea"'.[36]

In such ways the processes of commodification through language, imagery and agency that are shown in the distinctive encounters between 'inside' and 'outside' interests are made known through the presentation of landscape in Mary Linskill's fiction. The novels and their immediate concerns may not, in themselves, have lasted. However, by investing their landscapes with evangel-ical, spiritual and regenerative moral powers they are still part of that discursive shaping of local identity and wider regional self-consciousness that took place in and around Whitby over a protracted period of time. Though on the surface their moral and social perspectives may appear inflexible now, their picturesque constructions of a place and its people betray the shifting contours that were closely bound up with the experience of a modern world.

---

[35] J. S. Fletcher, *A Book about Yorkshire* (London, 1908), p.272.
[36] Mrs R. Stawell, *Motor Tours in Yorkshire* (London, 1909), p.95.

18

Cullercoats: An Alternative North-Eastern Landscape?

LAURA NEWTON

This chapter explores the discrepancies in the nation's figuring of two groups of the North East's working classes during the late nineteenth century – the industrial worker and the Cullercoats (Northumberland) fisherfolk – using verbal and pictorial imagery from a variety of contemporary writings. It suggests that the impossibility of presenting a naturalistic visual representation of the industrial worker and his milieu led to the local appropriation of Cullercoats imagery as an alternative North-Eastern landscape which could be projected as part of the region's positive 'repackaging' of itself.

The North East

Given the growing importance of the North East as a region of industrial and economic wealth during the second half of the nineteenth century, it is perhaps not surprising that it attracted regular notice from widely read magazines such as *The Graphic*, *The Art Journal* and *The Magazine of Art*, as well as from writers on such subjects as local history, geography and travel. But, with few exceptions, it is apparent from the style and handling of the writings that the interest was generated not because of the region's achievements or positive attributes, but because it was regarded as a curiosity, somehow 'different'. Richard Welford's article 'Newcastle Upon Tyne' noted that 'smoke from the manufactories and steamers is allowed to pollute the air unchecked, while fumes from the chemical works stunt vegetation and destroy the beauty of what was once a delightful landscape',[1] while *The Graphic* in 1884 described how:

> The inky water laves the windings of the banks, with their wharves and slips, and the dismal stretches of blackened soil on the edges of the shore, laden with ooze, and strewn with scurf and refuse. It is a flood unutterably foul. ... Nothing is yet visible of houses ashore, through the irritating and suffocating fog-cloud, but close at hand there is the deafening strike, strike, of a thousand hammers on sullen metal, from the ship-building yards hard by ... tall chimneys belching sulphurous fumes; – black wooded erections, like gigantic

---

[1] R. Welford, 'Newcastle upon Tyne', *Art Journal* (1882), p.293.

Figure 18.1. Robert Jobling/William Lionel Wyllie, *General View of Albert Edward Dock* (North Shields), (*The Graphic*, 23 August 1884, pp.192–3).

scaffolds, with a running wheel high in air and mighty beam rising and falling in the pit's mouth – blighted fields beyond, with leafless hedge rows, and stunted trees gaunt in deformity.[2]

Similarly, the writer Vernon Lee, the lifelong friend of John Singer Sargent, declared:

one of the most impressive of all spectacles, short of hell – the Tyne at Newcastle. ... A vast mass of leaden water, polluted with every foulness, flowing heavily, or scarce seeming to flow at all, between lines of docks and factories, their innumerable masts and innumerable chimneys faint upon the thick brown sky, faintly reddened with an invisible sun, and streaked in various intensities of brown and grey and black, with ever rising curls of smoke. This river flows, most often as deep as a gorge, between banks of blackish cinders, of white poisonous chemical refuse, or worst of all, of what was once pure live soil, now stained and deadened into something unnatural, whereon the very weeds refuse to grow.[3]

The uniformity of these terrifying word-pictures is remarkable. Although the first quote was by a local writer, all were written for a national audience. The *Graphic* article had specially commissioned illustrations by W.L. Wyllie and the Cullercoats artist Robert Jobling. Wyllie was well known for depictions of similar Thames scenes, but Jobling was, outside the region, completely unknown. However, his work seems to have fitted easily into the style adopted by Wyllie, although the illustrations hardly do justice to the prose (Fig. 18.1).

Yet, not all writers on the North East regarded the situation in a purely negative light. In a special edition of *The Graphic*, to mark the centenary of George Stephenson's birth, the journalist and critic Aaron Watson not only sang the praises of Newcastle's 'noble streets' but reminded his readership that 'it is a vulgar error to suppose that Newcastle is in Scotland. The inhabitants neither speak Gaelic nor wear kilts.'[4] His next article, 'The Coaly Tyne', for *The Magazine of Art* in 1883, is still more celebratory. Presumably mindful of the different audience he addresses, he makes a direct appeal:

it is a painter's river; ... it abounds in pictures from its source to the sea. ... The sun sometimes builds up superb effects with those vapours in which the prosaic observer sees but suggestions of stygian caves forlorn. Those quick-flowing waters, so inextricably associated with the products of the mine, are often very brilliant and attractive to the eye.[5]

The entire article abounds with images aimed at whetting the appetite of artists:

It [Jarrow] is a place where you may see a pillar of cloud by day and a pillar of fire by night; for it is a town of shipyards and blast furnaces and Cyclopean industry ... Where the shipyard slopes down to the river is a row of iron

---

2 'Down Tyneside', *Graphic* (23 August 1884), p.195. Another example can be found in W.J. Palmer, *The Tyne and its Tributaries* (London, 1882), p.261.

3 V. Lee, 'The Tyne at Newcastle', from *Juvenilia* (c.1878) in I.C. Willis (ed.), *A Vernon Lee Anthology* (London, 1929).

4 *Graphic* (4 June 1881), p.554.

5 A. Watson, 'The Coaly Tyne', *Magazine of Art* (1883), p.115.

skeletons, growing rapidly into steamships under the continuous hammering of swarming crowds of workmen, who look as small among the curving ribs of metal as the Lilliputians must have seemed to Gulliver.[6]

Peter Quinn has maintained that this article was a specific attempt by Watson to encourage local artists to depict the industrial scenes of the region.[7] But Watson's message was surely more subtle:

> When Mr. W.L. Wyllie exhibited in last year's Academy an admirable painting of the Thames below bridge, and called it 'Our River', the critics almost unanimously agreed that, because there was a great deal of smoke in the air, and of dilapidation on the banks, and of mud in the water, it must be a picture of the Tyne. This was a new illustration of the proverb of a dog and a bad name.[8]

In making this point Watson was naming one of the few artists who regularly portrayed industrial or river scenes with success. It was a national, not merely local, failing of the nation's artists to seek their subject matter among such scenes. It is telling, therefore, that the article was illustrated by Jobling using specially commissioned works rather than reproductions of existing works by him or others. Jobling's workers are true Lilliputians, mere indicators of scale in the urban/industrial panorama.

Watson was not alone in trying to put forward a more positive interpretation of the region. R.J. Charleton's *A History of Newcastle upon Tyne* also indulged in the imagery of 'smoke-laden skies', the fiery light of ironworks at night, the hammers of the shipyards ringing out and so on, but in addition turned it into symbols of the heroism of the local population:

> A sterner task it is, and one calling for all the hardy and daring qualities of their ancestors, to ransack the bowels of the earth, and, in the face of danger and death in some of its most horrible forms, to bring forth her buried treasures for the use of man; and no child's play is it to compel the brittle, stubborn iron into ductility, and frame it into a thousand useful and terrible shapes. To make of it the stately merchant ship, the swift locomotive, the cunning engines of all kinds, the stable anchor, the mighty warship, and the death-dealing gun – all this is labour for Titans.[9]

Jobling's imagery does not, unsurprisingly, reflect any of these scenes and issues, but instead sticks to conventional views of the more picturesque corners of the city. Vernon Lee's account of the workforce is very different:

> There are men who live among all this by the thousand ... black, red-faced, and blistered, or with flesh in pale creases under the grime, their clothes engrained with dirt, shiny with grease, often tattered, the filthy wisp of comforter round their necks; men who sat silent and morose, scarcely exchanging a word, and who are yet human beings, intelligent and sensitive, who get treatises on

6   Ibid.
7   P. Quinn, 'Picturing Locality: Art and Regional Identity in the North East of England, 1822–1900' (unpublished PhD thesis, University of Sunderland, 1997), p.342.
8   Watson, 'Coaly Tyne', p.115.
9   R.J. Charleton, *History of Newcastle upon Tyne* (London, c.1885), p.16.

political economy from the free library, in order to see why things should be so very queer and uncomfortable down here.[10]

She swipes at the injustice of the situation, playing on the fears of the 'polluted' souls of the 'well-dressed' that perhaps they will not continue to enjoy their privileges unchallenged by the 'red faced and blistered' for much longer.[11] The unknown writer of the *Graphic* article did not share Lee's wary optimism. Instead, Tyneside's 'habitual dweller ... must, sooner or later, inevitably sink to the level of his surroundings – must either become in temper monotonous and unlovely' or 'become somewhat given to inflamed eyelids, a bloated countenance generally, and characteristic twitching at the mouth corners'.[12] Although bordering on the caricature, the entire tone of this article depicts a life not of Titans, but of those without hope. This aspect of the article in particular exposes the glaring anomalies between the rhetoric and the illustrations. Overall, the language used to describe Tyneside, by writers positively or negatively disposed towards the region, displayed remarkable similarities, while the pictures produced by local and non-local artists alike adopted an almost standardised imagery which refused to confront the human implications of the scenes described by the text.

Cullercoats

So, how does all this compare with the literature and imagery about Cullercoats? By the time Aaron Watson wrote his account of the North-East-coast fishing industry for *The Magazine of Art* in 1882, readers of popular illustrated magazines were very familiar with images and tales of the quiet heroism of the Cullercoats fisherman.[13] Reproductions of paintings such as J.D. Watson's *The Lifebrigade Man* were a regular feature of *The Graphic* from its inception in 1869.[14] Similarly, the art-viewing public would have been familiar with Cullercoats fisher-life from pictures such as Frank Holl's *No Tidings from the Sea* (1871), A.H. Marsh's *Baiting the Lines* (1870), *The Missing Boats* (1871), *The Signal, Breakers on the Bar* (1872) or *Harvest of the Sea* (1877), and W.Q. Orchardson's *Toilers of the Sea* (1870).

Aaron Watson's short account of Cullercoats functions within a longer article as a comparison to the more cosmopolitan port of North Shields. Watson describes the village and its long history as a fishing community. Its people 'might trace a direct descent from the Vikings' and are characterised as having 'changed little in dress, in manners, or in speech' since the days of the Armada.

---

10 Lee, 'The Tyne', p.118.

11 Ibid., p.119. These ideas may have been influenced by Ruskin's *Fors Clavigera*, 8 vols (Orpington, 1871–84), addressed to 'The Workmen and Labourers of Great Britain'.

12 *Graphic* (23 August 1884), p.195.

13 A. Watson, 'After the Herring', *Magazine of Art* (1882). Part I of this article deals with fisher life in the Scottish village of Burnmouth and the north Northumberland village of Cresswell. Part II deals mainly with North Shields as an important fishing port, but contrasts it with a description of Cullercoats. See especially p.455.

14 'The Lifebrigade Man', *Graphic* (February 1870), p.274. Other similar illustrations by Watson included *The Fisherman's Darling* (February 1871), *Saved* (December 1871) and *Duck Shooting* (February 1870). Other artists contributing similar illustrations to the magazine included A.H. Marsh and John Charlton.

The women are described as 'the working bees. Stout, hardy creatures, with petticoats of blue flannel, and such a common agreement in their style of dress as to seem as if they wore a uniform.' The paragraph ends with a blatant advertisement for the artistic possibilities of Cullercoats:

> Cullercoats lifts the fisherman's calling into the region of poetry, from which indeed it is seldom far withdrawn. In Cullercoats everything is primitive. As a fishing station, Shields is going through a rapid process of development; but, though it is only two miles away, Cullercoats has been untouched by the waves of change.[15]

The key features of this account – the village's primitive qualities of work, dress, custom and speech – seen in opposition to the development of Shields were concerns which recur again and again in other accounts, not only of Cullercoats, but of other artists' colonies in England and abroad. For example, in Staithes 'the dress of the fisherfolk is as quaint and paintable as it has ever been for many generations',[16] while the fisherman of Hastings has 'the blood of Jutish sea-dogs and Danish Vikings running still through his veins'.[17]

In 1886 R.J. Charleton produced an article on Cullercoats for *The Magazine of Art* which from the outset lays claim to the place as an artist's haven. 'There are not many places in England that can show a better record of service in the cause of art than can the comparatively unknown little fishing village of Cullercoats.'[18] This article bears direct comparison with similar ones littering the art magazines during the 1880s and 90s, directing artists to little-known sketching grounds (Clovelly, Whitby, the Norfolk Broads, Cambridge, Walberswick, Holland) or existing artists' colonies (Fontainebleau, Barbizon, Newlyn, Grez, St Ives). Charleton lists a number of well-known artists and works associated with Cullercoats, including Watson, Holl and Winslow Homer. Significantly, Charleton takes issue with artists who have depicted scenes of rural labour as dehumanising:

> We cannot see that there is anything essentially melancholy in the weariness which comes of labour undertaken and faithfully performed. There is, on the contrary, something noble and hopeful in the sight of the labour of tilling the earth. ... Yet, take it at its noblest and best, it lacks the fascination which the element of danger adds to the calling of the toilers of the sea.[19]

Of course, this echoes his 'labour for Titans' rhetoric, positioning his opinions firmly in the Ruskinian mould – a belief in the nobility of toil, as epitomised

[15] Watson, 'After the Herring', Part II, p.455. Watson actually distorts the truth of the village's history in order to make the tradition of fishing here appear longer established. He refers to Cullercoats as having been a fishing village since the time of the Armada, i.e., the late sixteenth century. However, W.W. Tomlinson (see his *Historical Notes on Cullercoats, Whitley and Monkseaton, etc.*, London, 1893) and others claim that Cullercoats did not become a settlement until the early seventeenth century, when it was established as an export harbour for coal and salt. It was only after these industries moved to other harbours during the early eighteenth century that fishing became the important industry at Cullercoats.
[16] *Whitby Gazette*, August 1901, cited in P. Phillips, *The Staithes Group* (Marlow, 1993), p.17.
[17] G. Allen, 'On and Off Shore', *Art Journal* (1883), p.287.
[18] R.J. Charleton, 'Cullercoats', *Magazine of Art* (1886), p.456.
[19] Ibid., p.461.

in the paintings of Jules Breton, rather than the Zola-esque vision of the sub-human peasant who inhabits the world of Courbet. Unfortunately, we have no way of knowing who Charleton specifically had in mind, but it is interesting to consider A.B. Blake's article on Fontainebleau and Barbizon in *The Art Journal* of 1882, where the Barbizon peasant was described as having 'coarseness of feature and sluggish animalness of movement' because labour had made him 'a human beast of toil'.[20]

Charleton again used Jobling to illustrate his article, but this time at least one of the images, *The Sands at Evening* (Fig. 18.2), was derived from an existing painting, *The Day is Done and Darkness Falls from the Wings of Night* (Royal Academy, 1886).[21] Although the figures play a significant role, Jobling concentrates on creating 'atmosphere' and a sense of 'place' rather than depicting Charleton's idea of the heroism of their lives. The change of title of this image suggests an interesting anomaly. The verse of the Longfellow poem ('The Day is Done', 1844) to which the painting seems to allude runs: 'I see the lights of a village/Gleam through the rain and the mist,/And a feeling of sadness comes o'er me/that my soul cannot resist.' This sentiment contradicts Charleton's assertion that there is nothing 'essentially melancholy in the weariness which comes of labour'. As a result of the change of title and the fact that the reproduced image was in black and white, the poeticism of the original was successfully converted into a more naturalistic image of fisher life, in keeping with the other illustrations and with Charleton's rhetoric.

During the period 1886–7 the writer and journalist Lillias Wasserman, widow of the merchant-turned-Cullercoats artist J.C. Wasserman, produced two related pieces of work on Cullercoats. The first took the form of a weekly serialised fictional account of an artist in Cullercoats, written for *The Newcastle Weekly Leader*,[22] while the other appeared as a factual article in *The Art Journal*.[23] Both draw on the same material, but the differences in handling are astounding, especially when dealing with the fisherfolk themselves. Both accounts describe the fisherlasses as upright, graceful, strong, with grey eyes and masses of golden hair, and their habit of walking along the banks at night, arms entwined, singing ballads. But in the *Art Journal* article she then adds:

> it is true that the most intelligent of them can neither read nor write. Of course the limited intercourse with the world which arises in consequence has drawbacks. It renders them narrow, prejudiced, unreasoning. But these are blemishes easily forgiven in the general interest they awaken. ... They have a rugged independence which makes them intolerant of patronage; but meet them as man to man, and, above all, avoid letting them imagine that you are talking down to them, and it is not difficult to win their hearts.[24]

---

[20] A.B. Blake, 'Fontainebleau and Barbizon', *Art Journal* (1882), p.327.

[21] The painting is in the Laing Art Gallery, Newcastle upon Tyne.

[22] L. Wasserman, 'Where the North Wind Blows. Part VII, A Cullercoats Artist', *Newcastle Weekly Leader*, 25 December 1886; 1, 8 and 15 January 1887.

[23] L. Wasserman, 'Some Fisher Folk', *Art Journal* (1887), p.57.

[24] Ibid., p.58.

Figure 18.2. Robert Jobling, *The Sands at Evening* (*The Magazine of Art*, 1886, p.457).

Wasserman's patronising tone, which reduces the fisherfolk to little more than a sociologically fascinating subspecies, seems incredible coming from the pen of someone who had lived among these people for a number of years. Her anthropological dissection continued with an account of their superstitions and local funeral customs, all of which are regarded as further evidence of their ignorance. The discrepancy between the accounts can be understood in terms of the perceived readership of each piece, but perhaps in her anxiety to stress the uniqueness of the fisherfolk to a national audience Wasserman's exaggerations toppled over into caricature.

Again, Jobling's pictures were used to illustrate the *Art Journal* article. All show scenes typical of Jobling's by now more naturalistic output – baiting lines, pulling up the cobles, launching the lifeboat, and one, *Singing Ballads*, which is almost certainly derived from his *A Fisher Song*, in which the lasses perform the ritual of the moonlit promenade. The other illustrations concentrate on the ordinary, everyday tasks. Even the potential drama of the lifeboat picture is dissipated by the composition and scale of the figures – their heroism is almost mundane.

Cullercoats, its fisherfolk and its art colony continued to attract attention from writers, often those engaged in writing guidebooks, histories and semi-factual tales. Examples include James Runciman's *Romance of the Coast* (1881), W.W. Tomlinson's *Historical Notes on Cullercoats, Whitley and Monkseaton, etc.* (1893) – which includes a large section on artists at Cullercoats – and John Robinson's *Illustrated Handbook to the Rivers of the Tyne, Blyth and Wansbeck* (1894). Although very different books, they all seem to have been designed to attract visitors to the area and can be regarded as part of the larger body of work promoting Cullercoats as a worthwhile destination. W.G. Larkins's 'Reminiscences of Artistic Cullercoats' in *The Tyneside Magazine* of December 1894 was unusual for combining the standard fisherfolk rhetoric with meaningful critiques of various artists' works, but is likely to have reached only a local readership rather than the national art-loving public.

Cullercoats artists also featured prominently in Rudolf Dircks's article 'Northumberland and Some Artists' in *The Art Journal* of 1904. Unfortunately, however, Dircks made no mention of the colony but instead concentrated on the supposed independence and insularity of the region's artists, who, he claimed, have 'rarely sought London, as a French student seeks Paris'.[25] This notion is perhaps another manifestation of the perceived 'difference' of the region. While these artists were 'self-reliant' it was only as a necessary result of their conscious rejection of the London art scene, a decision made usually after having experienced it. But such a charge of insularity does not bear scrutiny. The region's artists were always well versed in the latest technical developments through personal contacts and the annual Bewick Club exhibitions in Newcastle.[26] So, while the overall tone of the article was positive, Dircks failed to convey any sense of a community of artists at Cullercoats.

'Difference'

In the broadest terms it would seem that the North East and Cullercoats received their fair share of notice in contemporary literature of various kinds. Accounts of Newcastle and the Tyne seem to have descended into hackneyed responses to the industrial landscape into which the industrial worker was inserted, negatively or positively. But the artistic community, nationally and locally, refused

---

[25] R. Dircks, 'Northumberland and Some Artists', *Art Journal* (1904), p.305.

[26] See L. Newton, 'Artists of the Cullercoats Colony c.1870–1914' (unpublished PhD thesis, University of Northumbria, 2001), esp. chapters 3 and 5, and *Cullercoats: A North-East Colony of Artists* (exh. cat., the Laing Art Gallery, Newcastle upon Tyne, 2003).

to be provoked into any serious depiction of the industrial landscape and its inhabitants, despite Aaron Watson's call to do so. The notion of the industrial North East was maintained but without taking on the threatening aspects which the pictorial depiction of an industrial workforce may have unleashed.[27] There is little evidence to support Quinn's claim that 'The local artist became figured as the depictor of people and place in all its variety ... artists and writers advocated the depiction of the industrial and the urban as a specifically North-Eastern subject.'[28]

Articles on Cullercoats, on the other hand, seem to have conformed to a general pattern applicable to other coastal colonies and sketching grounds in their emphasis on the pre-industrial workers of ancient stock, heroically maintaining their customs, costumes, superstitions, religious beliefs, work practices and pre-industrial landscape in the face of an ever-encroaching urban, industrial threat. Accompanying these accounts are images which metamorphose from pictures of heroic lifebrigade men in classical poses during the late 1860s and 1870s to more naturalistic pictures of fisherfolk at work or leisure with the focus on accurate depictions of dress, work practices and place during the 1880s and 1890s.

But how can we account for the discrepancies between these two sets of accounts of the North-Eastern worker? Prior to the nineteenth century it is perhaps easy to understand the positioning of 'the North' as 'different' quite simply because of its geographical distance from the metropolis. Yet this became increasingly untenable with the advent of rapid forms of transport and communication during the nineteenth century. However, during this period 'the North' also became equated with industrialism, reinforcing its 'difference' from the southern urban experience. It is obvious, of course, that this notion was to a large extent an intellectual, 'high culture' fiction, maintained in order to deny and displace the urban industrial experience to a location other than 'the South' or, more specifically, London. This helped to maintain the myth of London as the cultural jewel set among a southern rural idyll. The denial of an industrial south is demonstrated by critical refusal to recognise Wyllie's industrial Thames scenes as such. The myth is further exposed in the writings of those such as William Morris, who rejected the metropolitan experience or who sought to improve conditions within it.[29]

During the late nineteenth century middle-class anxiety about the urban experience increasingly manifested itself in 'terra incognita'-type writing, such as that by Sir Charles Trevelyan, Robert Sherard, Charles Booth and Rider Haggard, in which the perceived degenerating effects of urban life on the working classes was a major theme. This anxiety was partly prompted by the realisation that the

[27] This was a time of such social unrest as evidenced by the Bloody Sunday Riots (November 1887) and the Dock Strike (1889).

[28] Quinn, 'Picturing Locality', p.316. Quinn offers no serious examples of such industrial depictions. He talks of T.M. Hemy's *Elswick Works* (1886), painted for Lord Armstrong, but by his own admission the foregrounding of the river modulates the industrial landscape in the background so that it is fit for Armstrong's consumption.

[29] See, for example, W. Morris, 'Art and Socialism' (1884), quoted in J. Marsh, *Back to the Land* (London, 1982), p.15.

nation's manhood did not measure up when called upon during the Crimean War and the following period of imperial expansion. Intellectuals such as Charles Kingsley, Thomas Carlyle, F.D. Maurice and J.A. Froude promoted hero figures from England's past as models to which men should aspire.[30] Their writings also frequently stressed the racial superiority of the Anglo-Saxon race as part of the ideological justification for the nation's colonial exploits.

Of course, there were both verbal and pictorial depictions of the urban working classes. But, as Alan Woods points out, while fictional examples, such as those found in Dickens, Gaskell or Eliot, could resolve scenes of working-class discontent within the scope of the narrative, other strategies had to be adopted in visual depictions. Woods pinpoints a number of these: the use of anecdote; putting the subject 'in the past' and therefore resolved by history; emphasising the aesthetic values of the picture – what he calls 'the attractive nature of rags in sunlight'; or concentrating on an individual such that he becomes divorced from his surroundings and is thus transformed from a threat into an object of pity or charity.[31] None of these strategies seems to have been used to depict the North-Eastern industrial worker, but would certainly seem to apply to at least some of the images of Cullercoats fisherfolk.

Arguably, however, the Cullercoats imagery is more complex than that. Stephen Daniels has suggested that national identities are often largely defined by what he terms 'legends and landscapes' – stories of a Golden Age, traditions, heroic deeds, and so on – which give shape to the 'imagined community' of the nation.[32] Thus the literature about and output of the Cullercoats colony – encompassing subjects of heroism, shipwrecks, virile masculinity, female stoicism, traditional customs and costumes, all set within a pre-industrial landscape – provided an ideal working-class paradigm which could be appropriated by British intellectuals to construct certain notions of 'Britishness'.

The place of the Cullercoats fisherfolk as a paradigm was reinforced by a wealth of material from other popular and high art sources. In the first six months of its life *The Graphic* contained images and critiques of pictures on fisher life and sea rescues in virtually every edition. Photographers such as Frank Meadow Sutcliffe in Whitby and Lewis Harding in Cornwall were producing images of fisher life which could be widely disseminated.[33] Caricaturists such as George du Maurier in *Punch* magazine poked fun at the nation's obsession with fisherfolk. And, of course, such subjects were seen on the walls of the Royal Academy and in the pages of the art press, from the work of The Hague School artists in the early 1860s to the large-scale works still being produced by Newlyn artists after the turn of the century.

---

30 See, for example, J.A. Froude, 'England's Forgotten Worthies' (first published in *Westminster Review*, 58, July 1852), C. Kingsley, *Westward Ho!* (London, 1854) and *The Heroes* (London, 1855) and T. Carlyle, *On Heroes, Hero Worship and the Heroic in History* (London, 1840–41).

31 A. Woods, 'Doré's London: Art and Evidence', *Art History*, 1:3 (September 1978), p.349.

32 S. Daniels, *Fields of Vision: Landscape Imagery and National Identity in England and the U.S.* (Cambridge, 1993), p.5. Daniels uses Benedict Anderson's phrase from *Imagined Communities: Reflections on the Origin and Spread of Nationalism* (London, 1983).

33 Sutcliffe took many photos of Staithes and Runswick Bay, which serve as useful comparisons to the art produced there. For examples of Sutcliffe's Staithes photographs and du Maurier's cartoons see Newton, *Cullercoats: A North-East Colony*, figs 22 and 23, p.33.

This large body of material is also allied to the international preoccupation with the fate of the rural labourer, which had been gathering pace in Britain since at least the beginning of the industrial revolution.[34] Like the fisherfolk, the rural labourer was also outside the (southern) urban/industrial experience and could therefore also provide an acceptable working-class image – distanced not by geography but by associations with a past rural arcadia.[35] By the end of the nineteenth century this was manifesting itself in images by George Clausen, H.H. La Thangue, Edward Stott and P.H. Emerson; the writings of Thomas Hardy, Edward Carpenter and Alfred Austin;[36] the music of Frederick Delius, Sir Edward Elgar and Ralph Vaughan Williams; and in organisations determined to preserve aspects of rural life, such as the English Dialect Society (1873), the Society for the Protection of Ancient Buildings (1877), the Folk Lore Society (1878) and the English Folk-Song Society (1898). The ideological interchange-ability between fisherfolk and labourer is also manifest in the works of many artists at Cullercoats, Staithes and Newlyn by the turn of the century.

All this suggests an astonishing level of complicity on the part of artists, writers, photographers, fisherfolk, labourers and public to maintain an accept-able image of working-class 'difference', which, despite regional fluctuations, was obviously a national and international phenomenon. Robert Colls and Philip Dodd have suggested that this was part of a general policy of inclusion, at once embracing yet marginalising, thereby neutering possible disruptive groups such as the working classes, women, the Irish, and so on.[37] During the 1860s Matthew Arnold put forward the idea that provincial cultures were allowable, but only as peripheral to the core 'metropolitan' English culture.[38] Dodd uses the example of Newlyn and its colonists to draw attention to this relationship. The artists' positioning of Newlyn fisherfolk within a Celtic framework, while ignoring the contemporary problems of mass emigration, the decline of tin mining and the decimation of the fishing industry by European competition, was 'the necessary complement of the artists' affiliation to metropolitan institutions, especially the Royal Academy'.[39]

[34] See A. Hemingway, *Landscape Imagery and Urban Culture in Early Nineteenth Century Britain* (Cambridge, 1992), for earlier examples.

[35] Indeed, Raymond Williams charts this nostalgia for a better, rural age back to Hesiod (c.900 BC); see R. Williams, *The Country and the City* (London, 1973), esp. chapter 1. For the interweaving of work-forces see P.J. Waller, *Town, City and Nation: England 1850–1914* (Oxford, 1983), esp. chapter 5.

[36] Carpenter's writings, such as *Civilisation: Its Causes and Cure* (1889) gave momentum to the widening 'back to the land' movement, rejecting the unhealthy stifling urban experience for a primi-tive rural lifestyle bringing health, happiness and freedom. Carpenter's admirers included E.M. Forster, C.R. Ashbee and Havelock Ellis. Hardy's work, on the other hand, recognised that rural life had changed forever and could no longer be regarded as existing in splendid isolation, but was instead increasingly bound up with urban life in mutual interdependence. See T. Hardy, *The Dorsetshire Labourer* (London, 1883).

[37] For more, see R. Colls and P. Dodd (eds), *Englishness: Politics and Culture 1880–1920* (London, 1986).

[38] M. Arnold, *Complete Prose Works III*, ed. R.H. Super (Michigan, 1970), pp.295–345.

[39] P. Dodd, 'Englishness and the National Culture', in Colls and Dodd, *Englishness*, p.14.

'Northern-ness'

To what extent can this also be applied to Cullercoats imagery, however? The crucial difference between the artists at Cullercoats and those at other colonies was that the majority of them were local artists producing works to be exhibited and sold at North-Eastern venues. In other words, the region's artistic output addressed a primarily regional audience. So to what extent did they deliberately set out to construct a 'northern' image based on Cullercoats, and was this because of an awareness of similar subjects from other colonies, or dictated by a rejection of the alternative local subjects – that is, the urban, industrial or rural? The urban and industrial seem to have been largely rejected. In 1885 a Newcastle newspaper made tantalising references to pictures in Jobling's studio exhibition showing industrial scenes along the Tyne.[40] Unfortunately, however, it has not been possible to locate any of these works. If Jobling did obey Watson's call to portray the industrial Tyne, all trace of his efforts has vanished. If the works proved unsaleable, Jobling, ever sensitive to market demands, is not likely to have repeated the experiment.

Yet the proximity of Newcastle *was* important to these artists, both as a centre of consumption and as a place from which to escape. The thirty-minute rail journey from Newcastle to Cullercoats signified a rejection of the urban/industrial landscape through which the artist had to travel to reach his destination, a symbolic shedding of the modern world to take a step back in time.[41] In her examination of rural artists' colonies Nina Lübbren highlights the fact that places were often chosen by artists because they filled a prior vision or expectation of particular available subject matter and that these preconceptions led to the creation of what she calls 'place-myths', whereby the artists, through repeated use of certain motifs, actually shaped the audiences' perception of that place.[42] (The bridge at Grez is an obvious example.) Cullercoats could have fulfilled such criteria, with its harbour, the narrow streets of fishermen's cottages and the distinctive outline of the Lookout House. Therefore, the subjects to be found at Cullercoats could supply a local market already well aware of similar work by Breton, Bastien-Lepage and The Hague School.

However, although we know that most of the important North-Eastern artists were regular exhibitors at the major British venues, they never attempted to present themselves as a group to the outside world in the way that the Newlyn or Glasgow artists did. Their failure to bombard the London market with Cullercoats pictures year after year in the manner of the Newlyn School, such that the place and its people became instantly recognisable (i.e., attained 'place-myth' status), meant that Cullercoats's identity as a colony or northern 'school' was never portrayed forcefully enough in the national art press. Rather than trying to

---

40 'R. Jobling's Studio Exhibition', *Newcastle Daily Chronicle*, 5 December 1885.

41 The nineteenth-century railway line from Newcastle to Cullercoats followed the modern Metro line, roughly following the river to Tynemouth before heading north. This takes the traveller through areas of what would have been among the highest density of industrial occupation.

42 N. Lübbren, 'Rural Artists' Colonies in Nineteenth Century Europe' (unpublished PhD thesis, University of Leeds, 1996) and *Rural Artists' Colonies in Europe 1870–1910* (Manchester, 2001), esp. pp.115–16 and 156–7. Lubbren points to Stanhope Forbes's choice of Newlyn instead of Manaccan, for example.

overcome the problems inherent in their distance from London, the Cullercoats artists concentrated their efforts on building up a buoyant local art market via new clubs and exhibition spaces throughout the region during the 1880s and 1890s. In this respect Quinn is correct in seeing Cullercoats as part of a larger attempt to foster a 'northern' identity and culture.[43]

This alternative northern culture had its roots firmly in the past, both actually and metaphorically. During the Romantic period the northern landscape had frequently been used to embody notions of the Sublime; a wild nature, attractive yet feared. In many ways these attributes were transferred onto the Cullercoats coastline and its inhabitants. Throughout the nineteenth century local newspapers, music hall, books, songs and poetry celebrated the region's dialects, often to recount tales of history and myth. ('The Lambton Worm' is one such famous product of the 1860s.) The recovery of the region's past was of crucial importance; here the Society of Antiquaries, the Literary and Philosophical Society and figures such as Dr J. Collingwood Bruce (editor of *Archaeologia Aeliana*), Robert Spence Watson (who wrote a monograph on the Saxon poet Caedmon in 1877), James Clepham (journalist and antiquarian) and Richard Welford (historian) played a large part. Magazines such as *The Northumbrian* and *The Tyneside Magazine* (1895) carried many articles on North-Eastern history – tales of Border reivers, Walter Scott, Harry Hotspur and Johnnie Armstrong. In his address to the Bewick Club in 1885, Spence Watson drew attention to the plentiful supply of artistic subjects to be found in the region, including Johnnie Armstrong, Collingwood, George Stephenson, Grace Darling, pitmen and, inevitably, lifebrigade men, fishermen and fishwives.[44] The industrial achievements of the North East were not ignored, but were celebrated either by heroising the inventors – Stephenson, Armstrong, Lothian Bell, Palmer, Hawthorn – or fetishising the invention – the *Rocket*, the Armstrong Gun, the High Level Bridge, the steam turbine. The attempts by Charleton, Welford and Aaron Watson to promote a more positive image of the region's industrial areas must be understood as part of this regional reinvention. The close relationship between Cullercoats colonists and local patrons, many of whom were writers, historians, politicians, journalists, inventors, industrialists and businessmen, meant that they were inevitably drawn into and bound up with this local drive to promote the North East in the national league-table of regions. The recovery of so many historically based local cultural manifestations, including Cullercoats imagery, must be seen as an attempt to create an alternative 'North-Eastern' image. But in order to subsume the urban, industrial Tyneside, the alternative image was largely regressive and inward-looking.

Despite the vitality and variety of national 'regionalism' during the nineteenth century, Jose Harris contends that by the end of the century there was a shift of 'the fulcrum of economic life away from the northern provinces to London, away

---

[43] Quinn, 'Picturing Locality', p.316.
[44] Henry H. Emmerson's *Johnnie Armstrong's Last Farewell* (1886) or *Grace Darling* (date unknown), and Ralph Hedley's *The Invention of the Lifeboat* (1896) or *Scottish Prisoners in the Tower of St Nicholas* (1899) are good examples of this trend.

from manufacturing industry to international finance'.[45] Culturally and intellec-
tually this meant that, as Quinn states, 'Local art was to become synonymous
with inferior and unimportant art in direct correlation to the deterioration in the
significance of the regions.'[46] In these circumstances the 'differences' presented
by fisherfolk or rural workers acquired negative connotations – custom and
belief became ignorance, honest toil became mundane degradation, tradition
and historicity became tedious backwardness. After the turn of the century the
art of all these British colonies lost its relevance as regionalism gave way to a
new British urban identity focused firmly on London.

David Lowenthal maintains that 'Since the early nineteenth century, national
identity has required having a heritage and thinking it unique. Heritage differen-
tiates, we treasure most the things that set us apart.'[47] If Cullercoats imagery can
be understood as part of this nineteenth-century heritage project, its reappraisal
– along with that of other British artists' colonies – is perhaps the next phase
in its historical recovery. Is it mere coincidence that this process has begun at
a time when the heavy industries, so studiously avoided by nineteenth-century
artists, have all but disappeared? Cullercoats imagery undoubtedly played its
part in the local construction of an alternative regional identity. Yet, perhaps
unwittingly, it also reflected the wider cultural and ideological changes of the
nation, from the expansionist 'New Imperialism' of the 1870s to Britain's loss
of status as *the* global economic power by the dawn of the twentieth century.
It is this duality which makes Cullercoats such a fascinating alternative North-
Eastern landscape.

---

[45] J. Harris, *Private Lives, Public Spirit: Britain 1870–1914* (Harmondsworth, 1993), p.19.
[46] Quinn, 'Picturing Locality', p.375.
[47] D. Lowenthal, 'British National Identity and the English Landscape', *Rural History*, 2:2 (1991),
      p.214.

Index

Page numbers in **bold** type refer to illustrations and their captions; superscript numbers refer to footnotes (for example, 253[34] indicates footnote 34 on page 253).

Regions and Regionalism in History

Volumes already published